SKYLEADERS

DC-1 through DC-7:

The Douglas propliners

First published in 2011 in the French language by Lela Presse.
This English-language edition published in February 2012.

A catalogue record for this book is available from the British Library.

ISBN 978 0 85733 157 1

Library of Congress control no. 2011935262

Published by Haynes Publishing,
Sparkford, Yeovil, Somerset BA22 7JJ, UK.
Tel: 01963 442030 Fax: 01963 440001
Int. tel: +44 1963 442030 Int. fax: +44 1963 440001
E-mail: saies@haynes.co.uk
Website: www.haynes.co.uk

Haynes North America Inc.,
861 Lawrence Drive, Newbury Park,
California 91320, USA.

While every effort is taken to ensure the accuracy of the information given in this book, no liability can be accepted by the author or publishers for any loss, damage or injury caused by errors in, or omissions from, the information given.

Printed in the USA by Odcombe Press LP,
1299 Bridgestone Parkway, La Vergne, TN 37086.

SKYLEADERS

DC-1 through DC-7:
The Douglas propliners

René J. Francillon

Preface and acknowledgements

The DC series of commercial airliners developed by the Douglas Aircraft Company, and their military derivatives, have been part of my life for some 67 years. The first to enter my consciousness were C-47s flying over Provence during the summer of 1944. Admittedly, they did not prove as exciting for a seven-year-old as the *Spitfires*, *Thunderbolts*, and *Liberators* which dared to drop a few bombs close to where my family lived in that not forgotten summer. In later years, while these wartime warriors had disappeared from the scene to be replaced by jets, DC-3s, DC-4s, DC-6s, and DC-7s continued to play a part in my life. As a teenager, I spent many an afternoon watching *Dakotas* of Air France at Nice-Le Var and then DC-3s of Swissair at Genève-Cointrin. But that was just a prelude for my first job. In 1956, I got to be around most of the DC propliners while working at Orly-Nord for the Aéroport de Paris. On my first day on the job, my boss, Anatole Rojinsky, took me on the tarmac and taught me how to quickly identify a DC-4 from a DC-6, and a DC-6 from a DC-7.

Then in the mid-1960s, after immigrating to the United States, I was hired by Douglas. There were few DC propliners left on the ramp at Long Beach Municipal Airport at that time but there were many old documents and photos of these aircraft that were being weeded out from files of colleagues with a limited interest in the history of our employer. Their losses were my gains. Those treasures have remained with me through many moves, long enough for many of the photos to get into this book.

By the mid 1970s, I was no longer with Douglas and had become an airport design consultant. But one that had yet to fly in a DC-3! This 'Gooney Bird' deficiency was, at last, disposed of when I got to fly between Boston and Portland, Maine, in a DC-3 of Provincetown-Boston Airlines and then, within a few weeks, in a DC-3 of SAETA (*Sociedad Ecuatoriana de Transportes Aéreos*) between Quito and Cuenca in Ecuador. Nevertheless, I have to admit that there is not a single DC-3 hour in a pilot's logbook with my name! Now, in my retirement years, the sounds of twin R-1830 radials are occasionally revived by a C-41 (N41HQ of Next Century Aviation Inc) trundling over the Carquinez Straight, right out my window.

All this to say that, for me, writing this book was a wonderful opportunity to travel down memory lane.

Book writing is never the work of a single individual. Whatever I accumulated in my files over the years would never have been enough to do justice to the DC propliners. But being older has advantages. One establishes relationships with friends around the world, whether met as the result of professional activities or a shared enthusiasm for aviation history. I owe a profound and most sincere gratitude to these friends, not just for what they contributed materially (such as super photos) but more so for their friendship and advice. In alphabetical order – and probably with omissions due to failing memory – I want to express my warmest gratitude to Cyril Avinens, William J. Balogh, Roger Besecker, Christian Boisselon, Alan Bovelt, Peter M. Bowers, Ken Buchanan, Martine Cabiac, Olivier Cabiac, Mário Roberto Carneiro, Humbert Charvé, Alex Cheminade, Benoit Colin, J. Corrigan, Alain Crosnier, Jean Cuny, Bill Curry, Ed Davies, M. J. Delgado, Jean Delmas, Jim Dunn, Jerry Edwards, Michel Fournier, Paul Genest, Richard Gennis, Kevin Grantham, Michael Gruenenfelder, Jacques Guillem, C. Hinton, Christian Jacquet-Francillon, Harry L. James, g.g.j. Kamp, Robert E. Kling, Rafael Koller, Frédéric Lert, Peter B. Lewis, Michel Marani, Frédéric Marsaly, David W. Menard, Steve Miller, Rick Morgan, Stéphane Nicolaou, Douglas O. Olson, David Ostrowski, Jorge Núñez Padìn, Lionel Paul, Alain Pelletier, George Pennick, Ruth E. Peters, Giuseppe Picarella, Carl E. Porter, Sam Prétat, Mervyn W. Prime, Harrison Rued, Daniel H. Schumann, R. Carson Seely, Martin E. Siegrist, Douglas Sloviak, Richard K. Smith, J. J. Tarsitano, Norm Taylor, Ronald H. Thompson, Barrett Tillman, Nick Veronico, and Simon Watson.

And, of course, the assistance and advice of many Douglas colleagues from the 'old days' and from today's Boeing archivists were absolutely vital to the completion of this work. Thank you my friends Harry S. Gann Jr, Patricia McGinnis, Mike Lombardi, Tom Lubbesmeyer, Jim Roberts, Jim Turner, Gordon Williams, and Tim Williams.

Although most of my previous books have been written for American and British publishers, this DC propliner story started as a French book published in 2010 by Lela Presse: *Les rois du ciel – Douglas DC-1 à DC-7*. In getting this book into print, I was fortunate to be able to rely on a cast of professionals at Lela Presse: Jean-Baptiste Delcambe, Jean-Marie Gall, Lionel Labeyrie, Michel Ledet, and Iulian Robanescu. Next, Mark Hughes and Jonathan Falconer at Haynes Publishing expressed an early interest in publishing an English edition and did everything to ease work on this edition. Whether you are on one side or the other of the Channel/Pas de Calais, I thank you all for making my task so pleasurable.

And then, there is the one who made it all possible, my friend, my confidante and my muse for more than 30 years: my wife Carol A. McKenzie. She is the first to admit that, for her, aircraft are simply transportation tools and are of little intrinsic interest to reasonable folks. Yet, when finally on her way to fulfill a dream – touching whales in the warm waters of Baja California – she remembered to photograph XA-UDY (ex C-47A-1-DK, 42-02396) for me! Then, with time to translate/adapt/improve the text from the French edition being rather short, she stepped in making it possible for me to complete the task in a timely fashion. Indeed, Carol does deserve much of the credit for the final results.

Vallejo, California
July 2011

C O N T

E N T S

Introduction

Douglas, a lasting legend

ABOVE *Donald W. Douglas Sr photographed in 1958 when he first flew in a DC-8. He had retired as president of the Douglas Aircraft Company the year before but was still chairman of its Board of Directors.* (Douglas)

BELOW *While attending the US Naval Academy at Annapolis, Maryland, Donald W. Douglas designed and built several model aeroplanes including this one which hung from the ceiling of his room at the Academy.* (Douglas)

For 25 years, the Douglas Aircraft Company, Inc., a company located in California since the early 1920s, built more piston-engined transport aircraft than any other manufacturer in the world. The jetliner-era proved to be far more difficult for Douglas. After being briefly in the lead as its DC-8 initially sold better than the Boeing 707, Douglas was quickly overtaken by Boeing and kept on trailing further and further behind the new commercial aircraft leader. The difficulties encountered during the jet era eventually led to a hurried merger in 1967, to give birth to the McDonnell Douglas Corporation. Thirty years later the new corporation was in turn taken over by Boeing. As we will see, the company's successes during the 1930s to 1950s, as well as the difficulties it encountered during the 1960s, can, to a large extent, be traced to the personality of its brilliant founder, Donald W. Douglas Sr.

Second son of an assistant cashier of the National Park Bank, Donald Wills Douglas was born in Brooklyn, New York, on Wednesday, 6 April 1892, and received his early education at Trinity Chapel School in New York City. At the age of 17, by which time he had acquired a great love for the sea, Donald Douglas followed in the footsteps of his older brother and entered the US Naval Academy in Annapolis, Maryland, in the autumn of 1909.

As it happened, that year was also most notable in the field of aviation. Some of the most significant events of that year were:
- 23 February 1909 – J.A.D. McCurdy flew the first aircraft in Canada;
- 17 June 1909 – The Wright brothers received a medal from the US Congress;
- 29 June 1909 – Orville Wright flew the first military aircraft at Fort Meyer, Virginia (an epochal event witnessed by Donald Douglas and his mother);

- 25 July 1909 – First crossing of the Channel by Louis Blériot;
- 1 August 1909 – First flight of an aircraft in California piloted by Glenn L. Martin;
- 2 August 1909 – The US Army purchased its first aircraft from the Wright brothers;
- 22–29 August 1909 – First international air meet in Rheims, France;
- 6 November 1909 – The French Consul General in New York decorated the Wright brothers with the Legion of Honor.

These events caught the attention of Donald Douglas. Once at the US Naval Academy, he began building and testing model aeroplanes (including at least one powered by a whiling wheel filled with gun powder) in spite of the disapproval of his instructors and many of the other naval cadets. Nevertheless, Douglas persevered. During his third year at the academy, with the approval of his parents, he opted to leave the US Navy to dedicate himself to aviation.[1] His interest was not in flying, however, but in designing flying machines. More down to earth, as befitted his Scottish origin, Donald Douglas intended to design and build aircraft in a professional manner. Consequently, being one of the first in the fledging industry to realize the importance of acquiring a solid academic background, he chose to pursue his studies at the Massachusetts Institute of Technology (MIT) in Cambridge, Massachusetts.

Given credit for his studies at the US Naval Academy, Donald Douglas was able to complete his MIT education in two years instead of the usual four. Moreover, while doing so he greatly impressed several of his professors, including Jerome Clarke Hunsaker, then one of the most brilliant theoreticians in the field of aeronautics. As a result, after graduating in June 1914, Douglas was invited to become a teaching assistant in the Department of Aeronautical Engineering at MIT. (For nine months of teaching he received $500[2] which is the equivalent of ±$11,000 today.)

An academic career, especially with such a modest salary, could not satisfy the compulsive young man who, after teaching at MIT for less than a year, joined the engineering staff of the Connecticut Aircraft Company in New Haven, Connecticut. In that position, he worked on the DN-1, the first dirigible for the US Navy. Talented and ambitious, Douglas then made a huge professional leap when he was hired in August 1915 as Chief Engineer of the Glenn L. Martin Co. at Griffith Park, Los Angeles. His first stay in California would have a profound impact on this dynamic man.

During his initial employment by Martin, he designed the Model S reconnaissance biplane and the Model R training and reconnaissance biplane, of which 14 and 16, respectively, were built between 1915 and 1917. A total of 14 of these two models became the first Douglas-designed aeroplanes to be exported, the customer being the Royal Netherlands East Indies Army (*Koninklijk Nederlands Indisch Leger*; KNIL.)

Still infatuated with the sea, the former Naval Academy cadet profited from his proximity to Santa Monica Bay to spend much of his free time sailing. During this period, Donald Douglas courted Charlotte Marguerite Ogg, a young lady from Indiana on vacation in California. They were married in June 1916, in Riverside, a city some 60 miles southeast of Los Angeles. Three months later, the newlyweds were forced to leave California when Martin decided to merge with Wright and Co., General Aero, and Simplex Automobile to organize the Wright-Martin Co in New Brunswick, New Jersey.

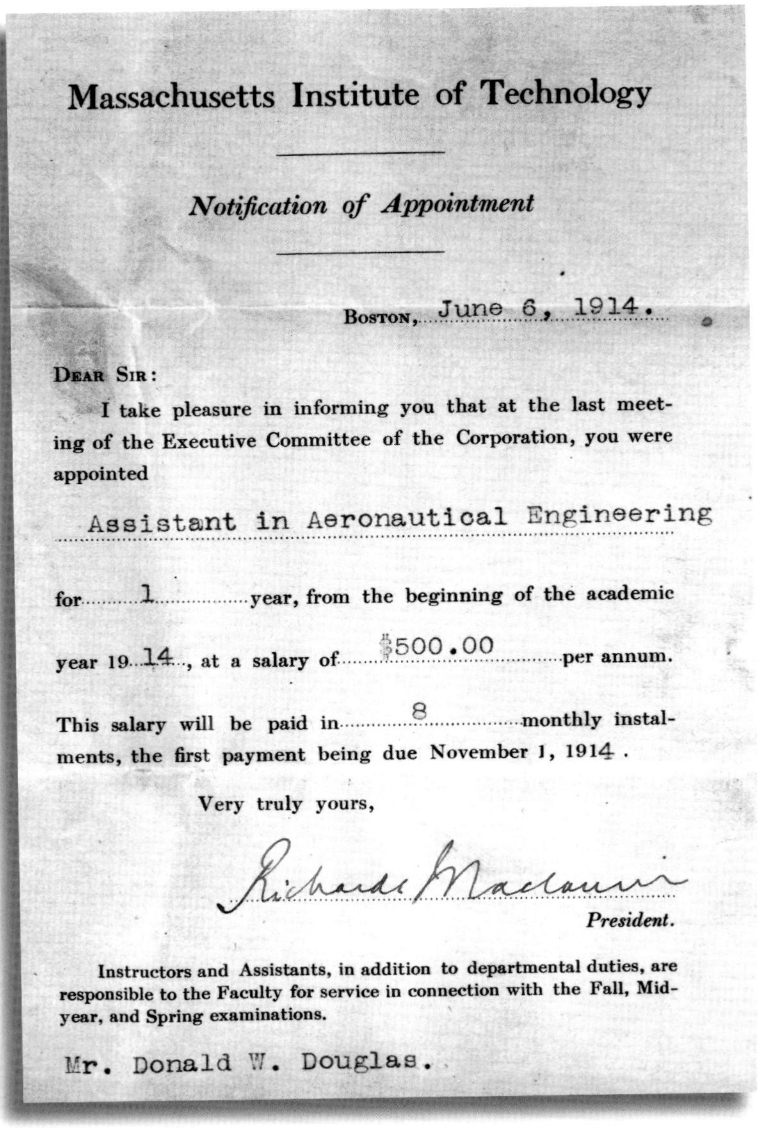

Massachusetts Institute of Technology

Notification of Appointment

Boston, June 6, 1914.

Dear Sir:

I take pleasure in informing you that at the last meeting of the Executive Committee of the Corporation, you were appointed

Assistant in Aeronautical Engineering

for 1 year, from the beginning of the academic year 19 14, at a salary of $500.00 per annum.

This salary will be paid in 8 monthly instalments, the first payment being due November 1, 1914.

Very truly yours,

Richard C. Maclaurin
President.

Instructors and Assistants, in addition to departmental duties, are responsible to the Faculty for service in connection with the Fall, Mid-year, and Spring examinations.

Mr. Donald W. Douglas.

ABOVE *Photocopy of the letter appointing Donald Douglas as an assistant in the MIT Aeronautical Engineering Department.* (Douglas)

This merger, however, was not felicitous and in December 1917 a new Glenn L. Martin Company was organized in Cleveland, Ohio.

Keen to further his career, Donald Douglas did not wait for the dissolution of Wright-Martin to move on as, in November 1916, he accepted an offer from the United States Army Signal Corps to become chief civilian aeronautical engineer for its Aviation Section. In this capacity he supervised the development of the 8-cylinder *Liberty* engine and its initial installation on a Lowe, Willard & Fowler (LWF) Model G. This water-cooled engine was then placed in mass production in its 12-cylinder version. Douglas also designed several combat aircraft. Unfortunately for him, a US political decision had been made to give priority to the manufacturing of training aircraft of US design and the production under license of combat aircraft of European design. Consequently, none of the Douglas designs were then built. Frustrated Douglas resigned from his government position and returned to work for Glenn Martin in Cleveland. Back as Chief Engineer, he earned $10,000 per year (±$170,000 in 2011). This was a rather impressive salary for a 26-year-old engineer and was 20 times what he had earned teaching at MIT three-and-a-half years earlier. The professional career of Donald W. Douglas was set.

For Martin, he designed the GMB (Glenn Martin Bomber)

---

1 According to rumours circulated in later years by some of his associates, Douglas was supposedly forced to leave the Naval Academy after one of his models crash-landed close to an Admiral! Although there appears to be no truth to that story, it fits nicely in the Don Sr. legend…

2 Unless otherwise noted, all amounts quoted in this book are in actual United States dollars. To provide readers with points of comparison, these amounts are also given in today's dollars, conversions being made by using the CPI – Consumer Price Index – compiled by the Bureau of Labor Statistics, US Dept. of Labor. No attempt was made to convert these amounts in pounds sterling or euros as doing so would be misleading due to constantly changing exchange rates with the dollar.

ABOVE *The Model S reconnaissance biplane was designed by Donald Douglas in 1915 for the Glenn L. Martin Co.* (Martin)

BELOW *Derived from the Douglas-designed GMB bomber, six Martin MPs were built for the US Post Office Department.* (Lockheed Martin)

to meet the requirements of the Aviation Section of the Signal Corps for a twin-engined aircraft that would be used as a bomber and a corps reconnaissance aircraft. Powered by 400hp *Liberty* engines, the GMB-1 first flew on 15 August 1918. Three months later, the end of the First World War curtailed plans for large scale production and only ten MB-1s (the military designation of the Martin twin) were built. The first nine were completed as combat aircraft (four as GMB-G reconnaissance aircraft with machine guns, three as GMB-M night bombers, one as the GMB-TA planned for an attempt at a transatlantic crossing, and one as the GMB-CA with a 37mm cannon on a flexible mount in the nose). The last was built as a military transport without armament and was designated at various times as the 12P (12 passenger), the GMP (Glenn Martin Passenger), and GMT (Glenn Martin Transport). This first Douglas-designed transport aircraft – 15 years before the DC-1 – was notable for its forward-located, fully-enclosed, cockpit with accommodation for a pilot and a co-pilot/navigator. Passengers sat inside the fuselage on 12 wicker chairs. Receiving the military serial number 62951, the GMT was completed in February 1920. Following test and evaluation at McCook Field in Dayton, Ohio (during which it carried the Engineering Division number P-110), it was intended for use by the Air Service to carry senior officers on inspection trips. That did not come to pass as the GMT was destroyed in an accident on 5 March 1920.

A civil derivative was designed in 1919 at the request of the Apache Aerial Transportation Company which intended to use it to start a transcontinental service linking New York and Los Angeles in four days. (Three overnight stops were planned as night flying was not yet practical as there were no navigational aids and instrument flying was still in its infancy.) Overly ambitious for the time, this project did not materialize but six aircraft with conventional open cockpits and a mail compartment in place of the passenger cabin were built as MP mailplanes for the Post Office Department. Nevertheless, the project for the Apache Aerial Transportation Company had greatly influenced Donald Douglas who thereafter could not wait until he was able to build aircraft purposely designed to carry passengers.

The beckoning of the sun

After moving to rejoin Glenn Martin, Donald Douglas found the weather in Cleveland to be harsh as the family had earlier enjoyed the sunnier climate of Southern California. Even though his wife was originally from the nearby state of Indiana, where winters can be as rude as in Ohio, she soon made it clear that she did not wish to settle in Ohio. In January 1920, asserting that the Ohio climate did not agree with their two sons, Mrs Douglas left for California where she was joined two months later by her husband.

Having just completed designing the MT torpedo bomber (another derivative of the GMB), Donald Douglas had left his well-paying job with Martin in the hope of establishing his own company under more clement skies. The young couple had some $600 in savings (±$6,200 in 2011), an amount that enabled them to survive without a salary for a few months but was insufficient to finance a new venture.

Certainly Donald Douglas knew that the California climate would be preferable for the health of his children and the happiness of his spouse. He also was confident that the milder winter temperatures would enable him to reduce heating costs for his factory. Moreover, the infrequent precipitation in Southern California would ease completion of aircraft outside of the factory during most of the year and would seldom interfere with flight tests. Finally, in those years California had plenty of manpower with salaries lower than was the case in the industrial East. For the

ebullient Douglas it only remained to find a sponsor to finance his new venture. That did not prove easy.

On 1 April 1920, Donald Douglas wrote to his MIT Mentor, Jerome Hunsacker as follows: '... *I have perhaps vain hopes of interesting capital in Southern California in an aircraft venture. California has long been a place where I wanted to live not only because of personal reasons, but because I have felt that if there is to be any civilian aeronautics it will be there that it will first attain real success...*'

Commander Hunsacker, who by then had become the chief of the Aircraft Division in the Bureau of Construction and Repairs of the US Navy, advised him to be prudent. He further suggested that Douglas join forces with William Boeing in Seattle. This advice fell on deaf ears, as for Donald Douglas and his wife the rainy climate of the state of Washington had no attraction whatsoever. Moreover, Douglas firmly intended to have his own company in which to build airliners.

Things were not easy, and his search for capital was unsuccessful for nearly three months. At last, thanks to a former colleague at Martin, Bill Henry, then a sports writer for the *Los Angeles Times*, Donald Douglas was introduced to David R. Davis. Although

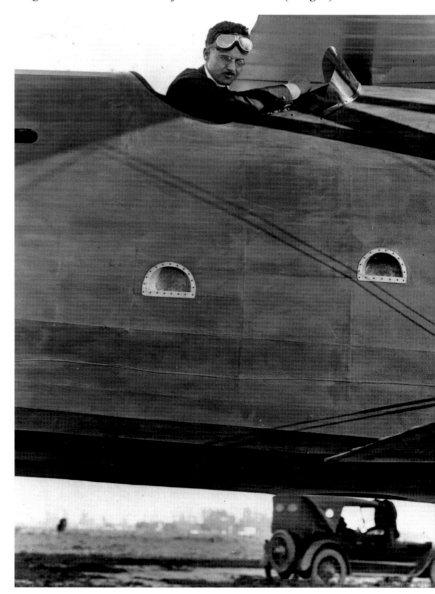

BELOW *David R. Davis sits in the cockpit of* The Cloudster; *20 years after financing this aircraft, Davis designed the high aspect ratio wing which Consolidated used for its B-24* Liberator. (Douglas)

this wealthy sport enthusiast was not interested in financing the design and production of transport aircraft, he was willing to invest $40,000 (±$415,000 today) if Douglas was prepared to design an aircraft capable of crossing the United States non-stop, a feat that had not yet been achieved.

The Davis-Douglas *Cloudster*

To undertake this work, the two partners organized a company which was registered on 22 July 1920 as the Davis-Douglas Company. Its 'Engineering Department' (if one can use such a grandiose name for a diminutive organization consisting of Douglas and five of his former Martin colleagues) was installed in the back room of a barber shop at 8817 Pico Boulevard, Los Angeles. While the record aircraft was being designed in this limited space, one of the five employees, George Strompl, purchased tools and materials for its construction and rented the second storey of the Koll Planning Mill at 421 Colton Street also in Los Angeles. Parts and assemblies built in that loft had to be lowered to the ground floor and trucked to Goodyear Field, 6.5 miles from downtown Los Angeles, where final assembly would take place in an airship hangar.

Relatively large for a single-bay equal span biplane, the aircraft had a span of 59ft 11in and a length of 36ft 9in. Although rather stout in appearance in order to provide space for two fuel tanks

BELOW *The fuselage of* The Cloudster *and its* Liberty *engine are loaded for transportation to Goodyear Field. Donald Douglas, Bill Henry, and Eric Springer are seated, from left to right, atop the fuselage; David Davis is sitting in the cockpit, and George Strompl and Henry Guerin are on either side of the aircraft's left wheel.* (Douglas)

containing a total of 560 Imp. gallons and a 41.6-gallon oil tank, the fuselage was remarkably clean for the time.[3] A 400hp 12-cylinder liquid-cooled *Liberty* engine was enclosed in the metal-covered nose with the radiator mounted underneath. The mid section of the wooden fuselage was finished with veneer panels and the aft section was fabric covered as were the wings and tail unit. The open cockpit with side-by-side seating was located aft of the trailing edge of the upper wing.

As Goodyear Field was constricted, the first take-off attempt in mid-February 1921 almost ended in a catastrophe when the pilot, Eric Springer, was forced to ground loop the aircraft. A second attempt was made on 24 February, with Springer and David Davis making an uneventful flight lasting some 30 minutes. Testing continued without problems during the following three weeks and, on 19 March, Springer flew *The Cloudster* to an altitude 19,160ft. This 'first' was followed in later years by many national and international records broken or set by aircraft bearing the Douglas name.

Due to the limited length of Goodyear Field, it was not possible for the aircraft to take off at its maximum weight of 9,600lb as required to fly non-stop between the West Coast and the East Coast of the United States. Accordingly, the attempt at making the first non-stop transcontinental flight was to start at March Field, a military aerodrome located near Riverside, and to end at Curtiss Field in Long Island, New York. As temperatures at mid-day would negatively affect the take-off performance, it was decided that the flight should start during the cool early hours of the day. Morning fog, typical and frequent at this time of the year, resulted in several postponements. At last, with Springer and Davis aboard, *The Cloudster* lifted from March Field at 6am on 27 June. Unfortunately,

---

3 In fact, the design was so clean that Eric Springer, who had been hired as test pilot, is said to have exclaimed: *'You've got a real cloud duster there, Doug'* when he first saw it. That turn of phrase appealed to the partners and the aircraft was named *The Cloudster*.

sanguine hopes were doused less than 10 hours later when, after *The Cloudster* had flown over Southern California and across Arizona, an engine failure resulted in an emergency landing at Fort Bliss, near El Paso, Texas.

Following this disappointment, David Davis lost interest in the venture and, after Donald Douglas succeeded in obtaining a first military contract, the partnership was dissolved. Having lost its *raison d'être*, the only product of the Davis-Douglas Company was temporarily forgotten. However, the basic design of *The Cloudster* – the first aircraft capable of lifting a useful load greater than its own empty weight – served as the starting point for both the first military aeroplanes to bear the name Douglas and the first aircraft to circumnavigate the world. Finally, as will be seen in Chapter 1, *The Cloudster* was sold and, after it was modified, became the first Douglas-designed aircraft to fly paying passengers.

The industrial débuts

With Jerome Hunsacker, Donald Douglas's professor and mentor at MIT, now in charge of aeronautical programs for the US Navy, the fledgling Davis-Douglas Company had no difficulty in being invited to submit a proposal in answer to a specification published on 1 February 1921 for a naval torpedo bomber. Having tendered a preliminary design derived from *The Cloudster*, the Davis-Douglas Company was awarded Contract No. 53303 for $115,850 (±1.375 million today) on 14 April. This amount covered the design, construction, and testing of three single-engined DT-1s (first Douglas torpedo bombers).

When the Davis-Douglas Company was dissolved, Donald Douglas had to search for capital to set up a new firm. Fortunately, the publisher of the *Los Angeles Times* and nine other California businessmen saw merit in the venture and agreed to co-guarantee a

ABOVE *Years after the event, the sign advertising the Engineering Dept of the Davis-Douglas Co. – incorrectly printed without the hyphen between the two names – was added in the window of the barber shop at 8817 Pico Boulevard, Los Angeles, to enable this publicity photograph to be taken.* (Douglas)

$15,000 (±$250,000 today) bank loan which enabled the Douglas Company to be organized in July 1921. Except for changing its name to Douglas Aircraft Company Inc. in 1928, the firm remained under the control of Donald Douglas and his family until 1967.

Like *The Cloudster*, the three experimental aircraft for the US Navy were built in the second-storey loft of the saw mill on Colton Street and assembled in a hangar at Goodyear Field. The single-seat DT-1 flew in November 1921 and was followed by two DT-2s which differed in having tandem cockpits. After the successful evaluation of these three machines, the US Navy ordered 40 Douglas DT-2s. They were built in new facilities located in a former movie studio of the Herrman Film Corporation at 2435 Wilshire Boulevard in the west of Los Angeles, on the edge of an open field suitable for air operations. In addition to ordering DT-2s from Douglas, the US Navy contracted with the Naval Aircraft Factory, LWF, and Dayton-Wright Company for 37 additional DTs. The last of these aircraft was withdrawn from use in November 1928.

For the first time Donald Douglas had the satisfaction of obtaining export orders, one from Peru for four DTBs and one DT-2B for Norway. In addition, Norway acquired a manufacturing license, the first for Douglas, and the *Marinens Flyvebatfabrik* went on to produce seven DT-2Bs. Finally, the DT torpedo bomber led to the development of the *Douglas World Cruiser* (DWC) for the US Air Service.

Construction of The Cloudster *is illustrated by three photographs: on the left, parts are being built in the shop of the sawmill at 421 Colton Street, Los Angeles; in the middle, the* Liberty *engine has been installed but the rear fuselage has not yet been covered; on the right, the fuselage has just been towed to Goodyear Field.* (Douglas)

OPPOSITE *The DT-1 at NAS San Diego, California, on 2 December 1921.* (USN)

RIGHT *When Douglas moved into what had been the studios of the Herrman Film Corporation at 2435 Wilshire Boulevard in Santa Monica, the setting was pastoral. Today, it is all asphalt, concrete, and glass.* (Douglas)

BELOW *Floats are being substituted for the land undercarriage of* two Douglas World Cruisers *during final preparations before the official start of the 1924 Round-the-World Flight at Sand Point Flying Field on the shores of Lake Washington.* (Army Air Service)

'First around the World'

In the years following World War One, flyers from around the world competed fiercely to become the first to cross oceans or to link ever more distant points. Circumnavigating the world by air then became an important goal for several nations (notably Argentina, France, Great Britain, Italy, and Portugal). In the United States, the War Department took the lead as, more than anything, the Air Service wanted to be ahead of the US Navy. Accordingly, either a Fokker T-5 or a modified Douglas *Cloudster* was to be acquired for testing in preparation for a round-the-world attempt. Instead of the modified *Cloudster,* requested by the Air Service, Douglas tendered a modified DT-2 with redesigned tail surfaces and interchangeable radiators of two sizes (the smaller for use in cold or temperate weather and the other for flight in the tropics). In addition, fuel capacity was increased from 98 Imp. gallons for the DT-2 to 536 gallons for the *World Cruiser* with petrol carried in a fuselage tank and three wing tanks. After testing the prototype (factory serial number 144, Air Service 23-1210), the War Department ordered four DWCs.

The four *World Cruisers*[4] departed Santa Monica on 17 March 1924, bound for Sand Point Flying Field, Lake Washington, near Seattle, from whence the flight was to start officially. Upon departure from that lake on 4 April, they set course to the north and then to the west. Two of the aircraft were lost, fortunately

4   Given Air Service serial numbers 23-1229 to 23-1232, they were numbered 1 through 4 and respectively named *Seattle, Chicago, Boston,* and *New Orleans.* They were crewed by Maj. Frederick L. Martin and SSgt. Alva L. Harvey, Lt. Lowell Smith and Lt. Leslie Arnold, Lt. Leigh Wade and SSgt Henry H. Ogden, and Lt. Erik Nelson and Lt. John Harding.

LEFT *Over the years, the Douglas logo commemorating the around-the-world flight was redesigned several times: that at the top was in use in the second half of the 1920s and that below some 10 years later.* (Douglas)

BELOW *This unarmed Douglas O-2B was assigned as a transport for Gen Mason M. Patrick, Chief of the Air Service.* (Air Service)

without fatalities, the *Seattle* crashing in Alaska on 30 April and the *Boston* having to be destroyed after alighting in the North Atlantic on 5 August. The other two, *Chicago* and *New Orleans*, reached Seattle on 28 September 1924, after covering 27,559 miles in 175 days (371 flight hours in 73 legs). Following this accomplishment, Douglas adopted the proud motto 'First Around the World' and used a logo bearing that claim for many years.

The following year the Douglas Company, the capital of which was then held by Donald Douglas and his father, experienced its first major business success. Its XO-2 biplane won the Air Service competition for a two-seat observation aircraft powered by a 420hp *Liberty* V-1650-1. A first contract covering 75 of these aircraft was awarded on 25 February 1925. Repeatedly improved and fitted with newer engines, this biplane family remained in production for 13 years. The 879th and last, an O-2MC-6 powered by a 575hp Wright R-1820-E radial engine, came off the Santa Monica line in 1938 to be delivered to China. This long lasting manufacturing run enabled Douglas both to survive the Great Depression which followed the 1929 crash and to remain in a profit position throughout the 1930s.

Often overlooked by aviation historians is the fact that the military O-2 became the first Douglas aircraft to obtain civil certification. Approved Type Certificate (ATC) No. 4 was awarded in June 1927 by the Aeronautical Branch of the Department of Commerce. Douglas was then producing *Liberty*-powered O-2Cs and O-2Hs which had not been designed to carry passengers either military or civilian.[5]

The first genuine Douglas transport aircraft

The Douglas C-1, a large single-engined biplane designed as a military transport, first flew on 2 May 1925. Twenty-six of these aircraft – the first to receive a military designation in the C (for cargo) category – were built for the Air Service. Even though these C-1s and C-1Cs were not used by airlines, they were covered by the

---

5   There were, however, a number of variants that were completed as unarmed staff transports. The O-2B and O-2J had *Liberty* engines, the O-25Bs were powered by Curtiss *Conqueror* liquid-cooled engines, and the O-38D had a Wright R-1820-E radial.

ABOVE *A spare* Liberty *engine is about to be loaded through the ventral hatch of the first Douglas C-1 during a demonstration at Wright Field, Ohio.* (WADC)

Approved Type Certificate No. 14 dated October 1927. Now Donald Douglas was positioned to design a civil transport aircraft first to carry mail and later paying passengers. A first step in that direction followed the issuance by the Post Office Department of a 1925 Request for Proposal for aircraft to replace the de Havilland DH-4Bs and DH-4Ms operated on its air network.

While the M-4, the last model in the postal biplane series, was

BELOW *Fitted with an enclosed rear cockpit, this modified Douglas M-3 mailplane was used as an instrument trainer by National Air Transport.* (United Air Lines)

being built in the plant at 2435 Wilshire Boulevard, Los Angeles, air operations were hindered by urban encroachments around the relatively small field at that site. Thus Douglas was forced to truck aircraft to Clover Field located on the edge of Ocean Park Boulevard in Santa Monica. This cumbersome arrangement was a temporary solution, and plans were begun for a permanent move to Clover Field. To build a new plant on this site, a corporate reorganisation and an increase in capital became necessary. Luckily, as the firm was financially strong, both of these steps were accomplished rapidly. On 30 November 1928, the Douglas Company gave place to the Douglas Aircraft Company, Inc. At that time two-thirds of its 300,000 shares were held by Donald Douglas and his father.

In these new facilities, Douglas began by building a small number of twin-engine *Dolphin* amphibians, including five that were sold and operated by two airlines. Moreover, with the exception of military derivatives of the DC-3 and DC-4, all DC-1 through DC-7 propliners were built at the Santa Monica plant.

During the late 1920s and early 1930s, Douglas did not limit itself to producing this small number of passenger transport amphibians, but continued to build numerous types of military aircraft. It also attempted, albeit without success, to move into the light aircraft market by building a prototype of both the *Commuter* and the DA-1 *Ambassador*. Fortunately, unabated production for the military enabled Douglas to remain solidly profitable during the Great Depression period when many other aircraft manufacturers went bankrupt. This gratifying situation allowed Donald Douglas to become a majority stockholder in a small company founded by John Knudsen 'Jack' Northrop, a brilliant engineer whose engineering genius did much for the success of the DC transport aircraft family.

The Wings of Northrop

For most, the name Northrop is synonymous with flying wings from the 1929 Model 1 bearing the experimental registration

X-216H[6] to the B-2 *Spirit* (one of the most important aircraft now in service with the USAF). Foremost, Jack Northrop deserves to be remembered for inventing and developing a construction method for conventional wings. Adopted by Douglas for its DC propliners, this wing design gave them a service life much longer than that of contemporary airliners, either built by Boeing or Lockheed in the United States or by various manufacturers in Europe.

Jack Northrop was born on 10 November 1895 in Newark, New Jersey, and came to California with his parents when he was nine years old. He made his aeronautical début in 1916 when, due to his talent as an industrial draftsman, he was hired by the Loughead Aircraft Manufacturing Company in Santa Barbara, California. There he began by designing the wings for the F-1 flying boat and doing the structural calculations for that aircraft. Later, still working for the Loughead brothers (who changed their corporate name to Lockheed in 1926), he designed a light aircraft biplane, the S-1. When this company went bankrupt in 1923, Jack Northrop joined the Douglas Company, where he designed new tail surfaces and radiators for the *World Cruiser* before becoming its chief engineer. In 1927, he went back to work for the restructured Lockheed for which he created the noteworthy *Vega* monoplane. A year later, Jack Northrop founded his first company, Avion Corporation in Burbank, California.

It was then that Northrop developed his multi-cellular wing structure and used it for his Model 1 flying wing which was tested at Muroc Dry Lake for over a year beginning in September 1929. Shortly afterward, the economic situation forced Jack Northrop to sell his small company to United Aircraft & Transport Corporation in Wichita, Kansas. To lead the Northrop Corporation, the purpose-created UATC subsidiary, he had to move to Kansas, where he produced 17 Northrop *Alpha* single-engined transports and two Northrop *Beta* single-engined light aircraft.

Jack Northrop, however, was no longer his own man. Moreover, he wanted to return to California to carry on his activities without corporate ties. It was his former boss and friend, Donald Douglas, who enabled him to achieve his goal by providing 51% of the capital of Northrop Corporation[7] in January 1932.

---

6 This aircraft was not a genuine flying wing as it had conventional tail surfaces mounted at the end of booms.

7 Douglas could afford making this investment as, in spite of the economic crisis in the United States, its sales and profit in 1931 amounted respectively to $3.8 million and $549,000 (±$54 million and $7.8 million). During that year, Douglas sold 245 aircraft, exceeding earlier benchmarks.

BELOW *This Northrop* Alpha *4A of Transcontinental and Western Air was fitted with an experimental radio transmitter with a tall mast aft of the cockpit.* (Stearman)

The new firm began work in its own facilities in El Segundo, on the edge of Mines Field, later to become the Los Angeles International Airport (LAX). The first aircraft built in this plant were single-engined aircraft carrying on the tradition of being named with Greek letters. As detailed in Chapter 1, several of these *Gammas* and *Deltas* were used commercially to carry passengers and mail. The Northrop Corporation, however, primarily built military aircraft (see Appendix 3) with the most important of these being A-17 attack aircraft for the Army Air Corps and carrier-based BT-1 dive bombers for the US Navy.

While production of the A-17s, a retractable landing gear version of the Northrop A-17, was underway at El Segundo, employees of the Northrop Corporation went on strike. Jack Northrop, being close to his staff, wanted to compromise. Donald Douglas, the majority stockholder, took a firmer position. Not surprisingly, what had to happen, happened. Douglas bought up the shares held by Jack Northrop and his friends to gain full control of the firm. On 5 April 1937, the Northrop Corporation became the El Segundo Division of the Douglas Aircraft Company. Strikers went back to work and this new division of Douglas went on to remain in operation until 1962. Among the many famous aircraft produced by the El Segundo Division during this 25-year period, were the carrier-based *Dauntless, Skyraider, Skyknight, Skyray, Skywarrior*, and *Skyhawk*.

Jack Northrop rebounded quickly from his disappointment in the loss of his company in 1937 and in August 1939 had the pleasure of organizing a new firm, Northrop Aircraft, Inc. in Hawthorne, again in the sprawling Los Angeles metropolis. He remained president of that company until his retirement in 1952. Jack Northrop passed away on 18 February 1981, but his company remains prosperous to this day. Renamed Northrop Grumman Corporation in 1994, following its merger with Grumman, the firm is a major naval, air, and space manufacturer in the United States. In recent years, it has grown by acquiring Westinghouse Defense Electronics in 1996, Logicon Corporation in 1997, Teledyne Ryan Aeronautical in 1999, Litton Industries and Newport News Ship Building both in 2001, and TRW, Inc. in 2002.

In the end, as far as the history of DC airliners is concerned, Jack Northrop's most significant contribution remains his multi-cellular wing design.

ABOVE *The Northrop* Delta *1D-7 became the RT-1 transport of the US Coast Guard.* (NA&SM)

A legend is born

When Donald Douglas became the majority stockholder of the Northrop Corporation in early 1932, the manufacturing activities of the nearby[8] Douglas Aircraft Company were centered on variants of its series of observation biplanes. O-25Cs powered by Curtiss V-1570-77 *Conqueror* liquid-cooled engines, O-38Bs with Pratt & Whitney R-1690-5 radials, and BT-2C trainers with Pratt & Whitney R-1340-1s were produced for the Army Air Corps and the National Guard, while O-2MCs for export to China had various radial engines. In addition, Douglas Aircraft was producing small numbers of *Dolphin* amphibians for civil and military customers, and had begun building twin-engined Y1B-7 and Y1O-35 parasol monoplanes for the AAC.

8 Air distance between Mines Field, on the edge of which Northrop was located, and Clover Field, home for Douglas, was only six miles.

BELOW *The Douglas XB-7 underwent armament trials at Wright Field, Ohio.* (Army Air Corps)

ABOVE *For 15 years, Donald Douglas had wanted to build airliners. He was able to enter this market after his company responded to a TWA request with the DC-1.* (Douglas)

While this was taking place, the US economy had entered a steep downward spiral with the gross national product falling from $103.6 billion in 1929 to $76.5 billion the following year. (GNP, expressed in actual dollars, dropped further in subsequent years to bottom out at $56.4 billion in 1934.) The unemployment rate was 15.8% at the end of 1931 and went up to 24.75% two years later. Under these conditions, the future of industrial companies, including Douglas Aircraft, appeared rather cloudy.

BELOW *The future of the Douglas Aircraft Company was further secured when its twin-engined light bomber/attack aircraft was ordered successively for the French, British, and American air forces. This is the first DB-7 for the* armée de l'Air. (Douglas)

Most opportunely, the company received a letter which would change the course of its history and finally enable its founder to undertake the manufacturing of airliners. Dated 2 August 1932 and signed by Jack Frye, Vice President in Charge of Operations at Transcontinental & Western Air, Inc. (TWA), this letter was identical to those sent simultaneously to Consolidated, Curtiss, Ford, and Martin. Boeing, the other major contemporary manufacturer, did not get that letter as, earlier, it had refused to deliver Boeing 247s to Transcontinental & Western Air before completing delivery of the 60 aircraft ordered by United Air Line, the principal competitor of TWA on transcontinental routes. In this letter, TWA expressed its intent to acquire at least 10 aircraft. In these years of financial drought, this was indeed a promising market. Consequently, the competitors sought to do better than what the client was requesting or that Boeing was providing to United Air Line with its Model 247. However, none were able to do better, or even as well, as Douglas with what became known as the DC-1 (Douglas Commercial 1).

The DC-1 first flew at Santa Monica on 1 July 1933, and flight testing proved its excellent performance. TWA ordered an initial

batch of 20 DC-2s, which was the production model of the DC-1 with one more row of seats to accommodate 14 instead of 12 passengers. In the end, the Santa Monica aeronautical firm built a total of 197 DC-2s and military derivatives before going on with the production of the DC-3, a variant with a wider fuselage. Including military models, Douglas built a total of 10,655 DC-3s and derivatives. Furthermore, this famous aircraft was built under license in Japan and the Soviet Union. (The DC-3 history is related in Chapters 4 and 8.) This activity enabled the Douglas Aircraft Company to hoist itself into first place among the world aircraft manufacturers as its revenues and profit increased rapidly. The latter went from $38,753 to $10,381,971 (±$625,000 to $165,200,000) between 1934 and 1940. During that same period, prototypes of the DF civil flying boat and of a first DC-4 (the future DC-4E, see Chapter 6) were realized. Note that Douglas did not neglect military programs during the second half of the 1930s. In Santa Monica, activities centered on the manufacturing of B-18 and B-23 bombers as well as on the development of the very large XB-19 bomber. In El Segundo, activities were reversed with emphasis being put on the manufacturing of single-engined military aircraft (Northrop A-17s for the Army Air Corps, Douglas 8As for export customers, Northrop BT-1s for the USN, and the first Douglas SBDs for the USN and the USMC) and twin-engined DB-7s for France and Great Britain. The exception to this military emphasis was the twin-engined DC-5 as related in Chapter 7.

In 1940, not surprisingly, activities were on the rise for the whole US aircraft industry. On one hand, airlines, mostly in the United States, continued to place large orders (for which Douglas was the principal beneficiary). On the other hand, beginning in 1938, France and Great Britain began ordering large numbers of military aircraft from US manufacturers.[9] Douglas received a first French order for 100 DB-7s in February 1939, with Great Britain following a year later by ordering 150 DB-7B *Bostons*. Furthermore, President Franklin D. Roosevelt requested that aeronautical manufacturing in the United States be rapidly increased.[10] Faced with orders of such magnitude, the aviation industry had to enlarge plants and/or build new ones. Financing of this expansion was made easier by the United States government.

First, the Emergency Plant Facilities program enabled manufacturers to obtain financing at favorable terms from the Reconstruction Finance Corporation. Furthermore, the government undertook to purchase these new plants at the end of a five-year period. Next, the Defense Plant Corporation was organized as a government entity to build new plants for leasing to aircraft and engine manufacturers for the duration of the war.

In the case of Douglas, the first of these programs saw a subsidiary, Western Land Improvement Company, acquire 200 acres on the edge of the municipal airport in Long Beach and the construction of a plant with an initial 1.5 million square feet of floor space. Under the other program, Douglas leased plants from the government which were located in Chicago, Illinois, and in Oklahoma City and Tulsa, Oklahoma.

The war years

In the months preceding and immediately following the entry into the war of the United States, the Douglas order book increased rapidly. Production was then divided between six plants: Chicago

ABOVE *With the exception of a few clerical employees, few women worked for Douglas during the 1930s. That changed rapidly during the war years with women accounting for 45% of the work force in 1944 (that number rising to 48% on the assembly lines).* (LOC)

(DC), El Segundo (DE), Long Beach (DL), Oklahoma City (DK), Santa Monica (DO), and Tulsa (DT).

Leased from the government, plants in Chicago and Oklahoma each built only one type of aircraft: Chicago produced 655 C-54-DCs (the military version of the DC-4) and the plant in Oklahoma City built 5,409 C-47-DKs and C-117-DKs (thus becoming the principal manufacturing center for DC-3 military variants.)[11] The last C-117 was delivered to the USAAF on 29 December 1945. Immediately after the war, when most military contracts were terminated, these two plants were returned to the government. That in Chicago disappeared several years later when the O'Hare International Airport was enlarged. In Oklahoma City, the former Douglas plant became one of the principal overall maintenance depots for the USAF, the Oklahoma City Air Materiel Area at Tinker AFB.

In the four other plants, production was more diversified. In Tulsa, also leased from the government, work began in 1943 to build 615 A-24B-DTs (a derivative of the SBD-5 *Dauntless* without a tail hook as ordered by the USAAF). These were followed by the assembly of Ford-produced components to deliver 964 Consolidated B-24D/E/H/J-DTs as part of the multi-company *Liberator Production Pool* which resulted in a total production of 18,482 of this four-engined aircraft. The first B-24E-DT (serial 41-28409) was delivered on 4 March 1943, and the first A-24B-DT (serial 42-54285) on 15 May 1943. Afterward, 1,291 A-26B/C-DTs, as well as one XA-26E-DT, were built in the Tulsa plant. This factory was returned to the government after the war, but was once again leased by Douglas during the Korean War to build Boeing B-47 *Stratojets* under the BLD program (Boeing, Lockheed, Douglas) and Douglas RB-66C-DT and WB-66D-DT *Destroyers*.

In the then new Long Beach plant, the first aircraft built, the

9 To obtain the rapid deliveries which they needed to face rising Nazi strength, France and Great Britain lent funds to airframe and engine companies, a fact which is too often ignored by the more jingoistic elements of the American population. In the case of Douglas, this financial infusion made possible the acquisition of additional tooling and an enlargement of the Santa Monica plant.
10 As early as 1938, the US aircraft industry had been urged to increase its annual output to 10,000 aeroplanes including 3,750 combat aircraft. In June 1940, President Roosevelt raised the annual production goal to 50,000 aircraft. It was again revised upward to 60,000 in 1942 and to 125,000 in 1943. In the end, production topped out in 1944 when 100,572 aircraft were delivered.

11 The first C-47A-DK, serial 42-92094, came off the assembly line in Oklahoma City in March 1943. The first *Skymaster* delivered from the Chicago plant (C-54A-1-DC, 42-72166) was accepted by the USAAF on 1 October 1943.

OPPOSITE *During World War Two, Douglas built Boeing B-17s in its Long Beach plant and Consolidated B-24s in its Tulsa plant. It then went on to build Boeing B-47s in Tulsa during the early Cold War years.* (USAAF)

ABOVE *The only aircraft built in the government-owned plant in Chicago were 655 Skymasters, including this C-54D-5-DC.* (Peter B. Lewis)

BELOW *After World war Two had ended, the Santa Monica plant was kept busy building DC-3Ds and DC-4s, and modifying surplus C-47s and C-54s to airline specifications.* (Douglas)

C-47-DL (serial 41-7722), was delivered to the USAAF on 1 February 1942. During the war, this plant produced 4,284 additional *Skytrains* and *Dakotas*, 999 Douglas A-20B-DLs, 3,000 Boeing B-17F/G-DLs, and 1,157 Douglas A-26B/C *Invaders*. Construction of the C-74 *Globemaster* was also begun in Long Beach but had not been completed when Japan surrendered. After the war, this plant was transferred to the government, but Douglas began reacquiring part of it in November 1946 to begin producing C-124-DL *Globemaster II*s. Later Douglas purchased the entire plant and greatly expanded it to house manufacturing halls for the DC-8s, DC-9s and DC-10s and its headquarters relocated from Santa Monica. Much later, when activities progressively diminished,

the size of the facility remaining in use was reduced. Finally, only manufacturing of C-17A *Globemaster III*s remained in Long Beach following the takeover by Boeing. These World War Two facilities and the Douglas headquarters in Long Beach have now been razed.

During World War Two, the traditional plants in Santa Monica (in use since 1929) and in El Segundo (opened in 1932) saw their activities divided respectively between production for the USAAF and for the USN (including, in both instances, Lend-Lease contracts). As a Navy plant, El Segundo focused its wartime activities on the production of the obsolescent SBD *Dauntless*. It also undertook the development and limited production of the less successful XSB2D-1 and BTD-1 and built prototypes of the XA-26 *Invader*, XTB2D-1 *Skypirate*, and XBT2D-1 *Dauntless II* (later to become famous as the AD and A-1 *Skyraider*). Finally, prototypes of the Bowlus troop transport gliders, the XCG-7 and XCG-8, were manufactured in El Segundo.

Controlled by the USAAF, the Santa Monica plant briefly continued building DC-3s for civil customers and then began producing minimum-change derivatives of the DC-3 under military contracts. During the war years, it was mainly responsible for the production of DB-7s and A-20s, and ended up delivering 5,998 *Havocs* and *Bostons* out of the total of 7,478 from all sources. It also built 589 C-54 *Skymasters*.

Whereas the Chicago, Long Beach, Oklahoma City, and Tulsa plants had only small numbers of engineers on staff to supervise production and develop minor modifications, the engineering departments in El Segundo and Santa Monica grew rapidly. In the case of the former, principal undertakings resulted in prototypes of the *Destroyer* (XSB2D-1), *Skypirate* (XTB2D-1), and *Invader* (XA-26). During that growth period, the engineering staff in Santa Monica designed the XB-42 and XB-43 bombers (the latter becoming the first US jet bomber), the XC-112 (the DC-6 military prototype as related in Chapter 10), and the XC-74 (which almost led to a first DC-7 development; see Chapter 12).

The Douglas Aircraft Company played a vital role throughout the Second World War. Between 1 January 1940 and 31 August 1945, its plants in California, Illinois and Oklahoma produced 30,903 aircraft to take second place behind North American (which built only single- and twin-engined aircraft). By total airframe weight, Douglas was number one with 306,573lb (15.3% of the US industry total).

BELOW *In 1944, two BTD-1s were modified into XBTD-2s with the addition of a turbojet mounted at a downward angle aft of the cockpit. They were the first Douglas aircraft fitted with jet engines.* (Douglas)

Postwar and the jet age

Even before the Japanese surrender in August 1945, the US government had begun cancelling military contracts. The end of fighting was followed by an acceleration of this procedure and led to massive layoffs. At Douglas, employment dropped from a high of over 140,000 in 1943 to only 24,900 in 1946. The plants in Chicago, Oklahoma City and Tulsa were closed and activities in Long Beach massively reduced. The number of aircraft delivered dropped from 11,598 in 1944 (the all time record for Douglas) to 5,353 in 1945 and 127 in 1946.

For the El Segundo division, survival came from Navy orders for the AD *Skyraider*, albeit barely keeping the production line open. Led by Edward Heinemann, the design team at that plant was fortunately able to obtain several contracts for the D-558-1 *Skystreak* and D-558-2 *Skyrocket*[12] transonic and supersonic research aircraft. The Navy also ordered prototypes of a jet night fighter (the XF3D *Skyknight*), an attack aircraft with coupled turbines (the XA2D-1 *Skyshark*), a carrier-based fighter of novel concept (the XF4D-1 *Skyray*), and a twin-engined carrier-based bomber (the XA3D-1 *Skywarrior*).

Postwar, commercial operators urgently needed to modernize their fleets, a task for which Douglas was better positioned than other manufacturers as large numbers of C-47s and C-54s became surplus to military requirements and were available for modification into airliners. In addition, a smaller number of airframes, left unfinished due to military cancellations, were completed in Santa Monica as DC-3Ds and DC4-1009s.

Long-term, the civil market appeared equally promising for Douglas as it had a range of aircraft which had been developed as part of military contracts. They included the pressurized-cabin DC-6 (which, still carrying its USAAF XE-112-DO designation, flew in February 1946); the large capacity Model 415 (derived from the XC-74); and the Model 1004 (which, offered as the DC-8 *Skybus*, relied on the aerodynamically clean layout of the XB-42 with two inline engines in the fuselage driving contra-rotating propellers aft of the tail unit). Indeed, after overcoming problems during its first year in operation, the DC-6 became a huge success, giving birth to numerous civil and military variants as well as to the DC-7 series (see Chapters 10 and 13). Conversely nothing came about from Model 415 which was too large and costly and Model 1004 which was too ambitious. Douglas then attempted to rejuvenate its DC-3 by turning it into the Super DC-3:

12 On 20 November 1953, the *Skyrocket* became the first aircraft to fly at twice the speed of sound.

however, it was simply not competitive with the faster and larger Convair offerings.

The first flight of a Douglas aircraft fitted with a jet engine was made in May 1944 at the Los Angeles Municipal Airport (ex Mines Field). Retaining the Wright R-3350-14 radial of the BTD-1, the XBTD-2 added a 1,500lb st Westinghouse WE-19 XA mounted at an angle in the rear fuselage. The next Douglas jet, the XB-43 with two 3,750lb st General Electric J35-GE-3s, first flew at Muroc Army Air Base on 17 May 1946.

Whereas the El Segundo design team launched itself enthusiastically into the development of aircraft with turbine, turbojet, or rocket engines, the more conservative team at Santa Monica did not begin testing another jet-powered aircraft, the X-3 *Stiletto*, until September 1952. This overly prudent attitude led Douglas to hesitate for a long time before undertaking the financially-risky development of a first jetliner, the DC-8. Even though the development of this jetliner had been announced in August 1952, Douglas only confirmed that decision three years later. This was a costly error as Boeing had no such hesitation.

During the 1950s, the conflict in Korea and the Cold War resulted in renewed military activities for aircraft manufacturers. For Douglas, its El Segundo team benefitted the most with substantial Navy orders for AD *Skyraiders* and A4D *Skyhawks*. Conversely, the design teams in Santa Monica and Long Beach obtained only smaller production contracts for C-124 *Globemaster II*s, B-66 *Destroyers*, and C-133 *Cargomasters*. Douglas also received a contract for 262 Boeing B-47 *Stratojets*, with license manufacturing taking place at the Tulsa plant that had reopened at the end of 1951.

The end of a legend

Since the beginning of the firm, Donald W. Douglas had been both its president and Chairman of its Board, and for many years the Douglas family held a majority of the company shares. In 1957, Donald W.

ABOVE *Northwest Airlines ordered five Douglas DC-8-32s. Disappointed with their performance, this carrier did not re-order DC-8s and traded its five for Boeing 707s.* (Douglas)

Douglas Jr[13] succeeded his father at the presidency while his father remained as Chairman of the Board while progressively reducing his involvement in operations. In search of greater financial returns, father and son sold a majority of their company shares to invest in real estate after their lucrative participation investment in Western Land Improvement Company, the subsidiary which had been formed in 1940 to acquire land for the Long Beach plant. With real estate development in nearby Orange County booming, they anticipated better and more rapid opportunities to increase their wealth than continuing to depend on the cyclical aircraft market. Paying less attention to their aircraft business and having become minority stockholders in the Douglas Aircraft Company proved nefarious.

Proud successor of the long line of Douglas propliners, the DC-8 was first flown on 20 May 1958 and it appeared to have a brilliant future. Unfortunately, several major and costly difficulties prevented early production DC-8s from meeting performance guarantees. Douglas did what was necessary to correct these shortcomings, but heavy losses were incurred (a total of ±$390 million today dollars for the years 1959 and 1960, the first losses ever for the company). These difficulties prevented Douglas from financing the development of a second jetliner, the Model 2067, to compete against the Convair 880 and 990 and the Boeing 720. In an attempt to hold its competitive position while minimizing

13 Donald Wills Douglas Jr was born on 3 July 1917 in Washington, D.C. Although he studied mechanical engineering at Stanford University and aeronautical engineering at the Curtiss-Wright Technical Institute, he did not graduate from either. Joining his father's company in 1939, he first worked in its strength group before gaining further experience working in various departments. Appointed manager of flight test in 1943, he later became director of the testing division. He was promoted vice president of the Douglas Aircraft Company in 1951, elected to its board of directors in 1953, and named president in 1957. Following the merger with McDonnell 10 years later, he served as senior vice president for MDC until retiring in 1974. He remained on the board of Directors of the McDonnell Douglas Corporation until 1989. He passed away on 3 October 2004.

investments, Douglas reached an agreement with France's Sud-Aviation to market its twinjet *Caravelle* in most of the world. Should demand so justify, production under license would take place in Santa Monica. Boeing reacted decisively by offering its 727 trijet with better performance and more suitable due to its properly dimensioned belly holds. The Boeing 727 quickly pushed the *Caravelle* into second place. Sales petered out, and Douglas had no reason to build the French jetliner.

The Long Beach team fared even less well in the military field as, after winning its last production contract in 1954 (for the C-133), it lost several major competitions (including those for the Lockheed C-141 in 1961 and the C-5 in 1965). While Santa Monica and Long Beach struggled, El Segundo kept Douglas in military contention, mainly thanks to its A-4 *Skyhawk*. Sadly, the ongoing rivalry between engineers in Santa Monica and El Segundo became increasingly petty. Finally, in 1962, Donald Douglas Jr[14] decided to bring an end to the design team which had been so effectively led by Ed Heinemann since the 1930s. The El Segundo plant closed and production of the *Skyhawk* was transferred to Long Beach with final assembly and testing undertaken at Palmdale, in the Mojave Desert, in facilities leased from the government.

Errors continued to mount. First, when the program that led to the DC-9 (and its updated MD-80, MD-90, and Boeing 717 versions) was launched, management failed to give credence to market research studies that had predicted a strong demand for twinjets. Industrial and financial planning were undertaken on a greatly minimized demand. The rapid and impressive sales success of the DC-9 beginning in 1965 caught his company by surprise. In Long Beach, production rates were repeatedly stepped up. Unfortunately, this required the hiring of additional personnel at

ABOVE *To this day, the Douglas DC-9 remains the champion of 'stretching.' The fuselage of the DC-9-30, illustrated by this PSA aircraft, was 14.4% longer than that of the DC-9-10. That of the MD-90 was 46.2% longer than that of the first DC-9.* (Douglas)

OPPOSITE TOP *Belonging to General Electric and registered N420GE, this* Caravelle III *undertook a demonstration tour in the United States with the names of both its manufacturer and its proposed licensee applied to the fuselage sides.* (Douglas)

OPPOSITE BOTTOM *The C-17 military cargo aircraft was designed and initially built by McDonnell Douglas in the old Douglas plant in Long Beach. It is still being built there, but it now is the 'Boeing' C-17.* (USAF)

a time when assembly line workers were much in demand due to increased military production resulting from operations in Vietnam. Douglas lost control over costs due to these needs. At the same time, it made the error of offering a large capacity double deck jetliner. Larger than the 747 proposed by Boeing, the D-950 and D-956 were simply ignored by airlines.

The Douglas Aircraft Company was in a bind, and the only solution was to merge expeditiously. It so happened that the McDonnell family then owned more shares in Douglas than did the Douglas family. Consequently, the Saint Louis firm gained control and the McDonnell Douglas Corporation came into being on 28 April 1967.

Although he had retired several years earlier, Donald Wills Douglas Sr became honorary Chairman of the McDonnell Douglas Corporation in 1967. He retained that title until passing away on 1 February 1981, 47 years and seven months after the first flight of the DC-1. Douglas disappeared when MDC was taken over by Boeing 16 years after the death of its founder.

---

14 Those familiar with father and son referred to them as 'Doug' and 'Junior.' Behind the latter's back, the moniker 'Bambi' was often used, notably by disgruntled former employees of the El Segundo Division.

Air transport in the 1920s and 1930s

One-third of the DC-1s through DC-7s were sold to export customers. Mainly, however, it was the needs of American carriers which proved determinant. The exception was the DC-5 which was developed at the request of KLM Royal Dutch, but of which only four actually were sold abroad. Hence, a summary of major air transport events in America during the 15 years which followed the First World War and preceded the entry into service of the DC-2 provides the required background to understand the development of Douglas propliners.

History records that the first passenger in a heavier-than-air machine was Henri Farman. On 21 March 1908, he was taken aloft at Issy-les Moulineaux, France, by his rival Léon Delagrange. On 8 July of that year, Delagrange took his companion, Thérèse Peltier, who thus became the first woman passenger during a short flight in Turin, Italy. In the United States, the first passenger was Charles Furnas, a mechanic for the Wright brothers, who was taken aloft by Wilbur Wright at Kitty Hawk, North Carolina, on 14 May 1908. These three had not paid for their flights, and it was only in January 1914 that a first 'paying' passenger discovered the joy of air travel under the Florida sun. During World War One, it was the transport of mail that became, at least in the United States, the primary justification for air transport. In Europe, aircraft had found a less altruistic use.

BELOW *Flying during the winter months on air mail routes in the Northern United States required that heavy protective clothing be worn, as does the pilot of a Waco 10 operating on CAM-11 between Ohio and Pennsylvania.* (LOC)

Air mail in the United States

Nevertheless, the first air mail flight was not made in America; Claude Graham-White did so on 10 August 1910 in Great Britain. Starting at Squires Gate near Blackpool, this seven-mile flight in a Blériot monoplane was essentially a stunt as it was not sponsored by the Royal Mail. During the following year, things became more businesslike with several experiments being officially sanctioned by postal authorities in Asia, Africa, and on both sides of the Atlantic. The first saw a Frenchman, Henri Piquet, carry 6,500 letters and post cards in a Humber biplane while flying the five miles between Allahabad and Nayni in India on 18 February 1911.

During the month of September 1911, there were several air mail flights:

• Between the 9th and 26th, to commemorate the Coronation of H. M. King George V, three pilots relayed each other to carry some 25,000 letters and 90,000 postcards between London (Hendon) and Windsor (Royal Farm). A Farman biplane and Blériot monoplanes made 20 flights during this financially profitable venture.

• Between the 13th and 20th, a quasi-official air mail flight was made in French Morocco to demonstrate that aircraft could be viable substitutes for ground transportation in countries with insufficient infrastructure. Henri Brégi took off from Casablanca on the 13th bound for Rabat in his Breguet III. On the 19th, he went on to Meknès in spite of coming under rebel fire and having to contend with a strong Sirocco wind. On the 20th, he landed at his destination in Fez after covering 200 miles in three flights.

• On the 19th, Achille Dal Mistro carried mail in a Deperdussin monoplane between Bologna and Venice, Italy, a distance of 90 miles.

In the United States, mail was first transported by air on 23 September 1911 between Nassau Boulevard in Long Island and Mineola (these two points in New York state being but 10 miles apart). Flying a Blériot *Queen*, Earle L. Ovington dropped a bag of mail in Mineola at the end of his first flight on the 23rd. On hitting the ground, that bag burst open and a wild chase ensued to retrieve the mail blown by the wind. In the following days, numerous flights were successfully completed, after the bags had been suitably reinforced. At the end of these trials, on 2 October, a total of 32,415 postcards, 3,993 letters, and 1,062 leaflets had been transported at no cost to the Post Office Department.

Other attempts at carrying air mail were undertaken in the United States during the following years but, in 1912, the Post Office Department was unable to obtain approval of the budget required to make these ventures consequential. Hence, the carriage of mail by air did not become official business until 1918, some 13 months after the United States had entered the war.

Regular flights for the Post Office Department began on 15 May 1918 between New York, Philadelphia and Washington D.C. with Curtiss *Jenny* biplanes then being flown by military pilots. Beginning on 12 August, the 220 miles between these three points were covered in about four hours, six days a week (except on Sundays) by Standard JR-1Bs flown by Post Office Department pilots. The air mail rate was 16 cents per ounce (or eight times the standard rate and equivalent to ±$2.00 today), but this surcharge was soon eliminated. Operations on this route ceased on 21 May 1921, after further funding was refused by Congress.

During this period, air mail operations were progressively extended across the United States, first between Cleveland and Chicago on 15 May 1919 and then between Cleveland and New York on 1 July. In 1920, links were opened between Chicago and Omaha on 15 May and between Omaha and San Francisco on 8 September. This last leg completed the opening of the first transcontinental air mail route, the *Columbia Route*. Letters sent by air across the country arrived at least 22 hours before those sent by the fastest land transportation available. It was a modest improvement, but to do better would require flying at night instead of making overnight stops.

In addition to this first transcontinental line, air mail was being carried on feeder routes, many of which were operated by private contractors. Initially, specially-modified de Havilland DH-4s were the most common for air mail flights. Among the other types in service were state-of-the art Junkers-Larson JL-6 metal monoplanes (an Americanized development of the German Junkers F-13) and the Douglas-designed Martin MP twin-engine.

As early as 1920, as stated above, it was evident that air mail would become a successful venture only if flights could take place at night as well as during daylight hours. Accordingly, in August 1920, the Post Office Department began installing radios, lights, and beacons along the major postal airlanes. Another significant improvement resulted from ordering specially designed mailplanes (the winner of this competition being the Douglas M[1]).

Carrying twice the load of the DH-4, the Douglas M flew faster

ABOVE *Before Henri Brégi could take off from Rabat, French Morocco, in a Breguet III on 19 September 1911, mail was duly stamped and inventoried.* (Musée de l'Air)

and had a longer range, resulting in a reduction in the number of refuelling stops. Moreover, specialized equipment on the ground enabled night flights to be undertaken, experimentally between Chicago–Iowa City–Omaha–North Platte–Cheyenne on 21 August 1923. Regular night operations began on 1 July 1924, reducing the time necessary for the transcontinental link to 35 hours from east to west and less than 30 hours in the opposite direction. Moreover,

BELOW *While officials posed for a photographer, Earle L. Ovington is handed the first bag of air mail carried in the United States on 23 September 1911.* (Bain News Service)

---

1 First delivered in May 1926, the Douglas M could carry either 1,000lb of mail or two passengers forward of the open cockpit.

ABOVE *Personnel and pilots of the US Post Office Department stand in front of a Standard JR-1B in August 1918.* (LOC)

LEFT *To replace its de Havilland DH-4Bs, the US Post Office Department acquired Douglas mailplanes, including this M-4 photographed in Santa Monica before being officially delivered.* (Douglas)

BELOW *Even though the Boeing 40C was powered by a Pratt & Whitney Wasp radial engine that was more powerful than the Liberty engines of the Douglas Mailplanes, the aircraft of the M series were better performing. The Boeing, however, could carry four passengers in an enclosed cabin whereas the Douglas could only accommodate two persons in an open compartment.* (Boeing)

reliability and flight safety were significantly improved as the result of a Post Office overhaul and modification program for the *Liberty* engines of the Douglas *Mailplanes*.

Once postal authorities had demonstrated that the air carriage of mail was a reliable activity, Congress decided that it should be privatized with various sectors being put up for bid. This was made possible by the Air Mail Act of 1925 (also known as the Kelly Act) which was signed by President Calvin Coolidge on 2 February 1925. On 7 October of that year, contracts for the first five CAM (Contract Air Mail) routes were signed to cover links feeding the transcontinental route. Contracts for more routes were then awarded, and the first commercial air mail flight was made on 15 February 1926 on CAM 6 (Detroit to Chicago) by Stout 2-AT single-engined airplanes[2] of the Ford Motor Company.

The two main sectors of the transcontinental route went to private companies in 1927. Commencing on 1 July 1927, Boeing Air Transport (BAT) was responsible for flights between Chicago and San Francisco with numerous stops and night operations only between Chicago and Cheyenne. National Air Transport (NAT) operated between New York and Chicago beginning on 1 September.[3] This completed the transfer of operations between the Post Office Department and air mail carriers. Several of these companies then also began flying passengers on their routes. This situation remained unchanged until 9 February 1934 when President Franklin D. Roosevelt cancelled all contracts.

Passenger transport in the United States

On 1 January 1914, the first paying passenger on a heavier-than-air machine was flown from Saint Petersburg to Tampa, Florida. The airplane, a Benoist XIV single-engined flying boat piloted by Tony Jannus and transporting A.C. Pheil, covered the 18 miles between these two Florida cities in 23 minutes. Over the next four months, more than 1,200 passengers were carried on this route across Tampa Bay for the one-way fare of five dollars (±$110 today). Once service ended on this overwater run, five more years went by before air transportation was again available in the United States.

ABOVE *On 1 January 1914, A.C. Pheil became the first paying passenger to fly in a heavier-than-air machine, this Benoist XIV that flew him across Tampa Bay, in Florida, in 23 minutes.* (Peter M. Bowers collection)

Three factors made this rebirth possible in 1919.[4] The first two, as was also the case in Europe, were the ready availability of both airplanes and pilots after the First World War. The third, however, was uniquely American. On 16 January 1919, the 18th article of Amendment to the Constitution of the United States of America was ratified. It forbade the production, sales, transport, and importation of alcoholic beverages.[5] Many Americans quickly sought to find ways around the Prohibition. This provided the impetus for several more-or-less scrupulous entrepreneurs to offer flights to nearby foreign destinations where those able to afford such travel could quench their thirst without fear of breaking US laws.

Beginning operations on 4 July 1919, before Prohibition-related air transport came into being, Syd Chaplin[6] Airlines began linking San Pedro (in the port district of Los Angeles) with Avalon Bay in Santa Catalina Island. Curtiss MF flying boats were used for these 34-mile flights until 1922 when Pacific Marine Airways, which had taken over from the Chaplin Airlines, placed Douglas-modified Curtiss HS-2Ls into service (see Chapter 1).

Also using HS-2L flying boats which had been adapted to carry passengers, but not by Douglas, Aero Ltd inaugurated a non-scheduled service between New York and Atlantic City, New Jersey, in August 1919. During the summer of that year, Aero Ltd became the first to provide flights for 'thirsty' clientele, with customers flown from Miami, Florida, to Nassau in the Bahamas. Other carriers followed with flights between Florida and Cuba, and between points in the state of New York and Montreal, another 'wet' destination. Appropriately nicknamed *High Ball Express*, flights from New York to South Carolina (Beaufort) and Florida (Miami and Key West), with extensions to 'wet' destinations in La Havana and Nassau, provided America Trans Oceanic Airways with the opportunity of becoming the principal provider of these specialized services.

---

2 It has often been written that operations on CAM 6 began on 13 April 1925. This appears to be erroneous as Ford was not awarded contracts for CAMs 6 and 7 until 21 October 1925. It is true, however, that earlier Ford had begun carrying freight by air for its own operations, and that this experience enabled it to start contract operations more swiftly than other awardees.
3 Flying from east to west, against the prevailing wind, air mail flights crossed the continent in 31hr 45min, including ground time.

4 In Europe, passenger operations started a few months earlier than in the United States, *Deutsche Luft Reederei* first carrying paying passengers, between Berlin and Weimar, via Leipzig, on 5 February 1919.
5 Amendment XVIII was repelled on 5 December 1933 when the Amendment XXI was ratified. Beer, wine, and hard liquors became once again readily available in the United States.
6 Syd Chaplin was the half-brother of the legendary comic actor, Sir Charles Spencer 'Charlie' Chaplin.

ABOVE *Before beginning scheduled passenger operations between San Diego and Los Angeles, T. Claude Ryan modified six Standard J-1 biplanes by fitting four seats in an enclosed compartment, behind the engine but in front of the cockpit.* (Ryan)

While entertaining, these 'wet' flights did less for the future of passenger air operations than those started by T. Claude Ryan in California. Beginning on 1 March 1925, he provided scheduled flights between San Diego and Los Angeles with six Standard J-1 biplanes fitted with a four-passenger enclosed cabin ahead of the open cockpit. As results were encouraging, Ryan added the Douglas *Cloudster* to his Los Angeles–San Diego Air Line fleet. As related in Chapter 1, Ryan modified *The Cloudster* by installing 10 seats in an enclosed cabin aft of the engine; one more passenger could be seated to the right of the pilot in the open cockpit. Using modified Standard J-1s and *Cloudster*, his airline carried 5,600 passengers in 1926. However, the following year Ryan lost interest in the airline, preferring to focus his activities on aircraft manufacturing (including the NYP *Spirit of St. Louis* of Charles Lindbergh).

The year 1926 was profitable not only for Ryan but also for many of the mail carriers operating under contract from the Post Office Department and several of them branched out to carry passengers occasionally. This was notably the case of Western Air Express (WAE) which flew its first passenger on 23 May 1926 between Los Angeles and Salt Lake City. The customer, however, had to sit uncomfortably in the open mail compartment forward of the cockpit of a Douglas M-2 (see Chapter 1). In spite of these various undertakings, air transport in America continued to lag behind European achievements. In part, this was due to the fact that available single-engined aircraft were uncomfortable and proved ill-suited to operations over the lengthier routes in the United States. Consequently, Americans then showed only limited interest in air transportation.

The situation changed rapidly after three-engined aircraft, better suited to carrying passengers, were put into service. Fokker

F.VIIa-3ms with an eight-passenger enclosed cabin were introduced by Philadelphia Rapid Transit (PRT) on 6 July 1926. This airline had to operate without the added revenue from air mail until it obtained the CAM 13 contract to carry mail between Philadelphia and Washington D.C. Four weeks later, Stout Air Services began flying Ford 4-ATs (with an enclosed cabin seating ten) on the Detroit–Grand Rapids route (CAM 14).

It was also in 1926 that the Air Commerce Act was promulgated. Among other provisions, this new law gave the responsibility for planning, building, and maintaining a radio communications and navigational air network across the nation to the United States Department of Commerce. Fledgling airlines thus were freed from the need to finance this costly system. Conversely, they lost some of their freedom of operation as the Department of Commerce was also given authority to regulate air transportation. Moreover, this 1926 Act created the Aeronautic Branch of the Department of Commerce which quickly initiated the Approved Type Certificate (ATC) system for civil aircraft.

For the most part, this was beneficial even though the Secretary of Commerce was also given almost dictatorial power over the air transportation industry. Soon, secretary Walter Folger Brown was accused by political opponents of exceeding his authority. This situation grew progressively worse and, after the 1932 presidential election put a Democrat in the White House, it became necessary to backtrack. On 9 February 1934, 11 months after becoming the 32nd president, Franklin D. Roosevelt cancelled all air mail contracts. During the ensuing *Air Mail Emergency,* postal air operations became the responsibility of the Air Service of the United States Army. Deprived of air mail revenues, airlines would have great difficulties to survive. Fortunately, the upset was of short duration and, following the signing on 12 June 1934 of a new Air Mail Act, the situation returned to normal.

Celebrating the crossing of the North Atlantic by Charles Lindbergh in May 1927 with considerable enthusiasm, the American public found new interest in air transportation. Soon benefitting from this development, airlines took the necessary steps to attract

a growing number of passengers by placing faster and more comfortable aircraft into service. This was notably the case of the three-engined Fokker F-10 and Boeing 80 which entered service respectively with Western Air Express on 26 May 1928 and Boeing Air Transport on 30 October 1928. Next, the four-engined Fokker F-32, the first American airplane to carry 30 passengers, was added by Western Air Express on 13 December 1929. Moreover, several of these airlines began offering improved services: cold meals were first served by co-pilots of Western Air Express F-10s in May 1928; the first male flight attendants (then called *couriers*) began serving hot meals in Ford 5-ATs of Stout Air Services in July 1929; and stewardesses made their appearance in May 1930 aboard Boeing 80As of Boeing Air Transport.

With night flying remaining precarious, the first passenger line across the United States was opened on 7 July 1929 using a combination of air and rail transportation. Passengers left New York aboard trains of Pennsylvania Railroad which took them during the night to Columbus, Ohio. In the morning, they boarded Ford 5-ATs of Transcontinental Air Transport (TAT) bound for Waynoka, Oklahoma (with intermediate stops in Indianapolis, Saint Louis, Kansas City, and Wichita). During the night passengers were transported to Clovis, New Mexico by Santa Fe Railroad. There another TAT aircraft took them to their destination, Los Angeles, with refueling stops being made in Albuquerque, New Mexico and Winslow, Arizona. The air-rail trip was made in 48hr 26min (as against 80hr by train only) with a one-way fare of $339.98 (±$4,200 today). In October 1930, when Transcontinental & Western Air (which had succeeded to TAT) dispensed with rail links, travel time from east to west was reduced to 35hr 9min (34hr 18min in the opposite direction). Flights from Newark[7] to Los Angeles still required 11 intermediate stops, but one-way fares fell to $200 (a 40% reduction in one year).

The end of the 1920s was a period of unfettered capitalism

ABOVE *Ford* Tri-Motors *were among the most significant airliners in use in the United States prior to the DC era. This one is a 4AT-A operated on the Detroit–Cleveland route by Stout Air Services.* (Peter M. Bowers collection)

during which several major financial groups became interested in civil aviation and created conglomerates to bring together airlines, aircraft and engine manufacturers, as well as related companies. The principal of these conglomerates were:

- The North American Aviation Company which, led by General Motors, regrouped two airlines (TAT and Eastern) as well as several companies producing aviation equipment (the most important of which being the Fokker Aircraft Company of America) in December 1928.
- United Aircraft & Transportation Corporation (UATC) which was organized two months later and was comprised of aircraft manufacturers (Boeing, Chance Vought, Northrop, and Sikorsky), an engine manufacturer (Pratt & Whitney), propeller manufacturers (Hamilton and Standard), and an airline (Boeing Air Transport).

Conglomerates such as these were looked upon favorably by Republicans who had been in power since 1921 but worried Democrats. The situation got increasingly bitter in 1930 when Secretary Brown in the Republican administration of Herbert Clark Hoover encouraged further consolidation among airlines. This led on 21 July 1930 to the organization of Transcontinental & Western Air (TWA) following a three-way shotgun wedding between TAT, WAE, and Pittsburg Aviation Industry Corporation.

Two months after acquiring National Air Transport, UATC organized United Air Lines on 1 July 1931 by combining NAT and BAT. The new airline was then the only one offering transcontinental service on the most direct route, that between New York, Chicago, and San Francisco. As indicated earlier, TAT (later TWA) flew between the two coasts along the *Lindbergh Route* linking New York and Los Angeles by crossing the country in its middle along a slightly longer path.

---

7   Newark, in New Jersey across the Hudson River from New York City, was then the airport used by carriers serving the greater New York area. The New York Municipal Airport-La Guardia Field and the New York International Airport (now JFK) came into use respectively in October 1939 and July 1948.

ABOVE *Ellen Church became the first 'air hostess' on 15 May 1939 while working aboard a Boeing 80A of Boeing Air Transport. A male cabin attendant, then called a 'courier', had first flown on 7 July 1929 aboard a Ford 5-AT of Transcontinental Air Express. His name has long been forgotten.* (Boeing)

BELOW *Transcontinental and Western Air came into being in 1930 when three carriers (TAT to which belongs this Ford 5-AT, WAE, and PAIC) were encouraged by the government to merge. TWA changed its name to Trans World Airlines 20 years later.* (Ford)

A third player on transcontinental operations made its appearance in January 1930 when American Airways was organized by the Aviation Corporation (AVCO) which regrouped several airlines. By combining the air mail contracts of the companies from which it had been organized, American was able to offer service between New York and Los Angeles along a route further south. However, as that route was longer American Airways (which became American Airlines in 1934) began by offering a mixed air and rail service. Afterward, American followed the lead of Eastern Air Transport by using sleeper-planes for night flights, hoping that the comfort provided by these Curtiss *Condors* would offset the longer travel time.

While the air transportation industry was at last making fast progress in America, a well-publicized accident had lasting consequences. On 31 March 1931, shortly after taking off from the Kansas City Municipal Airport, NC999E, a Fokker F-10A of TWA, crashed into a corn field near Bazaar, Kansas, after losing a wing in flight. The six passengers and two crew members were killed. One of the passengers was Knute Rockne, the legendary American football coach of the Notre Dame University team, who was travelling to Hollywood to become technical consultant in the production of a sport movie. A media frenzy resulted. Fokker F-10As and other aircraft with wooden wings saw their use as passenger transport planes subjected to new and costly regulations in the United States.

ABOVE *After one of its Fokker F-10As broke up in flight on 31 March 1931, TWA urgently needed to modernize its fleet. This requirement gave birth to the long lines of Douglas Commercial aircraft.* (H. Hazelwinkel collection)

To replace them, a new generation of airliners became desirable. The three transcontinental airlines took the lead by pushing Boeing and Douglas to develop aircraft that soon were to revolutionize the air transport industry. United put the Boeing 247 in service on 30 March 1933, TWA followed with the Douglas DC-2 on 18 May 1934, and American added the DST beginning on 25 June 1936.

Chapter 1

Commercial début

The DC-1 (Douglas Commercial One) was the first in the lasting series of airliners developed and built by the California airframe manufacturer. It was not, however, the first Douglas aircraft to carry paying passengers. The following aeroplanes became the first 'Douglas'[1] aircraft to have that distinction.

- In 1919, US Army officers were flown in the Martin GMP, a transport version of the GMB bomber which had been designed by Donald Wills Douglas for the Glenn L. Martin Company. With its fully enclosed cockpit in the nose and a 12-seat cabin

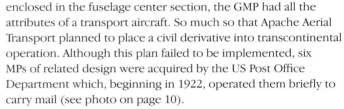

1   In this instance, 'Douglas' has to be written in quotation marks as the GMP was designed, not built, by Donald Douglas, while the other three were rebuilt by Douglas to designs by others.

enclosed in the fuselage center section, the GMP had all the attributes of a transport aircraft. So much so that Apache Aerial Transport planned to place a civil derivative into transcontinental operation. Although this plan failed to be implemented, six MPs of related design were acquired by the US Post Office Department which, beginning in 1922, operated them briefly to carry mail (see photo on page 10).

- Also in 1922, 11 years before the maiden flight of the DC-1, two Curtiss HS-2L flying boats were modified by Douglas for Pacific Marine Airways to carry passengers between Wilmington (in the port district of Los Angeles) and Santa Catalina Island, thus becoming the first Douglas-engineered aeroplane in commercial service.

- Next the Davis-Douglas *Cloudster* was twice modified to carry passengers: first by Douglas for two California businessmen, Thornton Kinney and Benjamin Brodsky, and then by T. Claude Ryan for his airline.

LEFT *The first paying passengers to fly in a 'Douglas' did so neither in the DC-1 nor its DC-2 production version, but in two Curtiss HS-2Ls which had been built by Boeing and modified by Douglas. The second of these flying-boats had an enclosed cabin whereas the first had six seats in an open space (see photograph on page 323).* (Douglas)

BELOW *The Martin GMP (or GMT) was the first transport aircraft designed by Donald Douglas, but it was not used to carry paying passengers.* (Air Service)

Production for others and by others

While working on the DT torpedo bombers and the DWC record aircraft, the newly organized Douglas Company undertook to modify two Boeing-built Curtiss HS-2Ls to turn them into passenger transport aircraft using Aeromarine drawings and new parts built by Douglas in his installation at the Koll Planing Mill. The first of these single-engined flying boats, the former BuNo A-4237 of the US Navy, was transported by land from NAS San Diego to Los Angeles on 27 March 1922, and was fitted with a four-seat open cabin in the forward portion of the hull. The former A-4251 followed suit on 22 April and differed only in having an enclosed cabin in the same location.

The modified flying boats entered service in early summer 1922 with Pacific Marine Airways. They were used to fly passengers between Wilmington and Hamilton Cove, a small bay near Avalon on Santa Catalina Island. The one-way fare for the 34-mile 20-minute flight was $12.50 (±$160.00 today). A third HS-2L modified by another contractor was added to the fleet. All three

ABOVE The airframe of the first Boeing-built HS-2Ls (BuNo A-4327) was delivered to the Davis-Douglas Company in March 1922. Donald Douglas is standing, hatless and hands in pockets, in front of this flying boat. (Douglas)

remained in use on this seasonal route until Western Air Express took over Pacific Marine Airways in June 1928 and replaced these ageing flying boats with Loening C-2H amphibians. A record 3,500 passengers were carried by the three HS-2Ls in 1927. Not a single accident was recorded in six years of operation.

Donald W. Douglas and David R. Davis had gotten together in June 1920 for the express purpose of building *The Cloudster* with which Davis hoped to become the first to fly non-stop across the

BELOW The Cloudster *was modified for Thornton Kinney and Benjamin Brodsky by replacing some of the fuel tanks with two open cabins.* (Ryan)

ABOVE *Ryan replaced the two open cabins of* The Cloudster *with an enclosed compartment with ten seats. In this modified configuration, the cockpit was moved forward of the wings.* (Ryan)

ABOVE *This picture shows the enclosed cabin of the Ryan-modified* Cloudster. (Ryan)

BELOW *The modified* Cloudster *was also used to carry beer barrels in Baja California during the prohibition years.* (Ryan)

United States. Following the abandonment of that attempt on 27 June 1921, Davis lost interest in the venture, and *The Cloudster* was brought back to California where it remained unused for several months. In May 1923, it lost its *raison d'être* when the Air Service made the first non-stop crossing using a Fokker T-2.

The Cloudster was then sold to two real estate developers, Thornton Kinney and Benjamin Brodsky, in Venice, a tourist destination on the coast of Los Angeles. The two men wanted this aircraft to be modified to carry prospective real estate customers and tourists wishing to ogle sunbathers and admire the spectacular California views. To this end, two of the large fuel tanks between the *Liberty* engine and the cockpit were removed to provide space for twin open-air compartments. Each could accommodate two to four passengers with an additional passenger sitting next to the pilot in the cockpit.

When this business venture failed after a few months, *The Cloudster* was sold to the Ryan Flying Company of San Diego. This firm had been organized in March 1924 by T. Claude Ryan and Benjamin 'Frank' Mahoney to use six military-surplus Standard biplanes to link San Diego with Los Angeles, the first air route in the United States to be operated year-round on a regular schedule. The one way fare on this 120-mile trip was $17.50 (±$225.00 today).

Having acquired *The Cloudster* at the end of 1925, the company was reorganized by Mahoney as Ryan Airlines, the name Ryan being retained even though T. Claude Ryan had withdrawn from the venture. Shortly thereafter, the aircraft was damaged in a heavy landing. Douglas rebuilt it using a new upper wing and the fuselage that Ryan had modified to obtain a genuine airliner. The cockpit was then relocated forward of the wing just behind the engine. Aft of it, a ten-passenger enclosed cabin was provided with five seats on each side of the central aisle. Access to this cabin was by means of an upward-hinged door on the left side of the upper fuselage. The *Liberty* engine installation was also modified first by adding a tall pipe to carry exhaust fumes above the wing and then by dispensing with the propeller spinner and installing a new radiator around the propeller shaft to improve cooling during the hot summer months.

In its new configuration, *The Cloudster* was used in 1926 not only

for scheduled flights between the two Southern California cities but also for charter flights between San Diego and San Clemente Island. In December 1926, when the Mexican road between Enseñada and Tijuana had been washed away, *The Cloudster* was used to transport beer and whisky thus ensuring an uninterrupted supply of alcoholic beverages to the Baja California border town, a 'critical' need for those living north of the border during Prohibition. In a less questionable use, *The Cloudster* flew a Chinese businessman on the return trip to Enseñada. On that occasion, the pilot was unable to reach his destination before nightfall and chose to land on a beach. During the night, the rising tide destroyed it. The wreck of *The Cloudster* remained on the beach when the tide withdrew, an ignominious ending for the first Douglas aircraft.

The Cloudster, as modified by Ryan, and the two HS-2Ls modified by Douglas went without a successor for several years. Surviving by producing military aircraft and mailplanes, the Douglas Company had to wait to make its entry in the airliner business.

The mailplanes

Needing to replace the DH-4Bs and DH-4Ms which constituted the bulk of its air mail fleet, in 1925 the Post Office Department invited manufacturers to submit proposals for new mailplanes. This provided Douglas with the opportunity of entering the civil aircraft market by developing a mailplane derived from its observation biplanes. The resulting Douglas Air Mail 1 (DAM-1) retained the O-2 airframe and its *Liberty* engine, albeit with a revised radiator installation. The cockpit was moved aft, to what had been the radio-gunner station in military aircraft. This provided space aft of the engine for a fire-proof, aluminum-and-asbestos lined compartment with a capacity of 55.8cu ft for 1,000lb of mail loaded through two hatches atop the fuselage. Bearing the factory serial number 169,[2] the DAM-1 was first flown at Santa Monica on 6 July 1925 by Eric Springer, and was leased for one year to the Post Office Department for operational testing. During this period, it was fitted with a 150,000-candle power landing light under each lower wingtip and two 30,000-candle power parachute flares; in addition, individual exhaust stacks on both sides of the cowling were replaced by long collective pipes to reduce glare in the cockpit

during night operations. Once it had been so modified, the DAM-1 was flown by Post Office pilots on the transcontinental mail route, mostly between Chicago, Illinois, and Elko, Nevada. While leased to the Post Office Department, the DAM-1 was damaged. It was then returned to Douglas which rebuilt it to M-2 production[3] standard before delivering to it Western Air Express in June 1926.

As we have seen earlier, the United States Government decided to privatize air mail operations before the DAM-1 was put into service by the Post Office Department. After President Calvin Coolidge signed the Kelly Act, five mail routes feeding into the transcontinental trunk line were awarded on 7 October 1925 to private companies. More contracts were then quickly awarded.

Although powered by a *Liberty* engine as were its main competitors, the Curtiss Model 40 *Carrier Pigeon*, and the aircraft it replaced, the US-built DH-4, the first production version of the Douglas mailplane performed substantially better than either. The M-2 had a top speed of 145mph versus only 125mph for the *Carrier Pigeon* and 123mph for the DH-4M. Carrying a full load, the M-2 had a range of 645 miles compared to 525 miles for the *Carrier Pigeon* and 350 miles for the DH-4M. Moreover, the M-2 carried 1,000lb of mail, twice the load of the DH-4M. Consequently, Douglas mailplanes quickly became the principal aircraft used for postal service and enabled their manufacturer to build up a solid reputation with many air carriers.

Western Air Express was one of the first companies that were awarded a contract by the Post Office Department. It had been purposely organized in Los Angeles to bid for Contract Air Mail 4 (CAM 4) linking Los Angeles with Las Vegas, Nevada, and Salt Lake City, Utah, a distance totaling 625 miles. To operate on this route, WAE began by ordering five Douglas M-2s in December 1925. They differed from the DAM-1 principally in being fitted with a frontal radiator as had been designed by Douglas for the O-2BS[4] in order to operate as a floatplane. Their mail compartments, forward of

---

2   *The Cloudster*, the first aircraft to receive a Douglas fsn, had been numbered 100 in a futile attempt to make believe that the company had already produced 99 aeroplanes. Thus, the DAM-1 was actually the 70th aircraft produced by a Douglas company.

3   Whereas production models of the Douglas mailplane received M-2 through M-4 designations, the first, the DAM-1, never was officially referred to as the M-1 in order to avoid confusion with the mailplane of another manufacturer, the Ryan M-1 monoplane which had first flown on 14 February 1926.

4   The O-2BS was a special modification of the O-2B command aircraft of the Air Service that was built as a civil aircraft for James McKee. This Pittsburgh businessman used it to realize the first single-pilot trans-Canada flight between 11 and 19 September 1926.

ABOVE *The Douglas Air Mail One (DAM-1) is shown in its original configuration.* (Douglas)

ABOVE *This is one of the Douglas M-2s with which Western Air Express began operations. Photographed at Vail Field, Los Angeles, in 1926, it has been configured to carry one passenger and 500lb of mail in addition to the pilot.* (Western Airlines)

the cockpit, could seat two passengers in open tandem cockpits. As indicated above, the fledgling airline later obtained a sixth M-2 as well as the DAM-1 which had been rebuilt to M-2 standard by Douglas after suffering damage during earlier operations.

Operation on CAM 4 began on 17 April 1926, when two mail-carrying M-2s flown by Charles 'Jimmy' James and Maurice 'Morry' Graham took off, one from Salt Lake City flying toward the southwest and the other from Los Angeles flying in the opposite direction. Two passengers, Ben F. Redman and J. A. Tomlinson, were carried from Salt Lake City to Los Angeles on 23 May 1926 in an M-2 flown by Jimmy James. The one-way fare for this eight-hour flight was $90.00 (±$1,000 today, or about the current economy class round-trip fare from London to Los Angeles). For the first time, a Douglas designed and built aircraft had carried paying passengers. It was the unheralded beginning of a long line. In June 1927, the Aeronautics Branch of the Department of Commerce issued the ATC No 5 to this Douglas airliner.

BELOW *With engine warming up, this M-3 of National Air Transport was about to depart for a flight on CAM 17 (Chicago to New York). Note the large radio mast aft of the cockpit.* (United Airlines)

With the last of its own air mail operations continuing until the summer of 1927 while route transfer to private contractors proceeded slowly, the Post Office Department needed to replace DH-4s reaching the end of their useful life. This led to a government order for ten Douglas M-3s being placed in March 1926, followed shortly thereafter by one for 40 M-4s. Essentially similar to the M-2s of Western Air Express, the M-3s added landing lights, flares, and long exhaust pipes for night operations as first retrofitted to the DAM-1. To improve performance (particularly weight lifting) under high altitude and hot temperature conditions, such as prevailing in the summer in the mid and western United States, M-4s received wings of increased span and area.[5] After being operated by the Post Office for a relatively short period, M-3s and M-4s were sold to the private companies which had obtained air mail contracts, principally National Air Transport which went on to operate Douglas mailplanes until October 1930.

The first Douglas military transport aircraft

Funds for Contract AC810 were included in the budget for fiscal year 1925 (from 1 July 1924 to 30 June 1925) to cover the acquisition of nine Douglas C-1s, the first purpose-designed transport aircraft for the *Air Service* and the first to be ordered from Douglas. Powered by 435hp *Liberty* engines, they were outwardly similar to the O-2C observation aircraft with non staggered wings of equal span. They were, however, significantly heavier, more corpulent, and larger, with the fuselage length increased from 28ft 6in for the first O-2 to 35ft 4in for the C-1. Pilot and assistant-pilot or mechanic sat side-by-side in an open cockpit aft of the engine, slightly ahead of the wing's leading edge. Behind them, a 10ft-long, 3ft 10in-wide, and 4ft 2in-high enclosed cabin could be arranged with eight individual seats for military personnel or with five litters plus a seat for a medical attendant. Alternatively 2,500lb of cargo could be carried, loading and unloading of bulky items, such as a spare engine, being made through a ventral hatch.

Nine C-1s and 17 C-1Cs saw extensive use with the Air Service and the Air Corps but seldom carried civilian passengers. The notable exception occurred in 1926 on the occasion of an aviation rally sponsored by the Ford Motor Company (The National Air Tour for the Edsel B. Ford Reliability Trophy or simply the Ford National

5   Span went from 39ft 8in for the M-2s and M-3s to 44ft 6in for the M-4s, with a resulting increase in wing area from 411 to 465sq ft.

ABOVE *For this April 1927 publicity shot, the 'passengers' in the cabin of an Army Air Corps C-1C are Douglas employees.* (Douglas)

ABOVE *Boarding steps eased access to the C-1 cabin.* (Douglas)

BELOW *This ski-equipped C-1 was photographed at Wright Field, Ohio, on 21 April 1926.* (Douglas)

Reliability Air Tour) that took place between 7 and 21 August 1926. Prior to the start of the tour, journalists and officials were taken on a 2,600-mile circuit covering 10 central states. This single civilian use was, perhaps, what led the Aeronautics Branch to award ATC No 14 retroactively to the Douglas C-1 in October 1927.

The Douglas *Dolphin*

In 1930, Douglas flew the *Sinbad*, a twin-engined flying boat for two pilots and up to eight passengers. At the beginning of the following year, this prototype was sold to the US Coast Guard while Douglas began building *Dolphin* amphibians. Retaining the layout of the *Sinbad* flying boat, the *Dolphins* differed in having both a retractable undercarriage mounted outside the hull and their engines raised further up above the wings to keep the propellers out of the water spray. Planned as a luxury 'air yacht' and offered with a choice of radial engines, the *Dolphin* initially attracted the attention of two wealthy Americans: the inventor and industrialist Powel Crosley Jr, and the candy and gum manufacturer William Wrigley Jr.

The 58th and last *Dolphin* was delivered in 1934 with manufacturing of these amphibians having been undertaken in a quasi-artisanal manner with aircraft in many configurations in spite of the limited production. Notably, no fewer than 16 different 300 to 550hp models of Pratt & Whitney and Wright radial engines powered *Dolphins,* with some of these aircraft having wooden wings while others had fabric-covered metal wings. Non-US government customers, six wealthy private operators (among them the previously-mentioned Crosley and Wrigley), the Standard Oil Company, and the Argentine Navy (*Armada Argentina*), all demanded customized interiors, finishing and equipment. In spite of the willingness of the manufacturer to satisfy conflicting customer requirements, sales of *Dolphins* to civil and export customers were disappointing during the Great Depression years. In the end Douglas avoided taking a financial bath only due to the fortuitous success of the military versions of its amphibians: 24 *Dolphins* being built for the Army Air Corps, 11 for the USN, and 11 for the US Coast Guard. The remaining four were built to carry paying passengers.

ABOVE *Drilling rigs at the Long Beach oil field provided the backdrop for this Dolphin 114 of Wilmington-Catalina Airlines.* (Peter M. Bowers collection)

Located close to the coast of Southern California, Santa Catalina Island has a temperate climate much appreciated by residents of the Los Angeles metropolis during the early fall when desert winds bring land temperatures to an unpleasantly high level. Much of the land on Santa Catalina was owned by the chewing-gum-fortune Wrigley family which wanted to make access to this island easier for tourists and those wishing to build vacation homes. The first flight from the coast to this island was made on 10 May 1912, by Glenn L. Martin. Then, as related in the preamble, airlines began transporting passengers aboard Curtiss MFs, Douglas-modified HS-2Ls, and Loening C2Hs.

To replace the Loening amphibians, two six-passenger *Dolphin 1s* were acquired by the Wilmington-Catalina Airline. A third Douglas amphibian (that which William Wrigley Jr had acquired earlier for his own use) was quickly added to the fleet. In spite of the difficult economic situation during the 1930s, business for this small airline prospered, requiring that cabin seating be increased from six to ten with an 11th passenger sitting in the cockpit on the right-hand seat. With flights lasting but 12 minutes, this 'high density' configuration did not attract many customer complaints. One-way and round-trip fares in the mid-1930s were respectively $4.75 and $8.00 (±$70.00 and $120.00 today). From 1932 until December 1941 when America entered the war and operations ceased, the Wilmington-Catalina Airline carried over 200,000 passengers in the course of some 38,000 crossings all without a notable incident.

On the other side of the Pacific, two *Dolphins* were operated by the China National Aviation Corporation (CNAC). Having acquired 45% of its capital in March 1933, Pan American Airways supplied

OPPOSITE *These two views show the same* Dolphin 114 *of CNAC, the Chinese affiliate of Pan American Airways. The ground shot was taken in Santa Monica and the other shows NC14240 flying over Shanghai on 5 January 1935.* (Douglas)

several aircraft to this Sino-American company. Delivered to Pan American in August 1934, the two *Dolphins* for CNAC were shipped to Shanghai. With a six-seat cabin, they were mainly used between this port and Canton, via Wenchow, Foochow, Amoy, and Swatow. After Shanghai fell to the Japanese at the end of 1937, CNAC transferred its operations to Hong Kong. By then, however, the two *Dolphins* were no longer in use, having likely been destroyed in Shanghai during Japanese bombing and straffing raids.

Gamma and Delta

Jack Northrop was the main proponent of single-engined passenger and mail monoplanes in America. He started in this line of business by designing for Lockheed the remarkable *Vega* high-wing monoplane which flew in July 1927 and became a major success. Three years later, for the Northrop Aircraft Corporation (then a subsidiary of United Aircraft & Transportation Corporation), he came up with the *Alpha* mail-carrying monoplane and the *Beta* sport monoplane. In 1932, after Donald Douglas had helped him to set up the Northrop Corporation, he continued this activity by developing the *Gamma* and the *Delta* which had wings similar to those of the *Alpha*.

Although conceived as a mailplane, the *Gamma* was essentially hand-built so that aircraft in the series could be quickly finished in a variety of configurations. The first, the *Gamma 2A*, was a single-seater acquired by the Texaco Oil Company for its record breaking pilot Frank Hawks. Northrop then built 59 additional *Gammas* as racing aircraft, bombers, advanced trainers, test beds, etc. Only three of these, the *Gamma 2D*s, were delivered as mailplanes to TWA with a cargo compartment ahead of the single seat cockpit.

Jack Frye flew NR13757, the first of the *Gamma 2D*s, on 13 and 14 May 1934 to set an 11hr 31min transcontinental record

(Los Angeles to Newark with a refueling stop in Kansas City), the flight being made on the day airlines again flew postal flights following the *Air Mail Emergency*. The next *Gamma 2D* was modified by TWA as a high altitude, overweather research airplane. The main modification consisted of substituting a 775hp Wright SR-1820-F532 with a General Electric turbocharger, for the original 710hp SR-1820-F3 radial. In addition, space for a flight test engineer and recording equipment occupied what had been the mail compartment. With the exception of the sole *Delta 1E*, the *Deltas* differed essentially from the *Gamma* in having the cockpit moved forward, just behind and above the engine, followed by an eight-seat enclosed cabin. When the *Delta 1A* was first flown in May 1933, Northrop and Douglas had high hopes for a major commercial success. Unfortunately, in October 1934, the US Government mandated that single-engined airplanes no longer be used to transport passengers at night or over routes where an emergency landing would be difficult. Consequently only three of the 32 *Deltas* built by Northrop and, under license, by Canadian Vickers, went to airlines as passenger transports:

- The first was a *Delta 1B* put into operation by *Aerovías Centrales S.A.* in Mexico in August 1922.
- The Swedish airline *A.B. Aerotransport* ordered two *Deltas* on 21 April 1934. Its passenger-carrying *1C* set a record between Stockholm and Paris by linking the two capitals in 4hr 55min at an average speed of 200mph. The other, the *1E* mailplane, was a two-seater looking much like a *Gamma*.
- The last to carry passengers was a *Delta 1D2* which remained in use with *Líneas Aéreas Postales Españolas* until March 1939.

The design and construction process[6] of the *Gamma* and *Delta* contributed much to the commercial success of the first DCs. In particular the DC-3 and its military versions were to prove exceptionally sturdy and long lasting thanks to Jack Northrop.

BELOW *The second Northrop* Gamma 2D *of Transcontinental and Western Air is shown before its modification into a high-altitude research aircraft.* (Northrop Institute of Technology)

---

6   The all-metal wings were of typical Northrop multi-spar construction with the no-dihedral cen-tre section built integrally with the fuselage and the outer panels, with dihedral and fabric-covered control surfaces, bolted to the center section.

ABOVE *The Northrop Delta 1B of* Aerovías Centrales S.A. *was registered X-ABED in Mexico.* (Douglas)

BELOW A.B. Aerotransport – Swedish Air Lines *acquired two Northrop monoplanes in 1934: SE-ADI, on the left is a* Delta 1C *with single-seat cockpit and an eight-seat passenger cabin; SE-ADW, on the right, is a* Delta 1E *with two-seat cockpit and mail compartment between the engine and the cockpit.* (SAS)

Chapter 2

DC-1 – The founder of the dynasty

Following the crash of the TWA Flight 599 (a Fokker F-10A registered NC999E) on 31 March 1931, the Bureau of Air Commerce instructed operators to undertake frequent inspection of the wing structure of all airliners with wooden spars and ribs such as used for F-10As. As such inspections would prove excessively costly and time consuming for fledgling US airlines, most opted to replace wooden-winged aircraft with newer designs as soon as possible. At the lower end of the market (aircraft with no more than eight seats), the Lockheed *Orion* which had been flying since March 1931 found favor with several carriers. It combined a

fuselage primarily built of wood with metal wings, had a retractable undercarriage, and was powered by radial engines, either Pratt & Whitney *Wasps* or Wright *Cyclones,* enclosed in NACA cowlings. Maximum speed ranged between 215 and 225mph depending on engine selection.

The pioneer aircraft with more seats came from the Boeing Airplane Company. Since February 1929, this firm had been part of the United Aircraft & Transportation Corporation which also included an airline, Boeing Air Transport, and an engine manufacturer, Pratt & Whitney. On 6 May 1930 and 12 April 1931, respectively, the Seattle aircraft manufacturer had flown prototypes of two new low-wing monoplanes:

- The Model 200 *Monomail* was an all-metal, single-engined aircraft designed to carry 220lb of cargo and mail in a compartment ahead of the single-pilot open cockpit. Equipped

BELOW *Photographed during one of its early flights, X223Y displays the fairings between the forward fuselage and the engine nacelles as initially mounted on the DC-1.* (Douglas)

with partially retractable undercarriage and ground-adjustable propellers, this *Monomail* was built for Boeing Air Transport (which became United Air Lines in 1931) and was later modified as the Model 221A to carry eight passengers in lieu of mail. The Boeing airline later acquired a revised six-seat *Monomail*, the Model 221.

- The company financed prototypes for both the Model 214 and Model 215 twin-engined bombers incorporated modern features similar to those of the Model 200 but had four open cockpits. The Army Air Corps then acquired five improved Model 246 bombers which carried the Y1B-9A military designation.

Experience gained by its aircraft manufacturer with the *Monomail*, and more so with the twin-engined bombers, convinced UATC that a high-performance airliner powered by two of the radial engines from its Pratt & Whitney subsidiary would give a significant competitive advantage to its Boeing Air Transport/United Air Lines. Thus, as the development of the new airliner and its operations would remain with members of the conglomerate, UATC authorized Boeing in 1932 to proceed with its design.

Incorporating the structural and aerodynamic features of the *Monomail* and the B-9 bomber, the Model 247 had low-mounted wings, anodized skin, a sound-proofed and heated passenger cabin and an electrically-operated retractable undercarriage. Townend rings were fitted over the cylinders of its Pratt & Whitney *Wasp* radials. Truly, the Boeing 247 was a revolutionary aeroplane when it first flew at Seattle on 8 February 1933.

Entering service 50 days later, on 30 March, the new Boeing immediately rendered obsolete the Boeing 80 biplanes and Fokker F-10 and Ford 5-AT monoplanes, all of which were trimotors with fixed undercarriage, that had entered service only five years earlier. Although they had gone into service just five weeks before the Model 247, the Curtiss T-32 *Condor* biplane also proved no longer competitive in spite of its retractable undercarriage.

ABOVE *With its low-mounted metal-structure wings, retractable undercarriage and close-fitting engine cowling, the Lockheed* Orion *(here a 9E of TWA) was an exceptionally clean aircraft for its day.* (Lockheed)

BELOW *Contractually obligated to hand over 60 Model 247s to its affiliated company, United Air Lines, before delivering others to competitors, Boeing had to turn down a TWA request. That refusal opened the door for Douglas to enter the airline market.* (Boeing)

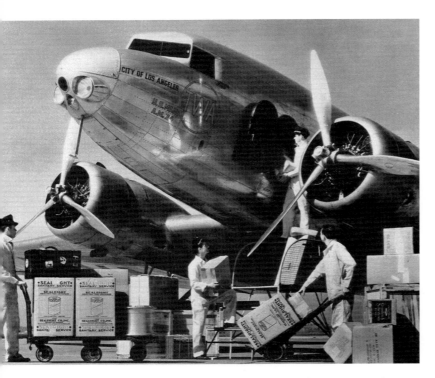

ABOVE *In preparation for a proving flight on the TWA network, cargo is being loaded in the DC-1.* (TWA)

BELOW *The letter sent by TWA on 2 August 1932 has been called 'The Birth Certificate of the DC Ships'.* (Douglas)

Rivals of United Air Lines on the transcontinental route found themselves at an immediate competitive disadvantage. In particular, Transcontinental & Western Air was heavily affected due to the operating restrictions which had been imposed on its Fokker F-10As following the 31 March 1931 accident.

When it learned that the Model 247 had been ordered by United Air Lines, TWA attempted to order some of these new twin-engined aircraft in the hopes that it would be able to take delivery soon after its rival. Unfortunately, Boeing was contractually obligated to deliver all 60 Model 247s ordered by its affiliate before supplying other customers, particularly one competing with United on the prestigious transcontinental route. After briefly contemplating designing a three-engined derivative of the Model 247 to meet the particular performance requirements of TWA, Boeing demurred.

Transcontinental & Western Air lost little time before its Vice President in Charge of Operations, Jack Frye, sent a letter to Consolidated Aircraft Corp., Curtiss-Wright Corp., Douglas Aircraft Co., General Aviation Manufacturing Corp., Stout Metal Airplane Co. (Ford), and Glenn L. Martin Co. In this letter, Frye asked the six manufacturers if they would be interested in building 60 three-engined airliners meeting the specifications of TWA and how long it would take before flight tests. All six manufacturers responded with alacrity even though the 'General Performance Specifications' attached to the letter request – the 'birth certificate' for the DC-1 – contained a difficult to meet demand: 'this airplane, fully loaded, must make satisfactory take-offs under good control at any TWA airport on any combination of two engines.'

TRANSCONTINENTAL & WESTERN AIR INC.

10 RICHARDS ROAD
MUNICIPAL AIRPORT
KANSAS. CITY. MISSOURI

August 2nd,
19 32

Douglas Aircraft Corporation,
Clover Field,
Santa Monica, California.

Attention: Mr. Donald Douglas

Dear Mr. Douglas:

Transcontinental & Western Air is interested in purchasing ten or more trimotored transport planes.

I am attaching our general performance specifications, covering this equipment and would appreciate your advising whether your Company is interested in this manufacturing job.

If so, approximately how long would it take to turn out the first plane for service tests?

Very truly yours,

Jack Frye

Jack Frye
Vice President
In Charge of Operations

JF/GS
Encl.

N.B. Please consider this information confidential and return specifications if you are not interested.

SAVE TIME — USE THE AIR MAIL

TRANSCONTINENTAL & WESTERN AIR, INC.

General Performance Specifications
Transport Plane

1. **Type:** All metal trimotored monoplane preferred but combination structure or biplane would be considered. Main internal structure must be metal.

2. **Power:** Three engines of 500 to 550 h.p. (Wasps with 10-1 supercharger; 6-1 compression O.K.).

3. **Weight:** Gross (maximum)   14,200 lbs.

4. **Weight** allowance for radio and wing mail bins   350 lbs.

5. **Weight** allowance must also be made for complete instruments, night flying equipment, fuel capacity for cruising range of 1080 miles at 150 m.p.h., crew of two, at least 12 passengers with comfortable seats and ample room, and the usual miscellaneous equipment carried on a passenger plane of this type. Payload should be at least 2,300 lbs. with full equipment and fuel for maximum range.

6. **Performance**

Top speed sea level (minimum)   185 m.p.h.
Cruising speed sea level - 79 % top speed   146 m.p.h. plus
Landing speed not more than   65 m.p.h.
Rate of climb sea level (minimum)   1200 ft. p.m.
Service ceiling (minimum)   21000 ft.
Service ceiling any two engines   10000 ft.

This plane, fully loaded, must make satisfactory take-offs under good control at any TWA airport on any combination of two engines.

Kansas City, Missouri.
August 2nd, 1932

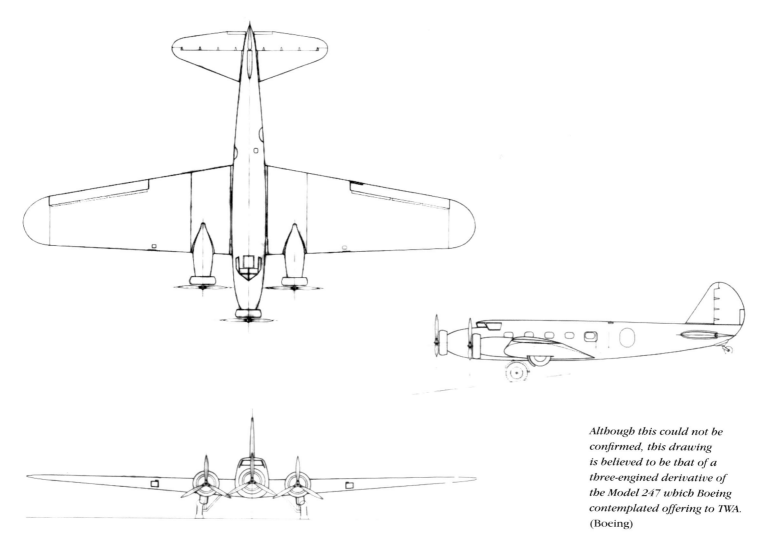

Although this could not be confirmed, this drawing is believed to be that of a three-engined derivative of the Model 247 which Boeing contemplated offering to TWA. (Boeing)

A swift response

When Jack Frye's letter was delivered to 3000 Ocean Park Boulevard in Santa Monica, Donald Douglas immediately discussed it with his closest associates (James H. 'Dutch' Kindelberger, chief engineer, Arthur E. Raymond, deputy chief engineer, and Harry Wetzel, the Santa Monica plant director). It took little time for these men to conclude that this was an exceptional business opportunity, all the more so as the country was deep in the Great Depression. Douglas notified TWA that it would submit a proposal and requested that Harry Wetzel and Arthur Raymond meet with the airline. Things moved very quickly as the two representatives from the California manufacturer took the train for New York just 10 days after Jack Frye had sent his letter.

Before departing for New York, a ten-person team led by Arthur Raymond and supervised by 'Dutch' Kingleberger studied three-engined configurations (as requested by TWA) as well as twin-engined designs. The team quickly concluded that:
- even though TWA was asking for a three-engined aircraft, Douglas would offer a twin-engined design with performance equal or superior to what the airline had specified;
- the all-metal low-mounted wing would use the Northrop multi-cellular design with stressed skin;
- the undercarriage would be retractable; and
- passenger comfort, cruising speed, and flight operation safety would be of paramount importance.

Consequently it was on a twin-engined proposal that Arthur Raymond continued working during his transcontinental rail journey. Additional technical details were telephoned from Santa Monica by team members thus enabling Raymond and Wetzel to be well prepared when meeting with Transcontinental & Western Air representatives: Richard W. Robbins, President; Jack Frye; and TWA technical consultant, Charles Lindbergh. Meeting simultaneously with representatives from four other manufacturers offering three-engined designs, the TWA managers were quickly impressed with the twin-engined Douglas proposal. In particular, Jack Frye was favorable to the Douglas proposal as he had gained first hand experience with the strength of the Northrop multi-cellular wing design while flying the *Alpha*. On the other hand, Charles Lindbergh proved less easy to convince as he kept expressing doubts a twin-engined airplane would be able to take-off successfully from high temperature/high elevation airports in the event of an engine failure. Working feverishly, Arthur Raymond, in New York, and his colleagues in Santa Monica checked and rechecked their calculations until they were satisfied that the aircraft would indeed be able to fly on one engine anywhere on the TWA network. Hence, Douglas agreed, albeit with some fear, to a contract provision guaranteeing this critical performance.

A deal was reached on 20 September 1932 with TWA[1] ordering a first aircraft for $125,000 (±$2,000,000 today) and taking an option on 60 additional aircraft at the unit price of $58,000 (±$932,000 today). Seventeen years after he had made his debut in the aircraft industry, Donald Wills Douglas would at last realize his dream of undertaking serious production of civil airliners.

---

1 As a safeguard against the possibility of the twin-engined DC-1 failing to meet requirements, General Motors Corporation (which then controlled TWA and owned General Aviation Manufacturing) instructed its aircraft manufacturers to proceed with the design of the three-engined GA-38X. Construction of a prototype was begun in Dundalk, Maryland, but work ceased before it was completed.

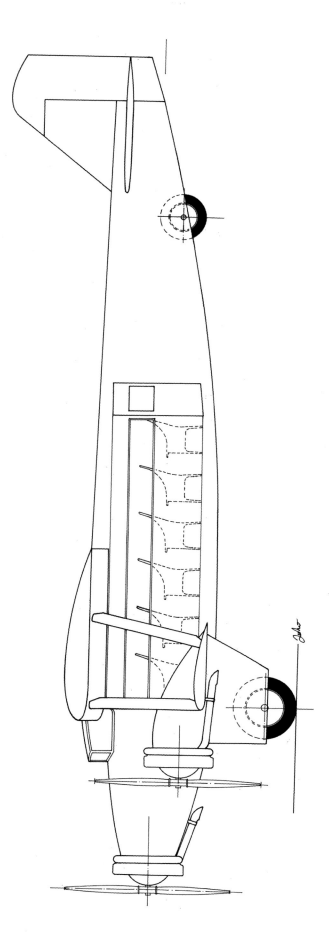

Side-view drawing of a three-engined design studied before Douglas settled on a twin-engined layout for its DC-1. (Iulian Robanescu)

ABOVE AND RIGHT *The Northrop multi-cellular wing structure used for the DC-1 and its successors was submitted to harsh testing.* (Douglas)

BOTTOM *In 1958, a quarter of a century after the maiden flight of the DC-1, several members of the original design team were photographed at Long Beach in front of a DC-3. From left to right, they are Arthur Raymond, Lee Atwood, George Strompl, W. Bailey Oswald, 'Dutch' Kindelberger, Donald Wills Douglas, Ed Burton, and Frank Collbohm. The person on the right is unidentified.* (Douglas)

Design and development of the first Douglas Commercial

Having returned to Santa Monica with a signed contract from TWA for the DC-1, Arthur Raymond was designated the project manager. In undertaking the detailed design of the DC-1, he was assisted by a strong team with additional support from consultants highly regarded in the industry. Jack Northrop, while still managing the Douglas subsidiary in El Segundo, supervised structural design activities. Ed Burton, who would become the company chief engineer during World War Two, was assisted by Frank Collbohm who designed the main undercarriage,[2] while Fred Thearle undertook that of the tail wheel. Ivar Shogran headed the power plant team that evaluated offerings from Pratt & Whitney and Wright for their nine-cylinder *Hornet* and *Cyclone* engines. He chose a version of the latter, the SRG-1820-F, to power the DC-1 and specified three-blade, fixed-pitch metal propellers for initial installation. Design of the 12-volt electrical system was entrusted to Warren Boughton.

Reliance on wind tunnel testing during the initial design phase was a first for a transport aircraft. Undertaken at the California Institute of Technology (Caltech) in Pasadena, under the

2　The hydraulically-powered main gear retracted aft into the engine nacelles with the wheels protruding beneath the nacelles to provide protection in the event of a gear up landing.

LEFT *A ¹/₁₁th scale model of the DC-1 was tested in the GALCIT (Guggenheim Aeronautical Laboratory of the California Institute of Technology) wind tunnel at Pasadena.* (Douglas)

MIDDLE AND BOTTOM *These two views illustrate the cabin of the Boeing 247 (encumbered by wing spars) and the clean cabin of the DC-1.* (Boeing and Douglas)

OPPOSITE *Taken in Santa Monica on 16 March 1933, this photograph shows the DC-1 fuselage under construction.* (Douglas)

supervision of Dr Clark L. Milligan and Dr Arthur L. Klein, with a ¹/₁₁ scale model, these tests revealed that the aircraft would be unstable with the planned wing geometry. To eliminate the problem, the wing leading edge was swept back, resulting in the characteristic shape of the DC-1 wings (and later those of the DC-2, DC-3 and DC-4E). Performance calculations were the responsibility of Dr W. Bailey Oswald, another Caltech professor. The soundproofing consultant was Dr Stephen J. Zand of the Sperry Company, his objective being to keep cabin noise to a level not exceeding that in contemporary Pullman rail cars.

When preliminary information on the Boeing 247 was published in the monthly magazine *Popular Mechanics*, Raymond had copies of the article posted in the design office and kept admonishing his team 'to do better than Boeing.' That they did. In particular, by using the Northrop wing design with the flat center-section bolted to a recess beneath the fuselage, the Douglas engineers kept the cabin floor flat, whereas the cabin aisle of the Boeing 247 was encumbered by the wing spars. Moreover, they adopted a cabin height sufficient to enable a majority of the passengers to circulate without having to bend their heads down.[3] Conversely, the width of the aisle between the two rows of six individual seats was only 16in. Fortunately, that was not much of a problem as the girth of most passengers then was significantly less than what it is today.

Other carefully considered choices concerning accommodation and comfort saw the adoption of partially-reclining seats, a novelty, with backs that could be tilted either fore or aft to enable pairs of passengers to sit facing each other for ease of conversation. Heating, ventilation, and soundproofing also received much attention, making the DC-1 and its twin-engined derivatives more 'passenger friendly' than either the Boeing 247 or the Lockheed 10 *Electra*.[4] The wise design decisions made by Arthur Raymond, his team, and his consultants were to earn for Douglas a lasting and favorable reputation with many important customers.

Challenging trials

When it was wheeled out of the assembly hall, the DC-1 (fsn 1137 and bearing the temporary registration X223Y) was powered by 700hp Wright *Cyclone* SGR-1820-F radial engines enclosed in still novel NACA cowlings. Although appearing to be there either to reduce vibrations or to smooth airflow in the narrow confines between engines and the forward fuselage sides, streamlined fairings were installed to house sensor cables provided to record additional engine parameters during early tests.

On Saturday, 1 July 1933, test pilot Carl Cover and flight test engineer Fred Herman had to wait until late in the morning for the seasonal fog in Santa Monica Bay to lift before getting on their way for the maiden flight of the DC-1. After a long warming up period to get the *Cyclone* engines readied and several runs made

3 Cabin height was 6ft 4in, something much appreciated by the TWA Technical Advisor, the notably tall Charles Lindbergh.
4 Seating 10, like the Boeing 247 but two and four less than the DC-1 and DC-2 respectively, this twin-engined transport first flew on 23 February 1934.

NACA cowling

Beginning in 1926, engineers at the National Advisory Committee for Aeronautics (NACA) in Langley, Virginia, began studying ways to reduce drag around cylinders of radial engines. Led by Fred Weick, they analyzed several configurations of streamlined, low-drag engine cowlings before starting wind tunnel tests with a Wright *Apache* biplane powered by a nine-cylinder, single-row Wright J-5 *Whirlwind*. Results being promising, NACA then fitted a symmetric, circular airfoil cowling around the *Whirlwind* radial engine of a Curtiss AT-5A biplane.

Flight tests with the modified AT-5A demonstrated a 60% reduction in drag around the engine. Top speed of the aircraft with its NACA cowling was 137mph versus only 118mph without it. Quickly, this type of cowling was universally adopted, not only in the United States but also abroad, to reduce the drag of radial engines.

This Curtiss AT-5A was the first aircraft fitted with a NACA engine cowling. (NACA)

ABOVE *With the X of its experimental registration appearing on the tail over a white background, the DC-1 was photographed at Clover Field before its momentous first flight on 1 July 1933.* (Douglas)

at progressive speeds back and forth on Clover Field, the aircraft lifted off at 12:36pm. By then, only light clouds remained in the blue California sky and wind was light.

As the DC-1 gained altitude, the left engine coughed and lost power. Carl Cover rammed forward the throttle for the right *Cyclone* and, fortunately, that engine roared, enabling the aircraft to regain some altitude. However, shortly thereafter power was lost on both engines. Putting the nose down to keep airspeed about stall margins and succeeding in restarting both engines, Carl Cover avoided the impending disaster temporarily. As the DC-1 climbed once again, power was again lost. Donald Douglas, and all those assembled at Clover Field to observe the first flight, feared the worst. With Carl Cover struggling with the recalcitrant power plant, the DC-1 continued to gain altitude for brief periods before descending again as engines kept acting up. Nevertheless, through skillful piloting, Cover managed to get the DC-1 to rise to 1,600ft above the field before deciding that it was time to make a precautionary landing. Touchdown was hard but the valuable prototype had been saved and its crew was safe.

Once on the ground, concerns were high, especially after it was determined that fuel contamination, the expected culprit for the engine difficulties, was not the cause. Ivar Shogram and the power plant team spent the following week running the Wright engines but could not replicate the failure on the ground. In the end, it was the experienced test pilot, Carl Cover, who came up with a likely cause: malfunctioning carburetors. When that assumption proved to be correct, it was determined that the carburetors had been mounted backwards, thus shutting down fuel flow to the engines as the aircraft climbed. After the carburetors were remounted properly, the Wright *Cyclones* no longer proved temperamental.

During the second flight, on 7 July, the DC-1 once again ran into troubles as it had a propensity for fishtailing. To eliminate this disturbing flight characteristic, the rudder and its linkage were slightly modified, thus restoring directional stability and enabling flight testing to proceed rapidly. For the manufacturer's testing Carl Cover was joined by Edmund T. 'Eddie' Allen, the already

well-known engineer and test pilot. Shortly afterward, the aircraft was evaluated for TWA by Jack Frye and D.W. 'Tommy' Tomlinson. Les Hollobeck and Joe Marriott, pilots for the Bureau of Air Commerce, were assigned to the check flight characteristics and to undertake the pre-certification testing program.

Although loaded weight had risen to 17,000lb, a 20% increase over the 14,200lb goal set by TWA in August 1932, all of these experienced pilots reported favorably on the handling characteristics and performance. Their only significant criticisms concerned the aft-setting of the center of gravity and the hard landing characteristics of the DC-1.

To ascertain the cause for the latter, the DC-1 was taken to nearby Mines Field where touch-and-go landings were performed on 7 August. For these tests, the pilots – Eddie Allen in the left seat for the manufacturer and Tommy Tomlinson on his right for the customer – were joined by Frank Collbohm and 'Doc' Bailey Oswald as observers. For the first iterations, Collbohm stood behind the pilots in the cockpit to lower and raise the undercarriage when directed by the pilots. During the landings, and while lying on his belly, Oswald observed the left gear and wheel through the removed entrance door on the left side of the fuselage. A proverbial oversight resulted in Oswald not being informed that he was expected to lower the gear. The result was predictable: the non-retractable tail wheel touched down first and the DC-1 set down on its belly. Fortunately, damage was slight as the main wheels partially protruding under the engine nacelles limited damage to bent propellers and minimal skin scrapes on the belly.

Rather than limiting itself to making these repairs, Douglas decided to undertake a series of modifications to improve performance and correct some of the remaining deficiencies. This work included replacing both the SGR-1820-F with the 710hp SGR-1820-F3 and the fixed-pitch propellers with two-pitch units in order to bring take-off and single-engine performance up to the TWA specified level even though gross weight had now risen to 17,500lb. Other modifications included the redesign and enlargement of the fin and rudder, as well as the removal of the fairings between the fuselage sides and the engine nacelles to improve local airflow and reduce the drag slightly.

Now ready to undertake additional testing and demonstrate that it would meet the TWA performance requirements while operating from high elevation airfields even in periods of elevated

temperatures, the DC-1 saw its registration changed from X223Y (in which the X stood for experimental) to R223Y (with R for restricted).

For the all-important single-engine test, the DC-1 was taken to Winslow, Arizona, where the airfield used by TWA on its transcontinental route was 4,850ft above sea level and where summer temperatures frequently exceeded 90°F, thus significantly reducing lift and engine power. With water ballast bringing take-off weight to 18,000lb, and with a crew of four (Allen, Tomlinson, Collbohm and Oswald), the DC-1 was lined up on the runway on the morning of 4 September 1933. During the takeoff run, Tomlinson confidently shut down the right engine instead of just reducing power as had been planned. Eddie Allen, ever a consummate test pilot, reacted quickly and pushed the throttle of the right engine to the wall while applying rudder to keep the aircraft rolling and taking off in a straight line. After lifting off,

ABOVE *The DC-1 made its first belly landing on 7 August 1933 while making touch-and-goes at Mines Field. Damages were minimal.* (Douglas)

the DC-1 was taken slowly to its 8,000ft cruising altitude before continuing toward Albuquerque, New Mexico. At the end of this 280-mile flight on one engine, the DC-1 had demonstrated that it fully met the most stringent of TWA requirements. There was nothing further to delay TWA from ordering the aircraft into

BELOW *Photographed in front of the Grand Central Air Terminal, the DC-1 shows the revised tail surfaces that were fitted in August 1933.* (Douglas)

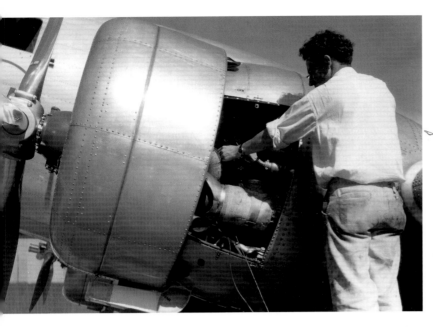

ABOVE *Temporarily re-engined with Pratt & Whitney* Hornet *SD-G radials, the first Douglas Commercial was redesignated DC-1A.* (P&W)

production, especially as United Air Lines had placed the Boeing 247 on its transcontinental route three months earlier. From east to west, the Boeing twin crossed the country in 21hr 30min (including technical stops) while the older three-engined aircraft of TWA required 28hr 43min between New York and Los Angeles. Transcontinental & Western Air exercized one-third of the options it had taken and ordered 20 DC-2s derived from the DC-1 and featuring a longer fuselage to seat 14 instead of 12.

New engines and a slew of records

Once the TWA order had been firmed up, Douglas sought additional customers. As several potential clients favored Pratt & Whitney, the Santa Monica firm leased the DC-1 back from TWA

to test a P&W installation. After the *Cyclones* had been replaced by 700hp *Hornet* SD-G radials, the aircraft was redesignated DC-1A. With *Hornet* engines, it obtained approval from the Bureau of Air Commerce on 8 November 1933. However, 40 days later, it made another belly landing, this time at Clover Field. Once again, damages were minimal and, after being re-engined with 760hp Wright SGR-1820-F52s, the aircraft was returned to TWA as a DC-1.

Meanwhile the political situation in the United States had undergone significant changes. The recently elected president Roosevelt, a Democrat, quickly took steps to correct alleged fraudulent mail contract awards by the preceding Republican administration. On 9 February 1934, he cancelled all contracts and ordered the Army Air Corps to begin carrying the mail ten days later. Without revenues from mail contracts, airlines would have considerable difficulty to survive.

To demonstrate that they had better equipment and could do better than the Air Corps, Transcontinental & Western Air and Eastern Air Transport (both of which were then controlled by North American Aviation Company) chose to make a spectacular flight on the occasion of the last TWA mail flight on the transcontinental route.

With Jack Frye and Eddie Rickenbacker[5] as pilots and carrying mail, the DC-1 took off from Burbank on 18 February 1934. After crossing the Rockies, Frye and Rickenbacker made a technical stop in Kansas City, Missouri, before continuing to their destination in New Jersey. During the next leg, they climbed to a maximum of 14,100ft[6] to avoid turbulence and take advantage of favorable winds higher up. They landed in Newark early on 19 February as the 13hr 2min flight set a new transcontinental speed record. During the following 14 months, by which time it was registered NC223Y as it was now allowed to carry passengers, the DC-1 was used by TWA for limited commercial operations. Mostly, however, the airline used it on proving flights in preparation for placing the DC-2 into service.

Wishing to publicize the superior performance of American airliners, the National Aeronautic Association (NAA) sponsored a series of modifications for the DC-1. More powerful engines, 875hp Wright SGR-1820-F25s were fitted, while additional fuel tanks were installed in the fuselage to increase capacity up from 425 to 1,749 Imp. gallons. As this additional fuel brought take-off weight to a new high – 28,500lb, well above safe margins and twice what TWA

---

5 Edward Vernon 'Eddie' Rickenbacker had become the top scoring American fighter pilot during World War One by bringing down 22 German aircraft and four observation balloons. In 1934, he was General Manager of Eastern Air Transport and later was the CEO of Eastern Air Lines.
6 Had the DC-1 carried passengers, it would not have been able to fly at that altitude as the aircraft was neither equipped with drop-down oxygen masks nor fitted with a pressurized cabin.

BELOW *The DC-1 set its first transcontinental record on 19 February 1934.* (Douglas)

had asked in its original specifications – valves had to be installed to dump fuel quickly from the fuselage tanks in the event of an emergency. For its ferry flight to the NAA on the East Coast on 30 April 1935, the DC-1 was once again registered R223Y. With a crew of three (Tommy Tomlinson, H.B. Snead, and Peter Redpatch), the aircraft broke its own transcontinental speed record. The flight from Grand Central Air Terminal in Glendale, near Los Angeles, to Newark took 11hr 5min including time for a fueling stop in Wichita, Kansas. This was but a beginning.

Operating from Floyd Bennett Field, the re-engined DC-1 was then flown on a New York–Washington–Norfolk circuit on 16, 18 and 19 May 1935 by Tommy Tomlinson and Joseph S. Bartles to set or break 11 national records and eight world records.

Coming after the remarkable performance of a DC-2 during the 1934 MacRobertson Trophy Air Race from England to Australia (see Chapter 3), these DC-1 records did much to convince skeptical Europeans, particularly in Britain, that the Americans were now the world leaders for airliners. However, and even though most British airlines were still flying biplanes replete with struts and fixed undercarriage, several editors in the UK continued to express doubts about the performance of the Douglas commercial aircraft.

Unclear situation

After setting this series of records, the DC-1 was not used extensively for one year. Instead, it mainly served to test constant speed propellers and automatic pilots for NACA and the Army Air Corps. Now disposing of enough DC-2s, TWA sought to find a customer for the DC-1.

Not wanting to attract attention on his plans, the secretive Howard Hughes acquired the DC-1 in September 1936 through a front company, Western Aero & Radio Company in Burbank. By then well-known for his speed records in his H-1 *Racer* and the Northrop *Gamma* 2G, Howard Hughes contemplated having auxiliary fuel tanks installed in the DC-1 before using it for a record attempt around the world. Already quite quirky, Hughes quickly changed his mind and decided to use the specially modified Lockheed 14-N2 for the round-the-world flight. Once again, the DC-1 was up for sale.

On 4 January 1937, during the Spanish Civil War, the Vimalert Company, Ltd. in New York requested an export license to ship the DC-1 to Spain, the intended customer being the Republican government. As the required export license had not been issued, the DC-1 was not aboard the SS *Mar Cantábrico* when this Spanish

DC-1 Records

American Records Broken	
1,000km, without load	191.764mph
1,000km, 1,000kg load	191.764mph
2,000km, without load	190.906mph

American Records Set	
1,000km, 500kg load	191.764mph
1,000km, 2,000kg load	191.764mph
2,000km, 500kg load	190.906mph
2,000km, 1,000kg load	190.906mph
2,000km, 2,000kg load	190.906mph
5,000km, without load	169.03mph
5,000km, 500kg load	169.03mph
5,000km, 1,000kg load	169.03mph

World Records Broken	
1,000km, 1,000kg load	191.764mph
1,000km, 2,000kg load	191.764mph
2,000km, 500kg load	190.906mph
2,000km, 1,000kg load	190.906mph
2,000km, 2,000kg load	190.906mph
5,000km, without load	169.03mph

World Records Set	
5,000km, 500kg load	169.03mph
5,000km, 1,000kg load	169.03mph

Note: Distances and weights are given in metric units as these are the units used by the *Fédération Aéronautique Internationale* which certify all records. For readers having difficulties with the metric systems the equivalent for the numbers above are as follows:
1,000km, 2,000km, and 5,000km are, respectively, 641.4, 1,242.7, and 3,106.9 miles
500kg, 1,000kg, and 2,000kg correspond to 1,102.3, 2,204.6, and 11,203.1lb.

ABOVE *Then registered to Western Aero & Radio Company which had acquired it on behalf of Howard Hughes, the DC-1 is shown landing at Oakland, California, in 1936.* (International News Photo)

LEFT *The DC-1 was wrecked at Malaga, Spain, in December 1940 after making its 'unlucky' third emergency landing.* (DR)

BELOW *The DC-1 was only briefly operated by TWA, mostly for route proving for the DC-2s.* (AAHS collection)

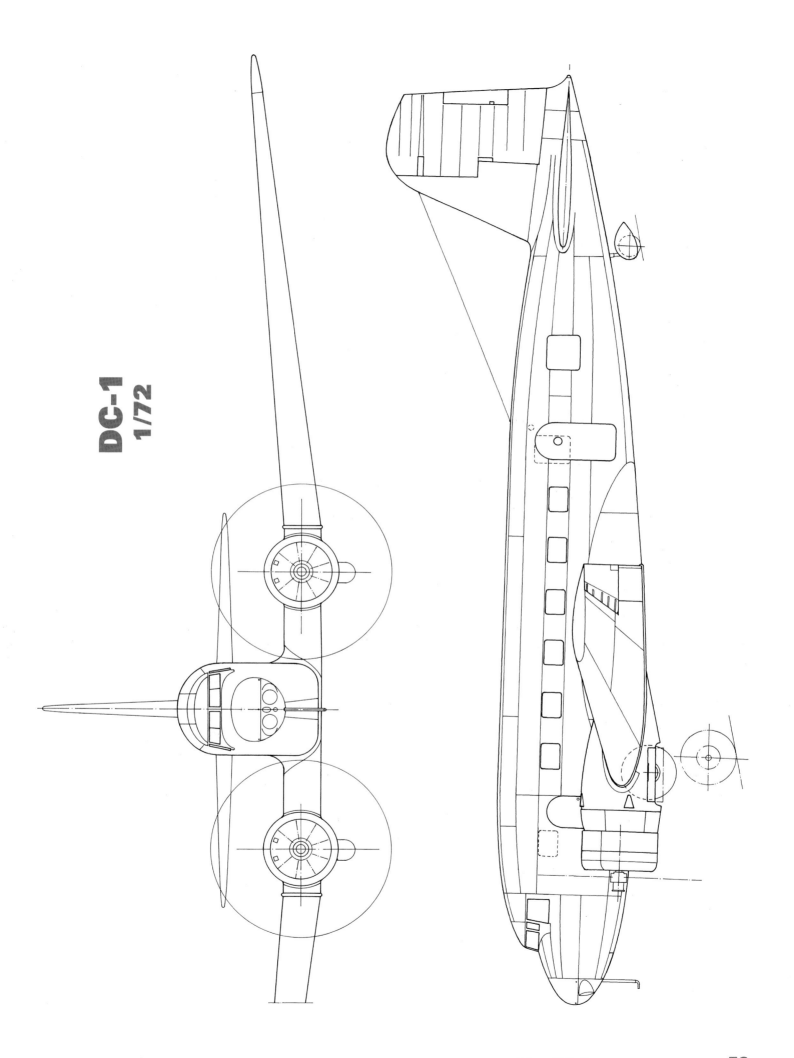

DC-1
1/72

vessel sailed from Brooklyn to Bilbao on 5 January. For the next 16 months nothing further was heard about the DC-1.

It was then acquired in May 1938 by Viscount Forbes, the Earl of Granard, who briefly contemplated flying it across the Atlantic to be registered in the United Kingdom. In the end, the DC-1 was not flown but shipped to Britain. Reassembled at Croydon, the DC-1 became G-AFIF on the British registry. It then made a few publicity flights, including one to Bavaria in September 1938, when Viscount Forbes took journalists to report on the signing of the Munich Accords. Having logged some 1,400 hours in the previous five years, the DC-1 disappeared shortly afterward from the British registry.

Apparently as the result of some questionable activities by a French broker, the DC-1 reappeared in Spain in October 1938 where it was registered as EC-AGN for *Líneas Aéreas Postales Españolas (LAPE)*. During the next five months, it made several flights to France carrying political refugees as well as some of the gold reserve of the Spanish Republican Government. In April 1939, after the Civil War had ended, the DC-1 was reregistered as EC-AAE for *Sociedad Anonima de Transportes Aéreos (SATA)*.

Things always happen in threes

Having survived two previous forced landings – on 7 August 1933, at Mines Field and on 18 December 1933, at Clover Field – the DC-1 was not so fortunate the third time. When taking off from Malaga, the intermediate stop on the Seville to Tanoan route in December 1940, EC-AAE experienced an engine failure. The pilot quickly set the aircraft down past the end of the runway; unfortunately the ground was strewn with stones. Although passengers and crew walked out safely, the DC-1 was destroyed. According to legend, the first Douglas commercial was then broken down with its aluminum parts being used to build an Anda, a stretcher-like platform on which Our Lady of Malaga, a statue of the Madonna, was carried during religious processions. Neither this element of the story nor the exact date of the accident ending the DC-1 career have been confirmed.

For Douglas, the DC-1 operation ended with a financial loss as design, manufacturing, and testing costs totaled $307,000 (±$4.9 million today). As contractually provided, TWA only paid $125,000 (±$2.0 million today). Fortunately for the manufacturer, the $182,000 (±$2.9 million today) loss was offset by profits from other programmes thus keeping it in a profit position. Thereafter annual profits rose rapidly thanks to hefty sales of DC-2s and DC-3s. Above all, the DC-1 went on to be remembered for being the first in a most successful line of airliners that sustained its manufacturer for several decades.

Data for the DC-1

Dimensions: Span, 85ft; length, 60ft; height, 16ft; wing area, 942sq ft.
Weights: Empty, 11,780lb; loaded, 17,500lb.
Accommodation: Two pilots and 12 passengers.
Power plant: Two 710hp Wright *Cyclone* SGR-1820-F3 nine-cylinder, air-cooled radials driving three-blade, variable pitch metal propellers with a diameter of 11ft 6in. Fuel tanks in the wing center section with a capacity of 425 Imp. gallons.
Performance: Maximum speed, 210mph; cruising speed, 190mph at 8,000ft and 200mph at 14,000ft; initial rate of climb, 1,050ft/min; service ceiling, 23,000ft; normal range, 1,000 miles.

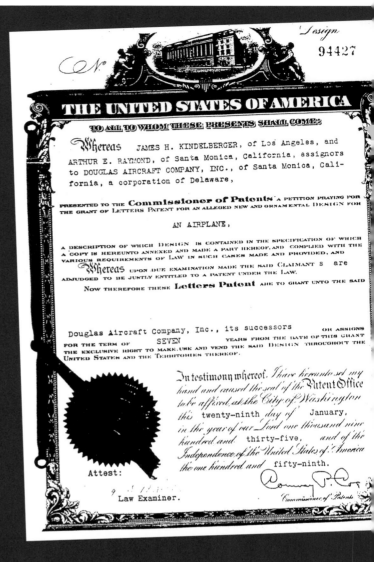

A rather skimpy patent application

On 9 April 1934, 'Dutch' Kindelberger and Art Raymond filed a patent application on behalf of the Douglas Aircraft Company for the conceptual layout of the DC-1 and DC-2. This application had a skimpy basis as the claimants only requested a patent for 'an alleged new and ornamental design for an airplane'. In spite of the rather esoteric nature of this application, a patent was issued in 1935.

As this patent only was for the 'United States and Territories thereof', numerous twin-engined transport aircraft visibly inspired by the DC-1 and DC-2 soon followed elsewhere: the Bloch 220 in France, the Fiat G.18 in Italy, the Mitsubishi MC-20 in Japan, and the Tupolev ANT-035 in the Soviet Union. *Imitation is the most sincere form of flattery.*

Jan. 29, 1935. J. H. KINDELBERGER ET AL Des. 94,427

AIRPLANE

Filed April 9, 1934 2 Sheets—Sheet 1

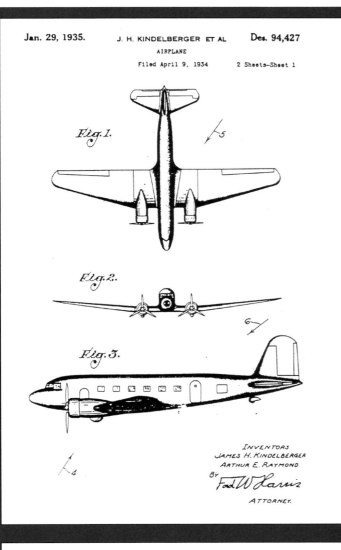

Fig. 1.

Fig. 2.

Fig. 3.

INVENTORS
JAMES H. KINDELBERGER
ARTHUR E. RAYMOND
BY
Fred W Harris
ATTORNEY.

Jan. 29, 1935. J. H. KINDELBERGER ET AL Des. 94,427

AIRPLANE

Filed April 9, 1934 2 Sheets—Sheet 2

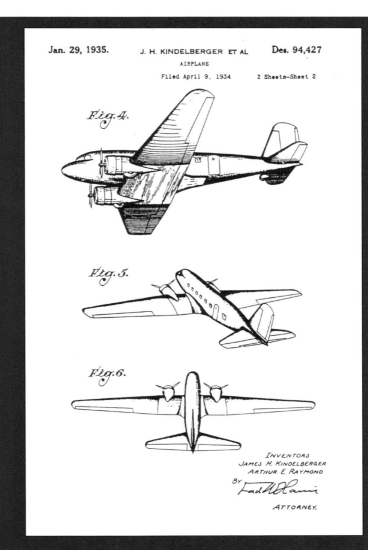

Fig. 4.

Fig. 5.

Fig. 6.

INVENTORS
JAMES H. KINDELBERGER
ARTHUR E. RAYMOND
BY
Fred W Harris
ATTORNEY.

Patented Jan. 29, 1935

Des. 94,427

UNITED STATES PATENT OFFICE

94,427

DESIGN FOR AN AIRPLANE

James H. Kindelberger, Los Angeles, and Arthur E. Raymond, Santa Monica, Calif., assignors to Douglas Aircraft Company, Inc., Santa Monica, Calif., a corporation of Delaware

Application April 9, 1934, Serial No. 51,364

Term of patent 7 years

To all whom it may concern:

Be it known that we, James H. Kindelberger and Arthur E. Raymond, citizens of the United States, the former residing at Los Angeles, in the county of Los Angeles and State of California, and the latter residing at Santa Monica, in the county of Los Angeles and State of California, have invented a new, original, and ornamental Design for an Airplane, of which the following is a specification, reference being had to the accompanying drawings, forming part hereof.

Fig. 1 is a top plan view of an airplane;
Fig. 2 is a front elevational view;

Fig. 3 is a side elevational view;
Fig. 4 is a perspective view taken as indicated by the arrow 4 of Fig. 3;
Fig. 5 is a perspective view taken as indicated by the arrow 5 of Fig. 1; and
Fig. 6 is a perspective view taken as indicated by the arrow 6 of Fig. 3, showing our new design for an airplane.

We claim:
The ornamental design for an airplane, as shown.

JAMES H. KINDELBERGER.
ARTHUR E. RAYMOND.

Chapter 3

DC-2 – The first major success

ABOVE *The first DC-2 – fsn 1237, NC13711 – is ready to be towed onto the apron on 11 May 1934. Note that the assembly of a dozen more DC-2s is already well underway.* (Douglas)

BELOW *Of the 192 DC-2s built by Douglas, only three were powered by Pratt & Whitney Hornet engines: I-EROS, a DC-2-115B for Avio Linee Italiane; NC14285, a DC-127 for Standard Oil (as shown in this photograph); and PH-AKT, a DC-2-115H for KLM.* (Douglas)

The first Douglas Commercial model to be placed in full production, the DC-2, entered service on 18 May 1934 on the TWA route between Columbus, Ohio; Pittsburgh, Pennsylvania; and Newark, New Jersey (the main airport in the New York area). Eight days later another TWA DC-2 became the first to fly between Newark and Chicago. That flight took five hours, which was thirty minutes less than United Air Lines could do with its Boeing 247. Next, beginning on 1 August, DC-2s were used on the Newark to Los Angeles route reducing travel time in that direction to 18hr, including time for intermediate stops in Chicago, Kansas City, and Albuquerque. Previously the Ford Tri-Motor of TWA took twice as long (36hr 22min) to fly across the continent from east to west, with eight technical stops required. One-way fare was $160.00 (±$2,600 today). Air travelers quickly appreciated this better service and other airlines – with the notable exception of United Air Lines which was still too closely tied to Boeing and operating a large fleet of 247s – rushed to order DC-2s. For Douglas the risks taken in going ahead with the DC-1 development were rewarded, particularly so as sales abroad contributed significantly.

The most significant difference between the DC-1 and the DC-2 was the longer cabin with improved accommodations. By adding one row of seats, overall length was increased from 60ft to 61ft 11¾ in with seating going from 12 to 14. Span and wing area remained unchanged. With minor structural strengthening being incorporated, maximum take off weight went from 17,500lb for the DC-1 to 17,880lb for the DC-2 in the configuration initially approved by the Aeronautics Branch of the Department of Commerce. The ATC No 540 was issued belatedly, on 28 June 1934, 41 days after the DC-2 had entered service without an ATC approval.

Civil DC-2 variants

In all, 130 DC-2s were built for civil and government customers in the United States and abroad in three separate series differentiated by the type of power plant with which they were fitted. Two models of the DC-2 itself were powered by variants of the nine-cylinder Wright SGR-1820 radial driving three-blade, variable pitch Hamilton-Standard propellers. Those for US customers came under the previously mentioned ATC No 540, while the DC-2s for most export customers were covered by ATC No 555 issued on 28 August 1934. Take-off power for the *Cyclone* variants (SGR-1820-F2, -F2A, -F3, -F3A, -F3B, -F52, and -F53) which powered all but five of the DC-2s ranged between 710 and 875hp. Covered by ATC No 570, dated 20 May 1935, the DC-2As were powered by Pratt & Whitney *Hornet* engines (700hp SD-G, 875hp S1E-G, or 800hp S2E-G). Ordered by the Polish airline LOT, two DC-2Bs were equipped with 750hp Bristol *Pegasus VIs* built under license by Skoda. Strictly an export model, the DC-2B was not covered by an ATC.

To identify the specific configuration chosen by customers, all of these twin-engined transport aircraft were further identified by three-digit model numbers added after their DC-2 designations. Intended for TWA, General Air Line, and Eastern Air Line, the first production aircraft were DC-2-112s. The DC-2-267, the last to come

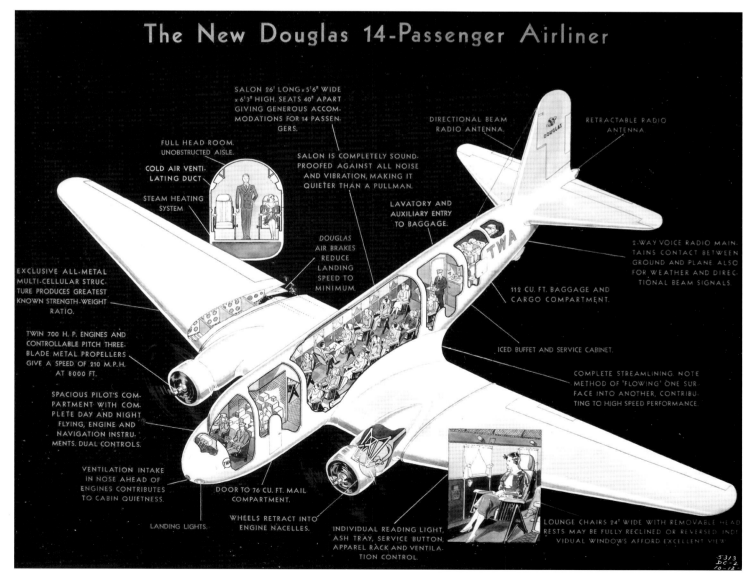

The New Douglas 14-Passenger Airliner

off the production line in Santa Monica, was the only C-42 built for the Army Air Corps.

Maximum take-off weight for the DC-2s powered by Wright SGR-1820 engines was progressively increased from 17,880 to 18,200lb, before being finally raised to 18,560lb. Both the DC-2As with Pratt & Whitney *Hornets* and the DC-2Bs with *Pegasus* engines had a maximum take-off weight of 18,200lb. Most of these aircraft had two fuel tanks located in the wing center section with a combined capacity of 150 Imp. gallons of 87-octane petrol. Customers requiring longer range from their aircraft had the option of having two 62.5 Imp gallon auxiliary tanks fitted to bring fuel capacity to a maximum of 275 Imp. gallons.

As shown in the October 1933 Douglas cutaway drawing reproduced on the preceding page, two landing lights and an air intake for cabin ventilation were located in the nose of the aircraft. Pilot and co-pilot sat side-by-side in an enclosed cockpit with a two-panel windshield center and two sliding side windows. Aft of the cockpit, on the right-hand side, a 75cu ft compartment was provided for mailbags. Loading and unloading was accomplished through a small door on the left side of the forward fuselage. The main cabin, with an access door to the cockpit forward, was 26ft long, 5ft 6in wide, and 6ft 4in high. Standard accommodation was provided for 14 passengers (7 seats on each side of the center aisle with 40in pitch). These 24in wide seats[1] were equipped with a removable headrest and their backs could be swung to enable passengers to face either forward or aft. At the aft of the cabin, a food storage compartment with dry ice was on the left side and a lavatory on the opposite side. Further aft, a 120cu ft baggage compartment could be accessed

1   Today's economy seats vary between 17 and 18.5in in width, and between 30 and 34in in pitch.

in-flight. Passengers and crew boarded the aircraft through a door usually provided on the left of the rear fuselage; however, airlines had the option of ordering their aircraft with the entrance door on the opposite side (as was the case for American Air Lines). A folding seat for a steward or stewardess (the term 'cabin attendant' did not come into use for another three decades) was at the cabin's rear.

For long flights across continents, such as those by KLM and KNILM between the Netherlands and the Dutch East Indies, a radio-navigator was added to the crew and sat immediately aft of the pilot. The aircraft for these two carriers were also unique as they were provided with a downward firing flare launcher on the left side of the cockpit. The cabin of the aircraft used on these long routes had fewer seats, first five then seven (four on the left and three on the right) to provide space for an additional refrigerated compartment located behind the last right-hand side seat. Passengers could recline their seats almost to the full horizontal position (this long before today's airlines started bragging about their 'lie flat beds' in business class).

DC-2s with even more comfortable accommodations were ordered by non-airline customers. Aircraft in this category were a DC-2-124 for the Swiftlife Corporation, a DC-2A-127 for the Standard Oil Company of California, and a DC-2-190 for Captain George Whittell, a wealthy California investor. The only foreign customer for one of these specially fitted aircraft was the Austrian Government, which ordered a DC-2-115D for Chancellor Engelbert Dollfuss.

BELOW *The cockpit of a DC-2-115F was photographed in Santa Monica on 2 July 1935.* (Douglas)

US DC-2 customers

The second operator of Douglas Commercial aircraft was General Air Lines which, beginning in August 1934, briefly operated four DC-2s between San Diego, Los Angeles, Las Vegas, and Salt Lake City. When General Air Lines was reorganized into a new Western Air Express, its DC-2s were sold to Eastern Air Lines to bring the fleet of this carrier to 14 of the new twin-engined airliners. Heavily advertised under the name 'The Great Silver Fleet' which was boldly applied on their sides, Eastern's DC-2s were operated on the East Coast route between New York, Washington, Charleston, Jacksonville, and Miami. Next American Airlines began flying DC-2s between New York and Chicago in December 1934, before placing its first Douglas twin-engined aircraft on its transcontinental route. Although the DC-2 proved substantially safer and more reliable than previous airliners, losses were nevertheless incurred by these airlines.[2]

Pan American Airways, then the principal US international airline, was the first to operate DC-2s on its Latin American network. It went on to acquire 16 more, including those for its affiliates, Pan American-Grace Airways (Panagra) and China National Aviation Corporation (CNAC). Having acquired DC-2s to replace flying boats between Florida and Brazil, Pan American started using them for weekly flights on that route. Southbound flights departed from Miami at 7:45am on Thursday and arrived in Rio de Janeiro the following Monday at 4pm. Along the way, the DC-2s made technical and commercial stops in Cuba, Haiti, Puerto

2   The first US registered DC-2 to be lost was NC13785, a DC-2-112 of TWA which crashed on 6 May 1935 near Macon, Missouri, when the pilot attempted an emergency landing after running out of fuel. Out of the occupants, 10 survived, but three others, including New Mexico Senator Bronson M. Cutting, died.

ABOVE *Taken on 21 June 1934, this publicity photograph of the cabin of a DC-112 of TWA is misleading as it gives the impression that coffee and consommé would not spill over. The DC-2 flew well, but in turbulence at low altitude...* (Douglas)

BELOW *Eastern Air Lines was a major customer for Douglas and operated its 'Great Silver Fleet' of DC-2s on routes from the Northeast to Florida.* (Eastern)

ABOVE *Ordered by the Pan American Aviation Supply Corporation for delivery to Panagra, NC14268 crashed at Arajuno, in the Ecuadorian rainforest, on 31 July 1944.* (Douglas)

Rico (where they remained overnight in San Juan), the Virgin Islands, the French Antilles, Trinidad and Tobago (for a second overnight layover in Port of Spain), the Guyanas, and then 15 stops in Brazil (including overnight stops in Belem and Recife). In December 1936, the one-way fare from Miami to Rio de Janeiro was $438.00 (±$6,750.00 today).[3] After using its DC-2s on other parts of its network (notably in Alaska) Pan American disposed of the last of these aircraft in 1941. During the last quarter of that year, crews from its subsidiary, PAA-Africa, ferried DC-2s for the Royal Air Force on the new trans-African route, from Takoradi in the Gold Coast – today's Ghana – to Khartoum in the Anglo-Egyptian Sudan.

Panagra, which was 50% owned by Pan American, used DC-2s on its route along the western coast of South America, from Cristobal in the Panama Canal Zone to Santiago, Chile. Flights continued across the Andes toward Buenos Aires and Montevideo. Panagra last flew DC-2s in 1947. CNAC, the Chinese affiliate of Pan American, operated its DC-2s between Shanghai, Peking, Canton, Chungking, and Hong Kong as well as to Burma. Its last DC-2 crashed in Kunming on 14 March 1942 after attempting to take off in an overloaded condition. Of the 17 occupants only four survived the crash.

Major air carriers in the continental United States disposed of their DC-2s in 1940–41 after replacing them, in most instances, with DC-3s, which were more economical to operate. These DC-2s were either sold to the British Purchasing Commission and the Royal Australian Air Force or were impressed by the USAAF which gave them the C-32A designation. Five other ex-TWA DC-2s were acquired in April 1942 by Northeast Airlines, and were fitted by this carrier with the longer wing outboard panels of the DC-3. Notwithstanding this modification, they also ended as C-32As with the USAAF.

In 1942, when US airlines operated a total of 322 aircraft, only eight of them were DC-2s, five with Braniff Airways and three with TWA. After the war, surviving DC-2s and C-32As released by the USAAF were only used by small airlines or in other than passenger carrying roles. This was notably the case of an aircraft which Johnson Flying Service in Missoula, Montana, operated for transporting smokejumpers to fight forest fires in terrain difficult to access from the ground.

---

3   In those days, only the wealthiest could afford air travel. Furthermore, it was far from being as comfortable as it is today with, for example, the DC-2s of Pan American cruising at between 6,000 to 8,000ft through the hot, humid, and often turbulent tropical air; all without the benefit of cabin air conditioning. Clearly our grandparents and great grandparents were better travelers than we have become. Let us not forget also that our grandfathers were traveling in suit and tie and our grandmothers wore hats and gloves.

BELOW *This DC-2-115B, fsn 1368, was built for Pan American Airways. It belonged to the Donald Douglas Museum and Library when photographed over St Louis, Missouri, on 3 August 1988.* (Harry S. Gann, Jr)

Breaking into the international market

Prior to its spectacular participation in the October 1934 MacRobertson Race, the DC-2 had not attracted much attention in Europe. The most notable exception was provided by the Netherlands where the leading manufacturer, Fokker, and the leading airline, KLM, vied with each other to purchase DC-2s or acquire the manufacturing rights for the new American twin-engined airliners. Realizing that the new Douglas would quickly render obsolete aircraft built by his company, Anthony Fokker was successful in securing both the manufacturing rights and the sales exclusivity in Europe for the DC-2. In the end, *NV Koninklijke Nederlandsche Vliegtuigenfabrik* (Fokker) did not undertake license manufacturing of the DC-2 but it did sell sub-rights to Airspeed Ltd which contemplated assembling DC-2s in Great-Britain under its A.S. 23 designation. The registration G-ADHO was reserved for the first A.S. 23 but, in the end, nothing came of this project. Thus, the only DC-2 on the British registry was G-AGBH, a DC-2-115L of KLM (ex PH-ALE, fsn 1584), which took refuge in Great Britain on 16 May 1940 when Germany invaded the Netherlands. Earlier, another refugee (ex SP-ASL, fsn 1378) of LOT Polish Airlines had been expected to become G-AGAD but was detained in Romania while on its way to safety.

Accepting its first DC-2, fsn 1317, on 25 August 1934,[4] Fokker immediately turned it over to KLM which intended to enter the DC-2 in the MacRobertson Trophy Air Race being organized to celebrate the Centenary of Melbourne, Victoria. Sixty-four competitors were announced but only 20 aircraft showed up for departure from Mildenhall, Suffolk, on 20 October 1934. Bound for Melbourne they were required to make five stops (in Iraq at Baghdad, in India at Allahabad, in Singapore, and in Australia at Darwin and Charleville) and could make as many technical stops as they required. The £10,000 prize went to C.W.A. Scott and Tom Campbell Black flying one of three purpose-built de Havilland D.H.88 *Comet* racers. The two British pilots had linked England to Australia in 71hr 0min 18 sec, including time spent on the ground. Eight other aircraft reached their destination, 10 others (including another *Comet*) were forced out of the race. H.D. Gillman and J.K. Baines died on 22 October, the second day of the race, when their Fairey *Fox I* crashed near Palazzo San Gervasio in Italy.

However, the most notable performance was not that of the *Comets* which arrived in first and fourth places, but that of two

ABOVE *Contrary to what has been frequently written, Fokker did not build the DC-2 under license. Although it had acquired the manufacturing rights for the DC-2, the Dutch company only acted as the European sales agent for Douglas. The 'Fokker-Douglas' DC-2s were built in Santa Monica for delivery to customers in Europe.* (Fokker)

American airliners which placed in the two middle spots. A Boeing 247D with a crew of three (Roscoe Turner, Clyde Pangborn, and Reeder Nichols) which, carrying no load, had covered the 11,123 miles in 92hr 55min 38sec to place third. Still more remarkable was the achievement of the DC-2 flown by K.D. Parmentier, J.J. Moll, B. Prins, and C. Van Brugge. Carrying three paying passengers and mail bags, their PH-AJU *Uiver* (Stork) flew over the usual KLM route to the Dutch East Indies before continuing on to Australia. Forced to make a precautionary landing in Albury, New South Wales, the KLM DC-2 lost some time but still placed second with an elapsed time of 90hr 13min 36sec (flying time being 81hr 10min 36sec).[5] Until then the Douglas name had remained relatively unknown in Europe (even though two of its *World Cruisers* had been the first to fly around the world in 1922). But, all of a sudden, Douglas became world-famous.

---

4   The aircraft was flown from Santa Monica to New York where it was partially dismantled for shipping. The same procedure was used to deliver Fokker-distributed DC-2s and DC-3s to customers in Europe as described on page 97 in the DC-3 chapter.

5   The second place DC-2 crashed on 20 December 1934 near Rutbah Wells (Ar Rutbar in Al Anbar province), Iraq, while making a special holiday flight to Batavia in the Dutch East Indies (today Jakarta, Indonesia).

BELOW *Few expected that the passenger- and mail-carrying DC-2, seen prior to departure from Mildenhall on 20 October 1934, would be in second place – behind a purpose-built de Havilland Comet racer – at the end of the MacRobertson Trophy Air Race from England to Australia.* (KLM)

ABOVE *SP-ASL, the second of two DC-2Bs of LOT, is shown here about to depart from Warsaw on the first flight to Greece by the Polish airlines on 3 October 1936.* (DR)

LEFT *During World War Two, when it continued flying to Germany and the rest of Nazi-occupied Europe, Swissair applied red-and-white stripes to its aircraft to help them being identified to a neutral nation. This DC-2-115B, HB-ITE, displays its nose and tail markings in this photograph taken at Zürich-Dübendorf.* (Rafael Koller)

In addition to the notorious PH-AJU, KLM and KNILM,[6] its associate on the East Indies route, obtained 20 additional DC-2s through Fokker. Only one of them PH-AKT, *Toekan* (Toucan) was powered by Pratt & Whitney engines. Most of these aircraft were used initially on the long route to Batavia on the northeast coast of Java.[7] Between May 1935 and June 1937, when they were replaced by DC-3, DC-2s flew on this route 290 times. On entering service to Batavia, the DC-2s had reclining seats for only five passengers. Two seats were added when the installation of more powerful *Cyclone* engines allowed take-off weight to be increased. The 9,000-mile trip between the Netherlands and the East Indies took five and a half days with overnight stops being made in Athens, Baghdad, Jodhpur and Singapore. Each day numerous technical stops had to be made, with the DC-2s, their crews, and their passengers averaging 10 flight hours per day.

Other clients acquiring the new twin-engined airliners through Fokker were:
* the Austrian and French Governments, one DC-2 each,
* Swissair, five DC-2s,
* LAPE (*Líneas Aéreas Postales Españolas*), five DC-2s,
* CLS (*Ceskolovenska Letecka Spolecnost*), five DC-2s,
* LOT (*Polskie Linie Lotnicze*), two DC-2Bs,
* A.L.I. (*Avio Linee Italiane S.A.*), one DC-2A, and
* DLH (*Deutsche Luft Hansa*), one DC-2.

Bearing fsn 1333 and registered F-AKHD, the DC-2-115B ordered by the French Government was delivered in August 1935. On arrival it was sent to the CEMA (*Centre d'essais du matériel aérien*) at Vélizy-Villacoublay where it was praised. This led Renault, the French automobile manufacturer, to contemplate acquiring the manufacturing license and replacing the American engines with its own engines, but this came to naught. In 1939, the French DC-2 was briefly operated by Air France between Paris and Algiers before disappearing from the French registry during the war. A second DC-2, fsn 1332, went on the French registry in December 1959. It was the former HB-ITO of Swissair which had become ZS-DFX of Phoenix Airline before being registered F-BJHR in France. It was withdrawn from use at Nice in October 1961.

In addition to the aircraft delivered abroad through Fokker, Douglas directly exported 14 DC-2s, including four each to Australia and China. Another (fsn 1413) was sold to the Soviet Union where it was registered USSR-M-25; it was destroyed as a result of an explosion in flight near Bucharest on 6 August 1937. The remaining five, fsn 1418/1422, were shipped to Japan under a manufacturing license acquired in May 1935 by Nakajima Hikoki K.K. for the sum of $80,000.00 (±$1.3 million today).[8] The first of these aircraft completed acceptance testing at Santa Monica before being shipped to Japan. It was followed by sub-assemblies and parts for four others which were assembled at Ota. The first of these flew in February 1936. After being tested by the Japanese Navy, the DC-2s were placed in commercial service by *Nihon Koku K.K.*

---

6 *Koninklijke Nederlandsch-Indische Luchtvaart Maatschappij* (KNILM) was organized in 1928 by Dutch East Indies investors without the financial participation of KLM.
7 The first commercial flight on this route was made, not without great difficulties, between 1 October and 25 November 1924 by a single-engined Fokker F.VII registered H-NACC. Afterward, KLM used various Fokker three-engined aircraft (F.VIIb/3m, F-VIII, F.XII, and F.XVIII) until replacing them with DC-2s in May 1925.

8 In the early1960s, while doing research for his first book, *Japanese Aircraft of the Pacific War*, the author wrote to the Douglas Aircraft Company seeking to obtain information concerning the manufacturing licenses for the DC-2 and DC-3 which had been sold to Japan. His letters remained unanswered as the manufacturer was still leery attracting attention to this transaction. Some five years later, after the author had joined Douglas in Long Beach, he had to do company research in the Santa Monica archives. The badge identifying him as belonging to management attracted the attention of the archivist. Noting the name on the badge, the archivist said nothing but went to a filing cabinet from which he quickly retrieved the author's unanswered letters. Attached to them were photocopies of the Japanese licenses. For the author, the mystery was solved.

(later *Dai Nippon Koku K.K.*). Early during the war, at least one was used by the Japanese Army Air Force thus leading the Air Technical Intelligence Unit (ATIU) to assign the code name *Tess* to Japanese DC-2s.

Head-on competition

DC-2s of Swissair began operating between Zurich, Basel, and London on 1 April 1935. Seven weeks later, on 23 May, KLM began flying DC-2s to Batavia. For many other European airlines this was truly a shock, as they were mostly operating older and, in some cases, frankly obsolete aircraft. In that year, only the most loyal subjects of His Majesty King Edward VIII could take genuine pride when seeing Boulton Paul P.71As, de Havilland D.H.86s, Handley Page 45s, and Short L.17s – all of which were heavily strutted biplanes with fabric covering and fixed undercarriage – sharing the tarmac at Croydon with DC-2s. The French and the Germans had no reason for complacency as their airlines then relied primarily on three-engined aircraft with fixed undercarriage, Wibault 282s or 283T.12s for the former and Junkers Ju 52/3ms for the latter.

Manufacturers, airlines, and government authorities in Europe had simply ignored signs that a technical revolution was well underway in the United States. Shocked, they reacted first by developing a series of record-breaking airplanes masquerading as future airliners but, in fact, serving as prototypes for a new generation of bombers:

*   In Italy, the prototype of the Savoia-Marchetti SM.79 was flown on 28 September 1934;
*   In Germany, the Dornier 17 A and Heinkel 111 C flew in 1934/1935;
*   In the United Kingdom, the Bristol 142, *Britain First*, was airborne in April 1935;
*   Finally, it was France's turn with the first flight of the Amiot 340 in December 1937.

Although these European aircraft were streamlined and fast, they all lacked the economic performance required from genuine airliners. Modern European airliners were ready at last to enter service in 1936 (Fiat G.18s in Italy), in 1938 (Block 220s in France), and 1939 (de Havilland *Flamingo* in Britain). Certainly, one would have hoped that there was no further reason for Europeans to feel inferior as those three airliners compared favorably with the Boeing 247, Douglas DC-2 and DC-3, and Lockheed 10/14/18. In the meantime, however, American transport aircraft manufacturers had not remained idle and, if anything, the gap between the

ABOVE *By the early 1940s, the United States aircraft industry had taken a commendable lead with its airliners. This is exemplified by this line-up of a DC-2, a DC-3 and a Boeing* Stratoliner *of TWA.* (TWA)

aeronautical industries on the opposite sides of the North Atlantic had increased. To use a publicity claim now made trite by Boeing with its bombastic claims when launching the 787, the DC-2 was indeed a genuine 'game changer' for the international air transport industry.

For its manufacturer, financial losses incurred with the DC-1 and the initial batch of DC-2s for TWA were more than offset with profits realized by selling DC-2s to other American clients and export customers. Moreover, the success obtained with the DC-2 earned for Douglas W. Douglas and his team the 1935 Robert J. Collier Trophy for 'the most significant progress in aviation'.

BELOW *President Franklin D. Roosevelt congratulates Donald W. Douglas during the award ceremony for the Robert J. Collier Trophy at the White House on 1 July 1936.* (Douglas)

ABOVE *Two R2D-1s went to the USMC and were operated by squadrons VJ-6M and VMJ-1, both based at MCAS Quantico, Virginia. Three went to the USN.* (USMC)

Military derivatives

The first customer for a military version of the DC-2 was the US Naval Aviation. Of the five aircraft ordered three were DC-2-125s and two were DC-2-142s, but all were R2D-1s for the USN and USMC. Powered by 710hp Wright R-1820-12s, BuNos 9620/9622, 9993, and 9994 were delivered between November 1934 and December 1935. They were operated as special transports for the Secretary of the Navy, the Chief of Naval Operations, the Commandant of the Marine Corps, and flag officers and their staffs. Four R2D-1s were lost while in naval service, but BuNo 9993 was stricken by the Navy in 1944. In 1983 it was restored in the markings of PH-AJU, the DC-2 entered by KLM in the 1934 MacRobertson Race.

As the Army Air Corps had performed poorly during the Air Mail Emergency, and as many aircraft and human losses had then incurred, a government committee was organized to review the situation. Chaired by Newton D. Baker, a former Secretary of War,

BELOW *Two aircraft of the 10th Transport Group during manoeuvres in 1943: that in the foreground is a C-33, the other being a DC-3 impressed from an airline.* (USAAF)

it recommended that civil transports be procured for the Army Air Corps. The first of these new aircraft was a DC-2-153 which, powered by 750hp Wright R-1820-25s, became the XC-32 with the serial number 36-1. After military trials at Wright Field, Ohio, it was sent to Langley Field, Virginia, for use by the GHQ Air Force. Similar to civil DC-2s when delivered, this aircraft was progressively upgraded with new radio and navigation equipment, pneumatic deicers, and small propeller spinners. Designated C-32 while at Langley, it remained in use until heavily damaged in a landing accident on 4 September 1942. Two basically similar aircraft, differing only by their cabin installation, were delivered as YC-34s (but later simply became C-34s). Given serials 36-345 and 356-346, they remained in use until 1942. In 1942, 24 civil DC-2s were impressed and became C-32As in USAF nomenclature.

Their serial numbers (42-53527 to -53532, 42-57154 to -57156, 42-57227, 42-52228, 42-58071 to -58073, 42-61095, 42-61096, 42-65577 to -65579, 42-68857, 42-68858, 42-70863, 42-83226 and 42-83227) were seldom applied. Those which survived military operations were returned to the civil registry in 1944–45.

The first tactical transport version of the DC-2 to be built was the C-33 of which 18 were ordered in March 1935 with serial numbers 36-70 through 36-87. Specifically intended to carry 2,400lb of cargo and military equipment, the C-33s were fitted with a two-panel door on the left side of the fuselage. Cargo loading, handling, and unloading was eased further by installing (1) the cabin floor section at the cargo door at an angle so it was parallel to the ground when the aircraft was parked; (2) attachment points by the door for a tripod hoist assembly; and (3) a cable and pulley system, and tie-down points in the cabin. In addition to their large cargo door, C-33s differed externally from DC-2s in having the enlarged fin and rudder of the DC-3 but without the dorsal fin of the latter aircraft. They were powered by 750hp R-1820-25s as were the XC-32 and C-34s.

After acceptance trials, the first C-33 (36-70) was modified in January 1938 and was then designated C-38 (instead of C-33A as had been initially planned). Principal modifications consisted of installation of 930hp Wright R-1820-45s driving constant-speed propellers (earlier civil and military DC-2s having variable-pitch propellers), longer undercarriage struts, and a dorsal fin. After serving as the prototype for the C-39 variant, it was used to fly senior officers and VIPs until February 1945.

The 17 other C-33s enabled the Army Air Corps to organize its first specialized transport unit, the 10th Transport Group, which was organized at Patterson Field, Ohio, in May 1937. During

WW II, the Air Transport Command used its C-33s mostly in the United States before retiring them after the war ended.

The unofficial designation 'DC-2½' has often been used to describe aircraft combining features of both the DC-2 and DC-3. These hybrids were mostly C-39s (38-499 to 38-501 and 38-504 to 38-535) with the C-33 fuselage matched to the aft section and tail surfaces of the DC-3. The center section of their wings was similar to that of the DC-3, while the outboard panels were those of the DC-2. Moreover, the C-39s were fitted with the strengthened undercarriage of the C-38 and were powered by 975hp Wright R-1820-55s. They served with the USAAF until war's end. One of the C-39s, 38-515, is preserved in the collection of the National Museum of the United States Air Force at Wright-Patterson AFB.

The last military derivative of the DC-2 was the sole C-42 (38-503, fsn 2060) which was delivered to the Army Air Corps on 24 March 1939. Acquired as a transport for senior commanders and their staffs, it differed from the C-39s in having the cargo door replaced by a smaller passenger unit and in receiving comprehensive radio equipment. With its 1200hp Wright R-1820-53s, this was the most powerful aircraft in the DC-2 series. After the war, it was sold to commercial operators and sent to Latin America. While operated by *Transaer* and carrying the Argentine registration LV-GGT, it was too heavily damaged in a May 1960 accident to be economically repaired. During the early 1940s, two C-39s (38-513 and 38-528) were partially brought up to the C-42 configuration but retained their original designation.

DC-2s acquired from airlines and other civil operators were operated by the armed forces of the following countries:

ABOVE *Beautifully restored, this is 38-315, the C-39 in the collection of the National Museum of the United States Air Force at Wright-Patterson AFB. The NMUSAF staff has the commendable idea of photographing restored aircraft outside while avoiding visual evidences that the photo has been taken recently.* (NMUSAF)

- **Australia:** In 1940, the British Purchasing Commission in the United States obtained ten ex-Eastern Air Line DC-2s for the Royal Australian Air Force. With that service, they were given military serials A30-4 to A30-13. Most of them, however, were operated with pseudo-civilian registrations, such as VHCRA without the hyphen between VH and CRA as was the case for genuine civil registration. Entering RAAF service at the end of 1940, they were initially used by No 8 Squadron at Canberra for the training of paratroopers. Next they were distributed to four training schools, Nos 1, 2, and 3 WAGS (Wireless Air Gunner Schools) and No 1 Service Flying Training School. Surviving aircraft were sold at the end of the war.
- **Finland:** When the Soviet Union invaded Finland in 1939, rather limited assistance came from various sources. Notably, Count Carl Gustaf von Rosen from Sweden acquired a DC-2-115E for the Finns. This fsn 1354 was the ex-PH-AKG of KLM

BELOW *Named* Hanssin-Jukka *and initially numbered DC-1, this DC-2-115E (ex-PH-AKH of KLM) was modified as a bomber and fitted with armament.* (Ilmavoimat)

which had become the SE-AKE of AB *Aerotransport*. In Finland, it was quickly modified for military use, receiving a defensive armament consisting of a 7.7mm fixed machine gun in the nose and another of these guns in the dorsal turret. Racks for 24 12kg bombs were fitted beneath the wing center section. Although it was used by the *Ilmavoimat* for a few bombing missions, the modified DC-2 was primarily operated as a military transport. In Finnish service, it was named *Hanssin-Jukka*[9] and was given the identification number DC-1. However, as this was a misnomer for a DC-2, it became DO-1 in March 1942; two months later it was re-engined with Shvetsov M-62s. In 1949, *Ilmavoimat* obtained two other DC-2s, fsn 1582 and 1562, which became DO-2 and DO-3. In Finland, their Wright engines were replaced by 825hp Bristol *Mercury XVs*. DO-2, the last in service, was retired in April 1956.

- **Germany:** Early in World War Two, DC-2s fell into German hands when Poland, Czechoslovakia, and the Netherlands were invaded. Most went to *Deutsche Luft Hansa* with eight of these

9   Withdrawn from use in June 1955, this wartime veteran became a non-flying summer café between 1959 and 1981 before being reacquired by the Finnish Air Force for its museum at Tik-kakoski. Restoration has just been completed and, hopefully, it will fly again.

aircraft (seven ex-KLM and one ex-CLS) being subsequently transferred to the *Luftwaffe*. At the war's end, at least one was recovered by British forces.

- **Great Britain:** In 1939, when war broke anew, the Royal Air Force faced a critical shortage of transport aircraft particularly as it was called upon to provide logistical support to Commonwealth forces on many continents. As the British aeronautical industry had to give absolute priority to the production of combat aircraft, in 1940 and 1941, the British Direct Purchasing Commission in the United States sought to obtain the required transports as quickly as possible. Among the first it obtained for the RAF were 21 DC-2s (12 from American Air Line, 6 from TWA, and 3 from Pan American). Assigned serials AX755, AX767/AX769, DG468/DG479, HK820, HK821, HK847 and HK867, they entered RAF service in early 1941 and were primarily used in North Africa, Iraq, India, and Burma, by Nos 31, 117, and 267 Squadrons. In addition, at least one ex-C-32A (ex-Pan American and USAAF) was briefly used by No 31 Squadron. In 1943, the RAF transferred many of its DC-2s to the government of India and to Tata Airline. The last three DC-2s which had seen RAF service were broken up in 1945.

- **Japan:** At least one of the five DC-2s imported by Nakajima was briefly operated in Indochina by the Teikoku Rikugun Kokutai (JAAF) early in the war.

- **Spain:** During the civil war, the four DC-2s of LAPE were supplemented by two acquired abroad. They were operated both by LAPE and FARE (*Fuerzas Aéreas Republicanas Españolas*). One of these aircraft fell into Nationalist hands in July 1936 and was used as the personal transport of the Nationalist leader, Generalissimo Francisco Franco. After the civil war, the Nationalists got four of the other DC-2s and quickly handed them over to their new airline, *Iberia*.

LEFT *While being operated by the* Teikoku Rikugun Kokutai, *this Nakajima-assembled DC-2 was camouflaged and received full military markings.* (DR)

Data for the DC-2 and derivatives

	DC-2	DC-2B	R2D-1	C-33	C-38	C-39	C-42
Dimensions:							
Span, ft in	85 0	85 0	85 0	85 0	85 0	85 0	85 0
Length, ft in	61 11¾	61 11¾	61 9	61 11¾	61 6	61 6	61 6
Height, ft in	16 3¾	16 3¾	16 3¾	16 3⅜	19 7	18 8	18 8
Wing area, sq ft	939	939	939	939	939	939	939
Weights:							
Empty, lb	12,408	—	—	12,476	12,475	14,287	15,712
Loaded, lb	18,560	18,200	18,200	17,560	18,200	21,000	21,000
Maximum, lb	—	—	—	18,588	18,500	—	23,625
Power plant:							
Type (x 2)	Wright SGR-1820-F52	Bristol Pegasus VI	Wright R-1820-12	Wright R-1820-25	Wright R-1820-45	Wright R-1820-55	Wright R-1820-53
Take-off rating, hp	875	750	710	750	930	975	1,200
Fuel tank capacity, Imp. gallons	150	152	—	—	110	155	155
Performance:							
Maximum speed, mph at ft	210/8,000	198/6,500	210	202/2,500	208/2,500	210/5,000	214/5,000
Cruising speed, mph at ft	190/8,000	185/12,000	—	171	170	156/5,000	170/5,000
Climb, ft/min	1,000/1	5,000/3	—	1,110/1	10,000/9.7	1,480/1	1,230/1
Service ceiling, ft	22,450	—	—	20,000	—	20,600	22,000
Normal range, miles	1,000	—	—	916	1,100	1,170	1,000
Maximum range, miles	—	—	—	—	—	1,600	1,600

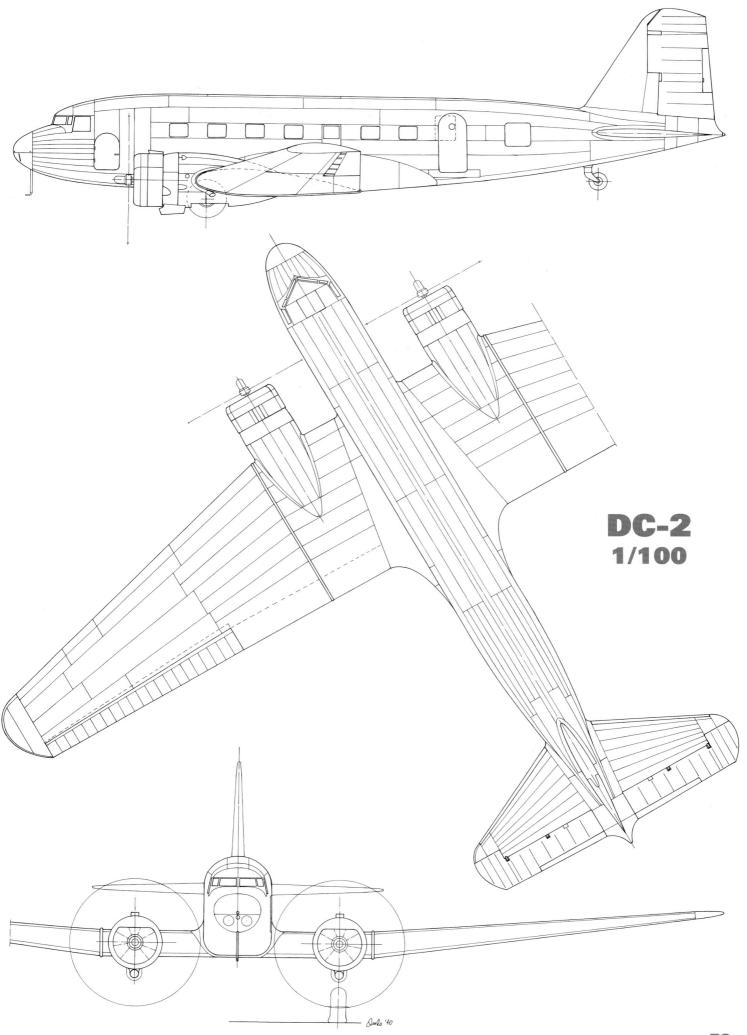

DC-2
1/100

CIVIL DC-2s IN THE UNITED STATES

LEFT *Photographed at the Chicago Municipal Airport (now Chicago-Midway) in 1934, NC14274 was the first DC-2-120 of American Airlines. (American Airlines)*

LEFT *This DC-2-120 of American Air Lines was acquired by the British Direct Purchasing Commission in 1940 and became HK867 with the Royal Air Force. It crashed in Sierra Leone on 7 September 1941 after colliding with a Hawker Hurricane. (American Airlines)*

BELOW *This Eastern Air Lines DC-2-112 went to the Royal Australian Air Force in December 1940. After the war, it went on the Australian civil registry as VH-AEN of New Holland Airways. It crashed at Darwin on 9 May 1948. (Eastern Air Lines)*

RIGHT *Delta Air Lines did not purchase DC-2s directly from the manufacturer. NC14275, a DC-2-112, had been delivered to American Airlines in November 1934 and was sold to Delta in February 1941. Almost immediately, it was acquired for the RAF by the British Direct Purchasing Commission. (Delta Air Lines)*

ABOVE *General Air Lines operated four DC-112s for only a short period in 1934. (Douglas)*

RIGHT *Before being operated in Iraq by No 31 Squadron, Royal Air Force, during the second quarter of 1941, this DC-2-118B had been NC14271 with Pan American (as illustrated), XA-BJI with Mexicana, and again NC14271 with PAA-Africa. (Pan American Airways)*

RIGHT *Chinese-style lettering can be deceiving. This is not a CNAC DC-2 but a US-registered aircraft with markings applied to star in the 1936 Frank Capra movie, Lost Horizon. (Douglas)*

LEFT *Built as an R2D-1 for the US Navy, fsn 1404 (ex-BuNo 9993) had become N39165 of Mercer Enterprises before being photographed at the Burbank Airport in 1967.* (René J. Francillon)

ABOVE *The same fsn 1404 is shown here as N1934D after being refurbished for the Donald Douglas Museum and Library. It was photographed at the Los Angeles International Airport in front of the old terminal at Mines Field. It is too bad that the dark buildings in the background are not from the proper time period.* (Douglas)

LEFT *N1934D, fsn 1404, was later repainted in TWA colours.* (Harry S. Gann, Jr)

CIVIL DC-2s ABROAD

ABOVE *F-AKHD, fsn 1333, is shown while undergoing evaluation tests at France's Centre d'Essais du Matériel Aérien. (Jean Delmas collection)*

RIGHT *A second DC-2 found its way on to the French registry many years later. Registered F-BJHR it was used by* Airnautic *at the end of the 1950s. (Jean Delmas collection)*

RIGHT *Photographed in September 1934 before it was delivered to the Austrian Government with the A-500 registration, this DC-2-115D later was briefly HB-ISA in Switzerland and then EC-AGA in Spain. After being reregistered as EC-AAA it crashed in Spain in April 1946. (Douglas)*

ABOVE *The DC-2A acquired by Avio Linee Italiane was powered by Pratt & Whitney Hornet engines.* (DR)

LEFT *This DC-2-115E of KLM fell into German hands in 1940 and became D-ABOW with Lufthansa and then PC+EB with the Luftwaffe.* (KLM)

BELOW *Delivered to KNILM in May 1935, PK-AFJ was destroyed at Damo, Soerabaja, in December 1941.* (KLM)

RIGHT Lineas Areas Postales Españolas *took delivery of fsn 1330 in January 1935. After the Spanish Civil War ended, it became EC-AAD with Iberia but was damaged beyond economical repair in an accident in August 1940.* (Douglas)

RIGHT *D-ABEO, fsn 1318, was the only DC-2 purchased by Germany through Fokker. It was sold to LOT-Polish Airlines and, registered SP-ASJ, crashed on 25 November 1937 near Lazd Ricie in Romania.* (Lufthansa)

BELOW *Escaping from the Dutch East Indies in early 1941 when Japanese forces invaded that Dutch colony, PK-AFL of KNILM had become VH-ADZ of Marshall Airways before being photographed in the early 1960s.* (Mervyn W. Prime)

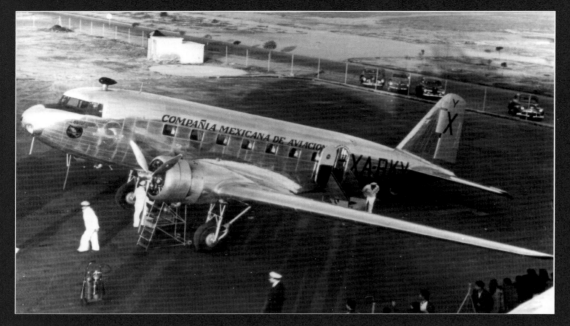

LEFT *XA-BKY, a DC-2-118B belonged to* Compañia Mexicana de Aviación, *a subsidiary of Pan American Airways.* (Douglas)

BELOW *Nakajima Hikoki KK assembled five DC-2s in Japan.* (DR)

BOTTOM *USSR-M25, a DC-2-152, was imported in the Soviet Union by Amtorg and was briefly used on the route between Leningrad and Sebastopol.* (Douglas)

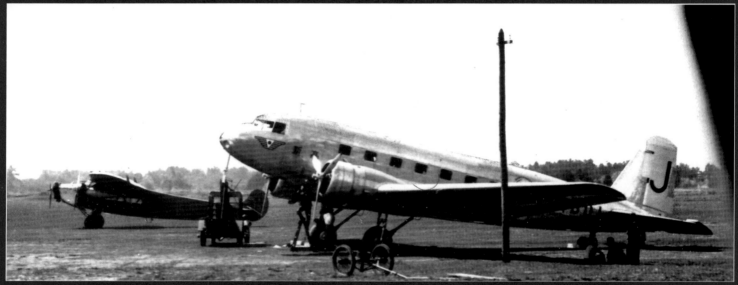

MILITARY DC-2s

TOP *This USN R2D-1 underwent testing at Langley, Virginia, with the National Advisory Committee for Aeronautics.* (NACA)

ABOVE *This photo shows the XC-32 in its original configuration.* (Army Air Corps)

RIGHT *Undergoing maintenance in an Army Air Corps hangar, 36-87 is a C-33 bearing on its fin the identification markings of the 4th Air Base Squadron.* (NMUSAF)

LEFT *The flag painted on the rear fuselage of this YC-34 (36-345) indicates that it was used to transport the Secretary of State for Military Aviation.* (William J. Balogh, David W. Menard collection)

ABOVE *Fitted with a test probe beneath the forward fuselage, this C-38 (36-70) was undergoing tests with NACA at Langley, Virginia.* (NACA)

LEFT *From this angle, this C-39 looks much like the larger C-47.* (NMUSAF)

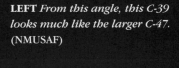

LEFT *With camouflage paint the C-42, 38-503 Happy Chief looks even more like a C-47.* (NMUSAF)

ABOVE *Bearing Spanish Nationalist markings, 42-1* Capitán Vara de Rey, *had originally been delivered by Fokker to LAPE.* (USAAF)

RIGHT *The former BuNo 9993 has been painted to represent PH-AJU of MacRobertson Race fame.* (DR)

BELOW *Luftwaffe markings (PC+EC) are being applied to fsn 1356, a DC-2-115E that had been PH-AKJ with KLM.* (Douglas)

Chapter 4

DC-3 – The money machine

Seventy-five years after the first Douglas Sleeper Transport (DST) flew in Santa Monica, nearly 200 of the more than 16,000 derivatives that followed it down production lines located in California and Oklahoma, as well as in the Soviet Union and Japan, were still flying. Yet, the success of this lasting product line was not

BELOW *Bound and determined to obtain DC-2 derivatives with a larger cabin that could be fitted with sleeper beds at night or more seats during the day, Cyrus R. Smith, President of American Airlines, kept pressuring Donald Douglas to commit to this program. Eventually, his persistency paid off for American Airlines which ended up operating 114 DSTs, DC-3s and ex-C-47s. NC25664* Flagship Rochester, *a DC-3-277B, was delivered on 28 March 1940.* (Boeing Historical Archives)

initially anticipated. Predictions were gloomy when American Airlines first expressed its wish to acquire larger derivatives of the DC-2.

Eventually acquiring 16 DC-2s, American Airlines placed its first Douglas airliner in service on 4 November 1934 between Newark and Chicago. On that route, its DC-2s competed with those of TWA and with the Boeing 247Ds of United Air Lines. Conversely, having to operate between the East and West Coasts over a route longer than those of its competitors,[1] American Airlines chose not to put its DC-2s in service to Los Angeles. Instead, it continued offering

---

1 American Airways was formed in January 1930 when several small airlines owned or controlled by the Aviation Corporation were merged into a single entity. From some of these, the new carrier had inherited several Contract Air Mail routes (CAM 4 from Fort Worth to Los Angeles, CAM 7 from Newark to Chicago, CAM 18 from Boston to Newark, CAM 21 from Boston to Cleveland, CAM 22 from Cleveland to Nashville, CAM 23 from Newark to Fort Worth, CAM 25 from Chicago to Washington DC, and CAM 30 between Chicago and Fort Worth). From various sectors of these mail routes, American Airlines (as American Airways had been renamed on 11 April 1934) cobbled up a less than direct transcontinental route.

ABOVE *The 10,655th and last aircraft in the DC-3 family built by Douglas was this DC-3D, fsn 42981, N1624. It was delivered to The Texas Company (Texaco) in April 1946.* (Douglas)

sleeper service with Curtiss *Condors* on the Dallas–Los Angeles segment on its transcontinental route.

When American Airlines began operating transcontinental services on 5 May 1934, its passengers went by overnight train to Cleveland, Ohio. From there, Ford 5-AT *Tri-Motors* made six stops while taking them to Dallas. The night flight from this Texas city to Los Angeles was made aboard Curtiss *Condor* biplanes with 12 sleeper beds. In the westerly direction, travel by train, day planes, and *Condors* required 38hr 45min. Although sleeper accommodations were comfortable, that was not enough to offset the fact that TWA's DC-2s took passengers from Newark to Los Angeles in just 18 hours. Not authorized to operate on a more direct transcontinental routing, American Airlines needed urgently to acquire better performing aircraft.

One week after the airline began offering its air/rail link between Newark and Los Angeles, its Board of Directors elected a new president, Cyrus Rowlett Smith (better known by his initials C.R.).[2] Although lacking a technical background, C.R. Smith knew how to work efficiently with the technical staff of the airline and its chief engineer, William Littlewood. He urged Littlewood and his assistant, Otto Kirchner, to draw up specifications for an aircraft matching the performance of the DC-2 with the comfort of *Condor* sleepers. The solution was soon obvious to the two American Airlines engineers; by increasing the fuselage cross-section of the DC-2, space would become available to install sleeper beds and development costs would be minimized. Clearly, the modified aircraft would have a higher take off weight, but that did not appear to be a problem as Wright was developing a new family of *Cyclones*, the SGR-1820-Gs, which were to be 35% more powerful on take-off than the SGR-1820-Fs powering DC-2s.

As initially envisioned by Littlewood and Kirchner, this 'steroid enhanced' DC-2 would retain an 85% part and component commonality with standard DC-2s. However, as available engine power kept increasing, American Airlines chose to increase its

performance requirement. In particular, C.R. Smith wanted payload to be increased in order to lower seat/mile cost in spite of the higher acquisition cost of the new aircraft. Moreover, Smith wished for the aircraft to be capable of flying non-stop between Newark and Chicago regardless of weather. Once these revised specifications were ready, Bill Littlewood was authorized by C.R. Smith to begin discussing them with Douglas.

A lukewarm reception

Donald Douglas, plant manager Harry Wetzel, and the manufacturer's engineers were not keen to go in the direction proposed by American. Firstly, their hefty DC-2 backlog was generating much profit. Secondly, they doubted that an aircraft with sleeper beds would have much of a market. Nevertheless, Arthur Raymond, who had just been promoted to chief engineer, put his team to work: Ed Burton was made responsible for the overall design, Lee Atwood for structural calculations, Bailey Oswald for performance calculations, and Harold Adams for the strengthening and modification of the hydraulically operated undercarriage.

Working in close cooperation with Bill Littlewood, the Douglas engineering team received much support from American Airlines. Notably, the airline flew one of its *Condors* to Santa Monica so that Douglas could study its sleeper arrangement. As work progressed, it became evident that the required modifications would necessitate more than fitting more powerful engines and increasing cabin width to fit either sleeper beds for night flights or more seats for day operations. With the predicted weight of the aircraft rising, it became necessary to enlarge the wings, span going from 85ft to 95ft and area from 939sq ft to 987sq ft. The fin and rudder also had to be enlarged to offset the wider fuselage and to correct the directional instability still plaguing the DC-2. Finally, the

---

2 Having earned an accounting diploma from the University of Texas, Smith held several business positions before becoming vice president of Southern Air Transport in 1929, a small airline taken over the following year by American Airways.

The DSTs and the DC-3s, as well as their military derivatives, retained the structural design of the DC-1 and the DC-2s. These four views illustrate the assembly process for the DC-3 and provide details on the multi-cellular wing structure developed by Jack Northrop. (Douglas)

undercarriage had to be redesigned to limit the footprint of the aircraft in spite of its greater maximum weight.

This last mentioned change well illustrates the prudence with which Donald Douglas undertook to design an aircraft for which he anticipated little demand (but which in fact was to become his greatest success). Believing that the DC-2 derivative would not sell well, the manufacturer did its utmost to minimize development and production costs. Thus instead of designing an all new undercarriage for proper weight distribution, he asked suppliers to come up with larger tyres which would not require much in terms of undercarriage modification. Specifically the diameter of wheel and tyres could not be increased. Goodrich and Goodyear both came up with tyres having a width of 17in instead of 15in for those of the DC-2. Consequently, the main undercarriage could remain mostly unchanged, exceptions made for increasing strut travel and substituting a full hydraulic gear retraction system for the manual pump of the DC-2.

Pilots also requested that the landing lights, which were mounted in the nose of DC-2s, be relocated to reduce cockpit glare while descending through clouds and fog. In the new aircraft, the landing lights were mounted in the wing leading edge, one on each side outboard of the engine. As a result of these modifications and improvements progressively introduced, the aircraft being designed for American Airlines ended up retaining only a 10% commonality with the DC-2. Moreover, new tooling would be required. Predictably, costs went up.

A list of modifications and a schedule of calculated performance were submitted to American Airlines on 10 May 1935. While Douglas remained skeptical regarding the project's chances of success, American Airlines knew that it badly needed this sleeper-equipped 'super DC-2' to compete with TWA. That left the airline president with the burden of changing the manufacturer's mind by convincing him of the viability of the venture.

In the course of a two-and-a-half hour telephone conversation between C.R. Smith in Chicago and Donald Douglas in Santa Monica, the president of the airline pleaded his case. Even though this call set the airline back $300 (±$4,700 today), C.R. Smith failed to overcome the fiscal conservatism of the California manufacturer of Scottish origin. Convinced that American Airlines lacked the financial resources to pay for the ten aircraft it planned to acquire, Donald Douglas remained non-committal. He did, however, authorize construction on a first aircraft in advance of a formal contract while urging his engineering and production staff to keep costs at the strictest minimum. It is only after American Airlines obtained a $4.5 million loan (±$70 million today) from the Reconstruction Finance Corporation[3] that Douglas finally agreed on 14 November 1935 to proceed with the project. Results soon proved that he had erred when failing to anticipate the sales potential of the DC-2 derivative as this transport aircraft soon went from success to success, and, to this day, remains the most built anywhere in the world.

Even before the first flight of the new aircraft, American Airlines doubled its order. Eight were to be delivered with sleeper beds as DSTs (Douglas Sleeper Transport), the remaining 12 as DC-3s with 21 seats for daytime operations. The final contract covering these aircraft was signed on 8 April 1936, four months after the first flight of the DST and two and one-half months before it entered service.

The prewar DST and DC-3

The DST prototype, fsn 1496 bearing the temporary registration X14988, was powered by two 1,000hp Wright SGF-1820-G5 radial engines. Although retaining only a 10% commonality with the DC-2, the new aircraft clearly resembled its forebear and was built along the same lines. On 17 December 1935, precisely 32 years after the Wright brothers had made their epochal flight at Kitty Hawk, North Carolina, Carl Cover lifted the DST from Clover Field, Santa Monica.

Even though trials had begun as the year-end holiday season was starting, X14988 made 25 more flights before the end of the month, logging 25hr 45min with the manufacturer's test pilots, Carl Cover and Elling Veblen, and with Dan Beard, the airline project pilot. No discrepancies of any significance were noted during these

BELOW *On display at the C.R. Smith Museum in Fort Worth, Texas, fsn 2202 is a DC-3-277B. It was delivered to American Airlines on 11 March 1940 and became its NC21798* Flagship Knoxville. (American Airlines)

3   The RFC was a US government agency organized in 1932 to help boost economic activities during the Great Depression by providing project financing at favorable terms. For the 10 new Douglas transports which American Airlines wished to order, the RFC agreed to provide 57% of the financing. Unit price for the new aircraft then was $795,000 (±$12.4 million today).

ABOVE *Photographed at Clover Field on 18 December 1935, one day after the maiden flight of the DST, X14988 shows the original configuration of the vertical tail surfaces without a dorsal fin and with the straight trailing edge of its rudder.* (Douglas)

early tests but, in January 1936, it became apparent that the fully loaded DST would require a take-off run exceeding the 1,000ft limit specified by American Airlines.

Having earlier decided that the aircraft would be displayed at the National Pacific Aircraft and Boat Show in Los Angeles between 1 and 19 February, Douglas took advantage of this downtime to

BELOW *Donald Douglas had been right when predicting that the sleeper-configured DST would not sell but, at first, he underestimated the sale potential of the DC-3.* (Douglas)

devise corrective measures. Careful analysis of engine performance revealed that the SGR-1820-G5s were not delivering the power promised by Wright. Fortunately, this was quickly and easily rectified by a minor modification of the crankshaft, enabling the aircraft to meet contractual performance guarantees.

Slightly damaged when landing at Mines Field on 5 March 1936, the first DST then had its original engines replaced by SGR-1820-G2s as planned for production aircraft. In addition, a small dorsal fin was added to improve directional stability during flights on one engine. Test flights were resumed on 27 March and were concluded on 29 April when the aircraft was ferried to Phoenix, Arizona,[4] to be handed over to American Airlines. It was, however, immediately flown back to Santa Monica where the airline staff was assisted by Douglas personnel while undertaking 50 hours of operational evaluation.

---

4   By accepting the DST in Arizona, American Airlines was able to avoid paying California taxes.

ABOVE LEFT AND ABOVE *During the mid- and late-1930s, air passengers traveled in style. No midriff t-shirt or cut-off jeans for these travelers shown in one of the double beds of a DST of American Airlines (with a rather proud young boy) and in the upper bed of a DST-A of United Air Lines.* (Douglas)

ATC 607 was obtained on 21 May 1936 for the initial DST model. Six other versions built for civil customers before the United States was forced into the war were covered by separate ATCs. All cabins had the following internal dimensions: length, 27ft 8in; width, 7ft 8in; and height, 6ft 4½in (the DC-2 cabin measuring 26ft x 4ft 10in x 6ft 3in).

Differences between the various DST and DC-3 models are as specified in the Approved Type Certificates below.

ATC 607: Issued on 21 May 1936, the first type certificate covered DSTs powered by Wright SGR-1820 engines with take-off ratings ranging from 1,000hp for the -G2s, -G2Es, and -G5s to 1,100hp for the -G102s, -G102As, and -G103As. Some DSTs were later re-engined with 1,200hp SGR-1820-G202As. All engine models drove three-blade constant speed propellers. Two 175 Imp. gallon tanks were installed in the wing center section between the fore and center spars. Two 167 Imp. gallon auxiliary tanks could be fitted between the center and rear spars. With 684 Imp. gallons in four tanks, the DST had a 1,250 mile ferry range.

As was the case for the DC-2, the cockpit of the DST was followed by a 35cu ft cargo and mail compartment on the right side with a door on the opposite side for loading and unloading. Aft of it, the cabin was divided into four compartments. The first, called 'Sky Room' and located on the right side, was relatively private and was fitted with two seats making into a bed, an upper bunk folding against the side and ceiling of the compartment during daytime, and a wash basin. Opposite to it was the galley in which hot meals, a novelty for airline passengers, could be prepared; the galley area also had a folding seat for a steward or stewardess. The next three compartments each had four 36in double seats on either side of the aisle and facing each other. At night, each pair of facing double seats was made into a 36in x 6ft 5in bed with a privacy curtain on the aisle side. In each of these three compartments, a 30in x 6ft 5in bunk bed was provided above each pair of convertible seats; it was folded against the compartment walls during daytime and was provided with a long and narrow window. During the day each of these three compartments could be occupied by eight passengers if they were prepared to sit side by side, enabling a maximum of 26 passengers to be carried by day. The design configuration for the DST, however, was for only 14 passengers, two in the 'Sky Room' and four in each of the three main cabin compartments.

At the rear of the cabin, a ladies lounge and a men's dressing room were provided, respectively on the left and right sides, both followed by their separate lavatory. Further back there was a 110cu ft baggage compartment which was loaded and unloaded through a door on the left side and was accessible in flight.

Twenty-one DSTs powered by Wright SGR-1820s were built in Santa Monica for American Airlines and Eastern Air Lines.

ATC 618: Aircraft covered by this type certificate dated 27 August 1936 were DC-3s. They differed from the DSTs by their cabin arrangement which was normally seven rows of seats of double seats with removable arm rests on the left of the 18¼in wide aisle and one single seat on the right. Seat pitch was 39in and each seat was 20in wide.[5] Other changes included relocating the galley to the aft of the cabin providing only one lavatory located forward on the right side, adding two compartments for a total of 148.5cu ft of mail and cargo, and enlarging the rear baggage compartment (156cu ft versus 110cu ft for that of the DST).

Several of these DC-3s were delivered in a so-called 'Club' configuration with 14 seats (seven on each side of the aisle). These seats could swivel 225° so that passengers could converse more easily. Later on, the seating in the standard day configuration was increased by reducing seat pitch and putting two seats on each side of the aisle. Post war, this enabled standard seating to be between 28 and 32 passengers.

The passenger access door was usually on the right-hand side of the fuselage but, at customer option, could be on the opposite side. From outside, DC-3 day planes were easily distinguished from DST sky sleepers[6] as they did not have the smaller upper-berth windows.

ATC 619: The 28 November 1936 type certificate was for the DC-3A. This model, like the preceding, was delivered in either the 21-seat standard configuration or in the 14-seat Club configuration.

Initially ordered by United Air Lines, a company retaining close ties with Pratt & Whitney (airline and engine manufacturer having earlier been UATC companies), the DC-3As differed from DC-3s in having 14-cylinder Pratt & Whitney twin *Wasp* engines instead of the 9-cylinder Wright *Cyclones* of the earlier model. Take-off power for the double row twin *Wasp* ranged between 1,050 and 1,200hp as detailed in a table at the end of this chapter. With these

5 Today's first and business class seats are wider and have more leg room but the width and spacing of the one-class seat of the late 1930s was more generous than those of today's economy seats.
6 The terms 'day plane' and 'sky sleeper' were those used by Douglas in its contemporary DC-3 and DST advertising brochures.

LEFT *In 'Club' configuration, the cabin of the DC-3 was fitted with 14 swiveling seats.* (Douglas)

LEFT AND BELOW *The Passenger entrance door of the DST and DC-3 was on the aft fuselage, either on the left (as shown by the photo of a DC-3A of Panagra) or the right (as on this DST of Eastern Air Lines) as specified by customers.* (Douglas and Eastern Air Lines)

engines the DC-3As had better performance at high altitude than the *Cyclone*-powered DC-3s, an important consideration for United with its Newark–San Francisco route going over the Rockies where elevations were higher than those encountered further south on the American and TWA routes.

ATC 635: The fourth version built before America's entry into the war was the DC-3B for which the ATC was issued on 3 May 1937. On delivery, they were powered by Wright SGR-1820-G102s (but, in most instances, were replaced by -G202As in March 1941). Ordered by TWA, the DC-3Bs were hybrids combining features of the DSTs with those of DC-3s. Their two forward compartments had the small upper windows of the DSTs and could each accommodate six passengers by night (or only four if the upper bunks were not used). The aft portion of the cabin received seven to nine seats (in 2 + 1 arrangement).

ATC 647: Aircraft covered by this ATC issued on 30 June 1937 were DST-A sleepers powered by 1,000hp Pratt & Whitney twin *Wasp* SB3-Gs. Cabin arrangement was essentially similar to that of the DSTs with Wright *Cyclone* engines.

ATC 669: Dated 30 September 1937, this type certificate initially covered a variant of the DC-3A powered by 1,050hp Pratt & Whitney twin *Wasp* S1C-Gs offering still more power at cruising altitude. Post war, the ATC 669 was also used for DC-3Cs (C-47s rebuilt by Douglas) and for DC-3Ds, the last of these Douglas twins to be built in Santa Monica.

Before civil aircraft production was interrupted by America's entry into the war, Douglas had delivered 442 DSTs, DST-As, DC-3, DC-3As, and DC-3Bs. In addition to ordering military versions of the DC-3 (mainly C-47s) for itself, the USN, and Allies, the USAAF then took over 137 aircraft ordered by civil customers but still under construction. These aircraft were given military designations (C-48, C-49, C-50, C-51, C-52, C-53, and C-68) as detailed in Chapter 8. Aircraft built for civil customers before the war in the late 1930s and the early 1940s were supplemented after the war by 28 civil DC-3Ds, the last of the breed.

Today, accustomed as we are to hear that several thousand Boeing 737s and Airbus A320s have been ordered, the less than

ABOVE *This view, looking toward the front of the aircraft, shows the cabin of a TWA DC-3B with 2 + 1 seating in the rear and sleeper accommodation forward of the padded partition.* (Douglas)

500 production number for the DST and DC-3 may appear insignificant. However, one ought to remember that, in the late 1930s and early 1940s, DSTs and DC-3s were the most-built airliners, and by far.

BELOW *Prior to the war, the Swedish airline AB Aerotransport, acquired three DC-3A-214s. This is the second of these aircraft, SE-BAB, fsn 1972, which was delivered through Fokker in September 1937.* (Douglas)

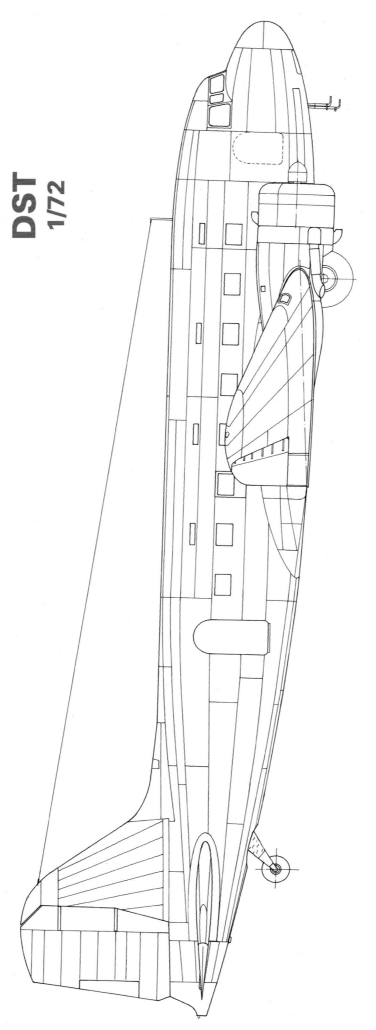

DST 1/72

Prewar operations in the United States

Having become NC14988 after the ATC had been issued, the first DST remained temporarily in California for operational testing. Hence, American Airlines first took full delivery of three other DST-144s in June 1936. The first, NC16001, *Flagship New York*, fsn 1495, was handed over to the airline on 7 June and flew its first revenue flight on 25 June 1936 between Newark and Chicago. Four days earlier, it had demonstrated its performance by flying round-trip non-stop between New York and Chicago in 8hr 7min. In regular operation the DST became the first aircraft to fly consistently non-stop from Newark to Chicago, something which TWA's DC-2s and United Boeing 247Ds could not do when operating against strong winds. During the summer of 1936, American also used its early DSTs on a 50-mile feeder service, from Lakehurst to Newark in New Jersey, for passengers of the German Zeppelin *Hindenburg*.

After receiving seven DSTs, American Airlines took delivery of its first DC-3-178, NC16009, *Flagship District of Columbia*, on 18 August 1936. With DC-3s now on hand, the airline transferred its DSTs to the transcontinental operation for which they had been designed. The first DST flight from Newark to Grand Central Air Terminal in Glendale on the outskirts of Los Angeles was made on 18 September 1936. By the beginning of 1937, American had taken delivery of all 20 aircraft it had initially ordered.

As modern travelers are used to transcontinental non-stop flights in wide-bodied aircraft, it is appropriate to consider how this was done seven decades ago. American's 12 DC-3s flew six daily flights in each direction on the Boston–Newark line and two daily flights between Chicago and Newark. Its eight DSTs enabled the airline to

ABOVE *NC16001* Flagship New York *made the first revenue flight for the DST on 25 June 1936. It was photographed a few weeks later at NAS Lakehurst, New Jersey, in front of the ill-fated* Hindenburg Zeppelin. (USN, Richard K. Smith collection)

make two daily flights between Newark and Los Angeles. Flight No 3, the *American Mercury*, departed Newark at 5:30pm. After dinner, the seats were made into beds and passengers got ready for the night.[7] The flight landed in Memphis, Tennessee, at 10:39pm local time (11:39pm in New York) having covered 940 miles. The 415 miles between Memphis and Dallas, Texas, were covered in 2hr 48min. Next, 5hr 1min were required for the 825 miles to Tucson, Arizona. Finally, after another 450 miles during which breakfast was served, the flight landed in Glendale at 7:51am. The three technical stops on the way lasted but 12 minutes each.

In the opposite direction *American Mercury* Flight No 4 departed Grand Central Air Terminal at 4:30pm and, after making the same three technical stops, landed in Newark the next morning at 11:20am. The other daily round-trip, the *Southerner*, was Flight No 7 westbound and 8 eastbound; it followed a slightly different

---

7   Safety rules were not what they are today: DST passengers could sit or lay down unencumbered by seatbelts!

BELOW *Two of the first DST-114 'Skysleepers' of American Airlines,* Flagship New York *(on the left) and* Flagship Huntington *(on the right) were delivered to this carrier respectively on 7 June and 18 July 1936.* (American Airlines)

ABOVE *After the first fatal accident for the new Douglas twin, the crash of NC16073 on 11 December 1936, this other DC-3A of United Air Lines underwent additional testing in Langley, Virginia, with the National Advisory Committee for Aeronautics.* (NACA)

route with 12-minute stops being made each way in Memphis, Fort Worth, and Phoenix.

With its DSTs and DC-3s, American Airlines no longer needed mail revenues to realize a profit. Moreover, in February

The first fatal accident

Registered NC16073, fsn 1913 was a DC-3A-197 delivered to United Air Lines on 11 December 1936. Unfortunately, it crashed less than two months later, becoming the first in the DST/DC-3 family to be lost.

Carrying eight passengers and a crew of three, NC16073 departed from Grand Central Air Terminal in Glendale, a few miles from downtown Los Angeles, shortly after nightfall on 9 February 1937. Weather was fine as the DC-3A approached its destination, the San Francisco Municipal Airport, after an uneventful flight.

Shortly past 9:00PM, while some 1¼ miles from the airfield, NC16073 went into a 45° dive and crashed into the waters of San Francisco Bay, killing all 11 persons on board. The wreck of the aircraft was recovered from the shallow waters during the following days, permitting a rapid commencement of the investigation into the cause of the crash. Initially, however, the fatal accident remained unexplained.

Five weeks later, an American Airlines DC-3 went into a dive as it was approaching Newark Airport. This disaster was averted as the crew managed to regain control. The dive had been caused by a set of headphones which, having been removed by the co-pilot and placed precariously on his control wheel, fell and jammed controls when it wedged at the base of the column. Quickly realizing what was happening, the co-pilot recovered his headset while the captain regained control of the aircraft and landed it safely. Armed with details of this incident, the team investigating the crash of the United DC-3A went back to work. Sure enough, they found a headphone set jammed at the base of the co-pilot's control column of NC16073.

To prevent similar accidents from occurring, a rubber boot was added at the base of both control columns.

1937, thanks to the added capacity provided by these aircraft, American became the first airline to carry one million passengers. Not surprisingly, its two main competitors were eager to find themselves in a similar situation. However, the next operator of the larger Douglas twins was another player, Eastern Air Lines. Already operating a large fleet of DC-2s, it added 38 DC-3s and six DSTs from December 1936, and initially flew them between Newark and Miami. Travel time was reduced as the newer aircraft required fewer refueling stops on the way.

Quite remarkably, it was United Air Lines, a former member of the Boeing group, which became the third carrier in the United States to put the new Douglas in service. However, it remained faithful to its former partner, Pratt & Whitney, and had its DC-3As and DST-As powered by *Twin Wasp* engines. Delivered on 23 December 1936, the first DC-3A-191 went into service between Newark and Chicago during the following month. After receiving additional DC-3As, United used them on its West Coast route between Seattle and Los Angeles with stops in Portland and San Francisco. First received in July 1937, DST-A-207s were put on the transcontinental route from Newark to San Francisco.

TWA, launch customer for the DC-2, was in less of a hurry to order DC-3s. However, faced with heavy competition from American and United on the transcontinental route, it had no choice but to follow suit. The first of its larger Douglas airliners were 10 DC-3Bs combining 'sleeper' features of the DSTs in the front of the cabin with 2+1 seating aft. They were delivered between April 1937 and January 1938, and, beginning in August 1937, were supplemented by Wright *Cyclone*-powered DC-3s with standard cabin arrangement.

Now operating transcontentally with their DSTs, DST-As, and DC-3Bs, the three competitors (the 'majors' – American, TWA, and United) were able to reduce one way fares from $160 (±$2,590 today) in May 1934 to $149.95 (±$2,240 today) two years later. The greater comfort of the DSTs and DC3s, their better performance, and their greater reliability were appreciated not only by these three 'majors' and Eastern, but also by other US airlines. For operations within the United States, nine of these carriers ordered 72 aircraft from Douglas (two DST-As, 47 DC-3s, and 23 DC-3As as listed on page 96). Likewise, the two US airlines operating outside of the continental United States, Pan American Airways and Pan American-Grace Airways (Panagra) acquired 11 DC-3s and 31 DC-3As for their Latin American operations.

When the United States was forced into World War Two, production of civil aircraft was temporarily halted. However, before this stoppage was implemented, 15 additional DC-3As came off the production line in Santa Monica. One went to a private customer, Swiftlife, Inc., another to the Civil Aeronautics Authority (CAA), and 12 were taken over by the Defense Supply Corporation (DSC) which allocated them to airlines operating under government control. The 15th became a C-53 and was allotted to Douglas to ferry staff and urgent parts between its Santa Monica headquarters and its plants in California, Illinois, and Oklahoma.

In early 1942, before airlines had to place a substantial portion of their fleets at the disposal of the government and the military, they operated 322 aircraft including 260 DC-3s and DSTs (more than 80% of the total) and eight DC-2s. The others were 25 Boeing 247Ds, 16 Lockheed 10 *Electras*, and 13 Lockheed 18 *Lodestars*.

Between 1934, when the DC-2 had entered service and, 1941, the last year with America at peace, airlines had made giant strides, principally due to their Douglas airliners. The following table summarizes the extent of progress.

Air transport growth in the United States between 1934 and 1941

(Domestic operations only)

	1934	1941
Miles of domestic airways in operation	28,084	47,703
Passengers carried	461,743	4,060,245
Express and freight carried (short tons)	1,066.5	9,605.0
Mail carried (short tons)	3,705.5	9,162.0
Airplanes in service and reserve	417	272

Source: *Statistical Abstract of the United States, 1942*
US Department of Commerce, Bureau of the Census

BELOW *Before the United States entered World War Two, Pan American Airways used its DC-3As primarily on its routes to the Caribbean and South America from ports of embarkation in Miami, Brownsville (Texas), and Los Angeles.* (Pan American)

DST and DC-3 – Pre-1942 US customers

Clients	DST	DST-A	DC-3	DC-3A	DC-3B	Total
American Airlines	15 (7 Jun 1936)		67 (18 Aug 1936)			82
Eastern Air Lines	6 (Feb 1940)		38 (18 Dec 1936)			44
United Air Lines		17 (9 Jul 1937)		46 (23 Dec 1936)		63
Transcontinental & Western Air Inc (TWA)			21 (9 Aug 1937)		10 (16 Apr 1937)	31
Western Air Express		2 (2 Jul 1937)		4 (Aug 1940)		6
Pan American Airways			8 (1 Oct 1937)	24 (31 Jul 1940)		32
Pan American-Grace Airways			3 (19 Oct 1937)	7 (Apr 1940)		10
Northwest Airlines				13 (22 Apr 1939)		13
Canadian Colonial Airways			6 (3 May 1939)			6
Pennsylvania-Central Airlines			20 (24 Oct 1939)			20
Braniff Aiways			11 (15 Dec 1939)			11
Chicago & Southern Air Lines			6 (14 Apr 1940)			6
Delta Air Lines			4 (Nov 1940)			4
SwiftLife Inc				1 (3 Feb 1941)		1
CAA				1 (1 Apr 1941)		1
Northeast Airlines				3 (4 May 1941)		3
Inter Island Airways				3 (23 Aug 1941)		3
Douglas				1 (unsold at end of 1941)		1
Defense Supply Corp.				12 (13 Apr 1942)		12
US total	**21**	**19**	**184**	**115**	**10**	**349**

NOTES:

Clients are listed in chronological order based on the delivery date of their first DST or DC-3.

Dates given in parentheses are those of initial deliveries.

ABOVE *NC25626, a DC-3-322 of Chicago & Southern Air Lines, is parked at the Chicago Municipal Airport (now Chicago Midway International Airport).* (DR)

LEFT *This DC-3-279A was delivered to Panagra in April 1940 and remained with this airline for 15 years. It then was flown by three other operators before being broken up for spares at the end of 1975.* (Douglas)

Prewar operations abroad

As had been the case with the DC-2, Anthony Fokker acquired the European distribution rights for the DC-3; 43 of these aircraft, all but three powered by Wright *Cyclones,* were built and tested by Douglas in Santa Monica. They were then shipped (see insert) to be reassembled by Fokker prior to delivery to customers in Belgium, Czechoslovakia, Ireland, the Netherlands, Romania, Sweden, and Switzerland.

Before war broke out in September 1939, the bulk of these aircraft were operated on European routes. The main exception was provided by KLM which used a number of its DC-3s for its service to Batavia. For the multi-stop flights to that destination,

these DC-3s only had 12 seats (four rows of 2+1) which could almost fully recline. As soon as it had enough aircraft, KLM offered three weekly flights departing Amsterdam every Saturday, Tuesday, and Thursday, with travel to the Dutch East Indies taking a full week. On the first day, the aircraft went from Amsterdam to Naples, via Marseilles. For the next six days the flight proceeded as follows: Naples–Athens–Rhodes–Alexandria; Alexandria–Lydda–Baghdad–Basra; Basra–Djask–Karachi–Jodhpur; Jodhpur–Allahabad–Calcutta–Rangoon; Rangoon–Bangkok–Penang–Medan–Singapore; and Singapore–Palembang–Batavia before a short ferry flight to Bandoeng where KLM and KNILM shared a maintenance center. Service ended in May 1940 with the German invasion of the Netherlands.

Export shipments

Whereas DSTs and DC-3s for US customers were delivered directly by air from the Santa Monica plant in California, DC-3s for customers in Europe and in the Pacific had to be dismantled and packed to be shipped across the oceans on commercial vessels. Those going westward to either Yokohama or Melbourne went aboard ships in Los Angeles. Sold through Fokker, DC-3s for European customers were flown from California to New York where they were prepared for shipment from the Port of New York either to Amsterdam, Antwerp, Cherbourg, or Rotterdam.

For maritime shipment, the aircraft had to be broken down in three lots. The first, which remained unboxed, was comprised of the fuselage, the wing center section, the engines, the undercarriage and the vertical fin. It measured 23ft 9in x 12ft x 59ft 10.5in, weighed 14,000lb, and its volume was 483.6cu ft. The second, which was packed into a 7ft 9in x 9ft 9in x 38ft 6in box, weighed 10,100lb and was comprised of the outer wing panels, the rudder, and the tailplanes. The third, in a 9ft 6in x 3ft 4in x 10ft 3in box weighing 2,216lb, contained the propeller and miscellaneous components.

Upon arrival, the three lots were trucked to the nearest airport where unpacking and reassembly took place. After acceptance flights, the aircraft was flown to the base of its intended customer.

The photo below shows the fuselage of OK-AIF, a DC-3-220A for CLS (*Ceskoslovenska Letecka Spolecnost*) being trucked in Antwerp from the port to Deurne aerodrome. DC-3s bound for Japan are shown at right being loaded on a ship at one of the Los Angeles harbours.

DST and DC-3 – Pre-1942 foreign customers

Clients	DST	DST-A	DC-3	DC-3A	DC-3B	Total
KLM			24 (21 Sep 1936)			24
USSR			21 (30 Nov 1936)			21
Swissair			5 (10 Jun 1937)			5
CLS			4 (19 Aug 1937)			4
LARES			2 (20 Sep 1937)			2
Airlines of Australia			4 (25 Oct 1937)			4
Japan			13 (6 Dec 1937)	9 (23 Nov 1937)		22
SABENA			2 (18 Jan 1939)			2
Air France			1 (7 Jun 1939)			1
CNAC			2 (1 Oct 1939)			2
ABA			1 (Nov 1939)	3 (23 Jul 1937)		4
Aer Lingus			2 (4 Mar 1940)			2
Total exportation	**0**	**0**	**81**	**12**	**0**	**93**

NOTES:
Clients are listed in chronological order based on the first delivery date.
Dates given in parentheses are those of initial deliveries.

Fifty other DC-3s, of which nine were powered by Pratt & Whitney *Twin Wasps*, were directly exported by Douglas. Seven of these aircraft went to foreign air carriers: Airlines of Australia, China National Aviation Corporation (CNAC), and Air France. In the case of the aircraft going to the French national carrier (fsn 2122, F-ARQJ), the sale did not go through Fokker as this DC-3-294 was handed over to Air France in Buenos Aires, Argentina, out of the distribution territory reserved for the Dutch company. Delivered on 7 June 1939, it went to *Comando de Aviación del Ejército* in January 1943. After 25 years in Argentine military service, it ended on that country civil registry until destroyed in February 1971.

Japan and the Soviet Union respectively obtained 22 and 21 Douglas-built DC-3s. In addition, both countries acquired the manufacturing rights for this Douglas twin, Nakajima and Showa building them as L2Ds while PS-84s and Li-2s came from Soviet government plants. The history of these Japanese and Soviet variants is covered in Chapter 8 as for the most part their 'Douglas' were used for military purposes.

TOP *OK-AIG, a* Cyclone-*powered DC-3-220B, was delivered to CLS in March 1939 but fell almost immediately into German hands when Czechoslovakia was overrun. Registered D-AAIG and operated during the war years by Lufthansa, it crashed off the Norwegian coast on 21 April 1944.* (Douglas)

LEFT *DC-3s operated by KLM between the Netherlands and the Dutch East Indies were fitted with only twelve seats, almost fully reclining, as shown.* (KLM)

RIGHT *In 1940, Douglas delivered the first French-registered DC-3 to Air France, then operating in Argentina. Postwar, and for the next three decades, DC-3s of various ancestry carried F registrations. Today, only two remain, including fsn 9172, an ex-C-47A-1-DL, which had* Aigle Azur *markings temporarily applied in 2006.* (Jacques Guillem)

The war years

Nine DC-3s fell into German hands: four from CLS when Czechoslovakia was invaded in March 1939, and five from KLM when the Netherlands was overrun in May 1940. All were then operated by *Deutsche Luft Hansa*, four being destroyed on the ground during the war, three crashing, and two surviving until Germany surrendered. Of the Dutch DC-3s not taken to Germany, four were destroyed during the fighting, five managed to escape to the United Kingdom, and seven were left to operate in the East Indies until Japan invaded the Dutch colony. Other KLM DC-3s which had been operating on the long routes to the Dutch East Indies remained based in Java and Sumatra until five were destroyed when Japanese troops landed in early 1942.

ABOVE *Next to the United States, the Soviet Union was the main operator of the DC-3 and its many variants. The first was this DC-3-196, USSR-M132, photographed in the USSR on 6 April 1938. The more numerous were PS-84s and Li-2s built in the Soviet Union.* (Douglas)

RIGHT *PH-ALI, a KLM DC-3-194, managed to escape to England in May 1940. By then carrying British registration, G-AGBB and leased to BOAC, it was shot down over the bay of Biscay on 1 June 1943 while on its way to Lisbon.* (Lufthansa)

The last two escaped to Australia to continue operating with the Allies.

During the war, neutral nations attempted to maintain a semblance of normality and kept much of their air network in use.

ABOVE *Aircraft registered in countries that remained neutral during the war did not escape attack. Even though it was carrying large neutrality markings, flags and letterings, identifying it as a Swedish aircraft, SE-BAF was shot down by German fighters on 27 August 1943.* (DR)

This was notably the case of Swissair which flew to Germany and German-occupied countries until the last year of the war. Similarly, AB Aerotransport kept flying to Great Britain. Even though the Neutrals had applied high visibility markings to their aircraft, wartime operations were not without risk. Two Swedish DC-3s were shot down by Luftwaffe fighters while flying from Scotland to Sweden: SE-BAF went down in the North Sea on 27 August 1943 and SE-BAG crashed near Hallo, Sweden, on 22 October 1943. All 20 occupants aboard these two DC-3s perished.

DC-3s had not been ordered by British carriers before the war thus, the first in the United Kingdom were two from Sabena and five from KLM which fled Nazi invaders in May 1940. The two ex-Belgian DC-3s were briefly operated by No 24 Squadron, RAF, but one was destroyed near Calais, France, almost immediately. The other was in British use for only slightly longer as it was in Algiers when the Royal Navy attacked the French fleet anchored at Mers-el-Kébir, French Algeria. Interned by Vichy French authorities, the

The saga of the Chinese DC-2½

Not all DC-3s or C-47s which came in harm's way ended tragically. One of the most fortunate was a Chinese DC-3 which, having been mauled by the Japanese, was returned to service after a bit of reconstructive surgery.

Douglas had delivered two DC-3s to China National Aviation Corporation, one in August 1939 and the other in November 1940. A third, which had belonged to Pacific Alaska Airlines, was added in July 1941. As Japanese forces kept advancing in China, CNAC DC-2s and DC-3s were worked hard from their new operating base, Kai Tak, in still unthreatened Hong Kong.

On 20 May 1941, fsn 2148, a DC-3-294A named *Omei Shan* and captained by 'Woody' Woods, took off from Kai Tak on its way to Chungking and Chengdu. The first leg of the flight was uneventful but, while continuing to his final destination, Woods was forewarned that a Japanese raid was expected in Chengdu. A precautionary landing was made in Suifu. Barely had the crew and passengers disembarked and taken refuge in a wood at the edge of the field than bombing began. A 100kg bomb went through a wing of the DC-3 before exploding. The outboard panel of the right wing was destroyed and the rest of the aeroplane was extensively damaged, but no fire started. The other DC-3 was dispatched from Chungking to pick up passengers and crew while the extent of damage received by *Omei Shan* was communicated to the CNAC engineering staff in Hong Kong.

The CNAC engineers determined that the aircraft was worth repairing and that, ultimately, a replacement outboard panel for the right wing would have to be obtained from Douglas. But, as the new wing panel would not arrive in Honk Kong for many weeks, a temporary solution had to be devised to retrieve *Omei Shan* and get it back to Kai Tak to be rebuilt. Necessity being the mother of invention, Zygmund Soldinsky and his staff of Chinese technicians came up with a daring solution: the aircraft would be temporarily fitted with the right outer panel of a DC-2 wing even though that would reduce span and area on that side. Solving the next problem, getting the DC-2 wing panel from Hong Kong to

Suifu, was also remarkably ingenious: the replacement panel would be mounted beneath the fuselage of the other DC-3. (Later Douglas adopted this procedure for military C-47s; see photograph on page 200.)

Carrying a full cabin load of passengers (including CNAC mechanics going to Seifu to make the repairs) and the spare DC-2 wing panel jury-rigged beneath the fuselage, the DC-3 made it safely to Chungking and then on to Suifu.

Eleven days after *Omei Shan* had been extensively damaged, the DC-2 panel was attached and holes patched, allowing Hal Sweet and Arnold Weier to ferry the lopsided DC-2½ to Chungking. As the aircraft flew right wing down, the pilots had to hold tight on their control wheels until pressure on the controls was reduced by hanging a heavy adjustable spanner on one of the wheels. No other difficulties having been encountered during the ferry flights, passengers and cargo were loaded in Chungking. Taking off at 2,200lb over approved gross weight, the DC2½ flew non-stop to Hong Kong.

After more comprehensive repairs and installation of the replacement wing received from Douglas, the aircraft was returned to service as a bona fide DC-3. Unfortunately, *Omei Shan* ran out of good luck on 13 February 1943 when its crew had to settle it down on the Yangtze.

ex-OO-AUH (fsn 2093, a DC-3-227B) then came into Axis hands, first in Italy and then in Germany. The Royal Air Force got it back at war's end but the aircraft was in poor condition and was scrapped.

The ex-KLM DC-3s were more fortunate except for the ex-PH-ALI (fsn 1590) which had become G-AGBB. While on lease from KLM, it was shot down on 1 June 1943 by a Junkers Ju 88 while on a BOAC flight to Portugal. All 17 aboard perished. Fortunately for British Overseas Airways Corporation, the British Government then provided it with Lend-Lease *Dakota* Is (ex-C-47s), IIs (ex-C-47As), and IVs (ex-C-47Bs).[8]

Until the Japanese attack on 7 December 1941, US civil air operations remained relatively unchanged even though the US Government had, during the preceding year, requested airlines to undertake a number of quasi-military activities. Thus, in October 1940, United Air Lines was contracted to begin training military mechanics at its technical center in Oakland, California. In 1940–41, Pan American Airways obtained even more government work, notably to build airfields in the Caribbean and to have a new subsidiary, Pan American Airways-Africa Ltd., open a trans-African route to ferry aircraft and transport military personnel and cargo, first for the British and then for the Allies (see page 174 for further details).

After the United States entered the war, airlines participated in the war effort even more actively by:
- Developing and operating air routes outside the United States on behalf of the Air Transport Command and the Naval Air Transport Service;
- Managing and operating personnel training centers and modification centers; and
- Placing crews at the disposal of the military to fly transport aircraft and ferry combat aircraft.

---

8 For the origin of the name *Dakota*, see page 170.

ABOVE *This DC-3-385 was built for Delta Air Lines and was photographed by the manufacturer in the markings of this airline. However, it was taken over by the USAAF which gave it the 41-7690 serial as a C-49A. Transferred to Australia, it was registered VHCDC (no hyphen during the war) and operated by Australian National Airways when it was shot down near Tacloban, Leyte, the Philippines, on 13 November 1945.* (Delta)

In addition, these carriers had a large portion of their fleets taken over, and their operations within the United States were placed under military control. By increasing working hours for their personnel and flying hours for their reduced fleet, they more than offset the reductions in personnel and equipment. So much so that air transport activities within the US grew impressively during the war. Even though they had only 279 operational aircraft in 1944 versus 358 in 1940, airlines flew 388,618 passengers in 1944 (30.7% more than in 1940) and carried 33,006 short tons of freight and express (more than five times what they had carried in 1940). This last result was made possible by undertaking all-cargo operations, with Pennsylvania-Central Airlines being the first with an inaugural flight between Washington, D.C. and Chicago in March 1942. Whether passenger (a large number of whom were flying on official business or under special priority status) or cargo, the majority of that traffic went aboard DC-3s.

Purely military DC-3 operations are described in Chapter 8 on the C-47 and other DC-3 military variants.

BELOW *During the last months of World War Two, transport aircraft were returned by the USAAF to civil operators. This was the case for N68544, an ex-C-53-DO (42-68762) which went to TWA in June 1945.* (Jacques Guillem collection)

ABOVE *Ozark Airlines, based in the central United States, was one of the many local service carriers which flew DC-3s. N132D – a former C-53-DO (42-15533) which had taken part in* Operation Husky, *the Allied invasion of Sicily in July 1943 – was photographed in St. Louis, Missouri, 25 years later.* (Peter B. Lewis)

Postwar operations

At war's end, the massive reduction in military forces placed a considerable number of C-47s and their military variants at the disposal of airlines in the United States as well as all over the world. However, with American carriers these prewar twin-engined airliners were rapidly supplanted on main routes by a new generation of four-engined airliners with better performance and increased comfort level. Initial DC-4 service began with Western Airlines on 18 January 1946 and service with Lockheed Constellations commenced on 3 February 1946 (Pan American to

BELOW *As the ageing DC-3s lost much of their passenger appeal, the last scheduled operators in the United States sought to offer compensations. Mohawk Airlines resorted to having its stewardesses wear low-cut period dresses and to offering free beer and cigars to delighted male passengers.* (Mohawk)

Bermuda) and 1 March 1946 (TWA on its transcontinental route). Next came the Douglas DC-6 (United Air Lines on 27 April 1947) and the Boeing *Stratocruiser* (Pan American on 2 April 1949).

Nevertheless availability of this newer transport did not result in the rapid disappearance of DC-3s and ex-C-47s from the fleet of major airlines.

Postwar, the large-scale modification of C-47s and other DC-3 military variants was undertaken worldwide by airline engineering departments and by specialized companies. While most of these aircraft went to airlines, others were acquired by a wide variety of civil operators (charter operators, crop sprayers, civil contractors, and many others). These modification activities were fueled by the rapid availability of surplus military aircraft being offered at very attractive prices. In 1946, prices for former military 'DC-3s' ranged between $20,000 (±$236,500 today) for relatively weary C-47s to $43,500 (±$514,500 today) for almost brand-new C-117s. Nevertheless, a few airlines preferred paying full price for brand new DC-3Ds or for DC-3Cs which were zero-timed by Douglas in Santa Monica using military airframes. Unfortunately for Douglas, the number of companies that went this way was very small, and the California manufacturer ended up rebuilding only 21 C-47s into DC-3Cs and assembling 28 all new DC-3Ds using parts and components left from military contracts cancelled at war's end. The Douglas DC-3Cs and DC-3Ds differed from C-47s civilianized by others in not being fitted with cargo handling equipment (reinforced cabin floor, cargo latches, and double loading door). Consequently, they had slightly reduced empty weight and marginally better economic performance. The last two DC-3Ds were delivered in May 1946 to *Navegação Aérea Brasileira* and the last three DC-3Cs were delivered to Sabena in March of the following year. The final deliveries of DC-3Cs brought to an end US production of what is undoubtedly one of the most important airliners. In the Soviet Union, Lisunov Li-2 (DC-3 derivatives) remained in production for another six years (see Chapter 8.)

After twin-engined airliners with pressurized cabins entered service – Convair 240s with American Airlines on 1 July 1948 and Martin 404s with TWA on 5 October 1951 – DC-3s were pushed out of the fleet of trunk airlines.[9] The first to dispose of its DC-3 was American Airlines, the original customer for this celebrated aircraft, which did so in 1949. During the following decade however, other

---

9   Large US domestic airlines operating over the main routes were classified as 'trunk carriers' by the Civil Aeronautics Board. In the immediate postwar, they still numbered 16: American Airlines, Braniff Airways, Capital Airlines, Chicago & Southern Air Lines, Colonial Airlines, Continental Air Lines, Delta Air Lines, Eastern Air Lines, Inland Air Lines, Mid-Continent Airlines, National Airlines, Northeast Airlines, Northwest Airlines, Pennsylvania-Central Airlines, Transcontinental & Western Air, United Air Lines, and Western Airlines. These names were those in use in 1946. Subsequently, several disappeared through mergers while others changed their names (such as United Air Lines which became United Airlines – with airlines in one word – in 1974).

'No Force One'

As they aged, DC-3s were increasingly used for purposes quite different from that for which the DST had been developed. One of these unforeseen uses saw an ex-C-49J leased to transport the Libertarian Party candidate during the 1976 presidential campaign.

Not well known in Europe, the Libertarian Party was founded in 1971. In forty years, this party has never succeeded in having one of its members elected as a state governor, a representative or as a senator. Its showing in presidential elections has been even less fortunate, the best being in 1980 when Ed Clark garnered 1.1% of the popular votes.

In the 1976 presidential campaign, the Libertarian Party candidates, Robert Lea McBride and David Bergland, were on the ballot in only 32 of the 50 states. They ended in fourth place with 172,553 votes, the winners being the Democratic candidates, Jimmy Carter and Walter Mondale, who obtained 40.8 million votes.

During that campaign, Gerald Ford, the incumbent President and candidate for the Republican Party used Air Force One to tour the country, while Jimmy Carter relied on various jets leased for his use by the Democratic Party. The coffers of the Libertarian Party were not filled enough to lease a jet for Robert McBride. Instead, McBride had to contend himself with a venerable DC-3 which he quite often flew himself.

The aircraft was fsn 6343, a DC-3-454 ordered by Delta Air Lines but taken over by the USAAF to which it was delivered on 6 January 1943 as a C-49J with serial number 43-1988. It was released by the military in March 1945 and then went on the Canadian registry as CF-TDL, initially with Trans-Canada Airlines. Returning to the United States nine years later as N37F, this DC-3 had its Wright *Cyclone* SGR-1820-G202As (military R-1820-71s) replaced by Pratt & Whitney *Twin Wasp* engines. Over the years, the re-engined aircraft went through a number of owners before being leased in 1976 by the Libertarian Party. Fittingly, its registration was changed to N76LP for the electoral year and the political party. Having a good sense of humour, Robert McBride nicknamed his unpretentious transport 'No Force One' as a pun for Air Force One in which Gerald Ford travelled in style.

For five years after the election, fsn 6343 retained its N76LP registration even though it was no longer leased by the Libertarian Party. It was successively reregistered as N37FL, N125SF, N38CA, XA-SCF, and, again, N37FL. It ended derelict at the *Aeropuerto Internacional de Cancún* in Mexico.

BELOW *'No Force One' taxies at McClellan AFB, California, on 5 December 1976. Although the election had been lost one month earlier, N76LP was still marked 'Libertarian Presidential Campaign*. (Peter B. Lewis)

ABOVE *Photographed in Quito, Ecuador, with Mt Pichincha providing the background, this ex-C-47 was one of several still operated by* SAETA (S.A. Ecuatoriana de Transportes Aéreos) *in August 1974.* (René J. Francillon)

trunk carriers continued to fly DC-3s, assigning them increasingly to shorter and less traveled routes. In 1960, a few DC-3s remained with Braniff, Continental, Delta, Northeast, and United. Finally, Northeast Airlines, the last to fly DC-3s, ceased those operations.

The peak number of DC-3s in the fleet of American carriers was reached in 1946 when 470 were on domestic routes and 63 on overseas routes. Ten years later, the total was down to 336 and down to 235 in 1962. By then most of these aircraft were operated by a new category of carrier which had come into being in 1945 to operate regional routes. Initially called feeder airlines, these companies were redesignated local service carriers in May 1955. Three years later, 201 out of the 229 aircraft operated by these regionals were DC-3s. That number was progressively reduced until the last local service carriers' DC-3s were retired before the end of the 1960s. Some smaller operators kept flying DC-3s for several more years, the very last in US scheduled operations being

BELOW *Delivered to American Airlines on 27 February 1939, this DC-3-208A went through 13 operators during the next 25 years before being acquired by* Alas del Caribe. *Still with this Dominican carrier when photographed at Ciudad Trujillo in December 1975, HI-237 was destroyed when Hurricane David struck the Dominican Republic on 31 August 1979.* (René J. Francillon)

those of Air Molokai, in Hawaii, which went out in 1989. Thereafter, DC-3s in the United States were left with non-airline operators.

During the late 1940s, newspaper headlines the like of 'Another *Dakota* crashes' were rather frequent in Europe. It was not that DC-3s and ex-military C-47s were particularly unsafe but rather it was the consequence of having most commercial flights in Europe provided with *Dakotas* (in 1945 the name used by Commonwealth military forces had been quasi-universally adopted on the Continent). Consequently, each time an aircraft went down – a not so infrequent happening in post-World War Two years when airline safety levels were far from being what they are today – chances were high that it was a 'Dakota.' Notwithstanding these sensationalist headlines, DC-3s, whatever their origins, were reliable and well-liked by travelers at a time when roads and rail lines on the Continent were still in need of much repair. In postwar years DC-3s and *Dakotas* did much for the rebuilding and political integration of Europe.

With newer generations of airliners being introduced and high-speed rail gaining in popularity, ageing DC-3s were progressively used for lesser and lesser tasks. Begun in the United States, this trend migrated first to Europe and developed nations elsewhere, and then to Third World countries. Today, less than 200 DC-3s are in service worldwide (see table on page 111).

In the USSR, its Eastern European satellites, and other countries in the Communist sphere of influence, DC-3s were outnumbered by their Russian siblings, the Lisunov Li-2s. In the Soviet Union, Aeroflot operated Li-2s until 1962 while the type continued in service for another ten years with Polar Aviation and various government ministries. Outside of the USSR, Li-2s had even lengthier careers, those lasting the longest being those of the North Korean *Chosonminhang* (better known by the initial CAAK from its English title, Civil Aviation Administration of Korea).

Postwar upgrades and turbine engines

During the war years, air transportation had made truly remarkable technical and operational progress. Not surprisingly, as it was the aviation regulatory agency in the United States, the Civil Aviation Administration (CAA)[10] sought to capitalize on these developments immediately after the return of peace. More stringent regulations and certification requirements were developed by the CAA for new aircraft, and this administration also wanted to make some of its new demands retroactively applicable to older airliners, notably the DC-3. Quite quickly, the CAA contemplated requiring that performance improvements be incorporated in order for DC-3s to retain valid approved type certificates. Just as the DC-3 fleet

10 In 1958, the CAA was reorganized into the Federal Aviation Agency. It retained the FAA abbreviation when it was renamed Federal Aviation Administration in 1967.

was at its peak, its commercial future was threatened. Fortunately, reason prevailed as, in the case of the prewar- and wartime-built Douglas twins, economic considerations rendered impractical the implementation of some of the new CAA requirements. Operators, however, were fully conscious that the single-engine take-off performance of the DC-3 was marginal when compared to that of newer aircraft, particularly when operating at high gross weights from high-elevation, high-temperature airfields. Several modification programs were developed to correct this deficiency.

One of the simplest modifications consisted of fitting doors to enclose the main wheels fully and to smooth the engine cowlings, both of which reduced drag in the critical initial climb phase of flight. More comprehensive, but costlier, modifications included fitting squared-off wing tips which slightly increased span and area, and/or revising the main gear operating system to reduce retraction time. In other instances, performance was improved by replacing the standard 1,200hp *Twin Wasps* by engines offering more power on take-off and at higher cruising altitudes. Thus, some DC-3s and former C-47s were powered by a pair of Pratt & Whitney R-1830-75s or -94s rated at 1,350hp on take-off and 1,100hp at 7,500ft. Even better results were obtained by installing Pratt & Whitney R-2000-7M2s or -D5s (1,450hp on take-off and 1,100hp at 9,800ft) as was done for 'Hi-Per DC-3s' modified by the engineering department of Pan American for use by its affiliates, Panagra and *Aerovías Nacionales de Colombia SA* (Avianca).

To increase the range of DC-3s, various installations of auxiliary tanks in the wings were proposed. The most frequent was that of a 166.5 Imp. gallon in each outer panel.

In numerous other cases, DC-3s were modified for reasons other than performance improvements, such changes being made to ease

ABOVE *Built as a C-53-DO for the USAAF and then going to the USN as a R4D-3, N1075M was extensively modified (including new engine cowlings and large propeller spinners) for service with Virgin Islands Air Service in 1947–48. However, the pair of wheels seen under its rear fuselage was not part of the modification program.* (Peter M. Bowers)

BELOW AND BOTTOM *The single- and twin-installations of Turbomeca Palas auxiliary turbojets are illustrated by F-BEFF of UAT and F-BEIS of SNCASO.* (Michel Marani and Jean Delmas collection)

ABOVE *KJ839, a* Dakota IV, *was modified into the* Mamba-Dakota *prototype in 1949.* (DR)

operations, increase passenger comfort, or flatter appearance. Notably airlines and private operators had the double cargo door of their ex-C-47s replaced by a single passenger access door, often opening downward and provided with integral steps. Other DC-3s (or ex-military aircraft) had a single but larger rectangular window substituted for the first two windows on each side of the forward fuselage, a modification which was particularly appreciated when the aircraft were used for sightseeing. When operating in colder climes, operators also frequently replaced the original cabin heating system with a more efficient one. Finally, a notable external change was the addition of a rotating beacon at the top of the fin.

Seeking take-off performance improvements without having to replace the existing radials with more powerful engines, and also wanting to make use of low-thrust jet engines then

BELOW *G-AMDB, a* Dakota *re-engined with Rolls-Royce* Dart *turbines, was one of the* Dart-Dakotas *operated by British European Airways at the beginning of the 1950s.* (BEA)

being developed in France, *Société Nationale de Constructions Aéronautiques du Sud-Ouest* (SNCASO) devised two installations of 350lb st Turbomeca *Palas* auxiliary turbojets. In one case, a single *Palas* was mounted under the fuselage while in the other case two of these small turbojets were provided, one under each wing. Testing of both single and dual installations took place in 1951, but only a few DC-3s were so fitted in France and in Argentina. Toward the end of that decade, Steward-Davis Inc. in the United States proposed another jet-boosted variant. This 'Jet Pack 920' installation called for a 920lb st Continental J69-T-9 (a US produced version of the Turbomeca *Marboré*) to be mounted above the fuselage. However no Jet Pack 920 appears to have been flown.

The British aero-engine industry being the main proponent of turbine propeller engines, not unexpectedly it was in the United Kingdom that turboprops were initially adapted to re-engine DC-3s. The first was a *Dakota IV* (KJ389, fsn 25623, the former C-47B-16-DK with serial 43-48362) which had its *Twin Wasp* radials replaced by 1,425shp Armstrong Siddeley ASMa.3 *Mamba* turboprops. First flown on 27 August 1949, the *Mamba-Dakota* was used as an engine test-bed until 1958. Then registered G-APNX, it was again equipped with *Twin Wasps*. It was last reported in 1997 as N4797H in Florida.

Competing with the Armstrong Siddeley *Mamba*, the Rolls-Royce *Dart* was considerably more successful and is primarily remembered as the power plant of the Vickers *Viscount*. *Darts* were first fitted to another RAF *Dakota IV* (KJ829, fsn 25613) which got airborne with propeller-turbines on 15 March 1950. In 1956 it was purchased by Rolls-Royce and was successively registered G-37-2 and G-AOXI. Whilst this first *Dart-Dakota* was strictly used for experimental purposes, two aircraft – G-ALXN, fsn 29106, ex-KJ934, and G-AMDB, fsn 26432, ex-KJ993 – were fitted with Rolls-Royce *Darts* by Field Aircraft in 1951 to assist British European Airways with the engine development program for its V.701 *Viscounts*. Besides being operated as engine test-beds and to gain experience with turbine operations and maintenance, these two *Dart-Dakotas* were used by BEA for scheduled cargo service. The first of these commercial flights was made on 15 August 1951, when G-ALXN carried 1.5 tons of freight from Northolt to Hannover, Germany.

In December 1967, John M. 'Jack' Conroy[11] of Goleta, California, acquired a low-time C-53-DO (fsn 4903, 41-20133) which Remmert-Werner had re-engined with more powerful R-1830-75s. During the following year, Conroy replaced these radial engines with Rolls-Royce RDa.7 *Dart* 510 turboprops removed from a Continental Airlines *Viscount* 812 which had been taken out of service. For installation on the former C-53, now registered N4700C, power rating for the turboprops was limited to 1,350shp. Test flying of this Conroy *Turbo-Three* began on 13 May 1969 but no customers were found for it.

A more ambitious *Dart* installation was proposed by TAMCO (Turbo-Airliner Manufacturing Company) in 1976. The *Turbo-Commuter* was to have been extensively rebuilt with a pressurized cabin, a fully retractable undercarriage, and *Dart* RDa.6s or RDa.7s. But, once again, nothing came out of this proposal.

Turbine-engined DC-3s were again proposed after a new air transportation era had begun with the entry into service of the supersonic *Concorde*. This time, power plants were Pratt & Whitney Canada PT6 turboprops. First, Jack Conroy had Aircraft Technical Service and Specialized Aircraft Company replace the two *Darts* of his *Turbo-Three* by three 1,120shp PT6A-45 with five-blade propellers. Now registered N23SA and renamed *Tri-Turbo-Three*, it returned to flight status on 2 November 1977. Sold to Santa Barbara Polair, the *Tri-Turbo-Three* was fitted as an electronic test aircraft to evaluate the reliability of INS (Inertial Navigation System) and GPS (Global Positioning System) operations in the Polar Regions. Kept

---

11 Not to be confused with one of his contemporaries, another Jack Conroy (John Wesley Conroy) who was a notorious leftist American writer.

in non-flying condition between 1980 and 1986, the *Tri-Turbo-Three* was repaired after a ground fire and was last used during the 1990s for various tests on behalf of the USN.

In spite of its grandiloquent corporate name, United States Aircraft Corporation (USAC) was a small company at the Van Nuys Airport in California. It was at that location that in 1981 it had fsn 26744 (formerly C-47B-18-DK, 43-49483, and then KK160, a British *Dakota III*) re-engined with 1,020shp Pratt & Whitney PT6A-45Rs. It also had a 40in fuselage plug inserted forward of the wing to compensate for the light installed weight of its new power plant. Registered N300TX and called the DC-3 *Turbo Express*, the re-engined and lengthened aircraft first flew on 28 July 1982 and received a Supplemental Type Certificate (STC)[12] in December 1983. It then was used in Alaska until acquired in October 1987 by Basler Flight Services. This FBO (Fixed-base operator)[13] then obtained a second DC-3 *Turbo Three*, N607W. That was the start of the Basler success story related below.

Schafer Aircraft Modifications Inc (Schafer/AMI) of Waco, Texas,

---

12 The Federal Aviation Administration issues a Supplemental Type Certificate to modified aircraft instead of a Type Certificate (TC, previous ATC for Approved Type certificate) as it does to new aircraft types. The STC defines the product design change, states how the modification affects the existing type design, and lists the serial numbers of aircraft covered under the STC.
13 The Federal Aviation Administration defines an FBO as 'A commercial business granted the right by the airport sponsor to operate on an airport and provide aeronautical services such as fueling, hangaring, tie-down and parking, aircraft rental, aircraft maintenance, flight instruction, etc.'

ABOVE *Formerly 41-20133, a C-53-DO was fitted with Rolls-Royce* Darts *in California to become the Conroy* Turbo-Three. *(Douglas Sloviak)*

started its own DC-3 modernization program in 1985. It would entail replacing the radial engines with 1,424shp PT-6A-45ARs and, as had been the case for the USAC DC-3 *Turbo Express*, adding a 40in fuselage plug forward of the wing. Registered N70BF, the prototype for this DC-3-65TP (also, but seldom, called *CargoMaster*) was fsn 27085 (formerly C-47B-20-DK, 43-49824, and then KN219, a *Dakota IV* of the Royal Air Force). Flight tests began on 1 August 1986 and the DC-3-65TP was awarded its Supplemental Type Certificate one year later. Success eluded the DC-3-65TP at home but a ready market developed in South Africa.

With a large number of C-47s (and other DC-3 variants) still in service, the South African Air Force was eager to have these aircraft modernized and re-engined. It reached an agreement with Wonder Air (Pty) in Pretoria whereby this South African firm would upgrade SAAF aircraft under a license from Schafer/AMI.

BELOW *After its two* Darts *were replaced by three Pratt & Whitney Canada PT6A-45s, the* Turbo-Three *became the* Tri-Turbo-Three. *(DR)*

ABOVE *Built as a C-47A-15-DK with serial 42-92754, this aircraft went to the South African Air Force in April 1944. More than 53 years later, it became the first turbine-engine C-47TP modified as a maritime patrol. It was exported from South Africa to California to become N834TP with the US Test Pilot School in March 2003. It crashed on take-off at Mojave on 4 February 2009.* (DR)

BELOW *Placed at the end of the DC-3 text, this nostalgic photograph shows HB-IRB, a DC-3D delivered to Swissair in March 1946.* (Douglas)

This resulted in 38 SAAF aircraft being brought up to C-47TP standard. Two C-47TPs were further modified by Reutech Systems (Pty) to a maritime patrol configuration with (1) an Elta EL/M-2022 surveillance radar and its antenna in a radome beneath the rear fuselage; (2) a Kentron FLIR (Forward Looking Infrared sensor) in a ball mounting under the nose; and (3) the cabin being fitted with a TACCO (Tactical Coordinator) station, three stations for equipment sensor (acoustic detection, radar, and communications) operators, and bulged observation windows on both sides of the rear. In recent years, the SAAF disposed of many of its C-47TPs, many of which went on to the US civil registry. In addition, Wonder Air (Pty) modified four other aircraft for civil customers.

By far, the most successful modernization and turbine engine installation program for the DC-3 is that realized by Basler on the basis of the DC-3 *Turbo Express* initially developed by United States Aircraft Corporation. Established as a FBO in Oshkosh, Wisconsin, Basler Flight Services had been flying DC-3s since 1957 and, later, had acquired two DC-3 *Turbo Expresses*. Appreciating them and confident that there was a market for similarly modified turbine-engined DC-3s, Warren Basler acquired the rights from USAC and undertook to produce an improved version, the BT-67. Principal changes from the *Turbo Three* were: (1) 1,424shp PT6A-67R engines; (2) a composite material radome; (3) improved cockpit design with a new instrument panel; (4) the partition between the cockpit and the cabin moved forward to increase available volume; (5) redesigned leading edge near the wing tips; (6) revised wing tips increasing span by 8in; (7) metal, instead of fabric, covered control surfaces; (8) enlarged cargo doors to enable loading/unloading of LD-3 containers; and (9) fuel capacity increased by adding either a 166.5 or 333 Imp. gallon tank in each wing outer panels.

With these modifications, the BT-67 can carry 43% more payload, with seating being provided for 36 passengers (nine 2+2 rows) or 40 troopers on side benches. Cruising speed is increased by 24%. Supplemental Type Certificate SA840M was issued on 27 February 1990. To date, 54 DC-3s have been brought up to BT-67 with, according to some sources, 36 being currently operational (nearly one in five of the airworthy DC-3s in mid-2011).

More than 75 years after the first aircraft in this long line, DST X14988, first flew at Clover Field on 17 December 1935, Donald Douglas, Dutch Kindelberger, Arthur Raymond, and all those who worked designing, producing, and modifying these aircraft can be justly proud of the lasting success achieved by the world's most built transport aircraft.

RIGHT *Still carrying the US registration N387T when photographed on approach at McClellan AFB, California, on 24 May 1991, this Basler BT-27 was on its delivery flight to become TAM-38 with* Transporte Aéreo Militar *in Bolivia.* (René J. Francillon)

Elderly but still there when needed

At 4:53:10pm local time (21:53:10 UTC) on Tuesday, 12 January 2010, a 7.0 earthquake struck 15 miles WSW of Port-au-Prince, Haiti. As always when such tragedies occur, the world responded rapidly through governments and international organizations to come to the rescue of the victims. Aid providers pushed each other and news organizations competed with each other before assistance could be effectively orchestrated. In the midst of the initial chaos, the media was still getting its act together when the first aid arrived. No television cameras and gushing broadcasters were there when an elderly DC-3 became the first to land in Haiti with relief supplies.

Based at the St Lucie International in Fort Pierce, Florida, Missionary Flights & Services Inc. (more often referred to as MFI for Missionary Flight International) is dedicated to providing logistical support for religious and relief organizations. At the time of the 2010 Haiti earthquake its aircraft fleet was composed of a Cessna 310N light twin (N911MF) and three quite diverse DC-3s. N200MF was an ex-C-47A-35-ML which had been 'turbinised' as a DC-3-65TP, N300MF was an ex-C-47B-20-DK that was held in reserve, and N400MF was another C-47B-20-DK which had had its R-1830s engines replaced by Wright *Cyclone* SGR-1820-G-202As.

As soon as MFI got news of the earthquake, N200MF was readied and was sent to the Exuma International Airport in Georgetown to be loaded with 2.4 tons of tarps and water purification equipment that had been stored at that Bahamas site. Nine hours and 43 minutes after the earthquake, the DC-3-65TP lifted off from Exuma and set course for Port-au-Prince. When its pilots attempted to land at the Toussaint-Louverture International Airport in Port-au-Prince they found the field strewed with debis, forcing them to divert to the airport in Cap-Haitien on the north of the island. Tarps and water purification equipment were unloaded but N200MF was unable to refuel locally, forcing it to proceed to Provinciales Airport, in the Turks and Caicos Islands, before continuing to Florida to pick up its next load.

That same afternoon, N200MF returned to Haiti and, this time, was able to land at Toussaint-Louverture where it remained overnight before starting another round with reloading in Fort Pierce. This was just a start for MFI which went on to make 60 relief trips in two weeks, carrying 1,400 passengers (rescuers and medical personnel on the way in, and wounded and refugees on the way out) as well as 340 tons of medical supplies, food, and hygiene products.

BELOW The DC-3-65TP of Missionary Flight International was built as a C-47A-35-DL (42-23904). It later became a Dakota III (FD933) in the UK and a C-47TP (6879) with the South African Air Force. It was acquired by MFI in 2003 and was registered as N200MF on 4 April 2003. *(MFI)*

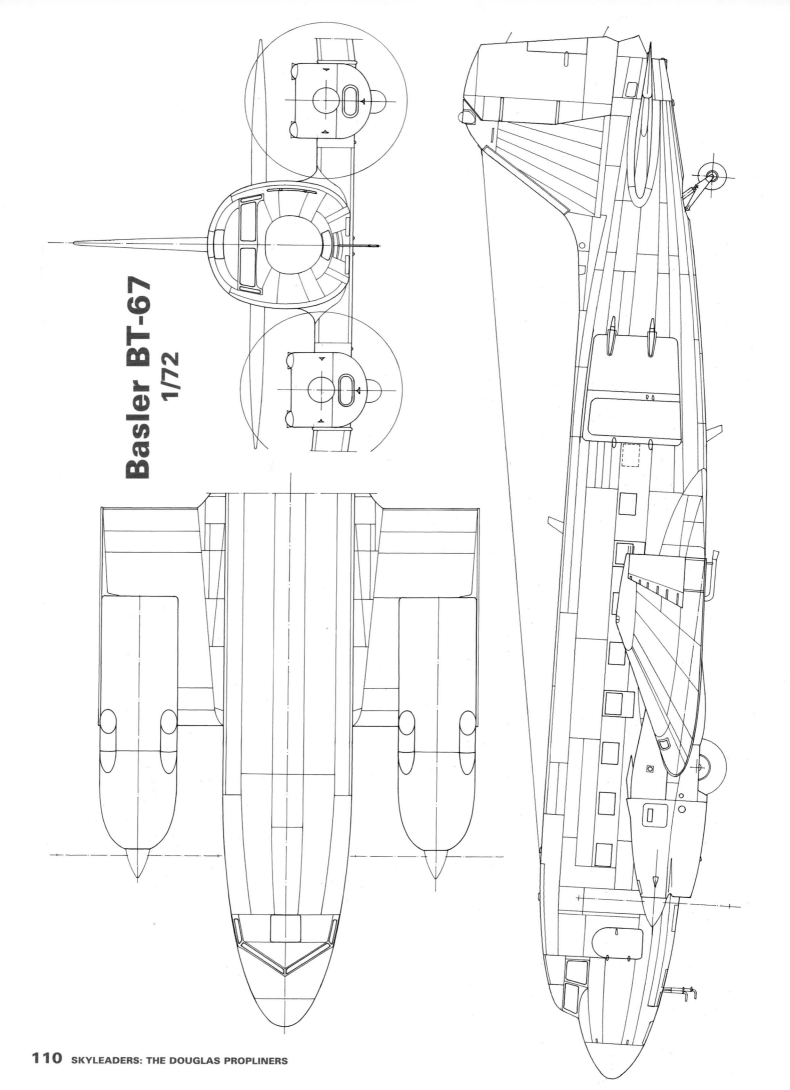

Basler BT-67 1/72

Where are they now?

Active DC-3s in June 2011

Country	DC-3 with radial engines		DC-3-65TP with PT6A-65AR		Basler BT-67 with PT6A-67		Total
	Civil	Military	Civil	Military	Civil	Military	
Argentina	1						1
Australia	7						7
Bolivia	1						1
Brazil	1						1
Canada	8				7		15
Chile	1						1
Colombia	14					9	23
Congo (Dem. Republic of)	1						1
Denmark	1						1
Egypt	1						1
Finland	1						1
France	2						2
Greece		2					2
Honduras	2	6					8
Iceland	1						1
India	4						4
Indonesia	3						3
Mali						1	1
Mauritania						1	1
Mexico	1	1					2
The Netherlands	2						2
New Zealand	2						2
El Salvador	1					2	3
Serbia		1					1
South Africa	6	1	2	10	1		20
Sweden	1						1
Switzerland	1						1
Thailand		2				8	10
United Kingdom	4	1					5
United States	57	1	4		7		69
Venezuela	1		1				2
Total	**125**	**15**	**7**	**10**	**15**	**21**	**193**

Source: *AeroTransport Data Bank* (http://aerotransport.org)

Notes: 1. In addition to these 193 active aircraft, 27 were undergoing major overhaul or being converted to turbine engines. They were expected to be returned to service.

2. Super DC-3s and ex R4D-8s are not included (see Chapter 11 for these aircraft).

Technical data for civil DC-3s

	DST (SGR-1802-G2)	DC-3A (S1C3-G)	DC-3C (R-1830-92)	Basler BT-67 (PT6A-67R)
Dimensions				
Span	95 0	95 0	95 0	95 8
Length, ft in	64 5½	64 5½	64 5	67 8
Height, ft in	16 3⅝	16 11	16 11	18 3
Wing area, sq ft	987	987	987	-
Weights and loadings				
Empty, lb	16,060	16,865	18,300	15,750
Loaded, lb	24,000	25,200	25,200	-
Maximum, lb	-	-	28,000	28,750
Wing loading, lb/sq ft	24.3	25.5	25.5	-
Power loading, lb/hp	5.4	4.8	4.8	10.1
Performance				
Maximum speed, mph at ft	212/6,800	230/8,500	237/8,800	247/12,500
Cruising speed, mph	192	207	170	236
Initial climb rate, ft/min	850/1	1,130/1	-	-
Service ceiling, ft	20,800	23,2000	-	25,000
Normal range, miles	-	2,125	1,025	2,140

LEFT AND BELOW *Civil cockpits then and now: the top photo shows the cockpit of NC16001, the first DST operated on scheduled service, when the aircraft was still in Santa Monica in the spring of 1936. The lower photo, taken in February 2006 during a flight in Baja California, shows the cockpit of XA-UDY of California-Pacifico (ex-C47A-1-DK 42-92396). The most significant difference in seventy years is the addition of a GPS on the centre frame of the windshield.* (Douglas & Carol A. McKenzie)

OPPOSITE *Prior to 1941, most aircraft in the DC-3 family were powered by nine-cylinder Wright Cyclone radial engines. Mass production of C-47s and other military variants saw 14-cylinder Pratt & Whitney R-1830 radials move decisively to the fore.* (Library of Congress)

The DC-3 engines

Wright *Cyclone* (nine-cylinder radial)

Type	Maximum rating	Take-off rating	Aircraft versions
SGR-1820-G2	850hp at 5,800ft	1,000hp	DST, DC-3
SGR-1820-G2E	-	1,000hp	DST, DC-3
SGR-1820-G5	850hp at 4,300ft	1,000hp	DST
SGR-1820-G102	900hp at 6,000ft	1,100hp	DST, DC-3
SGR-1820-G102A	900hp at 6,700ft	1,100hp	DST, DC-3
SGR-1820-G103A	-	1,100hp	DC-3
SGR-1820-G202A	1,050hp at 7,500ft	1,200hp	DST, DC-3, DC-3B
R-1820-71	1,000hp at 6,900ft	1,200hp	C-49, C-49A/B/C/D/F/J/K C-84, R5D-2
R-1820-79	-	1,100hp	C-49E, C-50C/D
R-1820-81	-	1,100hp	C-50B
R-1820-83	900hp at 6,700ft	1,100hp	C-51
R-1820-85	900hp at 6,700ft	1,100hp	C-50, C-50A
R-1820-97	1,000hp at 25,000ft	1,200hp	C-49G/H

Pratt & Whitney *Twin Wasp* (14-cylinder radial)

Type	Maximum rating	Take-off rating	Aircraft versions
Twin Wasp SB3-G	900hp at 6,000ft	1,000hp	DST-A
Twin Wasp SC-G	900hp at 11,000ft	1,050hp	DST-A, DC-3A
Twin Wasp SC3-G	900hp at 12,000ft	1,050hp	DST-A, DC-3A
Twin Wasp S1C-G	1,050hp at 7,500ft	1,200hp	DST-A, DC-3A
Twin Wasp S1C3-G	1,050hp at 7,500ft	1,200hp	DC-3A/C/D
Twin Wasp S4C4-G	900hp at 15,400ft	1,200hp	DST-A, DC-3A
R-1830-21	1,050hp at 6,400ft	1,200hp	C-41A
R-1830-51	1,050hp at 7,500ft	1,200hp	C-48A/B/C, C-52, C-52A/B/C
R-1830-75 ou -94	1,100hp at 7,500ft	1,350hp	Re-engined DC-3 & C-47
R-1830-82	1,050hp at 7,500ft	1,200hp	C-47
R-1830-90C	1,000hp at 14,500ft	1,200hp	C-47
R-1830-90D	1,100hp at 6,100ft	1,200hp	C-47
R-1830-92	1,050hp at 7,500ft	1,200hp	C-47
R-2000-4	1,100hp at 7,000ft	1,290hp	Re-engined DC-3 & C-47
R-2000-D5 ou -7M2	1,200hp at 6,400ft	1,450hp	Re-engined DC-3 & C-47

Armstrong Siddeley *Mamba* (axial-flow propeller turbine)

Type	Maximum rating	Take-off rating	Aircraft versions
Mamba ASMa.3	-	1,425shp	*Mamba-Dakota*
Mamba ASMa.6	-	1,590shp	*Mamba-Dakota*

Pratt & Whitney *Canada PT6* (axial- & centrifugal-flow propeller turbine)

Type	Maximum rating	Take-off rating	Aircraft versions
PT6A-45	-	1,120shp	ATSC *Tri-Turbo*
PT6A-45R	-	1,197shp	USAC *Turbo Express*
PT6A-65AR	-	1,424shp	Schafer DC-3-65TP
PT6A-67R	-	1,424shp	Basler BT-67

OPPOSITE *This DC3-65TP conversion is powered by 1,145shp Pratt & Whitney PT6A-65AR in closely-fitting cowlings and driving five-blade propellers.* (H.L. James)

ABOVE *Japanese-built DC-3 derivatives were powered by 14-cylinder Mitsubishi* Kinsei *radials with take-off power ranging from 1,000 to 1,560hp. This is a 1,300hp* Kinsei *51 on the right wing of a Showa L2D3. Note the additional cockpit windows of the Japanese aircraft.* (USN-NA)

Rolls-Royce *Dart* (centrifugal-flow propeller turbine)

Type	Maximum rating	Take-off rating	Aircraft versions
Dart 504	-	1,540shp	*Dart-Dakota*
Dart 505	-	1,540shp	*Dart-Dakota*
Dart 510	-	1,640shp	*Dart-Dakota*
Dart 510	-	1,350shp (downrated)	Conroy *Turbo-Three*
Dart 525	-	1,990shp	*Dart-Dakota*

Mitsubishi *Kinsei* (14-cylinder radial)

Type	Maximum rating	Take-off rating	Aircraft versions
Kinsei 43	1,065hp at 6,560ft	986hp	L2D2
Kinsei 51	1,183hp at 9,845ft	1,282hp	L2D-3, L2D3-1, L2D4, L2D4-1
Kinsei 53	1,183hp at 9,845ft	1,282hp	L2D3a, L2D3-1a
Kinsei 62	1,164hp at 19,030ft	1,537hp	L2D5

Shvetsov 62 (nine-cylinder radial)

Type	Maximum rating	Take-off rating	Aircraft versions
ASh-62IR	828hp at 4,920ft	986hp	PS-84, Li-2, TS-62 (re-engined C-47)
PZL asz-62IR	-	986hp	Airtech Canada DC-3/2000

LEFT *The Ash-61R radial engines of this Lisunov Li-2 in the markings of the* Magyar Honvédség Repûlo Csapatai *(Hungarian Air Defense Group) shows the removable cowling shutters that were used during cold weather operations.* (Iulian Robanescu)

BELOW *Photographed on the sand-packed runway at San Ignacio, Baja California, in February 2006, XA-UDY of* California-Pacifico *is an ex-C-47A-1-DK. Note the large rectangular window aft of the cockpit and the squared-off wingtips.* (Carol A. McKenzie)

Shvetsov 82 (9-cylinder radial)

Type	Maximum rating	Take-off rating	Aircraft versions
ASh-82FN		1,652hp	C-47 re-engined in USSR

Tumanski 88 (14-cylinder radial)

Type	Maximum rating	Take-off rating	Aircraft versions
M-88B		1,085hp	C-47 re-engined in USSR

Note: In the cases of Japanese and Russian engines ratings in metric hp have been converted to UK horsepower.

Turbomeca *Palas* (centrifugal-flow turbojet)

Type	Maximum rating	Take-off rating	Aircraft versions
Palas		350lb st	One or two auxiliary turbojets added to a small number of DC-3s

CIVIL DC-3s IN THE UNITED STATES

RIGHT *N22Z of Aspen Airways, an ex DST-A-207, was photographed in Denver, Colorado, on 4 July 1968.* (Peter B. Lewis)

RIGHT *Flying over Oklahoma City, N34 is ex-C-47B-35-DK of the Federal Aviation Administration which has been beautifully restored as shown by this 2003 photograph.* (DR)

BELOW *N130Q at Titusville, Florida, in March 1992: this is the only civil DC-3 – actually an ex-C-53-DO – that has been fitted with amphibian floats.* (Kevin Grantham)

LEFT *N 143D of Herpa Miniature Models at Oshkosh, Wisconsin, on 26 July 2006.* (Jim Dunn)

BELOW *N272R, an ex-C-47A-15-DK of Central America Airways Flying Service, is shown at Louisville, Kentucky, in January 1980.* (David W. Menard)

BOTTOM *N485, an ex-C-53-DO, of Bonanza Airlines, in 1962.* (DR)

RIGHT *N817NA, an ex-C-47H of the NASA Dryden Center, at Edwards AFB, California, in May 1981. (René J. Francillon)*

BELOW *N832PB, an ex-C-53B-DO of Naples-Boston-Provincetown Airlines, is parked at Boston's Logan Airport in 1975. (René J. Francillon)*

BOTTOM *N19912, an ex-C-53D-DO, of Pan American World Airways, in the 1950s. (William Balogh, David W. Menard collection)*

LEFT *N25627, a DC-3-222 of Chicago and Southern Airlines, in the early 1950s.* (William Balogh, David W. Menard collection)

BELOW *N25646, a DC-3-201C of Central Iowa Airlines in August 1979, was re-engined with Pratt & Whitney Twin Wasp radials in revised nacelles fully enclosing the main undercarriage after retraction.* (Ken Buchanan, David W. Menard collection)

BOTTOM *N28889 (an ex-C-47A-90-DL) of the Monroe County Mosquito Control District, at Marathon, Florida, on 7 October 1987.* (René J. Francillon)

RIGHT *N37465, a DC-3D of Pacific Northern Airlines, at Clover Field, Santa Monica in 1946.* (Douglas)

BELOW *N44587, an ex-C-47A-20-DK of West Coast Airlines, at Boeing Field, Seattle, on 19 July 1988.* (Peter B. Lewis)

BOTTOM *N44991, an ex-C-53-D-DO of United Air Lines, in the late 1950s.* (William Balogh, David W. Menard collection)

CIVIL DC-3s ABROAD

ABOVE *ZS-CRV, an ex-C-47A-25-DK/Dakota III of Rovos Air, at the Skukuza Airport, outside the Kruger National Park, in June 2006.* (Daniel H. Schuman)

RIGHT *ZS-ASN, an ex-C-47B-40-BK, was rebuilt and re-engined as a Basler BT-67. It is shown fitted for surveying mineral resources.* (DR)

RIGHT *ZS-GPL, an ex-C-47A-30-DL, of Springbok Flying Safaris.* (Frédéric Lert)

TOP *A bit of whimsy: 14+11, a C-47B-40-DK of the Luftwaffe, was given 'Royal Bavarian Air Force' markings.* (DR)

ABOVE *VH-ANR of Australian National Airways in 1946. It was a DC-3-194B which had been delivered to KLM in April 1937.* (Douglas)

LEFT *VH-PNM, an ex-C-47B-11-DK, was operated by Bush Pilot Airways between February 1972 and March 1974. The uniform worn by the pilots is well adapted to the local weather!* (Ruth E. Peters)

TOP *VP-BBT, ex-C-47B-16-DK, of Bahamas Airways during the 1960s.* (DR)

ABOVE *A CP-1742 of Trans-Oriente in Bolivia was a DC-3-279 re-engined with Twin Wasps.* (Mário Roberto Carneiro)

RIGHT *PT-KVC, a DC-3D of the Clube Nautico Agua Limpa, was based at the Santos Dumont Airport in Rio de Janeiro in 1976–88.* (Mário Roberto Carneiro)

ABOVE *CF-QCM, a C-43-DO re-engined with Pratt & Whitney R-2000s, of Quebec Cartier Mining in the early 1960s.* (William Balogh, David W. Menard collection)

LEFT *CF-QHY, an ex-C-47A-5-DK belonging to Plummer's Arctic Lodges, a hunting/fishing resort at Great Bear Lake, Northern Territories, Canada.* (Jim Dunn)

BELOW *HK-793, an ex-C-47-DL of Líneas Aéreas Taxader, at Santa Marta, Colombia, in June 1964.* (Jacques Guillem collection)

ABOVE *9Q-CTR, an ex-C-47A-30-DK of Air Kasaï, at Kinshasa-Ndolo on 21 September 2009. Registered in the Democratic Republic of Congo, this aircraft is unique for having been re-engined with PZL asz-62IR radials driving four-blade propellers.* (Alex Cheminade)

RIGHT *TI-AMS, an ex-C-53-DO of Aerovias Pontarenas S.A. in Costa Rica* (Jacques Guillem collection)

BELOW *TU-TIA, a DC-3D, was registered to Air Ivoire in June 1964 after having been used for more than 17 years by Pacific Northern Airlines.* (Jacques Guillem collection)

LEFT *Originally a prewar Cyclone-powered DC-3-313B of Pennsylvania Central, HC-AOP was registered in Ecuador for 16 years starting in June 1968. Belonging to CIASA when photographed at Quito in August 1974, it had by then been re-engined and fitted with cleaned-up nacelles and squared-off wingtips. (René J. Francillon)*

BELOW *Also photographed at Quito in August 1974, HC-SJI was an ex C-47B-50-DK of Servicios Aéreos Nacionales, S.A. (SAN). (René J. Francillon)*

LEFT *Bearing the markings of F-BBBE, a DC-3 (ex-C-47-DL) which was with Air France for 20 years beginning in 1946, this aircraft is in fact a C-47A-1-DL which belongs to the association France DC-3. Photograph taken at Auxerre on 28 April 2008. (Jacques Guillem)*

RIGHT *F-BEIS, an ex-C-53-DO after it had been fitted with two Turbomeca Palas auxiliary turbojets beneath the outer wing panels.* (Jean Delmas collection)

BELOW *Another view of F-AZTE, the superbly preserved aircraft of France DC-3, parked behind a replica of the Blériot XI at La Ferté-Allais, in 2007.* (Christian Jacquet-Francillon)

BOTTOM *9G-AAC, an ex-C-47B-40-DK of Ghana Airways, at Accra in January 1973.* (Jacques Guillem collection)

TOP *G-DAKK, the ex-C-47A-35-DL belonging to South Coast Airways, is about to land at Fairford on 24 July 1998.* (Richard Gennis)

ABOVE *Nothing fishy about TF-ISH, an ex-C-47A-DL, that flew with* Flugfèlag Islands *for 27 years.* (Jacques Guillem collection)

LEFT *EI-ACD, an ex-C-47-DL of Aer Lingus at Newcastle in 1961.* (Jacques Guillem collection)

TOP *When it entered service with* Transport Aérien du Mali, *this ex-C-53D-DO (fsn 11737, 42-68810) still wore its US registration number, N889P. In May 1993, it became TZ-AJW on the register of this Central African nation.* (Jacques Guillem collection)

ABOVE *XA-JOI, an ex-C-49J, of Aerolíneas de Monte Albán, at Oaxaca during the 1980s.* (Jacques Guillem collection)

RIGHT *XA-UDY, ex-C-47A-1-DK of California-Pacifico, at Tijuana, Baja California, in February 2006.* (Carol A. McKenzie)

TOP *LN-WND, ex-C-53D-DO of Stiftelsen Dakota Norway (Foundation Dakota Norway), at Duxford in July 2009.* (DR)

ABOVE *ZK-AZN Skyliner Napier, ex-C-47B-35-DK, of New Zealand National Airways.* (DR)

LEFT *ZK-AWP, ex-C-47B-30-DK, of Pionair Adventures Ltd.* (DR)

TOP *Still with an Australian registration and military-style folding seats on the sides of the cabin instead of airline seats when in service with* Air Niugini *in 1973, VH-SBB was an ex-C-47A-45-DL.* (Ruth E. Peters)

ABOVE *5W-FAA, an ex-C-47B-30-DK of Polynesian Airlines at Apia, Samoa, in 1965.* (Ruth E. Peters)

RIGHT *Perhaps not odoriferous but certainly colourful, HB-ISC, an ex-C-47A-40-DL of Classic Air AG, advertised Alrodo AG perfumes from St Moritz, Switzerland.* (DR)

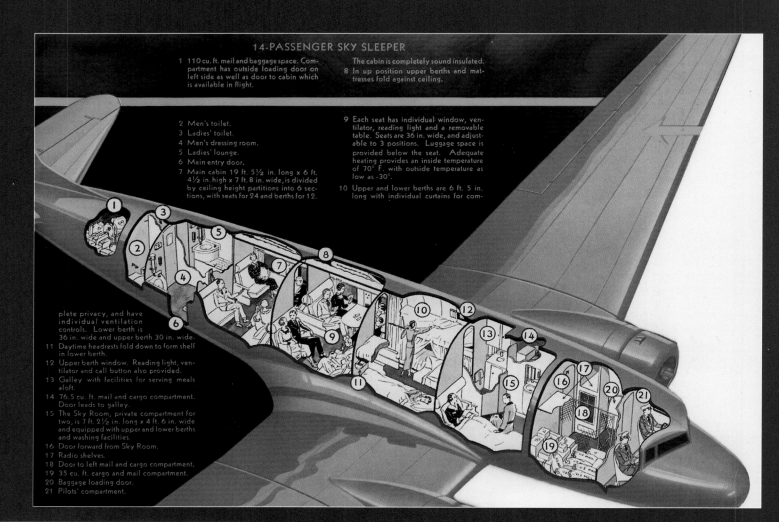

14-PASSENGER SKY SLEEPER

1 110 cu. ft. mail and baggage space. Compartment has outside loading door on left side as well as door to cabin which is available in flight.

The cabin is completely sound insulated.

8 In up position upper berths and mattresses fold against ceiling.

2 Men's toilet.
3 Ladies' toilet.
4 Men's dressing room.
5 Ladies' lounge.
6 Main entry door.
7 Main cabin 19 ft. 5½ in. long x 6 ft. 4½ in. high x 7 ft. 8 in. wide, is divided by ceiling height partitions into 6 sections, with seats for 24 and berths for 12.

9 Each seat has individual window, ventilator, reading light and a removable table. Seats are 36 in. wide, and adjustable to 3 positions. Luggage space is provided below the seat. Adequate heating provides an inside temperature of 70° F. with outside temperature as low as -30°.

10 Upper and lower berths are 6 ft. 5 in. long with individual curtains for com-

plete privacy, and have individual ventilation controls. Lower berth is 36 in. wide and upper berth 30 in. wide.

11 Daytime headrests fold down to form shelf in lower berth.
12 Upper berth window. Reading light, ventilator and call button also provided.
13 Galley with facilities for serving meals aloft.
14 76.5 cu. ft. mail and cargo compartment. Door leads to galley.
15 The Sky Room, private compartment for two, is 7 ft. 2½ in. long x 4 ft. 6 in. wide and equipped with upper and lower berths and washing facilities.
16 Door forward from Sky Room.
17 Radio shelves.
18 Door to left mail and cargo compartment.
19 35 cu. ft. cargo and mail compartment.
20 Baggage loading door.
21 Pilots' compartment.

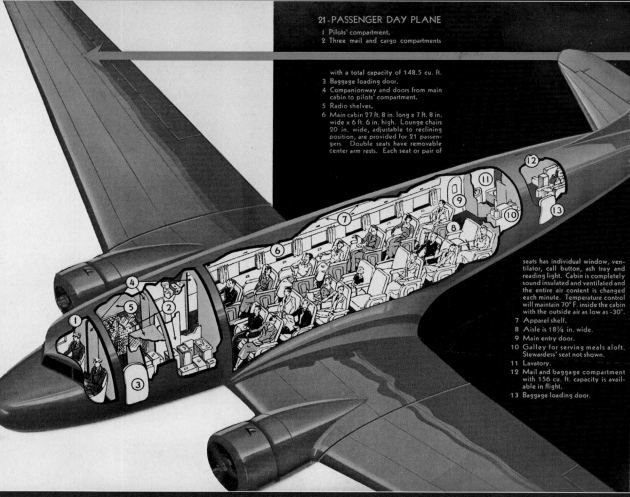

21-PASSENGER DAY PLANE

1 Pilots' compartment.
2 Three mail and cargo compartments with a total capacity of 148.5 cu. ft.
3 Baggage loading door.
4 Companionway and doors from main cabin to pilots' compartment.
5 Radio shelves.
6 Main cabin 27 ft. 8 in. long x 7 ft. 8 in. wide x 6 ft. 6 in. high. Lounge chairs 20 in. wide, adjustable to reclining position, are provided for 21 passengers. Double seats have removable center arm rests. Each seat or pair of

seats has individual window, ventilator, call button, ash tray and reading light. Cabin is completely sound insulated and ventilated and the entire air content is changed each minute. Temperature control will maintain 70° F. inside the cabin with the outside air as low as -30°.

7 Apparel shelf.
8 Aisle is 18¼ in. wide.
9 Main entry door.
10 Galley for serving meals aloft. Stewardess' seat not shown.
11 Lavatory.
12 Mail and baggage compartment with 156 cu. ft. capacity is available in flight.
13 Baggage loading door.

THIS SPREAD *Taken from a publicity brochure prepared for Douglas by The Essig Company Ltd. In the mid-1930s, these four cutaway illustrations show the DST cabin arrangement (134 top), the standard DC-3 cabin (134 bottom), a 'business' cabin arrangement (135 top), and the 'Club' configuration (135 bottom). (Douglas)*

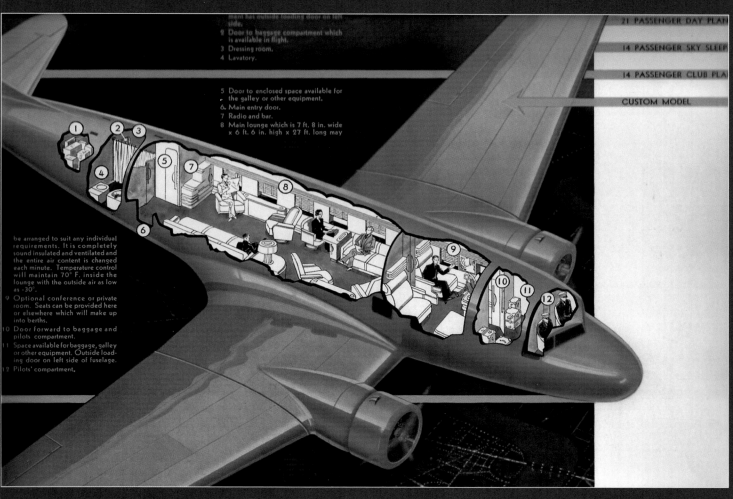

ment has outside loading door on left side.

2 Door to baggage compartment which is available in flight.
3 Dressing room.
4 Lavatory.

5 Door to enclosed space available for the galley or other equipment.
6 Main entry door.
7 Radio and bar.
8 Main lounge which is 7 ft. 8 in. wide x 6 ft. 6 in. high x 27 ft. long may

21 PASSENGER DAY PLAN

14 PASSENGER SKY SLEEP

14 PASSENGER CLUB PLAN

CUSTOM MODEL

be arranged to suit any individual requirements. It is completely sound insulated and ventilated and the entire air content is changed each minute. Temperature control will maintain 70° F. inside the lounge with the outside air as low as -30°.

9 Optional conference or private room. Seats can be provided here or elsewhere which will make up into berths.
10 Door forward to baggage and pilots compartment.
11 Space available for baggage, galley or other equipment. Outside loading door on left side of fuselage.
12 Pilots' compartment.

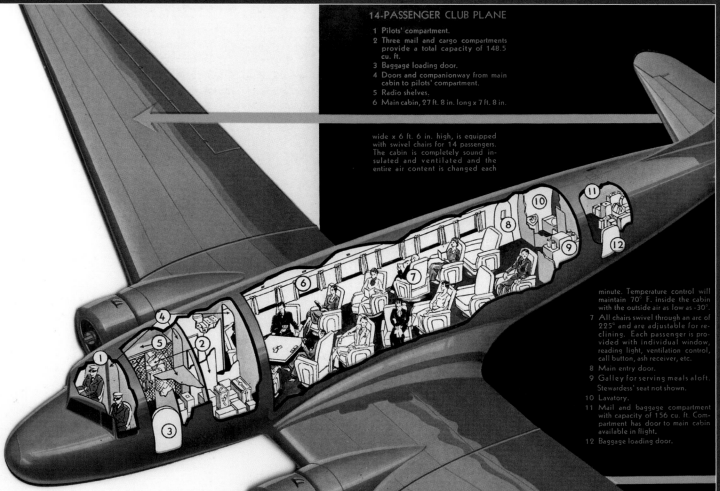

14-PASSENGER CLUB PLANE

1 Pilots' compartment.
2 Three mail and cargo compartments provide a total capacity of 148.5 cu. ft.
3 Baggage loading door.
4 Doors and companionway from main cabin to pilots' compartment.
5 Radio shelves.
6 Main cabin, 27 ft. 8 in. long x 7 ft. 8 in.

wide x 6 ft. 6 in. high, is equipped with swivel chairs for 14 passengers. The cabin is completely sound insulated and ventilated and the entire air content is changed each

minute. Temperature control will maintain 70° F. inside the cabin with the outside air as low as -30°.

7 All chairs swivel through an arc of 225° and are adjustable for reclining. Each passenger is provided with individual window, reading light, ventilation control, call button, ash receiver, etc.
8 Main entry door.
9 Galley for serving meals aloft. Stewardess' seat not shown.
10 Lavatory.
11 Mail and baggage compartment with capacity of 156 cu. ft. Compartment has door to main cabin available in flight.
12 Baggage loading door.

Chapter 5

DF – A last fling with the sea

Growing up in New York, Donald Wills Douglas and his two-year older brother, Harold, acquired a passion for the sea while on summer holidays in a house near the yacht club on Long Island Sound. There, the two boys were taught to sail by their mother. Eventually, their love of the sea brought both of them to attend the US Naval Academy in Annapolis, Maryland, Harold in 1907 and Donald two years later. Meanwhile, the younger brother had acquired an additional enthusiasm, that for aeronautics, which interfered with his intended naval career. Harold Douglas did become a naval officer but his sibling left the Academy after three years to study aeronautics at the Massachusetts Institute of Technology. From there, Donald Douglas went on to found and manage his own aircraft manufacturing company. Nevertheless, while pursuing his chosen career in the aviation industry, Donald Douglas did not lose his love for the sea and, once established in Santa Monica, became an avid yachtsman. So much so that in 1936 he was crewing the Six Metre racing yacht that won the Silver Medal for the United States at the 1932 Olympics in Los Angeles.

Successful as he was both as a yachtsman and as a manufacturer of landplanes, Douglas had difficulties transforming his love for the sea into achieving success when building seaplanes. While in business for himself, his first aircraft equipped to operate from water had been a civil derivative of the O-2 observation biplane, the O-2BS, with which James McKee made the first single-plane flight across Canada in September 1926. During the following year, the O-2BS was followed by twin-engined, float-equipped, T2D-1s and P2D-1s, and by twin-engined PD-1 flying boats (see Appendix III, pages 327 and 328). However, none of these twin-engined seaplanes had been designed by Douglas. Better, but still limited success, was obtained with the *Dolphin* series. None-the-less Donald Douglas was not discouraged, especially as the last two of these amphibians were ordered by Pan American for its Chinese affiliates, CNAC (see Chapter 1). His hopes rose in 1935 after he was elected to the board of directors of Pan American, an airline which had taken delivery of DC-2s starting in August 1934.

In the mid-thirties, Pan American made extensive use of flying boats (twin-engined Consolidated *Commodores* and four-engined Sikorsky S-40s and S-42s) on its over-water routes through the Caribbean and down the east coast of South America to Brazil and Argentina (continuing with landplanes to Chile). Moreover, it relied on larger flying boats (Sikorsky S-42s and Martin M-130s) when starting to operate across the Pacific. Donald Douglas thus had reasonable hopes that the airline of which he was a director would order flying boats from his Santa Monica plant.

BELOW *The first DF-151 taxying in Santa Monica Bay on 27 September 1936.* **(Douglas)**

It happened that, in 1935, the Douglas Aircraft Company was working on prototypes of two twin-engined flying boats. The smallest, the YOA-5, was developed for the Army Air Corps while the largest, the XP3D-1, was for the USN (see page 333). After the Army lost interest in its ill-conceived 'overwater bomber escort' program, the YOA-5 was soon forgotten. Conversely, the XP3D-1 was modified for the Navy into the XP3D-2 with engines moved from above the wings to their leading-edge. The modified flying boat did well during evaluation but, in the end, was rejected by the USN in favor of the cheaper Consolidated P3Y-1, the first of the famous *Catalina* series.

Nevertheless, the XP3D-2 configuration was well-suited to serve as the basis for a medium-range transport flying boat. Keen to offer such an aircraft to Pan American, Douglas decided to undertake the design for what became its DF (for Douglas Flying boat). The Santa Monica engineering team was confident that the DF would be well-suited to replace older Sikorsky flying boats and would fit well along with the DC-2s which Pan American and its affiliates were operating and which were soon to be supplemented by DC-3s. Unfortunately for Douglas, Pan American was advised by Charles A. Lindbergh. Properly, as it turned out, the hero of the first non-stop crossing of the Atlantic between the American and European continents had come to the conclusion that even the latest flying boats then under development would be made obsolete by a new generation of landplanes.

In December 1935, tired of being constantly observed, 'The Lone Eagle,' as Lindbergh was often called, had gone into self-imposed exile in Great Britain and, temporarily, settled down at Sevenoaks Weald. While in Kent, Lindbergh kept in regular contact with airlines retaining him as a consultant. In particular, he was a close confident of Juan Trippe, the founder and long-time leader of Pan American. That brought Lindbergh to write a letter to Trippe on 28 October 1936 (as reproduced on the right of this page).

In the second paragraph, he stated that he was 'glad that you are developing a land plane in addition to the new flying boats [the Boeing 307 Stratoliner and Boeing 314]. I believe it is probable that the landplane will replace the flying boat on all important routes in the future.' In the third paragraph, he went on to state: 'I believe that Pan American will otherwise be vulnerable [that is if Pan American did not obtain landplanes capable of flying the Atlantic routes] to competition by companies, either American or foreign, who operate landplanes of considerable higher performance than the Boeing flying boats.'

Charles Lindbergh proved remarkably prescient with these statements. Such foresight, unfortunately, was not in evidence in Europe, particularly in Great Britain and France where large civil flying boats were developed until after the end of World War Two (and where the 10-turboprop Saunders-Roe SR.45 *Princess*, the six-engine Latécoère 631, and the six-engine SNCASE SE.200 are still remembered with fondness by die-hard flying boat enthusiasts). By then, Douglas DC-4s and Lockheed *Constellations* were ruling over the North Atlantic.

Many have since argued that the downfall of flying boats came as the result of the wartime use of land-based aircraft on long overwater routes by the Royal Air Force Ferry Command (with much Canadian inputs), the Air Transport Command, and the Naval Air Transport Service. Yet, as predicted by Lindbergh, the switch to landplanes for transoceanic operations had started before the beginning of World War Two.

RIGHT *Photostat copy of the letter from Charles Lindbergh to Juan Trippe dated 28 October 1936.* (DR)

LONG BARN · WEALD · SEVENOAKS

Oct. 28, 1936

Dear Juan:

I have been in correspondence with Jack Frye in regard to the high altitude land transport which T.&W.A. is developing, and which, I understand, Pan American is taking part in.

I am glad that you are developing a land plane in addition to the new flying boats. I believe it is probable that the landplane will replace the flying boat on all important routes in the future. I think the only exception will

LONG BARN · WEALD · SEVENOAKS   2.

be in places where landing fields can not be obtained or where the traffic is so low that the construction of a field is not warranted.

In order to protect the company's interests, I believe it is extremely important that whatever landplane you develop is capable of flying the Atlantic routes with a reasonable pay load and a large fuel reserve. I believe that Pan American will otherwise be vulnerable to competition by companies, either American or foreign, who operate landplanes of considerable

LONG BARN · WEALD · SEVENOAKS   3.

higher performance than the Boeing flying boats, and which have supercharged cabins for carrying passengers above storms and in smooth air.

It is important to keep in mind that planes can now be built better, by a fairly large margin, than any we have yet ordered.

With best regards

Charles A. Lindbergh

ABOVE *The first DF-151 photographed on the ramp at Clover Field in September 1936 following its roll-out.* (Douglas)

But it was not only Europeans that failed to either anticipate or give credence to the wise prediction made by Lindbergh. In May 1935, while the DF was under construction, Donald Douglas confidently predicted a bright future for flying boats when he was invited by the Royal Aeronautical Society to give the keynote speech at the Twenty-Third Wilbur Wright Memorial Lecture. In his paper titled 'The Development and Reliability of the Modern Multi-Engine Air Liner with Special Reference to the Multi-Engine Airplanes After Engine Failure' he stated, when speaking about new American flying boats, that: 'With their four great engines it is difficult to imagine a flight failure due to engine trouble. Seaworthy hulls of large size seem adequate to permit safe landings under all conditions likely to be met. Comfort is even better served in these commodious hulls than in the smaller bodies of our land planes.' Fifteen years after Donald Douglas made this rosy prediction, the last major scheduled operation with flying boats came to an end when in November 1950 BOAC terminated its Southampton–Johannesburg service with Short *Solents*.

No future for a capable flying boat

As was the case for the DC-1 through DC-3 that preceded the DF, the wings of the flying boat were built in three sections with the center part having no dihedral. This section, however, represented a larger portion of the span and area than was the case with the land-based airliners. It provided room for six 225 Imp. gallon tanks. Retractable stabilizing floats were attached to the wing outboard panels which had two spars versus three for previous Douglas Airliners. Span was the same as that of the DC-3 but area was 31% larger.

Like other contemporary flying boats, the DF had its hull and cabin divided into compartments separated by watertight doors. Each of the four passenger compartments had eight seats (four rows of 2+2) for day operations, with these seats being made into four beds at night. Lavatories were located on each side of the center aisle between the forward compartment and that which followed. The galley and a seat for the steward or stewardess were aft of the last compartment, and were followed by baggage and mail compartments. A crew rest area was provided aft of the cockpit, above the first two passenger compartments.

Rolled-out in September 1936, the DF underwent ground

testing at Clover Field before being dismantled for transportation to the Santa Monica Bay where flight tests began before the month ended. Once again, the pilot for the early flights was Carl Cover. Trials were uneventful and the DF soon demonstrated remarkable performance even though its take-off weight was 20% higher than that of early DSTs and DC-3s but was powered by the same 1,000hp engines. Top speed and initial climb rate were down (178 versus 212mph, and 800 versus 850ft/min) but payload-range was up (32 passengers to 1,500 miles versus 21 passengers to 1,150 miles).

Unfortunately for Douglas, Pan American showed no interest in the DF even though it had much better performance than twin-engined flying boats then in service. Rather than ordering the new flying boat, the airline opted for relying on DC-2s, and then DC-3s, for its South American network. Operations of these landplanes became even more efficient once new inland airfields were built – notably that at Barreiras in the Brazilian state of Bahia, which opened in September 1940 – permitting a significant reduction in trip distance and travel time between the United States and Brazil as the DC-3s no longer had to follow the longer coastline.

With no forthcoming orders from Pan American or other US

Data for the Douglas DF

Dimensions: Span, 95ft; length, 69ft 10%⁄₁₆in; height, 24ft 6¼in; wing area, 1,295sq ft.

Weights: Empty, 17,315lb; loaded, 28,500lb; wing loading, 22lb/sq ft; power loading, 14.25lb/hp.

Crew: Two pilots, a radio-navigator and a steward.

Accommodation: Thirty-two seats by day, convertible into six beds for the night.

Power plant: Two 1,000hp Wright SGR-1820-G2 9-cylinder radials driving three-blade constant-speed propellers.

Performances: Max speed, 178mph at 6,800ft; cruising speed, 160mph; initial climb rate, 800ft/min; service ceiling, 13,900ft; range with 32 passengers, 1,500 miles; range with 12 passengers, 3,300 miles.

ABOVE *The HXD-2 at the Naruo plant of Kawanishi in Osaka.* (Komori)

carriers, the manufacturer was fortunate to obtain government authorization to sell the DF abroad. Two DF-191s, including the prototype, were then sold to Japan, allegedly for use by the national airline *Dai Nippon Koku K.K.* (for which registrations J-ANES and J-ANET were reserved). In fact, the DFs had been acquired at the instigation of *Dai Nippon Teikoku Kaigun Koku Hombu*, the headquarters of Japanese naval aviation, for evaluation. In Japanese naval service, the two were respectively designated HXD-1 and HXD-2 Navy Type D flying boat.

After it had been reassembled in Japan, the HXD-1 crashed during a test flight on 10 August 1938, near Shishi-Jima, a small island in the Inland Sea,[1] killing all six aboard. After being flight tested in Japan, the HXD-2 was dismantled to be studied carefully by *Kawanishi Kokuki K.K.* Information gathered during this evaluation was used by this Japanese flying boat manufacturer when designing the hull of the four-engined H8K1 flying boat (Allied code name *Emily* during the war) which first flew in January 1941.

The two other flying boats of this type built by Douglas were designated DF-195s but differed from the DF-191s only in minor

details. They were exported to the Soviet Union in 1937 and at least one was operated by Aeroflot between Moscow and Sebastopol until 1940.

For Douglas, this 'last fling with the sea' by its founder could have had serious financial consequences. Fortunately, DC-3 sales generated considerable revenues and substantial profits, offsetting several times over the loss from the DF program. The lesson had been learned and Douglas would never again venture into the flying boat market. Across the ocean, it was its DC-4, DC-6, and DC-7 propliners – later its DC-8, DC-10, and MD-11 jetliners – which, along with competitors from other manufacturers, would dominate air transportation over the oceans.

BELOW *One of the two DF-195s on the beach at Santa Monica in 1937. For some strange reason, the 'commisars' of the Soviet reception team are all sitting or standing at the extreme left.* (Douglas)

1   Many 'conspiracy advocates,' particularly in the United States, still claim that the first DF crashed while on a clandestine reconnaissance flight over a US Pacific base. Nothing has ever been provided to confirm this 'flight of fantasy.'

Chapter 6

DC-4E – Overly ambitious

By the mid-1930s, the conceptual phase of aircraft development had become a significantly different affair than it had been 10 or 15 years earlier. Not only had performance greatly increased but commercial aircraft were now fitted with more and more complex equipment and systems that had been either in their infancy or yet to be developed at the beginning of the previous decade (such as flaps, retractable undercarriage, variable-pitch propellers, radio, etc.). The path to progress was fast and enthusiasm ran high,

so much so that over confidence led to errors. This was notably the case of the fourth Douglas Commercial design which, overly complex and too costly to operate, was not put into production. This first DC-4 then became the DC-4E (E for Experimental), leaving the DC-4 designation available for what became another major success for the Santa Monica firm.

The starting point for the development of this one-off aircraft had been a request from United Air Lines in the fall of 1935 for an aircraft with twice the seating capacity of the yet-to-fly DC-3. This ambitious specification had come at a surprising time as the world economic situation was particularly depressed and as political and military tensions were on the rise. Following the October

BELOW *NX18100, the sole prototype of the triple-tailed DC-4, during a test flight in 1938.* (Douglas)

ABOVE *During a test on 5 October 1938, the crew of NX18100 feathered the propellers of engines Nos three and four to demonstrate the ability of the first DC-4 to fly in this extreme condition.* (Douglas)

1929 crash on Wall Street, the US economy had gone into a steep downward spiral. Gross National Product, which had reached a new high of $103.6 billion in 1929 (±$1,300 billion today), dropped 12% in 1930 and continued to fall until reaching a low in 1933 (after four years GDP was at nearly half its earlier level). The recovery was slow and it was only in 1940 that the GDP again reached the $100 billion mark (in current dollars), still below its 1929 high.

For Americans,[1] the Great Depression was a particularly difficult period with unemployment reaching a high of nearly 25% in 1933 and remaining above 14% until 1941. In spite of this national crisis, air transport in the United States went through a period of remarkable growth during these years. Two factors explain the growth of this industry while the rest of the Nation was suffering. Firstly, after a period of political turmoil leading to the 1934 Air Mail Emergency, US airlines had been reorganized and were then able to operate in sounder fashion. Secondly, three-engine aircraft with fixed undercarriage were being replaced by aerodynamically cleaner aircraft which were faster and markedly more comfortable for passengers. More importantly, the productivity of the newer aircraft far surpassed that of the trimotors they replaced.

Powered by three 420hp engines, the Ford 5-AT carried 15 passengers and cruised at 90mph. That conferred it an hourly productivity of 1,350 seat/miles, or 1.07 seat/miles per hp. With the Boeing 247, the Douglas DC-2, and the Douglas DC-3, hourly productivity per hp went up to 1.71, 1.77, and 2.02 seat/miles, respectively. Moreover, the twin-engine transports, particularly the DC-3, had a longer range when carrying their design load, a performance which enabled them to make fewer stops on the transcontinental route. Passengers – at least those who were not unduly suffering from the effects of the Great Depression – responded enthusiastically making it possible for airlines to generate increased revenues and profits.

In turn, the airlines got giddy. Notably the five major airlines in the United States reacted over enthusiastically to their improved financial position in what were difficult economic times for most other industries. These five air carriers were led by genuine 'captains of industry,' men who were brilliant and charismatic. At American Airlines, the head man was Cyrus R. Smith who had ultimately convinced Douglas to proceed with the development of the DST and DC-3. The leader at Eastern Air Lines was Eddie Rickenbacker, America's leading fighter ace in World War One and, earlier, a well-known race car driver and automotive designer. Those leading Pan American Airways, Transcontinental & Western, and United Airlines were the equally respected Juan Trippe, Jack Frye and William 'Pat' Patterson. It was the latter who took the leading role in pushing for an aircraft which would be twice as large as the not-yet-flown DC-3. Moreover, Patterson insisted that the new aircraft be faster than the DC-3 and that it cruise at higher altitudes, thus necessitating the use of cabin pressurization.[2]

When Pat Patterson communicated preliminary specifications for the new aircraft, the engineering interests of Donald Douglas were tickled. His business acumen, however, made him dubious about the commercial viability of such a large and advanced aircraft. In spite of the manufacturer's lukewarm reception to his suggestion, Patterson was not discouraged and, in fact, he contacted the leaders of the four other major air carriers to convince them to co-sponsor his challenging undertaking. Having determined their joint needs, they urged Douglas to come up with preliminary design details. As an enticement, they indicated that each of them planned on initially ordering four aircraft. This 20-strong potential order was enough for Douglas to go ahead.

---

1 It is not to say that Europeans and others fared better during the 1930s. However, it was the economic situation in the United States that impacted, or was expected to impact, more directly on decisions made by American airlines and aircraft manufacturers.

2 When Pat Patterson came with this unusual and demanding request, only two aircraft with pressurized cabins had been flown anywhere in the world. The first was a specially modified Dayton-Wright USD-9A (itself an American development of the de Havilland 9) which had been flown but once in 1921. The other was the two-seat, single-engine, Junkers 49 which was specially designed as a pressurized cabin research aircraft. It was first flown on 2 October 1931 and, four years later, was routinely flown at altitudes of up to 41,000ft.

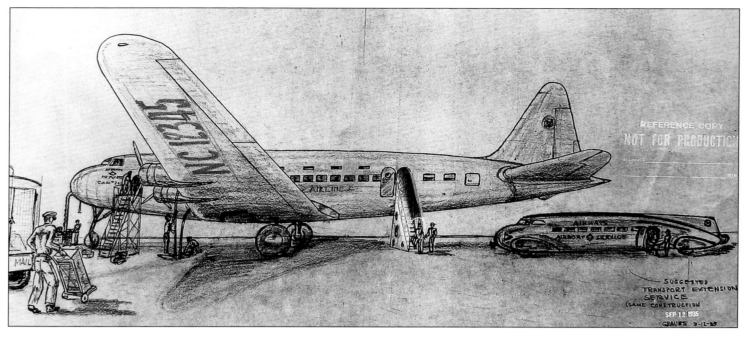

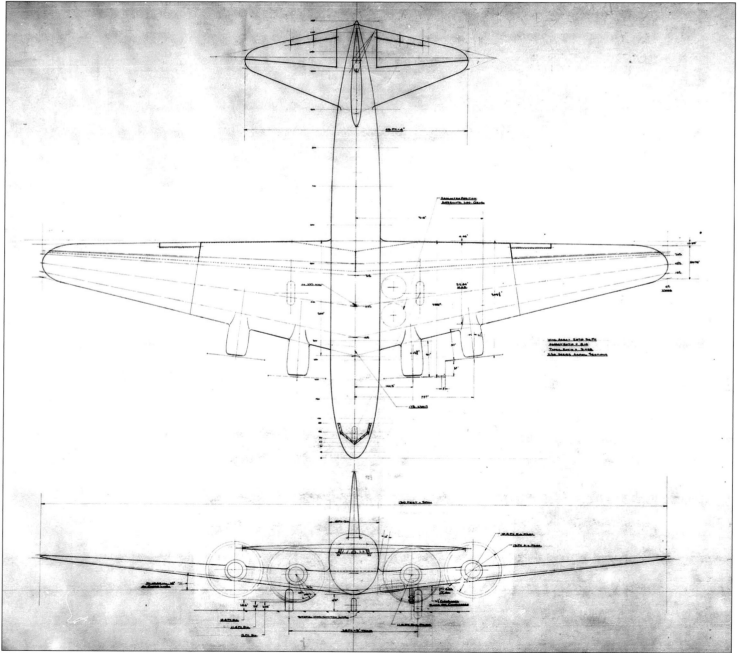

OPPOSITE TOP *Dated 12 September 1935, this company drawing shows one of the initial configurations for the tricycle variant of the DC-4. The aircraft was still shown with single vertical tail surfaces.* (Douglas)

Each undertaking to contribute $100,000 (±$1.6 million today), the five airlines signed a contract with Douglas for a prototype. Once manufacturer's tests were complete, the aircraft was to undergo 60 days of route proving with each of the five sponsoring carriers, commencing with United, the prime sponsor. The airlines were not obligated to order aircraft until satisfied with these tests.

Too many cooks

To satisfy the request of the five airlines, the team led by Arthur Raymond came up with a design remarkable for its size and weight. The first four-engine aircraft from Douglas, and its largest to date, the DC-4 was also notable on account of the diameter of its fuselage which was sufficient to install pairs of seats, convertible into beds, on both sides of the center aisle. Folding berths were to be provided above these seats/beds. Moreover, as the airlines desired, the fuselage was conceived to be pressurized at a later stage. In other respects, the new aircraft was quite conventional with a structure following on the lines adopted for the DC-1. The wing center section, to which two engines were to be mounted on either side, was to be bolted in a notch in the fuselage bottom. This

center-section and the two outboard panels were to have a multi-cellular structure with three spars. The engines were to be C-series Pratt & Whitney *Twin Wasp* radials developing 900hp at 10,000ft.

As shown in a September 1935 company rendering reproduced at the top of the preceding page, the use of a tricycle undercarriage was contemplated at the start of the project. However, a conventional gear was studied as an alternative. Both of these concepts were detailed in a report sent to the sponsors in March 1936 which also indicated that the manufacturer intended to use proven systems and equipment.[3] Unfortunately, this conservative approach was soon forgotten as the technical staffs of the five sponsoring airlines all came up with their favorite innovations. The conservative Douglas team sought, to no avail, to damper this unhealthy competition.

To begin with, the airlines opted for the use of a tricycle undercarriage.[4] Certainly, the tricycle design had the advantage both of keeping the cabin floor level and of easing operations. Conversely, by raising the rear fuselage, it brought the tail surfaces to a height incompatible with that of standard hangar doors. That led to a redesign of the tail to use triple vertical surfaces of lower height. Although it had been hoped that this would also improve directional control (particularly in an engine-out situation), this was not the case in spite of several redesigns. Using a tricycle configuration also necessitated moving the main gear legs aft.

As the design progressed, Douglas engineers and representatives of the airlines' technical departments agreed on other major upgrades. Notably, they decided to use a 115-volt direct

OPPOSITE BOTTOM AND BELOW *This March 1936 drawing shows that the aircraft was initially planned with conventional tail surfaces.* (Douglas)

3 This information differs from what has been stated previously, including in the author's prior work. The intent to have the aircraft fitted with single tail surfaces and conventional undercarriage, and to have it powered by *Twin Wasp* engines is confirmed by data included in a wind tunnel report from the Guggenheim Aeronautical Laboratory of the California Institute of Technology (GALCIT Report no 175 dated 8 June 1936).
4 To familiarize technical personnel and pilots with the peculiarity of the tricycle gear, Douglas leased an OA-4B amphibian from the Army Air Corps. That aircraft had its main gear locked in the down position and a nose strut and wheel added in the nose.

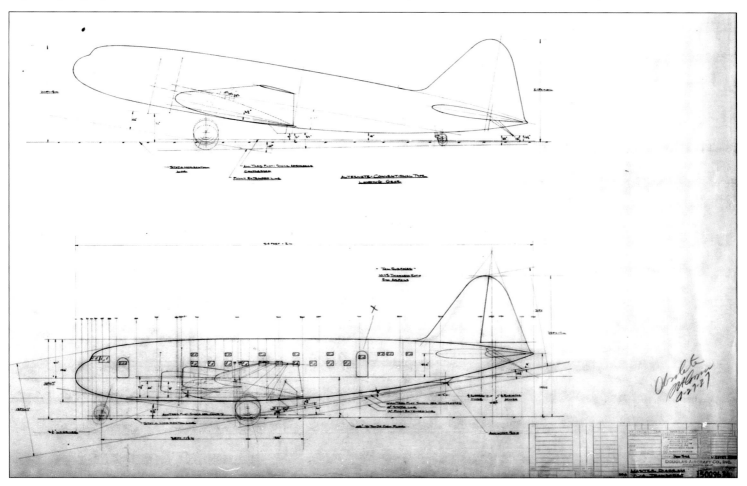

ABOVE *To gain experience with the tricycle undercarriage planned for the DC-4, Douglas modified an OA-4B by fitting it with a long-strut nose undercarriage.* (Army Air Corps)

LEFT *The Pratt & Whitney* Twin Hornet *radials powering the first DC-4 configuration proved unreliable and were not retained for later developments.* (Douglas)

BELOW *On the occasion of its roll-out, the triple-tailed DC-4 shares the ramp at Clover Field with a DC-3-194B of KLM (PH-ALN* Nandoe*) and a DC-2-112 of Eastern Air Lines (NC13737).* (Douglas)

current electrical system (instead of the 12- or 24-volt systems of the DC-2s and DC-3s) with generators driven by auxiliary engines aft of the main engines in the Nos 2 and 3 nacelles.

To offset weight increases, it was decided to replace the *Twin Wasps* with Pratt & Whitney *Twin Hornet* S1A-Gs (1,400hp on take-off and 1,150hp at 7,000ft) driving three-blade variable-pitch propellers with automatic feathering (another novelty). To improve controls in the event of an engine failure, the nacelles were angled out of the line of flight (2.5° for the inboard engines and 3° for those outboard) and down 1.5°. A total of 1,832 Imp. gallons of 100 octane petrol was to be carried in four 375 gal main tanks and four 83 gal auxiliary tanks, all of which were located between the pairs of engines. Pressure refuelling was to be accomplished through a single point under each wing panel (yet one more novelty).

The wings had a constant 7° of dihedral to the tips. Split flaps were fitted between the fuselage center line and the inboard engines while slotted flaps were provided between these engines and the joint line between the wing center section and the outboard panels. The latter had ailerons with trims. Flaps and ailerons were hydraulically operated (yet one more novel complexity). The horizontal tail surfaces had 9.5° of dihedral and the elevators had a combination of trim and servo tabs.

BELOW *This Douglas cutaway drawing shows the cabin arrangement as proposed by the Santa Monica manufacturer.* (Douglas)

Whereas the DC-1 had flown barely over eight months after a contract had been received from TWA, development of the new four-engine airliner kept falling behind schedule. This was not, however, the fault of the manufacturer. Simply put, this aircraft was the first aeronautical camel, a horse designed by a committee, as the staffs of the five customers kept vying with each other to put their own stamp on the final product. Consequently, the DC-4 was not ready to commence trials until 26 months after signature of the development contract.

Unfortunately for Douglas, as delays mounted and development costs increased, two of the sponsors lost interest before the aircraft flew. Having concluded that the DC-4 would be overly complex and difficult to maintain, and its operations unlikely to be profitable, Pan American and TWA opted out before having to pay their agreed $100,000 share of development costs. These two airlines then put their faith in the Boeing 307 *Stratoliner* and Lockheed 049 *Constellation* which respectively flew in December 1938 and January 1943.

Flight tests

To enable the aircraft to cruise at 200mph at 18,000ft (above-weather as publicists were keen to say), the five customer airlines had demanded that it be fitted with a pressurized cabin. However, before Pan American and TWA left the group, they had agreed to have the prototype completed without pressurization in order to minimize development costs.

DOUGLAS DC-4

NC 18100

(1) Radio Loop Antenna in non-metallic nose section.
(2) Location of retractable "nose" wheel of Tri-Safety Landing Gear.
(3) Pilot's Compartment.
(4) Flight Engineer, Radio and Navigation quarters.
(5) Forward Cargo Hold. 326 cubic feet of space for mail, baggage and express.
(6) Men's Dressing Room with toilet, three wash basins and couch.
(7) Electric Kitchen.
(8) Main Cabin 41 ft. long by 10 ft. 9 in. wide by 7 ft. 6 in. high. Forty lounge chairs are installed in pairs on each side of the center aisle.

These make up into single or double beds. Sleeping accommodations for 30 passengers are provided; 12 in comfortable upper berths. Cabin is steam heated, air conditioned and completely sound proofed.
(9) Berths can be made up for double occupancy or as single compartments with individual chair.
(10) Window in the sky. All berths, including uppers, have individual windows, individual reading lights and call buttons.

(11) Antenna.
(12) One of two rear Cargo Holds with a total capacity of 210 cubic feet.
(13) Seat and table arrangement permits home comforts.
(14) Check-room for clothing and hand luggage.
(15) "Bridal Suite". De luxe section with private facilities.
(16) Ladies' Lounge. Everything for milady's boudoir in spacious, elegant seclusion.

(17) Douglas Triple "S" Tail. Stability, Strength and Safety assured by this feature.
(18) In flight these huge wheels are hydraulically retracted.
(19) Four main power plants with full feathering propellers give the plane 5,600 h.p. for take-off.
(20) Auxiliary Engines. Two of these generate power for lighting, cooking and hydraulic control.

(21) Fuel tank section. Each engine has individual tank as well as interchangeable supply from total of 2,200 gallons of fuel.

Data for the DC-4E

Dimensions: Span, 138ft 3in; length, 97ft 7in; height, 24ft 6½in; wing area, 2,155sq ft.

Weights: Empty, 42,564lb; loaded, 61,500lb; maximum, 66,500lb; wing loading, 28.5lb/sq ft; power loading, 10.6lbhp.

Crew: Pilot, co-pilot, flight engineer, and two cabin attendants.

Accommodation: 42 passengers by night or 32 by night; maximum of 52 when the cabin was specially arranged.

Power plant: Four 1,400hp Pratt & Whitney *Twin Hornet* S1A1-G 14-cylinder radials driving three-blade variable pitch propellers with automatic feathering. Maximum fuel capacity, 1,832 Imp. gallons in four main and four auxiliary wing tanks.

Performance: Max speed, 245mph at 7,000ft; cruising speed, 200mph; initial climb rate, 1,175ft/min; service ceiling, 22,900ft; normal range 2,200 miles.

BELOW *During a test flight, NX18100 dumps colored fuel to demonstrate that this procedure was safe.* (Douglas)

The cockpit was arranged for a crew of three (pilot, co-pilot, and flight engineer) while two stewards or stewardesses were to take care of the passengers. Aft of the cockpit was the men's dressing room with an enclosed toilet, three wash basins, and a couch, followed by the electrical kitchen (galley). Next, the cabin was 41ft long, 10ft 9in wide, and 7ft 6in high. This was followed by a hall with the passenger entrance door on the left and faced by seating for the cabin crew. Further aft, the remaining space was divided between the 'bridal suite' with its private facilities on the right side, and the ladies' lounge with all expected amenities. Mail, cargo and baggage were carried in two belly holds with volume respectively being 326cu ft forward of the wing and 210cu ft aft.

The cabin was designed to receive ten rows of seats (two seats on each side of the aisle). For day use, seats could all face forward or could be arranged in facing pairs. For night use, the seats converted into 74in x 56in beds. The upper berths, which dropped from the ceiling like those of the DST, were 74in x 32in and were provided with narrow windows. The bridal room had its own double bed (made into seats during the day). Thus, standard accommodation was provided for 42 passengers by day or 32 by night. By replacing the men's dressing room and the ladies' lounge with lavatories, seating could be increased to 52.

Fitted with neither cabin pressurisation nor air conditioning, the prototype (fsn 1601 registered NX18100) was rolled out at Clover Field on 28 May 1938. As it was coming out of the hangar, the nose wheel broke through the pavement, fortunately without damage to

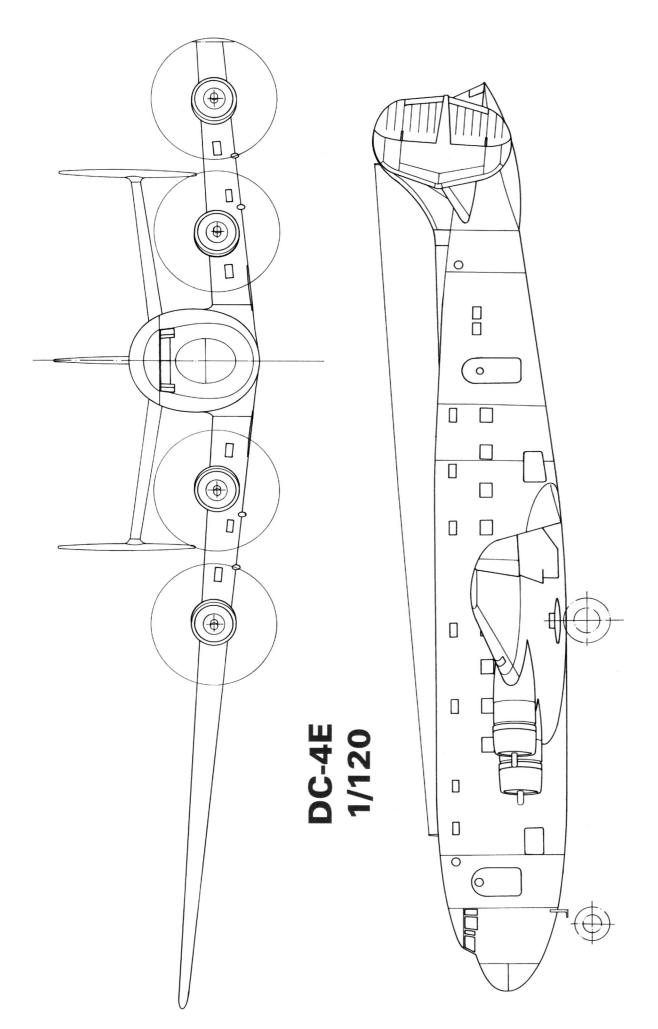

DC-4E
1/120

ABOVE *Bearing the markings of United Air Lines, the original DC-4 is shown here during a visit to Wright Field.* (Army Air Corps)

the aircraft itself. Following repairs to the nose wheel and ground testing, Carl Cover first flew NX18100 on 7 June 1938.

Except for longitudinal stability leaving a bit to be desired, flight handling was found fully satisfactory. Likewise, the tricycle undercarriage came in for much praise as it endowed the aircraft with improved take-off performance and eased handling in cross winds. Conversely, engines[5] and systems were found troublesome. Nevertheless, after the aircraft had logged 500 flight hours in six months in the hands of pilots from the manufacturers, the sponsoring airlines, and the Bureau of Air Commerce, it was judged ready for carrying passenger during route proving flights. No Approved Type Certificate was delivered and, for this proving period, the aircraft operated under a temporary dispensation.

Repainted in United Air Lines markings, bearing the title *Super Mainliner*, and carrying the permanent registration NC18100, the aircraft was operated for one month by the first of the three remaining sponsors. Passengers liked it and the media reported favorably. United, however, concluded that the aircraft had too many seats for the existing demand and that it was too costly to operate, primarily due to the complexity of its systems. The two other remaining sponsors, American and Eastern, did not even avail themselves of their right to operate the aircraft for one month. Instead, they joined United in asking Douglas to develop a new four-engine aircraft retaining the tricycle undercarriage but having single tail surfaces (this being made possible by the fact that new hangars would have taller doors). The result of this completely new design was the aircraft that took over the DC-4 designation and gained fame as the C-54 *Skymaster* during World War Two (see Chapter 9). The three-tailed aircraft then became the DC-4E.

A financial fiasco

For the manufacturer, this program ended with heavy financial losses. Design, development, and testing costs for the only Douglas

with triple rudders ran to a total of $1.7 million (±$26 million today) against which only $300,000 was received from American, Eastern, and United, the three sponsors remaining after Pan American and TWA had opted out. The only 'contributions' of the two non-starters had been entirely negative as their inputs had added both to conflicting demands from the other three and to the overall complexity of the program. Douglas avoided possible financial failure only because DC-3s were then being built in large number and as each delivery of this 'money machine' was contributing to its pecuniary well-being. The financial hole left after the DC-4E failed to enter production was also partially filled by its sale to Japan.

In 1938, *Dai Nippon Teikoku Kaigun Koku Hombu* (the headquarters of Japanese naval aviation) realized that it would likely require four-engined bombers with a range of 3,000 to 3,500 nautical miles. Performance such as this was then beyond the reach of the Japanese aeronautical industry. Consequently, the naval aviation headquarters began looking abroad. Its interest soon centered on the Douglas four-engined airliner which had just been rejected by its sponsors. When approached, Douglas was only too pleased to dispose of its white elephant, cover for the Japanese acquisition being provided by the national airline, *Nippon Koku K.K.*

Shipped as deck cargo from Alameda, California, the DC-4E was reassembled in Japan by Nakajima Hikoki K.K. After initial testing, the now Japanese DC-4E was used for several airline publicity flights intended to provide a cover for its ultimate military use as the LXD-1 (Navy Experimental Type D Transport). After the DC-4E disappeared from public eye, rumours were conveniently circulated that it had crashed into Tokyo Bay. In fact, it was dismantled and reverse-engineered by Nakajima which used the experience gained in that process to design its G5N1 (Navy Experimental 13-Shi Bomber) which was named *Shinzan* (Mountain Recess). That aircraft had wings of similar span, area, and geometry as the DC-4E but had a new fuselage, a twin tail, and horizontal tail surfaces without dihedral. Four G5N1s were built with 1,844hp Nakajima NK7A *Mamoru* 11 radials, and two as G5N-2s with 1,509hp Mitsubishi *Kasei* 12s. Two of the G5N1s were re-engined with *Kasei* engines and, along with the two G5N2s, were modified as transport aircraft with the G5N2-L designation.

---

5   So unsatisfactory were the *Twin Hornet* engines that they only powered two other prototypes, the North American XB-21 and the Stearman XA-21.

RIGHT *With outer tail panels and outboard wing panels removed, the DC-4 is being loaded at Alameda for transportation to Japan.* (Douglas)

BELOW *The original DC-4 is shown on approach to the Tokyo airport during its evaluation in Japan. Contrary to wartime propaganda, the aircraft did not crash in Tokyo Bay but was dismantled by Nakajima to be reverse-engineered.* (DR)

BOTTOM *Nakajima G5N2-Ls, such as this damaged aircraft photographed at Atsugi after the war had ended, retained the wing design and engine mounting of the first DC-4.* (USN, Giuseppe Picarella collection)

LEFT *The original DC-4 during final finishing before the control surfaces received their fabric covering.* (Douglas)

BELOW *NX18100 being towed out of the assembly hall on 18 June 1938.* (Douglas)

LEFT *The main wheel of the DC-4 had a diameter of 5ft 6in. Their tyres weighed 350lb.* (Douglas)

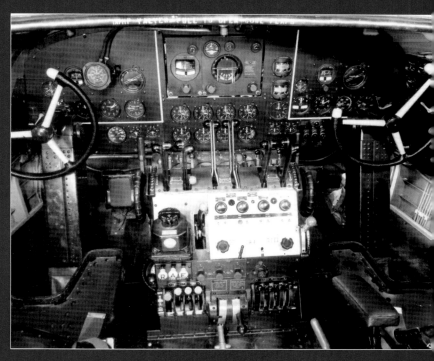

TOP LEFT *The cabin of the experimental DC-4 during its evaluation in Japan.* (Douglas)

TOP RIGHT *The cockpit of NX18100.* (Douglas)

BELOW *(photos 1, 2 and 3): Three views of the cabin of the experimental DC-4: (1) standard day accommodation with 2 + 2 seating (2) early proposal for providing recording equipment for business travelers and (3) twin berths.* (Douglas)

ABOVE *NX18100 parked in front of the terminal at Mines Field, Los Angeles.* (Douglas)

①

②

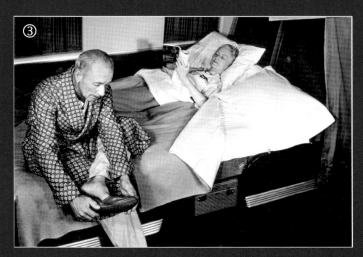

③

Chapter 7

DC-5 – Off the beaten path

ABOVE *After completing flight trials, the first DC-5 was modified into a corporate transport and sold to William E. Boeing, the retired founder of the Boeing Company. (Douglas)*

LEFT AND OPPOSITE *Before designing the DC-5, the El Segundo engineering team had studied the feasibility of developing mailplane aircraft from the DB-7 bomber (drawing at left) and the Model 10 (drawing on facing page), an all-new twin-engined design. (Douglas)*

The Northrop Corporation was delivered a hard blow in 1934 when the Aeronautics Branch of the Department of Commerce decided it would no longer authorize single-engined aircraft for use in carrying passengers at night or over routes with limited emergency landing facilities. Unfortunately, this Douglas subsidiary had hoped that its single-engined *Delta* would find a ready market with airlines in the United States. Furthermore, at about the same time, the entry into service of new twin-engined airliners enabled these same airlines to have enough mail-carrying capacity to eliminate the need for specialized mailplanes, thus depriving Northrop of yet another of its hoped-for markets, that for the *Gamma*. Saved from more serious difficulties by military contracts for its BT-1 carrier bombers and A-17 attack aircraft, Northrop still wanted to be a player in the civil market. However, buyers could not be found for either a series of small twin-engined airliners (studied first by the Northrop Corporation and then by the El Segundo Division of Douglas) or a derivative of the DB-7 light bomber (see page 339) proposed as the DC-7 mailplane. Nevertheless, Edward H. Heinemann, the chief engineer at El Segundo, remained convinced that the experience gained with the DB-7 and its tricycle undercarriage would eventually lead to the development and production of airliners. This conviction became a reality when Donald Douglas asked his El Segundo team to respond to a request from KLM.

By 1938, KLM had become the main foreign customer for Douglas as it had 18 DC-2s and 20 DC-3s in service, with more of the latter on order through Fokker. However, prior to becoming a Douglas customer, KLM had long relied on a series of high-wing Fokker aircraft and it believed that this configuration was preferred by passengers who could thus see the ground regardless of where they were sitting. This belief led the airline to communicate to Douglas its wish to obtain a high-wing airliner with performance comparable or superior to that of the DC-3 for use on its European network. Not surprisingly, as the Dutch airline was a good customer, its desiderata carried much weight with Donald Douglas. When the Santa Monica team showed only moderate interest in KLM's request as it was already overworked with existing programs and new projects, El Segundo jumped with alacrity on the opportunity to get back into the civil market.

The orphan from El Segundo

In response to the KLM request for a high-wing airliner tailored for European routes (i.e., with less range), Ed Heinemann and his team chose to retain the basic concept of the Northrop multi-cellular wing built in three sections but mounted high on the fuselage. The outer panels had 6° 30' of dihedral. The center section, with the engine nacelles and wheel wells for the main undercarriage, was without dihedral. Although that wing section was mounted high on the fuselage, spars did not penetrate the cabin making for a 72in unencumbered center aisle, high enough not to inconvenience most tall Dutchmen.

The fuselage of elliptical cross-section (with maximum external width of 8ft and maximum height of 7ft 6in) resulted in a cabin that was 20ft 9in long and 97in wide. Various accommodations were proposed with seating ranging from 16 passengers when installing a galley and lavatory, to 26 without these amenities. In both instances, there were two seats on each side of the center aisle. Depending on the number of seats fitted, two compartments provided between 155 and 244cu ft for baggage and freight. If requested by a customer, the cabin could be fitted with convertible seats/beds for 14.

While KLM was reviewing the specifications and drawings submitted by Douglas, an unexpected customer came onto the scene. Founded in 1935 through the merger of three smaller airlines, British Airways Ltd was a public company which had inherited a mix of ageing aircraft from its forebears. The new a airline began acquiring better performing aircraft from abroad in order to compete more effectively with the larger Imperial Airways which operated a fleet of antiquated aircraft. In 1937, British Airways put Junkers 52s and Lockheed 10 *Electras* in service before adding Lockheed 14s[1] during the following year. Then, with impending competition of the first modern landplanes from the local industry – the 22-seat de Havilland D.H.91 *Albatross* and the 17-seat D.H.95 *Flamingo* from the same manufacturer – British Airways contacted Douglas to obtain technical and pricing information for the DC-5.

While negotiations with British Airways were underway, KLM

---

1 Two of these aircraft gained some notoriety when used to transport Prime Minister Neville Chamberlin to/from Germany for meetings with Chancellor Adolf Hitler leading to the signing of the Munich Agreement in September 1938.

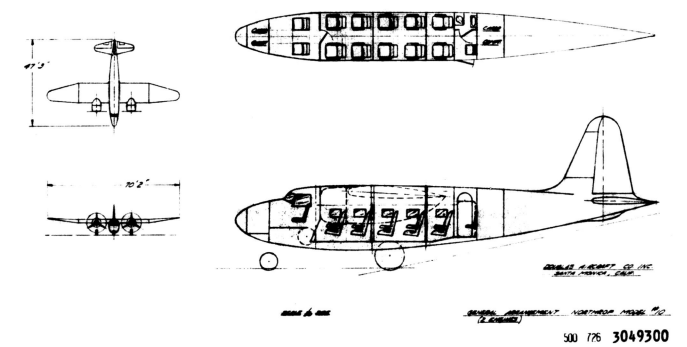

and Douglas signed a letter of intent on 13 December 1938 and, during the following month, the airline made public its intent to acquire four DC-5s. Still, the sale of these aircraft was not finalized for several months as Dutch public opinion and media were against KLM ordering yet another series of aircraft from the California manufacturer. In the end, overcoming public disapproval, KLM signed the definite contract on 22 May 1939.

Three months later, on 30 August, British Airways and Douglas signed a contract for nine aircraft calling for the airline to make a £27,912 (±£1.425 million today) deposit, an amount representing one-fourth of total contract value. The aircraft were to be shipped as deck cargo between December 1939 and March 1940 and were to be registered G-AFYG to G-AFYO. However, four days after contract signature, Britain declared war on Germany. The DC-5 contract was cancelled by the Air Ministry and the amount deposited was used to pay for other aircraft ordered by the British Purchasing Commission.

With the war in Europe creating fear and economic concerns, two additional orders for DC-5s were cancelled by airlines operating way out of the war zone, one for six aircraft from Pennsylvania-Central Airlines in the United States and one for two from *Sociedad Colombo-Alemana de Transportes Aéreos* (SCADTA) in Colombia. That left Douglas with only small orders from KLM, the USN, and the USMC.

The beginning

Registered NX21701 and bearing the Northrop/El Segundo Division fsn 411, the first DC-5 was rolled out in February 1939. Powered by 900hp Wright *Cyclone* SGR-1820-F62 radials, it was first flown by Carl Cover at Mines Field on 20 February. Flight trials continued without major difficulties, the most troublesome problem

BELOW *A DC-5 under construction at the El Segundo plant.* (Douglas)

stemming from poor control response when using the elevators. Fortunately, a quick solution was found and the horizontal tail surfaces were given 15° of dihedral to take the elevators out of the disturbed airflow generated by the high-mounted wing.

While the aircraft was in the shop to be fitted with its revised horizontal tail surfaces, El Segundo took advantage of the downtime to install more powerful engines – 1,100hp *Cyclone* SGR-1820-G102As – as specified by yet another unexpected customer. This time it was a private individual, William E. Boeing, the retired founder of the Seattle aircraft manufacturer. Bill Boeing also requested that the cabin of the aircraft be fitted with four pairs of seats, two three-place sofas, and a desk. Lavatory and baggage compartments were to remain unchanged. In 1940, after receiving an attractive paint scheme (as illustrated by the photo on page 152), being named 'Rover' by its new owner, and having its registration changed to NC21701, the first DC-5 became what we would call today a business aircraft. Bill Boeing had only made limited use of the aircraft when it was taken over by the US Navy in February 1942 to become the sole R3D-3 with BuNo 08005. In January 1944, the R3D-3 was transferred to NAS Banana River, Florida, where it was subsequently used to test blind landing equipment. Shortly after being withdrawn from military use at the end of June 1946, the first DC-5 was broken up.

The Dutch DC-5s

Planned to be used on KLM's European network in a 22-passenger configuration, the four DC-5s ordered by this airline were given Dutch registrations PH-AXA, -AXB, -AXE, and -AXG. However, they had not been delivered by the time the Netherlands was overrun by German troops in May 1940. Paid for and owned by the Royal Dutch Airline, two were diverted to Curaçao to be used on KLM's network in the West Indies (*West Indisch Bedrijf*) after being re-registered as PJ-AIW and PJ-AIZ. The other two went to KNILM in the Dutch East Indies where they were operated from Batavia as PK-ADA and PK-ADB.

After flying in the Caribbean for one year, the first two were sent to Batavia to become PK-ADC and PK-ADD with KNILM. They flew without incident over the network in the Dutch East Indies until 9 February 1942 when PK-ADA was damaged at the Batavia-Kemayoran airport during the first Japanese air attack. After temporary repairs, this aircraft was ferried to the technical base at Bandung where, unfortunately, it remained when the Japanese overran the last Allied defences on Java. The aircraft was then taken by the Japanese to Tachikawa, on Honshu, where it underwent flight testing for *Dai Nippon Teikoku Rikugun K k tai* (the Imperial Japanese Army Air Force) in 1942. Later, it was used as a military transport aircraft and as a radio-navigation trainer. It was still airworthy in February 1944 but its ultimate fate is not known.

The three other DC-5s were operated in the Dutch East Indies until they had to be evacuated to Australia in early March 1942. Down Under, they continued to be flown by KNILM crews until handed over to the Allied Directorate for Air Transport. Given USAAF designations (C-110A-DE) and serial numbers (44-83230 to 44-83232), they were mostly operated with pseudo-Australian civil registrations (VHCXA to VHCXC) by Australian National Airways and the USAAF 374th Troop Carrier Group. At war's end, the last got a bona fide civil registration, VH-ARD, and continued to fly with ANA until stored in July 1946.

In 1948, when Jewish patriots and sympathizers had arm dealers scrounging around discretely to acquire aircraft for the air force planned for the about-to-be-created State of Israel, the old KLM/KNILM/USAAF/ANA DC-5 went to New Holland Airways on 27 April. Almost immediately, ownership was transferred to Martin Allen Rybakoff and VH-ARD was ferried to Rome after leaving Australia on 10 May 1948. The aircraft was in Haifa 18 days later, where it was 'sold' to the newly created *Tsvah Haganah le Israel/Heyl Ha'Avir* (soon to become a formidable air force). Assigned to *Tayeset 102* (102 Squadron), first at Sde Dov and then at Ramat David, the Israeli DC-5 was used mostly as a transport; however, it also flew a few offensive sorties during which bombs were pushed out through the removed entrance door and for which it acquired the

ABOVE *The DC-5 prototype, NX21701, photographed at Clover Field, the site of the parent company in Santa Monica.* (Douglas)

nickname 'Bagel Bomber.' This last airworthy DC-5 was damaged in a heavy landing on 4 January 1949 and, although it never flew again, it was then used as an instructional airframe by the Tel Aviv Aeronautical Technical School until broken up, probably in 1955.

The military models

With war in Europe and the likelihood of the United Sates remaining out of the conflict increasingly in doubt, the US Navy and the US Marine Corps found themselves with even fewer transport aircraft than the Army Air Corps. To fill this void and

BELOW *PJ-AIW, one of the DC-5s that went to the West Indies division of KLM, was named* Wakago *(goose).* (Douglas)

TOP *PK-ADA, a captured DC-5 of KNILM, was tested at Tachikawa in 1942 by the Japanese Army Air Force.* (Peter M. Powers collection)

ABOVE *A R5D-2 of Marine Utility Squadron One (VMJ-1) at Saint Croix in the Virgin Islands.* (USMC)

LEFT *A Hollywood-style advertising photograph showing paratroopers around a R5D-2.* (LOC)

OPPOSITE *Two DC-5s were shipped to the Dutch West Indies as deck cargo aboard a Norwegian freighter.* (Douglas)

to help the Douglas El Segundo Division – one of its primary suppliers of carrier-based aircraft – overcome disappointing DC-5 sales, the Navy Department ordered seven of these aircraft for delivery in 1940. The first three went to the Navy as R3D-1s (BuNos 1901 to 1903) with 16 seats and larger cargo compartments (with a total of 278cu ft versus 155cu ft for those of the Dutch DC-5s). The others were delivered as R3D-2s to the Marine Corps (BuNos 1904 to 1907) with reinforced cabin floor and a double cargo loading door instead of the single passenger entrance door. Both naval models were powered by 1,000hp Wright R-1820-44 radials and had their fuel tank capacities increased from 458 to 541 Imp. gallons.

BuNo 1901 crashed before delivery, but the other two R3D-1s served with the Navy until BuNo 1902 was withdrawn from use in January 1946. The four Marine Corps R3D-2s were assigned as partial equipment to transport squadrons VMJ-1 and VMJ-151 on the East Coast, and to VMJ-2 and VMJ-252 on the opposite coast. The last three were withdrawn in October 1946.

Projected models

Hoping to increase market appeal of its DC-5, the El Segundo team proposed two rather different variants. The first was to retain the engines and configuration of the land-based DC-5s but was to have been fitted with twin Edo floats. The other, primarily intended to operate overwater, particularly in the Caribbean, was to have had the two radial engines replaced by four 600hp Ranger SGV-770B-7 12-cylinder, liquid-cooled engines. In this instance, maximum take-off weight was increased from 21,900 to 26,750lb but cruising speed went down from 192 to 180mph.

Export customers were also offered a twin-engined military variant that could be used to carry either 30 troops on bench seats on the sides of the cabin or 44 100lb bombs. Three flexible machine guns were to be fitted in nose, dorsal, and tail positions. No customer was found for this aircraft which had limited performance for combat operations.

America's entry into the war put an end to these projects as the El Segundo Division was instructed to give priority to large scale production of its SBD *Dauntless* scout bombers.

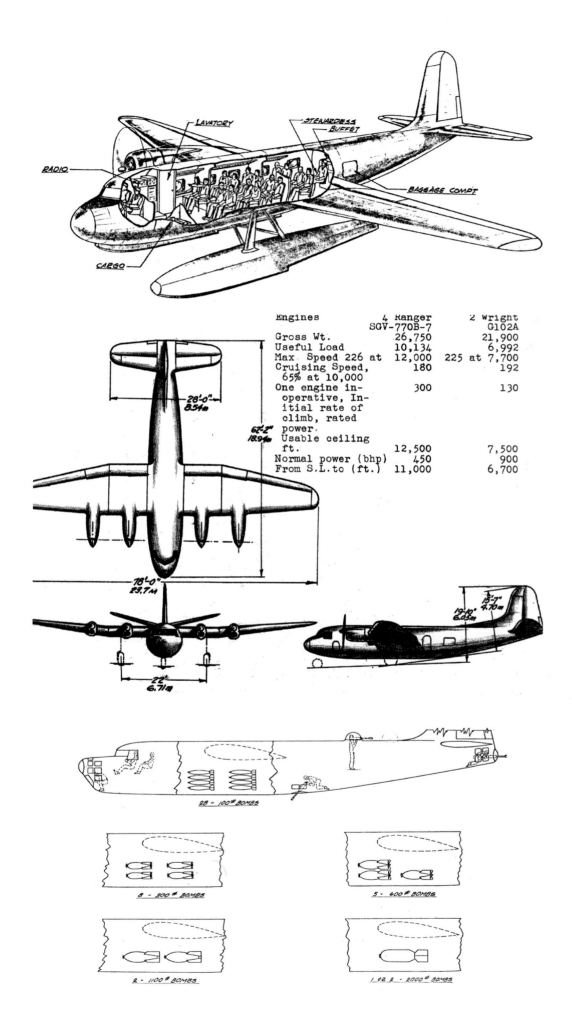

Engines	4 Ranger SGV-770B-7	2 Wright G102A
Gross Wt.	26,750	21,900
Useful Load	10,134	6,992
Max. Speed 226 at	12,000	225 at 7,700
Cruising Speed, 65% at 10,000	180	192
One engine in- operative, In- itial rate of climb, rated power.	300	130
Usable ceiling ft.	12,500	7,500
Normal power (bhp)	450	900
From S.L.to (ft.)	11,000	6,700

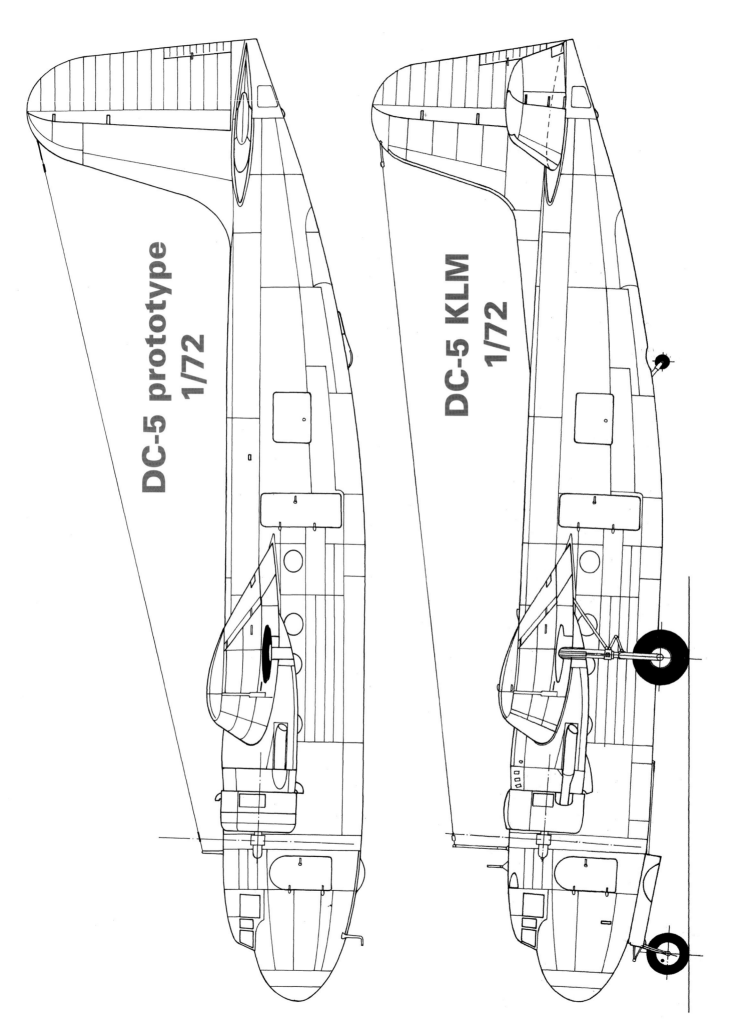

DC-5 prototype
1/72

DC-5 KLM
1/72

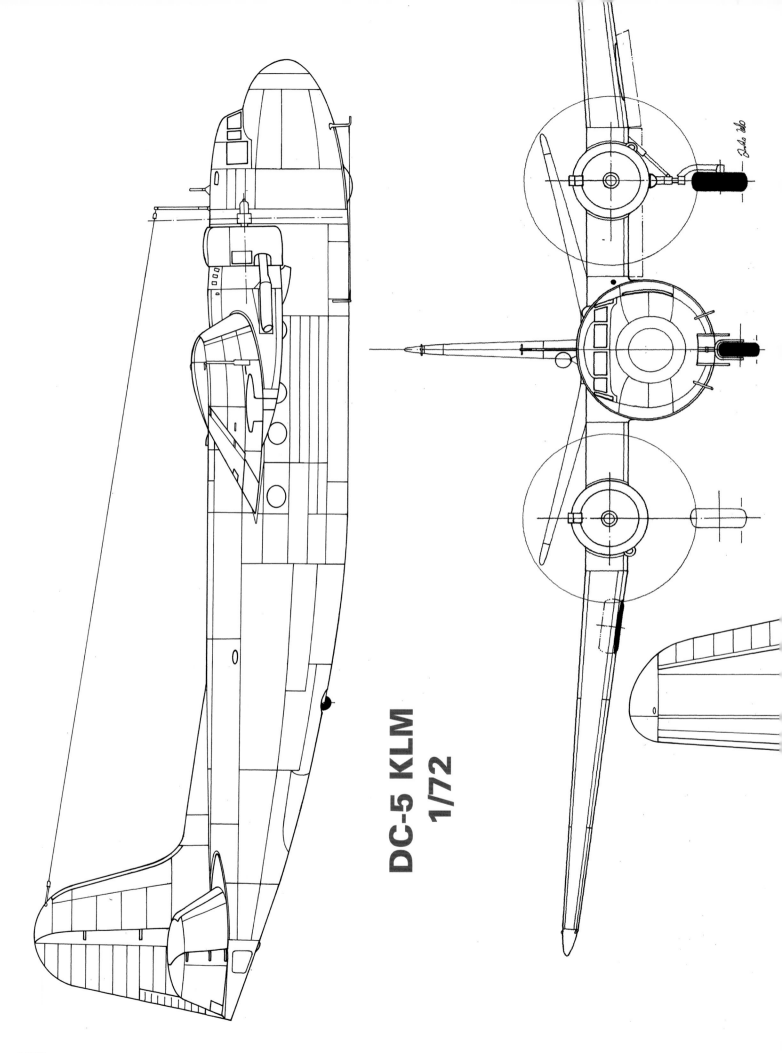

DC-5 KLM
1/72

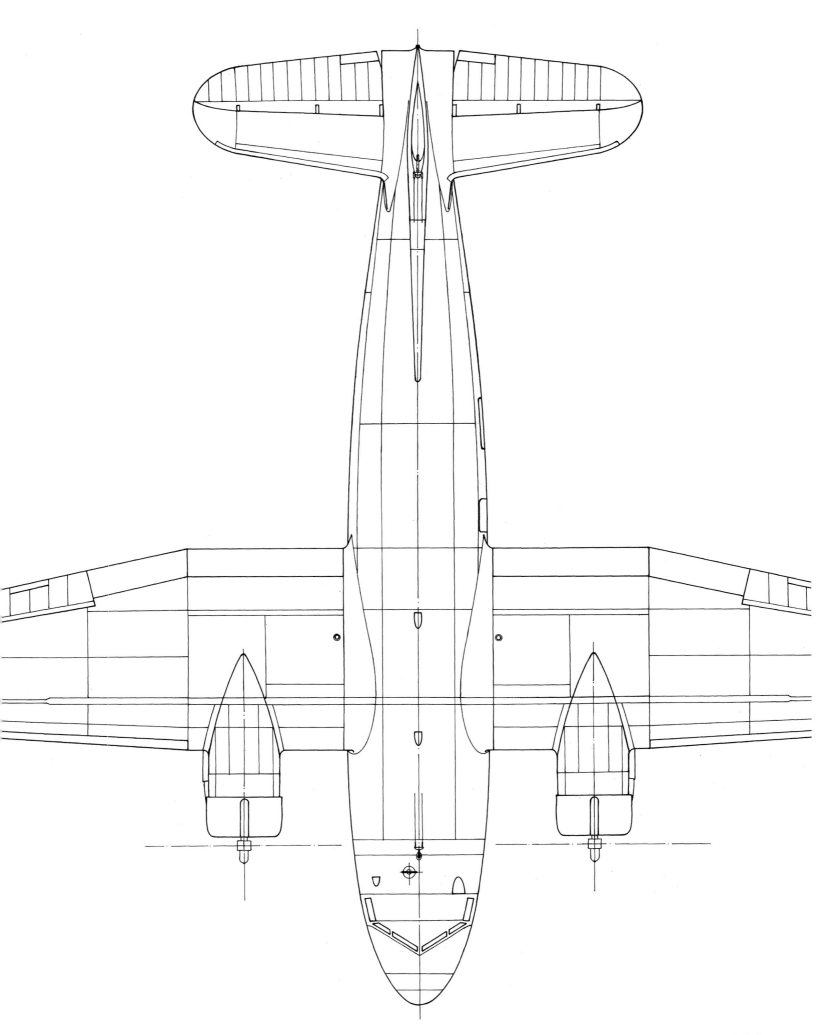

Chapter 8

C-47 – The war horse

Covering mostly military DC-2 models (35 C-39s and one C-42), contract AC 11137 from the War Department, also included the order for the first military derivative of the DC-3. This C-41 was acquired to become the transport for the Chief of the Air Corps, then Maj. Gen. Oscar M. Westover. Assigned serial 38-502, fsn 2053 was delivered on 22 October 1938, by which time Gen. Westover

BELOW *One of the principal missions assigned to Troop Carrier Squadrons of the USAAF, whether operating in Europe, the Mediterranean, the Pacific, or Burma, was the towing of gliders during airborne operations. Training for Douglas C-47 and Waco CG-4 pilots was initially provided by the 89th Troop Carrier Group (to which these three belonged) at Sedalia Army Air Base in Missouri.* (Boeing)

had been killed in an aircraft accident and had been replaced by Maj. Gen. Henry H. 'Hap' Arnold. As the C-41 was powered by two 1,200hp R-1830-21s, it was more of a P&W-powered DC-3A than a Wright-powered DC-3 in spite of appearing as a DC-3-253 in the manufacturer's records. Its cabin was fitted with 14 swivel seats and a work desk. The next military DC-3 derivative was a DC-3-253A, again with R-1830-21 engines, for the Secretary of War. Its cabin, essentially that of the DC-3B, had seats convertible into beds forward and 10 standard seats aft. This C-41A (fsn 2145, 40-70) was delivered in September 1939. Both the C-41 and the C-41A remained with the USAAF during the war before moving onto the US civil registry. Today these 'warbirds,' N41HQ and N341A, are still flying.

These two long-lived DC-3 derivatives were followed on Douglas production lines by no fewer than 10,183 military transport aircraft derived from the DC-3. Most were built in two related series: the

C-47 and R4D troop/cargo aircraft and the C-53 and C-117 troop/personnel transports. In addition, 149 DC-3s and DC-3As ordered by civil customers were delivered with military designations as they had been taken over by the US government before completion. Finally, 93 DSTs, DST-As, DC-3s, DC-3As, and DC-3Bs which had been delivered to US airlines were given military designations after they were impressed.

USAAF models built by Douglas

The satisfactory experience gained with its C-33s and C-39s prompted the Army Air Corps to adopt a derivative of the DC-3 as its standard all-purpose transport. These C-47s had a double cargo door, similar but larger than that of the C-39, and a reinforced cabin floor with snatch block, idler pulley, and tie-down fittings. A first contract, AC 15847, was signed on 16 September 1940, calling for 147 C-47s to be built in the new Long Beach plant. Over the next five years, this California plant turned out no fewer than 4,072 C-47/C-47A/C-47B-DLs ordered by the Army Air Corps/USAAF, as well as 66 R4D-1s ordered directly by the USN. In addition, 5,364 C-47A/C-47B/TC-47B-DKs and 17 C-117A-DKs were built in the government plant in Oklahoma City.[1]

As war clouds gathered and as the United States had undertaken to deliver aircraft to the United Kingdom under the Lend-Lease program, the War Department and the Navy Department concluded that they could not wait for production in Long Beach to get in full swing to obtain the required troop transport aircraft. Accordingly, the War Department supplemented the first C-47 contract with one (AC 18393 dated 24 June 1941) for an initial lot of 92 C-53s to be built in the Santa Monica plant.

ABOVE *The second military DC-3 was the C-41A in the Army Air Corps/USAAF record and the DC-3A-253A in that of the manufacturer. Its cabin was similar to that of the DC-3Bs of TWA with sleeping accommodations forward and airline type seats aft.* (Army Air Corps)

Three versions, C-47, C-53, and C-117, were built by Douglas under USAAF contracts.

C-47: Ordered in September 1940, 14 months before the Japanese attack on Pearl Harbor brought the United States into the war, this version was exclusively built in Long Beach (hence the DL suffix added to its full model designation). These aircraft were delivered with 1,200hp Pratt & Whitney R-1830-92 radial engines developing 1,050hp at 7,500ft, and 669 Imp. gallon fuel tanks.[2] In addition, up to nine 83 Imp. gallon auxiliary tanks could be installed in the fuselage for ferrying; not all were used for load-carrying flights over long sectors (particularly overwater). The C-47-DLs differed primarily from civil DC-3As in having a reinforced metal floor with cargo tie-downs and the passenger door on the left side replaced by a double door (7ft wide with height tapering from 5ft 10½in forward to 4ft 7½in aft). For loading/unloading cumbersome cargo (including vehicles such as Jeeps), both doors were opened against the fuselage side, one toward the nose and one toward the tail. For personnel transport, only the forward portion of this door was used. For dropping paratroopers, this portion of the door was simply removed. Compared with that of prewar DC-3As, the empty weight of the C-47 was up by nearly one ton, but cargo load was not reduced as maximum take-off weight rose to 31,000lb.

Starting with fsn 9000 – the C-47-DL 42-5693 delivered in January 1943 – late model C-47s and all C-47As, C-47Bs, and C-117s were fitted during production with strengthened wing tips.

---

1   The first C-47 contract for this Oklahoma plant, AC 28045 dated 19 September 1942, covered 1,799 C-47As and C-47Bs.

2   A wartime modification saw the unprotected wing tanks replaced by self-sealing tanks.

ABOVE *Before production of C-47s began in Long Beach, Douglas applied white tape on a DC-3 being built in Santa Monica to outline the modifications to be incorporated in the C-47. The size of the planned double door on the rear fuselage of the C-47 contrasts with the smaller opening for the passenger door of the DC-3.* (Douglas)

BELOW *The crew of a 75mm field howitzer poses without great enthusiasm for a staged photograph.* (Signal Corps)

Other easily spotted differences included the application of standard camouflage (olive drab for upper surfaces and neutral gray for lower surfaces), the addition of an astrodome aft of the cockpit, and the installation of cabin windows incorporating a punch-out center through which rifles could be fired in a rather utopian defense against fighter aircraft. Other changes incorporated early during production saw attachment points mounted beneath the fuselage to enable the external carriage of cumbersome loads or six parachute containers (a modification inspired by the adventure of the CNAC DC-2½, see page 100) and a glider towing hook[3] replacing the standard tail cone of airliners and early production C-47s.

Standard military crews for C-47s were comprised of a pilot, a co-pilot, a flight engineer, and a radio operator; for long flights, particularly over water, a navigator was added. Up to 28 airborne or parachute troops sat on folding benches (initially wood but later canvas webbing) on each side of the cabin. Alternative loads included either 18 or 24 stretchers for medical evacuees with three attendants or 6,000lb of military cargo.

The first of 965 C-47-DLs, 41-7722, came off the new assembly line in Long Beach in November 1941 and was officially accepted by the USAAF on 23 December. These first C-47s and later models were officially given the name *Skytrain*. However, in America they became universally known as 'Gooney Birds' as their appearance on approach and landing reminded people of the rather hilarious touch-down of Albatrosses. In the Commonwealth, and then in

3 Whereas the towing of military gliders by C-47s is well known (see photo on page 162), few details of a civilian experiment remain. In 1946, Winged Cargo Inc. of Philadelphia, Pennsylvania, acquired five surplus C-47As and at least one Waco CG-4 glider with the intent of providing cargo services in the US and the Caribbean. The only recorded glider-towing flight took place between Philadelphia, Miami, Cuba, and Puerto Rico on 24 April 1946.

much of the rest of the world, first military C-47s and then civil DC-3s, were almost universally called *Dakotas* (see footnote on page 170).

C-47A: The second model in this series was the one produced in the largest number: 2,954 C-47A-DLs in Long Beach and 2,299 C-47A-DKs in Oklahoma City. Like the C-47-DLs, they were powered by 1,200hp R-1830-92s fitted with a single-speed supercharger and rated at 1,050hp at 7,500ft. Conversely, they differed in having a 24-volt electrical system in lieu of 12-volt and hot air heating instead of steam heaters.

C-47B: To improve performance at higher altitudes, a critical consideration during operations across the Himalayas, 300 C-47B-DLs and 2,932 C-47B-DKs were powered by R-1830-90Cs. The two-speed supercharger fitted to these engines gave them maximum ratings of 1,200hp on take-off at sea level, 1,100hp at 6,100ft and 1,000hp between 12,500 and 14,500ft. In other respects, the C-47Bs were identical to the C-47As.

The last aircraft with a C-47 designation, serial 45-1139, a C-47B-50-DK, was delivered to the USAAF on 23 October 1945, a little over two months after World War Two had ended.

TC-47B: In the midst of C-47B production, the Oklahoma City plant built 133 TC-47B-DKs which were equipped as navigation trainers. They were identified externally by a row of astrodomes on top of their fuselage. In other respects, their airframe, systems, and power plants were those of C-47Bs.

XC-47C: Having to plan for providing logistical support during what promised to be a long campaign in the Pacific, the USAAF had to face the likelihood of not having airfields available, at least initially, on many islands where troops would have to be supported. The easiest solution to this problem was the fitting of floats to existing transport aircraft. Douglas was instructed to install a pair of Edo Model 78 floats to a C-47-DL (fsn 7365, 42-5671) which would be re-designated XC-47C-DL after modifications. Each of these

ABOVE *An early Jeep (a Willys Model MA) is driven aboard a C-47 during a loading demonstration on 18 February 1942.* (Douglas)

single-step metal floats was fitted with two retractable wheels and could carry 250 Imp. gallons of fuel.

Begun in July 1942, flight tests confirmed the feasibility of obtaining a fleet of float-equipped C-47Cs. In flight and on smooth water, the XC-47C handled satisfactorily but several deficiencies

BELOW *Field loading of bulky construction equipment was an arduous task for the men of the Army Corps of Engineers.* (USAF)

ABOVE *Having run off the runway at Amchitka in the Aleutians, this C-47A-50-DL of the 42nd Troop Carrier Squadon is about to be either removed for repair or to become a source of spare parts.* (NNAM)

during other phases of operation were identified. Notably, the float-equipped aircraft could operate only from the smoothest water, proved overly sensitive to cross winds and its tyres failed frequently during landings. Nonetheless, Edo received a contract for 150 sets of floats. Some were used to equip a small number of C-47s which were briefly operated in New Guinea, Alaska, and the Aleutians.

C-53: As a stopgap pending deliveries of all-purpose C-47s from the Long Beach and Oklahoma City plants, the USAAF ordered 221 C-53-DOs to be built as troop transports on the DC-3 production line in Santa Monica. Powered by R-1830-92s, C-53s did not have the reinforced cabin floor and double cargo door of the C-47s. Their cabin was fitted with 28 metal seats in seven rows of 2+2. They also had a towing cleat for use as glider tugs.

BELOW *Fitted with amphibious floats, this C-47A-75-DL has become a C-47C. Belonging to the 54th Troop Carrier Squadron, it was photographed in Alaska during the winter of 1944–45.* (Douglas)

XC-53A-DO: This was the designation given to a C-53 (fsn 4932, 42-6480) which, for test purposes only, had its trailing-edge split flaps replaced by full-span slotted flaps and a hot-air wing deicing system in place of the standard pneumatic deicing boots of the other military derivatives of the DC-3.

C-53B-DO: For operations in cold weather during the construction of the Alaska–Canada road in 1942, eight C-53-DO airframes were modified with winterized equipment, auxiliary fuselage tanks, and an astrodome.

C-53C-DO: Unlike the purpose-built C-53s and C-53Ds, and the modified XC-53A and C-53Bs, the 17 C-53C-DOs were civil DC-3As requisitioned while under construction and completed to military specifications (see table on page 168).

C-53D-DO: The USAAF also received 153 aircraft which differed from the C-53-DOs in having the metal troop seats replaced by benches on the cabin sides like those of C-47s.

C-117A-DK: As the war was coming to an end, fewer combat transports would be needed while more military passenger transports would be required. Accordingly, a July 1944 contract provided for 17 Oklahoma-built aircraft to be completed as C-117A-DKs. Essentially, their airframes and R-1830-90C engines were those of C-47Bs but they were completed without the reinforced cabin floor or the double cargo door, and their cabin was fitted with 21

airline-type seats, a galley and lavatory (amenities not provided in C-47s). They had a crew of four (pilot, co-pilot, radio operator, and steward) and some aircraft had a seat, aft of and between the two pilots, for a check pilot. The final C-117A, which was accepted by the USAAF on 29 December 1945, was the last new military derivative of the DC-3 built in the United States.

C-117B-DK: This designation was not that of new aircraft built by Douglas but rather was that given postwar to 11 C-117As which had their engines brought to R-1830-90D standard with single-speed supercharger.

XCG-17: Competing with the C-47C for the title of most unusual DC-3 derivative, the XCG-17 was an experimental troop-transport glider obtained by removing the engines and fairing over the nacelles of a C-47-DL (fsn 4588, 41-18496). Flatter gliding angle, lower stalling speed, and higher towing speed than conventional cargo gliders of the time were demonstrated during tests in the summer of 1944 from Clinton County Army Air Field in Ohio. However, by then the USAAF no longer needed combat gliders and the XCG-17 was stored until sold as surplus and rebuilt as a civil DC-3A in 1949. It was broken down in December 1993 after last serving with the *Fuerza Aérea Mexicana* as a C-47.

USN models built by Douglas

The Naval Air Transport Service was created on 12 December 1941, five days after the attack on Pearl Harbor, but had few aircraft. Naval Aviation did have a few transport aircraft (including four Douglas R3D-1s and -2s) and quickly added a few modified flying boats to commence overwater operations. But it still badly needed to add purpose-designed transport aircraft. Like the USAAF, the USN and the USMC went on to depend heavily on Douglas twin- and four-engined aircraft. The most numerous during the war years were DC-3 derivatives which were given R4D naval designations:[4] four models, the R4D-1s, -5s, -6s, and -7s as described below, were equivalent to C-47 variants; the R4D-2s and R4D-4s had started in production as civil DC-3s (see table on page 168); and the R4D-3s were C-53-DOs transferred by the USAF.

R4D-1: Sixty-six aircraft ordered directly by the Navy Department and 40 transferred by the USAAF were built in Long

---

[4] R4Ds still in service in September 1962 would be given new C-47 designations in accordance with NAVAIR Instruction 13100.7 implementing the use of the Department of Defense Model Designation of Military Aircraft, Rockets and Guided Missiles Book.

ABOVE *The engineless XCG-17 was stored at Davis-Monthan in Arizona between 1946 and 1949. After being taken out of storage, it was again fitted with* Twin Wasp *engines and ended up being broken up in December 1993 after last serving with* Escuadrón Aéreo de Transporte Mediano *of the* Fuerza Aérea Mexicana. *(Douglas)*

Beach. They were essentially identical to C-47-DLs except for some specific naval equipment, such as radios, and like the USAAF aircraft were powered by R-1830-92s. Deliveries to the USN began in February 1942.

R4D-5: Ordered under USAAF contracts, 81 C-47A-DLs and 157 C-47-A-DKs ordered under USAAF contracts were transferred to the USN and USMC directly from the Long Beach and Oklahoma City plants.

R4D-6: Corresponding to C-47B-DKs under which designation they were ordered, 150 aircraft became R4D-6s in naval service.

R4D-7: In addition to transport models, the Navy obtained the transfer of 41 TC-47B-DK trainers which became R4D-7s.

BELOW *An early R4D-1 is ready for delivery to the USN in the spring of 1942. (USN-NA)*

DC-3s in uniform

To supplement the aircraft ordered directly under USAAF and USN contracts with C-47, C-53, C-117, and R4D designations, the War Department, the Navy Department and the Defense Supply Corporation took over DC-3s ordered by airlines but still under construction. These aircraft were given the military designations as

ABOVE Assigned as the personal transport of a Major General (with a two-star flag on the rear fuselage), this C-49-DO was a DC-3-362 ordered by TWA but taken over by the military prior to delivery. (Army Air Cops)

shown below. Other DC-3 derivatives given military designations during World War Two were the civil DC-3s listed opposite.

Aircraft ordered by civil customers but completed for the military

USAAF designation	Douglas Spec. No.	Original customer	Engines	No. of seats	No. of aircraft	USAAF serial numbers
C-48-DO	DC-3A-197D	United	R-1830-82	21	1	41-7681
C-48A-DO	DC-3A-368	—	R-1830-82	10	3	41-7682/7684
C-48C-DO	DC-3A-414	Pan Am & associates	R-1830-51	21	7	42-38332/38338
C-49-DO	DC-3-384	TWA	R-1820-71	24	5	41-7685/7689
C-49-DO	DC-3-362	TWA	R-1820-71	24	1	41-7694
C-49A-DO	DC-3-385	Delta	R-1820-71	21	1	41-7690
C-49B-DO	DC-3-387	Eastern	R-1820-71	21	3	41-7691/7693
C-49C-DO	DC-3-357A	Delta	R-1820-71	28	2	41-7715 & 41-7721
C-49D-DO	DC-3-389	Eastern	R-1820-71	28	6	41-7716/7720 & 42-38256
C-49J-DO	DC-3-454	sundry	R-1820-71	28	34	43-1961/1994
C-49K-DO	DC-3-455	sundry	R-1820-71	28	23	43-1995/2017
C-50-DO	DC-3-277D	American	R-1820-85	21	4	41-7697/7700
C-50A-DO	DC-3-401	American	R-1820-85	28	2	41-7710/7711
C-50B-DO	DC-3-314B	Braniff	R-1820-81	21	3	41-7703/7705
C-50C-DO	DC-3-313B	Penn Central	R-1820-79	21	1	41-7695
C-50D-DO	DC-3-313B	Penn Central	R-1820-79	28	1	41-7696
C-50D-DO	DC-3-392	Penn Central	R-1820-79	28	3	41-7709 & 41-7712/7713
C-51-DO	DC-3-390	Can Colonial	R-1820-83	28	1	41-7702
C-52-DO	DC-3A-197D	United	R-1830-51	28	1	41-7708
C-52A-DO	DC-3A-394	Western	R-1830-51	28	1	41-7714
C-52B-DO	DC-3A-197E	United	R-1830-51	28	2	41-7706/7707
C-52C-DO	DC-3A-402	Eastern	R-1830-51	29	1	41-7701
C-53C-DO	DC-3A-453	United	R-1830-92	28	17	43-2018/2034
C-68-DO	DC-3A-414	Pan Am & associates	R-1830-92	21	2	42-14297/14298
No military designations	DC-3A-414	Pan Am & associates	R-1830-92	28	12	Contract by the Defense Supply Corp and aircraft delivered to Pan American
R4D-2	DC-3-388	Eastern	R-1820-71		2	BuNos 4707 & 4708
R4D-4	DC-3A-447	Pan Am & associates	R-1830-92		10	BuNos 07000/07003 & 33815/33820

Civil aircraft impressed by the military

USAAF designation	Douglas Spec. No.	Original customer	Engines	No. of seats	No. of aircraft	USAAF serial numbers
C-48B-DO	DST-A-207	sundry	R-1830-51	21	15	42-38324/38326 42-56089/56091 42-56098/56102 42-56609/56612
	DC-3A-296B	Northwest			1	42-56629
C-48C-DO	DC-3A-269C	Northwest	R-1830-51	21	1	42-38258
	DST-A-207D	United			1	42-38359
	DC-3A-363	SwiftLife			1	42-38260
	DC-3A-369	United			1	42-38327
	DST-A-207	United			1	42-78026
	DC-3A-197E	United			1	42-78027
	DC-3A-191	United			1	42-78028
	DC-3 A-367	Northeast			2	44-52990/52991
C-49D-DO	DC-3B-202	TWA	R-1820-71	28	1	42-38256
	DC-3-201	TWA			1	42-43624
	DC-3-201F	Eastern			1	42-65583
	DC-3-357	Delta			1	42-65584
	DC-3-322B	Chicago & So			1	42-68860
C-49E-DO	DST-114	American	R-1820-79	21	1	42-43619
	DST-217A	American			2	42-43620/43621
	DST-217C	American			2	42-43622/43623
	DST-144	American			1	42-56092
	DST-217	American			1	42-56093
	DST-144	American			4	42-56094/56097
	DST-144	American			1	42-56103
	DST-218B	American			1	42-56104
	DST-144	American			1	42-56105
	DST-217B	American			1	42-56106
	DC-3-270	Can. Colonial			1	42-56107
	DC-3-313B	Chicago & So			2	42-56617/56618
	DC-3B-202	TWA			1	42-56625
	DC-3B-270B	Penn. Central			2	42-56626/56627
	DC-3-270B	Can. Colonial			1	42-56634
C-49F-DO	DST-318	Eastern	R-1820-71	14	2	42-56613 & 42-56616
	DC-3B-202	TWA			2	42-56620 & 42-56621
	DC-3B-202A	TWA			1	42-56623
	DC-3-322 A	Chicago & So			1	42-56628
	DST-318	Eastern			1	42-56633
	DST-406	Eastern			1	42-56636
	DST-318A	Eastern			1	42-56637
C-49G-DO	DC-3-201	Eastern	R-1820-97	21	8	42-38252, 42-38255 42-56614/56615 42-56630/56632 42-56635
C-49H-DO	DC-3-277D	American	R-1820-97	21	2	42-38250/38251
	DC-3-313D	Penn. Central			1	42-38253
	DC-3-228	Pan Am			1	42-38254
	DC-3-270	Can. Colonial			1	42-38257
	DC-3-313D	Penn. Central			1	42-38328
	DC-3-313C	Penn. Central			1	42-38329
	DC-3-270B	Can. Colonial			1	42-38330
	DC-3-314B	Braniff			1	42-38331
	DC-3-227B	American			1	42-57506
	DC-3-277A	American			1	42-65580
	DC-3-277B	American			2	42-6581/65582
	DC-3-314	Braniff			3	42-68687/68689
	DC-3-313	Penn. Central			1	42-107422
	DC-3-194B	KNILM			2	44-83228/83229
C-52D-DO	DC-3 A-363	SwiftLife	R-1830-51	28	1	42-6505
C-84-DO	DC-3B-202	TWA	R-1820-71	28	4	42-57157 42-57511/57513

Dakotas for the Commonwealth

When the British Government declared war on Germany on 3 September 1939, neither the Royal Air Force nor other air forces in the Commonwealth had DC-3s on strength. This changed almost immediately, not in Europe as might be expected but in far-away Down Under where two *Cyclone*-powered DC-3-232s and two DC-3-232As belonging to Australian National Airways were impressed by the Royal Australian Air Force which had no transport aircraft. Assigned serials A30-1 through A30-4, these four DC-3s were operated in Australia by No 8 Squadron between September 1939 and June 1940 when they were returned to ANA. Later in the war, the RAAF received three *Dakota I*s[5] (A65-1, -3, and -4), 56 *Dakota III*s (A65-2 and A65-5/-59), and 65 *Dakota IV*s (A65-60/-124) and also operated on wartime loan 24 C-47s, C-49s, C-50s, and C-53s which retained their USAAF serial numbers. Postwar, the RAAF reduced the number of its *Dakotas* but retained others for several decades (including two from Transport Support Flight Butterworth sent to Vietnam on a humanitarian relief mission during the chaotic last weeks before the fall of Saigon in April 1975). Four aircraft were transferred in 1968 to the Royal Australian Navy but were withdrawn from use less than six years later. The last Australian military *Dakotas* were those of the Aircraft Research & Development Unit (ARDU) which were auctioned off in 2000.

Whereas the RAAF was the first to fly DC-3s, a former Commonwealth air force – the South African Air Force (*Suid-Afrikanse Lugmag*) – has the distinction of still operating DC-3 military derivatives. The SAAF, which received its first *Dakotas* in June 1943, eventually obtained 58 aircraft directly from the US and 26 transferred from the RAF, respectively numbered 6801 to 6858 and 6859 to 6884. They served during Word War Two with Nos 28 and 44 Squadrons before being operated during

ABOVE *This C-49C-DO, a DC-3-357A which had been ordered by Delta Air Lines, bears the orange markings (on the engine cowlings, around the rear fuselage, and on the rudder) which identified aircraft of the Air Transport Command operating in CONUS (Continental United States).* (USAAF)

BELOW *This* Dakota III *(C-47A-25-DL) was with No 40 Squadron, Royal New Zealand Air Force, in 1944–45.* (RNZAF)

---

5   When C-47s were first included among aircraft to be delivered to the United Kingdom under Lend-Lease, the new transport had to be given a geographical name in keeping with those of other RAF transport aircraft. Moreover, this name had to be American-themed as were others given to US-built aircraft. Nobody remembers who came up with Dakota, an Indian tribe for which two US states, North and South Dakota, are named. This choice was particularly clever as it was also the acronym of the letters DACoTA – Douglas Aircraft Company Transport Aircraft.

ABOVE N2-43 was one of the four C-47s which were transferred from the RAAF to the Royal Australian Navy. Fitted with an airborne intercept radar, it was used by 851 Squadron to train Sea Venom radar operators. (Mervyn W. Prime)

the Border and Bush Wars until 1989. Beginning in 1975, SAAF *Dakotas* saw extensive use in support of combat operations in Angola and Namibia. Deprived access to newer aircraft as a result of anti-Apartheid sanctions, the SAAF opted to have 38 of its C-47s re-engined with PT6A turbines (see page 107). In mid-2011, ten of these turboprop aircraft remained in SAAF service, five in the transport role, four for maritime surveillance, and one equipped for electronic surveillance (ELINT/COMINT).

Although the RAAF had been the first and the SAAF is now the last, it was the Royal Air Force that operated the largest number of Commonwealth DC-3s and *Dakotas*. The first DC-3s for a RAF unit were two Belgian refugees which saw service very briefly – not long enough to be given British military serials – with No 24 Squadron (see page 100). Next in RAF service were DC-3s acquired from US airlines by the British Purchasing Commission in 1940, most going to Nos 31 and 117 Squadrons operating in India and the Middle East. They were supplemented first by five DC-3s and one DC-3B obtained in the spring of 1942 from Pan American-Africa and then by three C-53s from the USAAF. These relatively few aircraft were followed by Lend-Lease *Dakotas*: 53 Mark Is (ex C-47-DLs and R4D-1s), nine ex C-53s as Mark IIs, 962 C-47As as Mk IIIs, and 896 C-47Bs as Mark IVs. After sterling service in World War Two (notably on D-Day and at Arnhem), RAF *Dakotas*, although in ever dwindling numbers, continued to prove most useful, notably during the 1949

Berlin Airlift and in Malaya until 1960. With *Dakotas* having served with some 46 RAF squadrons, the last operational aircraft, KN645, a *Dakota IV*, was retired on 1 April 1970. However, ZA947, a *Dakota III*, was returned to RAF service in March 1993 to become part of the Battle of Britain Memorial Flight.

Logistic operations in World War Two

During the Second World War, the American and Allied forces used their C-47s (and other DC-3 military derivatives) with equal success for strategic/logistic and tactical/combat

BELOW Already during World War Two, the performance of C-47s (here a C-47A-90-DL) was not spectacular. But, available in large numbers and dependable, the Douglas twin-engined transports were among the 'war winning' weapons as identified by General Dwight D. Eisenhower. (USAAF)

ABOVE *In December 1942, the USAAF took over the activities of Pan American-Africa, and its C-47s got to overfly the Gizeh pyramids in Egypt.* (DoD)

missions.[6] What follows is a necessarily brief overview of these operations.

Operations to transport personnel, deliver cargo, and ferry aircraft across much of the globe were initiated by Pan American before the United States entered the war. Three contracts between the airline and the War Department, and two between the airline and the British Government were signed on 12 August 1941. They called for Pan American to (1) establish a scheduled transport service between the United States and West Africa, (2) construct and operate an adequate airway across Africa, and (3) ferry Lend-Lease aircraft from the United States to the Middle East and Russia. The US government purchased from, and leased back to Pan American a Boeing 314 flying boat for operations across the South Atlantic and provided 24 DC-3s for operations by Pan American-Africa[7] on the trans-Africa route. Commencing in early October 1941 with the ferrying of a pair of DC-2s and one DC-3, operations on the route between West Africa and the Anglo-Egyptian Sudan[8] began in earnest on the 22nd of that month. Later, Pan American-

6   The Douglas twin-engined transports used by the USAAF for strategic/logistic operations were operated by Transport Squadrons and Groups, those supporting aircraft delivery operations by Ferrying Squadrons and Groups, and those for tactical operations by Troop Carrier Squadrons and Groups. The Naval Air Transport Service assigned its R4Ds to Air Transport Squadrons (VRs) while those of the USMC served with Marine Utility Squadrons (VMJs).

7   The first were militarized DC-3s (two C-48Cs and four C-49Hs). Over the 15 months of its existence, Pan American-Africa operated 79 impressed DC-3s, C-47s, and C-53s. Many of these aircraft were transferred 'in situ' to the Royal Air Force or the USAAF.

8   Operations between Bathurst in Gambia and Khartoum in Sudan were quite remarkable as they took place over vast distances without navaids and with minimal facilities for the aircrews and passengers in transit as well as for support personnel at the various intermediate stations: Freetown in Sierra Leone; Roberts Field in Liberia; Takoradi in the Gold Coast (now Ghana); Lagos, Kano, and Maiduguri in Nigeria; Fort Lamy in French Equatorial Africa (now N'Djamena in Chad); and El Geneina and El Fasher in Sudan.

BELOW *A C-53B-DO on the flooded field at Adak in the Aleutians in 1942. It was likely flown by airline personnel on military assignment as, then, the Air Transport Command was critically short of crews.* (USAAF)

ABOVE *Late in the war, support aircraft in the CBI, such as this C-47A-25-DK of the 1337th AAF Base Unit, were often given 'airline' names.* (USAAF)

Africa extended its reach to Egypt, Iraq, India, and China before its activities were taken over by the USAAF in December 1942.

Routine operations by land-based transport aircraft began over the North Atlantic on 4 May 1941 when a Consolidated *Liberator I* of the Royal Air Force flew from Montreal to Blackpool for the Atlantic Ferry Organization of the Ministry of Aircraft Production. British and Canadian Avro *Lancastrians* and USAAF Boeing C-75s, Consolidated C-87s, and Douglas C-54s were then used more and more frequently on this route. But these four-engined aircraft were not the only ones 'over the pond,' as Douglas DC-2s and DC-3s also contributed to the development of air operations over the North Atlantic. Operating under contract from the War Department, Northeast Airlines, one of the smallest trunk carriers, used a USAAF-provided Douglas C-39, one of the DC-2 military derivatives, for a flight on 11 January 1942 from Presque Isle in Maine to Gander in Labrador, via Moncton, Goose Bay, and Stephenville. This airline next extended its operations to reach Argentia in Newfoundland and Narssarssuaq (Bluie West-1) and Sondrestrom (Bluie West-8) in Greenland in April 1942; Iceland in May, and the New Hebrides in June 1942. Finally, between 2 and 4 July of that year, a C-47 operated by Northeast Airlines flew from Presque Isle, Maine, to Prestwick, Scotland.[9]

When Japan began its offensive in Southeast Asia and the Pacific in December 1941, the Allies found themselves with a critical shortage of transport aircraft and, more so, transport crews to undertake supply operations to war theatres in the far-flung corners of the world. In the United States, the War Department and the Navy Department had no choice but to turn to airlines for aircraft and experienced crews with which to set up a global network. Thus, Northwest Airlines, United Air Lines, and Western Airlines soon used DC-3s (including aircraft that had been impressed by the military only to be placed at the disposal to the airlines) on government controlled routes within the continental United States and to Alaska and the Aleutians where a Japanese advance threatened continental America and complicated the delivery of aircraft to the Soviet Union via the Alaska–Siberia route.[10]

Rapid Japanese advances in China and Burma at the beginning of 1942 created new logistical problems for the Allies as the Chinese forces of Generalissimo Chiang Kai-shek were now in danger of having their lifeline supply routes cut off. Building a road between Kunming, in Yunnan Province, and Lashio, in eastern Burma, had been an alternative but it was cut off by the Japanese in May 1942 and was not usable again until August 1944. Air resupply became the only practical alternative to keep the Chinese in the fight but it was not an easy one as it entailed flying over some of the world's highest mountains, weather was often a major impediment, and available aircraft were not well-suited for operations under such difficult conditions. Yet, there was great urgency to get personnel, weapons, equipment, and supplies to China over the 'Hump' route. Consequently, before better-suited aircraft such as the Consolidated C-87s, Curtiss C-46s, and Douglas C-54s became available, it was, once again, necessary to call on military variants of the DC-3 to fill the gap.

In January 1942, when the situation in China had taken a turn for the worse, President Roosevelt had instructed the USAAF to impress 25 civil DC-3s to equip a new unit to be deployed urgently to Asia. This First Ferrying Group was organized at Pope Field, North Carolina, on 3 March 1942, most of its flying personnel being airline employees called up as reservists. They

---

9 The importance attached by Northeast Airline to this pioneering flight is evidenced by the fact that the C-47 was captained by its vice-president for operations, Milton Anderson, and that the steward was none other than its president, Samuel Solomon!

10 During the war, the United States sent 8,058 aircraft (mostly Bell P-39s and P-63s, Douglas A-20s, and North American B-25s, but also 658 Douglas C-47s) over the ALSIB (Alaska-Siberia) route for delivery to the USSR. They were handed over to Soviet representatives in Fairbanks from whence *1 Aviatsionnaya Diviziya* (1 PAD) crews took them to Krasnoyarsk in Siberia. From there, the US aircraft were ferried to the front by operational crews. The 1 PAD crews were flown back from Krasnoyarsk to Alaska initially in Lisunov Li-2s (but also later in Lend-Lease C-47s) of the *8 Transportnaya Aviatsionnaya Polk* (8 TAP).

immediately began ferrying the impressed DC-3s to Asia via Central America, Brazil, Africa, and the Middle East. The first arrived in India in May 1942. Initial plans called for the First Ferrying Group to operate alongside CNAC (Pan American's Chinese affiliate) between Myitkina, in Burma, and China to avoid having to fly over mountains peaking above 12,000ft. However, the fall of Myitkina in May 1942 necessitated switching the departure point to Chabuan in India's Assam. Earlier, it was decided to call on Pan American-Africa to provide 10 DC-3s with crews as a stop-gap. Leaving Accra, in West Africa, on 9 April 1942, the aircraft of the Pan American affiliate reached Dinjan, India, before the end of the month. They were initially used to evacuate wounded and priority personnel from Lashio and Myitkina before these two Burmese bases fell to the Japanese. In addition the DC-3s of Pan American-Africa flew to Chinese destinations (Chengdu, Chungking, Kunming, and Weilin) before being sent back to Africa in mid-May 1942 when the aircraft of the First Ferrying Group arrived.

Operations over the 'Hump' itself commenced slowly with aircraft of the First Ferrying Group transporting 77 tons to China in July 1942 while the DC-2s and DC-3s of CNAC carried an additional 200 tons. One year later, with a growing number of C-47s being supplemented by the first Curtiss C-46s, the India–China Wing of the Air Transport Command airlifted 2,645 tons to China. Thereafter, the India–China Wing kept carrying more and more every month, until transported tonnage reached 17,214 in July 1944 and 64,448 one year later. By then, C-47s played only a very minor role over the 'Hump' as they had been progressively supplanted by better performing aircraft. 'Gooney Bird' performance over this difficult route had been improved with the introduction of C-47Bs with two-speed engine supercharger. Although C-47s did not perform as well as C-46s, they proved far more reliable. Unfortunately, 1,659 crew members and 590 aircraft of all types

were lost over the 'Hump'. Loss rate averaged almost one aircraft every other day during the three-year operations over this most difficult route.

Tactical operations in World War Two

The US Army did not organize its first airborne unit until July 1940, after the success of German operations in Europe (such as when Fort Eben-Emael in Belgium was rapidly overrun on 10 May 1940) demonstrated the capability of this new concept. To carry airborne troops, the Army Air Corps needed to acquire aircraft and set up dedicated transport units. The first was the 50th Transport Wing organized at Wright Field, Ohio, in January 1941 and equipped with a mix of Douglas twins (primarily C-33s, C-47s, and C-53s). Its squadrons and groups began training to airdrop paratroopers and tow combat gliders, and were ready when the first call came in the fall of 1942.

In preparation for *Operation Torch*, the landings in North Africa, three groups of the 50th Wing (the 60th, 62nd, and 64th Troop Carrier Groups) were sent to Great Britain. At 1:00am on 8 November 1942, 39 C-47s of the 60th TCG departed from St. Eval and Predannak on their way to Algeria with 531 men from the 2nd Battalion, 509th Parachute Infantry Regiment, USA. Several aircraft got lost on their way and had to divert, five were shot down by Dewoitine 520s from Groupe de chasse II/3, while others were forced to land on the dry lake at Sebra by the French fighters. In the end, only 10 C-47s of the 60th TCG dropped their paratroopers as planned. One week later, results were better as 304 men from the same regiment jumped at Youks-les-Bains where, assisted by French troops, they set up an advanced base near the Tunisian border.

In July 1943, US C-47s and C-53s, and British *Dakotas* joined forces both to carry paratroopers and tow gliders to Sicily. Unfortunately losses were heavy as many gliders, mostly British *Horsas*, landed in the water, drowning most of their occupants. In the Mediterranean Theatre of Operations, C-47s were next in large-scale action to drop paratroopers in Sicily (*Operation Husky*) in July 1943 and in Provence (*Operation Dragoon*) in August 1944. In April 1945, *Operation Herring* saw USAAF C-47s dropping Italian paratroopers in Northern Italy.

BELOW *A pair of C-47s fly over Provence in August 1945 during* **Operation Husky.** *These aircraft from the 81st TCS, 436th TCG, were then on detachment from the Ninth Troop Carrier Command in* **England.** (USAAF)

It was in the European Theatre of Operations that Douglas military derivatives gained the most fame. In preparation for *Operation Neptune*,[11] 14 groups of C-47s and C-53s (with a total of 1,022 aircraft) and 2,360 gliders (mostly Waco CG-4s but also a fair number of Airspeed *Horsas*) were assembled on airfields in England. During the night of 5 to 6 June, 821 C-47s and C-53s carried officers and men of the 82nd and 101st Airborne Divisions, USA, while 104 other Douglas twins towed gliders mostly loaded with equipment and ammunition to the Cotentin Peninsula. Sixteen of the troop-carrying aircraft and one towing a glider were brought down by the German flak while many of the liberating troops landed away from their intended drop zones. Nevertheless,

---

11 *Operation Neptune* was the main component of the better known *Operation Overlord*. It included an airborne component and a naval landing component. *Operation Overlord* also comprised diversionary phases: *Bodyguard, Dingson, Fortitude,* and *Servant*.

ABOVE *Not carrying weapons, these paratroopers aboard a C-47 are going for a training drop. The first US airborne troopers were those from the 509th Parachute Infantry Regiment.* (LOC)

they reassembled in the best manner possible to achieve most of their objectives. Further east in Normandy, *Operations Deadstick, Tonga, and Mallard* saw the 6th Airborne Division, British Army, flown into battle on 6 June by a mix of RAF aircraft (*Dakotas* as well as *Albemarles, Halifaxes,* and *Stirlings*) from Nos 38 and 46 Groups

BELOW *Bound for Normandy on D-Day, US paratroopers received final instructions before boarding a C-47A-80-DL of the 95th Troop Carrier Squadron, 440th Troop Carrier Group.* (USAAF)

ABOVE *This C-47A of the National Museum of the USAF at Wright-Patterson AFB, Ohio, has been repainted in the markings of the 88th TCS, 438th TCG, one of the units which dropped paratroopers in Normandy during the night of 5–6 June 1944.* (NMUSAF)

and in *Horsa* and *Hamilcar* gliders. In the course of the first night and first day on the Continent, the paras secured two key bridges on the Caen canal and the Orne River. After these momentous first 24 hours, the 6th Airborne Division remained on the frontline until brought back to Britain in early September. Whether in the Cotentin Peninsula or along the Caen Canal and Orne River, American and British airborne troops contributed effectively to the liberation of occupied Europe.

After successfully accomplishing this famous task, C-47s of the IX Troop Carrier Command remained busy ferrying troops and supplies to forward fields in Normandy and returning to Britain with wounded troops. Re-supply and medical evacuation continued until the fall of the Third Reich with more offensive missions taking place in between. This was notably the case in September 1944 when Field Marshall Montgomery sought to shorten the war and prevent Soviet troops from being the first in Berlin by mounting a major airborne operation in the Netherlands.

Operation Market Garden saw 34,600 troops from the 1st British Airbone Division, the 1st Polish Paratroop Brigade, and the 82nd and 101st US Airborne Divisions either air dropped or landed behind enemy lines by a transport armada mainly made up of C-47s from the IX Troop Carrier Command. They were to gain control of bridges over canals and rivers to provide the British XXX Corps with an easy access to the Ruhr. The initial assault made on 17 September 1944, saw 1,274 US C-47s, 164 British *Dakotas*, 321 British *Halifaxes* and *Albemarles*, and 3,140 gliders carry 20,011 paratroopers, 14,589 airborne soldiers, and 3,082 tons of ammunition, food and supplies. In spite of this massive undertaking and the gallantry of participating troops and aircrews,[12] *Market Garden* ended being a failure as XXX Corps could not move forward fast enough to relieve the airborne troops facing heavily armed and more numerous SS troops. British and Polish paratroopers took heavy losses before being forced to withdraw on 25 September.

Two other major airborne operations were undertaken in the

ETO before VE-Day. On 26 December 1944, 240 C-47s, some towing gliders, took advantage of clearing weather to resupply the besieged 101st Airborne Division at Bastogne. Three months later, on 24 March 1945, more than 17,500 British and US soldiers, respectively from the 6th and 17th Airborne Divisions, were landed by 2,861 aircraft and gliders[13] east of the Rhine, between Wesel and Hamminkeln. Over the next three days, *Varsity*, the largest airborne operation ever undertaken, resulted in the taking of 12 bridges over the Rhine and was concluded successfully when the airborne troops linked with the advancing 21st Army Group. Forty days later, Germany signed the act of surrender in Reims.

In the Mediterranean Theater of Operations, the most important airborne operation was that mounted on 15 August 1944, the first day of *Operation Dragoon*, the landing in Southern France. A total of 1,394 aircraft and glider sorties (most by C-47s) were needed to take the paratroops and air-landed troops of the 1st Airborne Task Force into combat. Results met expectations and losses were less than what had been predicted.

In the Pacific and in Southeast Asia, parachute and airborne operations were far less numerous than in Europe and, perhaps more significantly, were considerably smaller both in scope and numbers of aircraft and troops involved. Nevertheless, C-47s, *Dakotas* and other militarized DC-3s operated by American, Australian, British, Dutch, and New Zealander tactical squadrons did play a very significant role by transporting troops and supplies in theatres of operations where land communications were limited and where land and sea distances were much greater than in the ETO and MTO. The first notable parachute operation in the Southwest Pacific Area (SWPA) took place on 5 September 1943 when 96 C-47s dropped 1,700 paratroopers near Nadzab in New Guinea. Next came that on Nooemfor Island, off the coast of Dutch New Guinea, in July 1944, followed by a series of operations in the Philippines (at Corregidor, Tagaytay, and Los Baños in February 1945, and at Camalaniugan in July 1945).

In Burma, C-47s and *Dakotas* were called to support the Chindits[14] of Brigadier Orde Charles Wingate. *Operation Longcloth* began on 8 February 1943 when an initial contingent of 3,000 Chindits marched into Burma with supplies being parachuted or dropped from transport aircraft (mostly by militarized DC-3s of various origins). Next, a larger scale offensive behind Japanese lines was undertaken by Chindits and by Merrill's Marauders from the US. On 5 March 1944, the first wave of this *Operation Thursday* consisted of 26 USAAF C-47s each towing two gliders with troops, equipment, and supplies.

---

12 On 19 September 1944, Flight Lieutenant David S.A. Lord, was flying KG374, a *Dakota III* of No 271 Squadron, RAF, on a re-supply mission to Arnhem. Three minutes from the drop zone, the *Dakota* flew through intense flak and was hit twice on the starboard wing. The engine and fuel tank on that side burst into flames, but Flight Lieutenant Lord and his crew (three from the RAF and four Army dispatchers) continued to the drop zone where they proceeded to drop supplies, except for two containers that remained on board. Although knowing that the fiercely-burning starboard wing might collapse at any moment, Lord nevertheless made a second run to drop the last supplies, and then ordered his crew to bail out. Before they could do so, the *Dakota* crashed in flames. All but one of the crew perished. For his gallantry, Flight Lieutenant David Lord was awarded the Victoria Cross.

13 The aircraft included 1,588 C-47s and *Dakotas*, 72 Curtiss C-46s, and 42 Douglas C-54s; gliders were Waco CG-4s, Airspeed *Horsas*, and General Aircraft *Hamilcars*.
14 A British-Indian 'Special Force' which was officially the 77th Indian Infantry Brigade and then the Third Indian Infantry Division.

Thereafter, only one glider per C-47 became the norm, as pulling two gliders over-stressed the towing cable. To support *Operation Thursday*, the US Tenth Air Force organized its First Air Commando Group with two fighter squadrons, three liaison squadrons, and the 319th Troop Carrier Squadron (with C-47s and CG-4 and TG-5 gliders). The last major airborne mission supported by C-47s and *Dakotas* before the Japanese surrender was *Operation Dracula* in April 1945. On that occasion, two battalions of Indian paratroopers were dropped to capture airfields near Rangoon.

In addition to the air forces of Australia, Britain, Canada, New Zealand, South Africa, and the Soviet Union, those of four other nations received C-47s under Lend-Lease during the Second World War. Seventy-four C-47s went to China between 1942 and 1945, Dutch forces fighting in the SWPA got 16 during the same period,

the *Força Aérea Brasileira* (Brazilian Air Force) obtained 11 C-47s in 1944, and the Free French took in 53 during the last year of the war.

During the war, C-47s (and other military derivatives of the DC-3) had provided US and Allied forces with a degree of mobility unmatched by the Axis forces. Not surprisingly, Gen. Dwight D. Eisenhower included the C-47 among the war-winning weapons

BELOW *A squad of US airborne infantrymen waits to be towed aloft in a Waco CG-4A glider.* (Signal Corps)

BOTTOM *This CG-4A being towed off a forward field in Normandy was carrying wounded troops back to England in June 1944. An Army nurse, Lt. Suella Bernard, was in the right-hand seat next to the pilot.* (NMUSAF)

Tough birds

During their first war and thereafter over their long and not yet ended career, C-47s and their siblings had many occasions to demonstrate that they could survive severe damage, whether due to operational accidents or enemy action. The following story of an encounter with Japanese fighters and two photos taken after a midair collision illustrate the C-47's exceptional strength and survivability.

The 64th Transport Group was only a paper organization and had no aircraft when it was constituted at Duncan Field, Texas, on 20 November 1940. Transferred to California in July 1941, and successively based at March Field and Hamilton Field, the group and its three squadrons, the 16th, 17th, and 18th TCSs, were among the first to be equipped with C-47-DLs. In June 1942, they departed for Massachusetts where a fourth squadron, the 35th, was added before all continued to England. After four months at Ramsbury, Wiltshire, the 64th TCG took part in *Operation Torch*, first bringing US troops to Maison Blanche, Algeria, on 11 November 1942. During the remainder of 1942 and the first eight months of 1943, the four squadrons of the 64th dropped paratroopers in Tunisia, Sicily, and southern Italy. The group was based at Comiso, Sicily, in August 1943 when it was ordered to rotate squadrons to India. Between April and June 1944 it was the 17th TCS that got the Indian duty.

On 25 April 1944, one of the aircraft of this squadron (serial 42-24170, a C-47A-50-DL) took off from Imphal with Indian troops aboard. The four USAAF crew members were Capt. Hal M. Scrugham, pilot; 1Lt. Elmer J. Jost, co-pilot; Sgt. Clyde D. Ginder, radio operator; and Sgt Dean E. Durst, loadmaster. While en route, the C-47 was intercepted by radial-engined Japanese fighters (said to have been Navy A6M *Zeroes* but, more likely in this theatre, Army Ki-43 *Oscars*). While Capt. Scrugham and 1Lt. Jost manoeuvred violently one of the Japanese fighters collided with their C-47. The other enemy aircraft flew away. Although the top of the fin and rudder had been torn away in the

collision, the crew retained control and the damaged C-47 landed at Shamshenagar one hour later. *Gooney Bird*: 1, Zero (or whatever it was): 0!

No such details have been found concerning the operational accident illustrated by the accompanying photographs. Apparently, this C-47 belonging to a training unit of the First Troop Carrier Command collided in flight with another aircraft. In spite of losing a good bit of its upper fuselage, the aircraft was landed safely.

ABOVE AND BELOW *Inside and outside views of a C-47 from the First Troop Carrier Command that survived a mid-air collision.* (USAAF)

when he stated: '*Four things won the Second World War – the bazooka, the Jeep, the atom bomb, and the C-47 Gooney Bird.*' This praise for the Douglas twin-engined aircraft was apparently shared by one of the enemy powers and by a difficult ally, as both Japan and the Soviet Union operated their own versions in large numbers.

Postwar, and well into the 1990s in the case of aircraft re-engined with PT6A turbines, countless air forces acquired C-47s and/or Li-2s, with these DC-3 derivatives thus becoming the most widely-used military transports for several decades.

Made in Japan

Between November 1937 and February 1939, 22 *Cyclone*-powered DC-3s and nine *Twin Wasp*-powered DC-3As were shipped to Japan to be operated by Dai Nippon Koku K.K. While this purely commercial transaction was taking place *Mitsui Bussan Kaisha K.K.*, a Japanese trading company, purchased two DC-3As and acquired the rights to build and sell the DC-3 in the Empire of Japan and Manchukuo under a $90,000 contract (±$1.4 million today). Unbeknownst to Douglas, manufacturing rights had been acquired at the behest of the *Kaigun Koku Hombu* (Navy Air Headquarters) which had chosen the DC-3 to become the standard naval transport aircraft.

Reassembled in Japan by *Showa Hikoki K.K.* (Showa Aeroplane Co Ltd), a new but small manufacturer in Showa, near Tokyo, the two DC-3As (Douglas fsn 2055 and 2056) were delivered to the Imperial Japanese Navy in October 1939 and April 1940. Designated 'Douglas Transport Aircraft Type D' and receiving the short naval designation L2D1, the two imported aircraft underwent naval trials successfully, confirming that the selection of the Douglas design was well grounded. By then, two production lines had been set up in Japan, one in the plant of Showa Hikoki K.K. and the other in the Koizumi plant of the well-established Nakajima Hikoki K.K.

Designated Navy Type 0 Transport Model 11 (short designation L2D2), the initial Japanese version differed from the DC-3A in incorporating minor local manufacturing and in being powered by two Mitsubishi *Kinsei* (Gold Star) 43 twin-row radial engines rated at 986hp on take-off and 1,065hp at 6,560ft. Nakajima delivered

ABOVE *A line-up of C-47A-DLs of the 433rd Troop Carrier Group is shown at Finschafen, New Guinea, on 13 December 1943.* (USAAF)

72 L2D2s in 1940–42 before production was undertaken exclusively by Showa after its production line had gotten into full swing. The first Showa-built L2D2 was delivered in March 1941 and produced *Kinsei* 43-powered aircraft in two variants: the L2D2 for personnel/troop transport and the L2D2-1 troop/cargo transport

BELOW *Organised at Hailakandi, India, in March 1944, the 1st Air Commando Group immediately went into operations in Burma. Its 319th Troop Carrier squadron was equipped with C-47s, including this C-47A-65-DL.* (USAAF)

with a reinforced cabin floor and a double cargo door (smaller than that of the C-47 but opening inward, thus not requiring removal of one of the door panel sections when the aircraft was used by paratroopers).

The next personnel/troop transport models built by Showa were the L2D3 and L2D3a which differed from the L2D2 in being powered by 1,282hp *Kinsei* 51s and *Kinsei* 53s, respectively, and having three additional windows in the cockpit. Corresponding troop/cargo versions with reinforced cabin floor and double cargo door were designated L2D3-1 and L2D3-1a. These four L2D3 versions (with the full designation Navy Type 0 Transport Model 22) were produced in larger numbers than other Japanese-built Douglas twins. A few *Kinsei* 51-powered L2D4s and L2D4-1s (Navy Type 0 Transport Model 32) corresponded to the L2D3s and L2D3-1s but were fitted with defensive armament consisting of a 13mm machine gun in a dorsal housing and a 7.7mm Type 92 machine gun in a hatch on each side of the fuselage.

Finally, the L2D5 or Navy Type 0 Transport Model 33 was still under construction in 1945. This version, which was to have been powered by 1,539hp *Kinsei* 62 engines, featured a squared cross-section fuselage mostly made of wood and to have had smaller wing root fairings. By the time of the Japanese surrender, Showa had assembled the two DC-3As as L2D1s and produced 414 L2D2s through L2D5s, while Nakajima had built 71 L2D2s.

Soviet production

As a DC-2 had been imported in 1935 (see photo page 80), the *Soviet po trudoo i oborone* (STO, Labour and Defense Council) had been informed by officials of both the *Tsentrahl'nyy aero i glidrodinamicheskiy institoot* (TsAGI, Central Aero- & Hydrodynamics Institue) and the *Naoochno-issledovatel'skiy institoot Voyenno-vozdooshnykh seel* (NII VVS, Air Force Research Institute) of the interest that this aircraft and its newer derivative was generating in the Soviet Union. Accordingly, STO first approved the acquisition of one of the new Douglas twins on 21 March 1936 and then, three weeks later, followed with an instruction to acquire a manufacturing license for the DC-3. Two months after the signing of the licensing agreement on 15 July 1936, a first contingent of Soviet engineers arrived in Santa Monica to begin working with Douglas. As part of the agreement, the Soviets also acquired 21 *Cyclone*-powered DC-3s, with the first being shipped to Cherbourg,

OPPOSITE *Three recognition views of a Showa L2D2 powered by* Mitsubishi *Kinsei 43 radials* (USN-NA)

ABOVE *Photographed at Zamboanga, the Philippines, on 3 May 1945, this captured Showa L2D3 was undergoing evaluation with the Technical Air Intelligence Unit, SWPA.* (USN-NA)

France, to be handed over to X-Cello[15] on 30 November 1936. The next 20 were delivered through the European agent, Fokker, between August 1937 and January 1940. Of these 20, 18 were ready to enter service while one was partially assembled and another was supplied as knock-down components to serve as pattern aircraft for the Russian-built variant.

Production of DC-3s in Russia was entrusted to GAZ 84 (*Gosoodartsveny Aviatsiya Zavod*, 84, State Aeronautical Factory) located at Moscow-Khimki. The first aircraft – with its PS-84 designation indicating that it was a *Passajirski Samolet* 84 (Transport Aircraft from Factory 84) – was assembled in Khimki using Douglas-supplied parts and was powered by imported Wright *Cyclones*. Delivered in 1938, it was followed in 1939 by the first six aircraft for Aeroflot, five of which were powered by *Cyclones*. The sixth, the first wholly Russian-built DC-3 derivative, had Shvetsov M-62IR engines[16] as specified for the aircraft that were to be built first for the GVF (*Grazhdanskaya Vozdushnaya Flot*, civil aviation fleet) and then for the V-VS (*Voenno-vozdushniye Sily*, Soviet air forces).

Even Russian sources have now admitted that the PS-84s were not as satisfactory as the Lend-Lease C-47s, primarily due to the poorer quality of their instrumentation and radio equipment. Moreover the R-1830 installation of C-47s was better engineered than that of the M-62IR of the PS-84s and later the Li-2s. Consequently, the V-VS assigned C-47s in priority to its 8th Transport Aviation Regiment (8 TAP) which brought pilots and crew members of the 1st Aviation Ferrying Division (1 PAD) from Krasnoyarsk, Siberia, to Fairbanks, Alaska, to ferry Lend-Lease aircraft over the Siberian portion of the ALSIB route. Performance

---

15 This was a fictitious company set up for the occasion by Amtorg Trading Corporation, the Soviet trade representation in the United States. It also provided cover for intelligence agents of the GRU (Main Intelligence Directorate) and OGPU (All-Union State Political Administration).
16 This nine-cylinder radial engine was a development of the M-25, itself being a Russian-built version of the Wright *Cyclone* SGR-1820-F3 for which the Soviet Union had acquired the manufacturing rights in 1934. The M-62IR was rated at 986hp on take-off and 828hp at 4,920m. It was re-designated Ash-61IR in 1941.

ABOVE *This Lisunov Li-2T (23441605) was built in Tashkent in 1952. Fifty years later, this last of a breed, was restored to flight status; unfortunately, it crashed near Moscow on 26 June 2004.* (Michael Gruenenfelder)

of the PS-84 was also inferior to that of C-47s.[17] Conversely, as shown in the table below, the Japanese L2D3 was comparing favorably with American and Soviet derivatives of the DC-3.

The most obvious difference between American DC-3 variants and Soviet PS-84s was the shape of the engine nacelles (often fitted with shutters to regulate engine temperature during winter operations). Also readily visible when the PS-84 was on the ground was the replacement of the Y-shaped drag strut of the DC-3 main undercarriage by a V-shaped unit for increased strength (few of the fields from which PS-84s were called to operate had prepared

surfaces while the use of retractable skis was frequent in winter). In addition, the location and geometry of entrance doors were different, the standard installation for early PS-84s consisting of a single door on the starboard side of the aft fuselage which opened inward and aft (whereas most DC-3s had their entrance door on the port side, opening outward and forward).

The most produced wartime version of the PS-84 (and the later Li-2) was a multi-purpose transport aircraft for personnel, paratroopers, or cargo (up to 5,292lb of internal cargo or containers carried beneath the wing center-section and air-landed or air-dropped by parachute). PS-84s could also be adapted for medical evacuation by installing 18 stretchers and seats for two attendants. To perform these various roles, they were fitted with an additional double door on the starboard side which measured 5ft 5in x 5ft and opened outward and upward.[18] When used for air-drop operations, these versatile military transports carried 25 fully equipped paratroopers on back-to-back, side-facing benches in the middle of the cabin; the paratroopers could be dropped

17 Even though this was not 'politically correct', the Soviets opted to have Secretary General Joseph Stalin and his advisers flown in US-supplied C-47s instead of less reliable PS-84s when they went to Yalta to host the *Argonaut Conference* in February 1947. Prime Minister Winston Churchill and President Franklin Roosevelt did the Soviet leader one better by arriving in Crimea in four-engined transport C-54s, respectively a *Skymaster I* (British serial EW999, ex C-54B-1-DO, 43-1716) and the VC-54C. Wartime Allies, soon to be Cold War adversaries, were not immune to showing off.

18 Douglas had earlier fitted cargo doors to military versions of the DC-2 (the first with these doors being C-33s delivered in 1937). In the case of DC-3 variants with double cargo doors, development of the PS-84-K was authorized in July 1939 whereas C-47s were first ordered in September 1940.

	DST (SGR-1820-G2)		PS-84 (M-62IR)		C-47A-DL (R-1830-92)		L2D3-1a (Kinsei 51)	
Dimensions:								
Span, ft in	95	0	94	6	95	0	96	0
Length, ft in	64	5½	64	5	63	9	64	0
Height, ft in	16	3⅝	16	10⅞	17	0	–	
Wing area, sq ft	987		986		987		986	
Weights:								
Empty, lb	16,060		15,655		17,865		15,913	
Loaded, lb	24,000		23,150		26,000		27,558	
Maximum, lb	–		25,400		31,000		–	
Performance:								
Max speed, mph/ft	212/6,800		193/4,790		230/8,800		244/9,185	
Cruising speed, mph	192		–		160		150	
Climb rate, ft/min	850/1		–		10,000/9.6		16,400/16	
Service ceiling, ft	20,800		15,945		24,000		–	
Normal range, miles	–		–		1,600		1,865	
Ferry range, miles	–		1,450		3,800		–	

simultaneously from both sides of the aircraft using the standard port side entrance door and the forward section of the starboard cargo door which, for this purpose, opened inward and upward.

Early production PS-84s for Aeroflot had 14-seat cabins, but, over the years, passenger accommodation was increased to 21, 28, and finally 32. On entering airline service at the end of 1939, the aircraft were first used to evacuate wounded soldiers from the Karelian front during the Winter War with Finland. Scheduled passenger operations on the Moscow–Irkutsk route followed in January 1940. By the end of 1940, PS-84s were already outnumbering DC-3s (26 to 7) in the Aeroflot fleet. Six months later, when Germany invaded the USSR, civil PS-84s began operating alongside military variants.

The decision to adopt the PS-84 as the standard military transport was taken in late July 1939. At first, military PS-84s were configured as personnel transports and differed from the Aeroflot aircraft mostly in having Spartan accommodations. Rapidly, however, production switched to the more versatile model with double cargo door and removable troop benches or stretchers. Early during the war, these aircraft were fitted with defensive armament consisting of up to four 7.62mm ShKAS machine guns (one fixed, forward-firing in the nose, one a dorsal turret, and the two others on a flexible mount on each side of the rear fuselage). Later, the ineffective nose gun was removed and that in the dorsal turret was replaced by a 12.7mm Berezin UBT machine gun.

At the time of the Nazi invasion, the V-VS had virtually no bombers suitable for night operations, leading front line units to jury rig external bomb racks beneath some PS-84s. The success achieved with these makeshift bombers prompted Joseph Stalin to order the installation of bomb racks and other bombing equipment during production of a new version of the PS-84 to equip units of the *Aviatsiya dahl'nevo deystvia* (ADD, Long-Range Aviation). Carrying either four 551lb or two 1,102lb bombs on parallel racks beneath the wing center section, they were fitted with a NKBP-7 bombsight in a glass enclosure replacing the cargo door on the starboard side of the forward fuselage, just aft of the cockpit.

The first night bomber was tested in April 1942 and this new dual role, transport and bombing, model was almost immediately put into production replacing earlier versions. Later, bomb-carrying capability of the Li-2VP model was increased by fitting two racks in the fuselage, each taking five 220lb bombs stacked vertically. Li-2-equipped bomber regiments (*Bombardirovchnyi aviatsionniya polk*, BAP) performed brilliantly during the war with many of these regiments achieving 'Guards' status (*Gvardeiaskaya bombardirovchnyi aviatsionniya polk*, GvBAP) in recognition of their achievements.

In the paratroop transport role, PS-84s of the V-VS are best remembered for the role they played during a large scale operation behind German lines. It began during the night of 2 to 3 January 1942 when 43 PS-84s of *Aviatsionniya groopa osobovo naznacheniya* (AGON, Special Mission Aviation Group) dropped the first paratroopers of the 4th Airborne Group behind German lines at Vyaz'ma, 130 miles SW of Moscow. During the following days and continuing until 6 March, more soldiers from the 4th Airborne Group were dropped or landed by PS-84s and Tupolev TB-3s on captured airfields until 14,000 troops were committed. Even though relief forces never managed to reach them, the men (and some nurses) and local partisans succeeded in holding at bay far larger and better equipped German units. However, the last of them had to surrender to the *Wehrmacht* on 12 July 1942. In September 1943, the only large scale airborne operations mounted by the Soviet Army again relied mostly on PS-84s for transportation. During fighting near the Dnepr River losses were heavy and results meager.

While all this was taking place, production was transferred away

from advancing German troops when GAZ 84 was relocated from Moscow-Khimky, where its 411th and last PS-84 was delivered in October 1941, to Tashkent-Vostochny in the Uzbek SSR (today's Uzbekistan), where PS-84 deliveries commenced in January 1942. PS-84 production had also been initiated in 1940 at Kazan-Borisoglebskoye (GAZ 124) but only 10 aircraft were built before this plant in Tatarstan was given other war-related duties.

In September 1942, after Boris Lisunov had been appointed as chief engineer at GAZ 84, the Soviet derivative of the DC-3 aircraft became the Lisunov Li-2 to comply with a December 1940 directive to name aircraft in honor of the chief of the *Opytno-Konstruktorkoye Buryo* (OKB, Design Bureau).[19] However, it would appear that the PS-84 designation remained the most used during the war years.

After the Great Patriotic War ended, Li-2 production at Tashkent-Vostochny continued until the 4,331st and last was delivered in May 1953. The number of aircraft built in this plant and the date of final delivery are significant not only for the Soviet aircraft industry but also with respect to the history of the Douglas Aircraft Company. The number of PS-84s and Li-2s from the Tashkent plant (which retained the GAZ 84 numbering of the Khimki plant) was only exceeded by that of C-47s and C-117s built in Oklahoma City (5,381) while the last delivery of all-new DC-3s from a Douglas plant, a pair of DC-3Ds for a Brazilian customer, were delivered in May 1946, exactly seven years before the final Li-2. In postwar years, production of Soviet 'DC-3s' was also undertaken by GAZ 126 at Komsomolsk-na-Amure-Dzyomgi in the Ukrainian SSR, resulting in the delivery of 353 civil Li-2Ts between 1947 and 1950. Altogether, the total number of PS-84s and Li-2s built in these four plants is no fewer than 4,989.[20] That is more than what was thought to be the case before the fall of the Soviet regime.[21]

As alluded to earlier, local production of DC-3 derivatives had been supplemented during the war by the delivery of 658 Lend-Lease C-47s, out of a total of 707 which had been allotted to the Soviets. At war's end, like other Lend-Lease recipients, the USSR was supposed either to return aircraft still in service or to destroy them under US supervision. That did not happen as C-47s, quite a few re-engined with 986hp Shvetsov Ash-62IRs, 1,085hp Tumanski M-88Bs, or 1,652hp Shvetsov Ash-82FNs, remained in V-VS service until the early 1960s. During the Cold War years, with C-47s and Li-2s still being operated by the Soviet Armed Forces, the Air Standardization Coordinating Committee assigned the NATO reporting name 'Cab' to these aircraft. While the majority of these twin-engined aircraft were used in the transport role, many did get more exotic assignments. Notably, some were modified into UchShLi-2 navigation trainers, others served in support of cruise missile testing, one was used as a test bed for side-looking airborne radar (SLA), and one was experimentally fitted with tracked main undercarriages. Outside of the Soviet Union, the last military Li-2s appears to have been those of *Zhongguo Renmin Jiefangjun Haijun* (China's Aviation of the People's Navy) which were not retired until 1997.

19 When rights to manufacture DC-3s in the Soviet Union were acquired in 1936, the task of 'Russifiying' the American design was given to Vladimir M. Myasischev, the chief engineer at GAZ 84. But soon, this gifted designer ran afoul of the Party and, accused of harboring Capitalist sympathies, was sent in exile to work in an engineering work camp (a milder version of a *Gulag*). In 1938, his place at GAZ 84 was given to Anatoliy A. Sen'kov. When GAZ 84 had to be relocated away from advancing German forces during the summer of 1941, Sen'kov was in turn replaced by his deputy, I.P. Mosolov. Then, in 1942, Boris P. Lisunov, one of the key engineers sent earlier to work with Douglas, was put in charge of the design bureau at GAZ 84 and thus saw Russian 'DC-3s' named after him. He accomplished little else.
20 The July 1936 licensing agreement only had a three-year validity period but, as most PS-84s and Li-2s were built after this contract cut-off date, the Soviet Union ended up being able to build thousands of Douglas-designed aircraft without paying royalties to the California manufacturer. This only serves to prove that, perhaps, Capitalists – even those of Scottish ancestry – may not have been as good at business as they thought they were.
21 In 1974, a Soviet representative, passing himself as the 'Second Vice-Consul' at the San Francisco Consulate repeatedly assured the author that 'no DC-3 or derivatives had been built in the USSR.' He even denied that Lend-Lease C-47s had been delivered. A few months later, after having been identified as a GRU operative, this 'Vice-Consul' was extradited from the United States. Different times, different mores.

Designations given by the USAAF/USAF and the US Army to modified C-47s

Military designations before/after September 1962	Original version	Engines	Remarks
AC-47A / —	C-47A	R-1830-90B or -92	C-47As modified for navaids calibration.
EC-47A / —	C-47A	R-1830-90B or -92	C-47As modified as test beds (prefix 'E' for *Exempt*).
JC-47A / —	EC-47A	R-1830-90B or -92	C-47As temporarily modified as test beds.
NC-47A / —	JC-47A	R-1830-90B or -92	C-47As permanently modified as test beds.
RC-47A / RC-47A	C-47A	R-1830-90B or -92	C-47As equipped for photographic reconnaissance.
SC-47A / HC-47A	C-47A	R-1830-90B or -92	C-47As equipped for search and rescue.
TC-47A / —	C-47A	R-1830-90B or -92	C-47As fitted as crew trainers.
VC-47A / VC-47A	C-47A	R-1830-90B or -92	C-47As with upgraded accommodations for staff/VIP transport.
EC-47B	C-47B	R-1830-90C	C-47Bs modified as test beds.
NC-47B	C-47B	R-1830-90C	C-47B permanently modified as test beds for the US Army.
RC-47B	C-47B	R-1830-90C	C-47Bs equipped for photographic reconnaissance.
VC-47B	C-47B	R-1830-90C	C-47Bs modified for staff/VIP transport.
XC-47C and C-47C / —	C-47A	R-1830-92	C-47As fitted with Edo amphibian floats.
C-47D / C-47D	C/TC-47B	R-1830-90D	C-47Bs and TC-47Bs with engines modified as R-1830-90Ds by removal of one of the two superchargers from R-1830-90Cs.
AC-47D / EC-47D	C-47D	R-1830-90D	C-47Ds modified for navaids calibration.
— / AC-47D	C-47D	R-1830-90D	Designation given in January 1946 to the FC-47D 'gunship' (*Spooky, Puff the Magic Dragon*).
EC-47D / JC-47D	C-47D	R-1830-90D	C-47Ds modified as test beds (prefix 'E' for *Exempt*).
— / FC-47D	C-47D	R-1830-90D	Initial designation given to C-47Ds modified as 'gunships.' Became AC-47Ds in January 1966.
RC-47D / —	C-47D	R-1830-90D	This designation was first given to a C-47D fitted for electronic reconnaissance.
RC-47D / —	C-47D	R-1830-90D	Second use of the RC-47D designation, this time to identify five C-47Ds modified for photographic reconnaissance.
RC-47D / —	C-47D	R-1830-90D	Third use of the RC-47D designation, this time to identify a pair of C-47Ds equipped for navaids calibration.
— / RC-47D	C-47D	R-1830-90D	Unofficial designation given to a C-47D modified to serve as a radio relay station.
SC-47D / HC-47D	C-47D	R-1830-90D	C-47Ds equipped for search and rescue.
TC-47D / TC-47D	TC-47D	R-1830-90D	TC-47Ds fitted as crew trainers.
VC-47D / VC-47D	C-47D	R-1830-90D	C-47Ds modified for staff/VIP transport.
C-47E / C-47E	C-47A et C-47B	R-2000-4	C-47As and C-47Bs re-engined for the US Army.
RC-47N / EC-47N	Sundry models	R-1830-90D	Aircraft equipped as electronic reconnaissance platforms (ELINT/SIGINT/COMINT) which were mainly used to detect and record Morse code transmissions.
RC-47P / EC-47P	Sundry models	R-1830-90D	Aircraft equipped as electronic reconnaissance platforms (ELINT/SIGINT/COMINT) which were mainly used to detect and record voice and Morse code transmissions.
— / EC-47Q	Sundry models	R-2000-4	Re-engined aircraft equipped as electronic reconnaissance platforms (ELINT/SIGINT/COMINT) which were mainly used to detect and record voice and Morse code transmissions.
SC-47	C-47D	R-1830-90D	Designation, *without series letter suffix*, given to C-47S which were modified to improve their take-off and landing performance.

OPPOSITE *This Lisunov LI-2 is on display at the Belarusian Museum of the Great Patriotic War in Minsk.* (DR)

RIGHT *This C-47B-1-DK, one of the first delivered to the Free French Air Force, flies above the Channel in 1945. Its modified 'invasion' stripes are noteworthy.* (USAAF)

Civil Li-2s were also used in a wide variety of roles, a situation which often led to suffix letters being assigned as a means of identifying some of these variants. Notably, Li-2Ds were long-range passenger transport with additional fuel tanks, Li-2Fs and Li-2FGs were respectively for photographic and photogrammetry survey, Li-2GRs were early examples of 'combi' aircraft with cabins accommodating passengers and freight simultaneously, Li-2LPs were used for forest fire fighting, Li-2Ps were convertible passenger/cargo aircraft, Li-2PRs served on fishery patrol, Li-2-SKhs were crop dusters, Li-2Ts were the main passenger transport models, and Li-2Vs were aircraft for Antarctic research which were re-engined with Ash-62s with TK-19 turbosuperchargers and four-blade propellers.

Aeroflot retired its last Li-2s in 1962 but others remained longer in civil use, notably with the Russian Polar Aviation. Abroad, civil Li-2s were last operated in North Korea by *Chosonminhang* (Civil Aviation Administration of Korea, CAAK) into the mid-1980s.

Postwar modified versions

Aircraft 45-1139, the last of 9,666 C-47s, C-117s, and R4D-1s built by Douglas was taken on charge by the San Bernardino Air Depot, in California, on 23 November 1945. That event, however, did not bring an end to the appearance of new versions of DC-3 derivatives. As listed opposite and below, most were former military aircraft which were modified to perform new duties. In the case

Designations given by the US Navy and the US Marine Corps to modified R4Ds

Military designations before/after September 1962	Original version	Engines	Mission/Remark
R4D-5E / —	R4D-5	R-1830-90B or -92	R4D-5s modified as electronic test beds.
R4D-5L / LC-47H	R4D-5 / C-47H	R-1830-90B or -92	R4D-5s fitted with skis for operations in Antarctica.
R4D-5Q / EC-47H	R4D5 / C-47H	R-1830-90B or -92	R4D-5s equipped for electronic reconnaissance.
R4D-5R / TC-47H	R4D-5 / C-47H	R-1830-90B or -92	R4D-5s with seating for personnel transport.
R4D-5S / SC-47H	R4D-5 / C-47H	R-1830-90B or -92	R4D-5s modified as ASW trainers.
R4D-5T / —	R4D-5	R-1830-90B or -92	R4D-5s modified as navigation trainers.
R4D-5Z / VC-47H	R4D-5 / C-47H	R-1830-90B or -92	R4D-5s modified for staff/VIP transport.
R4D-6E / —	R4D-6	R-1830-90C	R4D-6s modified as electronic test beds.
R4D-6L / LC-47J	R4D-6 / C-47J	R-1830-90C, -90D or -92	R4D-6s fitted with skis for operations in Antarctica.
R4D-6Q / EC-47J	R4D-6 / C-47J	R-1830-90C, -90D or -92	R4D-6s equipped for electronic reconnaissance.
R4D-6R / TC-47J	R4D-6 / C-47J	R-1830-90C, -90D or -92	R4D-6s with seating for personnel transport.
R4D-6S / SC-47J	R4D-6 / C-47J	R-1830-90C, -90D or -92	R4D-6s modified as ASW trainers.
R4D-6T / —	R4D-6	R-1830-90C	R4D-6s modified as navigation trainers.
R4D-6Z / VC-47J	R4D-6 / C-47J	R-1830-90C, -90D or -92	R4D-6s modified for staff/VIP transport.
R4D-7 / TC-47K	TC-47B	R-1830-90C or -90D	TC-47B navigation trainers transferred to the US Navy.
— / C-47L	C-47H & C-47J	R-1830-90D or -92	Aircraft specially fitted for use outside the United States by naval attachés (ALUSNA).
— / C-47M	C-47H & C-47J	R-1830-90D or -92	Aircraft specially fitted for use outside the United States by personnel assigned to military assistance missions (MAAG).

RIGHT *Modified from a C-47B-10-DK airframe (that of 43-49029) this brightly-marked EC-47D of the 1869th FCS, Air Force Communications Service, was photographed at Chanute AFB in July 1965.* (Jacques Guillem collection)

ABOVE *Bearing a US civil registration (N64605), this SC-47H (ex-R4D-5 and then R4D-5S) had last served with the Naval Arctic Research Laboratory. It was photographed at Davis-Monthan AFB on 9 November 1976.* (David W. Menard)

LEFT *MM61765, an ex-C-53D-DO, was fitted in 1955 with an AI Mk 10 radar to be used in training radar operators for* Vampire NF 54s *of the* Aeronautica Militare Italiana. *When photographed in October 1978, it was used as a transport by the* 306° Gruppo. (DR)

BELOW *The 'Pinocchio' nose of this modified C-47B-15-DK of the Canadian Armed Forces indicates that it has been fitted with the R-24A NASARR as a trainer for CF-104 pilots.* (Jim Dunn)

of the C-47, this led to the use of the letter 'Q' as the last model identification suffix. It identified the Vietnam War-vintage EC-47Q variant which was re-engined with R-2004s and equipped as an electronic reconnaissance platform (ELINT/SIGINT/COMINT).

Colonial wars

The first batch of 22 C-47Bs handed over to the *armée de l'Air* in September 1944 at Medouina, French Morocco, was used to equip *Groupe de transport*[22] 1/15 *Touraine*. Other C-47Bs followed soon after for GT 2/25 *Anjou*, but these two units only flew in the logistical support role before the war ended. In September 1945, however, the French encountered opposition when attempting to reassert their authority in Indochina. After the wartime Japanese occupation, the return to *status quo ante* in this French colony was challenged by Communist forces led by Ho Chi Minh with fighting taking place in most of the French colony (but primarily in Tonkin, the region which became North Vietnam in 1954). Among the first aircraft to be sent to Indochina were six C-47Bs from the *escadrille de marche d'Extrême-Orient* (EMEO, Far East detached flight) which brought 150 soldiers and equipment from France. With the arrival of more aircraft this unit was brought up to squadron strength (as the GMTEO) before additional French C-47 squadrons were sent to Indochina as the

Communist led 'war of national liberation' intensified. There they provided much needed logistical support in a country with only a limited road and rail network, but they also took paratroopers into battle (doing so for the time in September 1946 near Luang Prabang in what became independent Laos), were used as makeshift bombers, flew aeromedical evacuation flights, and lit night battles with flares.

In Indochina, C-47s (and to a much lesser extent other transport aircraft, including impressed airliners) got further notoriety when in 1952 the French command adopted the concept of *'ilôts aéroterrestres'* (fortified air-land bases) to draw Viet Minh forces into chosen battle areas. French troops were to be concentrated in large fortified camps and provided with ample artillery and air support in the hope of inflicting disproportionally high casualties on the Communists. C-47s and other transport aircraft were to bring the initial units to these camps and then bring reinforcements and all supplies. This concept was proven at Na San (in what is now Vietnam's Son La Province) where the French scored a major victory in November–December 1952. Unfortunately for France, this first success could not be duplicated in 1954.

Operation Castor began in late November 1953 when 65 French C-47s and 12 USAF C-119s, loaned to France but flown by American crews, dropped paratroopers to commence work on a new fortified site at Diên Biên Phu, in northwest Tonkin near the Laotian border. An airstrip built by the Japanese during World War Two was

---

22 Although the literal translation of *groupe de transport* is transport group, it should be noted that, at the time, a French group was the equivalent in strength to a USAAF or RAF squadron.

C-47s in French Indochina

Six C-47s of the *armée de l'Air* arrived in Saigon on 12 September 1945 to begin operations in the French colony. Thereafter, the number of C-47s in service in Indochina increased progressively until topping the 100 mark during the last year of this colonial conflict. Yet, available aircraft were newer available in sufficient numbers, thus leading French forces to rely on chartered civil transport aircraft to makeup the deficiency.

BELOW *43-49665, a C-47B-20-DK of GT II/65 'Anjou' was photographed in flight over rice paddies in French Indochina.* (armée de l'Air, Jean Delmas collection)

LEFT *Taken at an unusual angle, this photograph shows rolls of barbed wire being unloaded from a French C-47 into a GMC CCKW truck.* (DR, Stéphane Nicolaou collection)

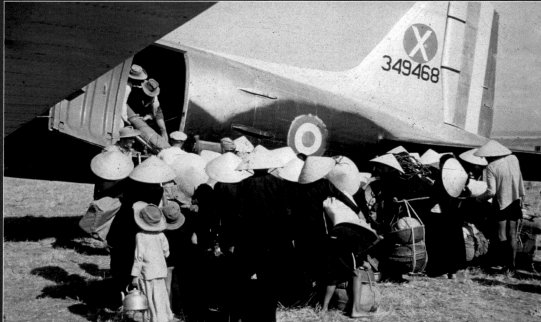

LEFT *Indochinese women wearing the traditional* áo dài *dress and* nón lá *conical hat stand by a GT I//64 'Béarn.'* (DR, Stéphane Nicolaou collection)

BELOW *For night re-supply missions, French C-47s, such as this aircraft from GT II/62 'Franche Comté,' had their lower surfaces painted black.* (DR, Stéphane Nicolaou collection)

RIGHT *Complementary pair, a C-47A and a GMC CCKW 'Deuce and a Half' in Indochina. Aircraft and truck had already established a strong record during World War Two.* (DR, Stéphane Nicolaou collection)

RIGHT *A trooper of the* Armée Nationale Vietnamienne *(Vietnamese National Army) stands guard by 43-49824, a C-47B-22-DK of GT I/64 'Béarn.'* (DR, Stéphane Nicolaou collection)

RIGHT *During the war in Indochina, French forces relied heavily on the support provided by private airlines such as* Aigle Azur *(to which F-BFGC, an ex C-47B-35-DK belonged).* (DR, Jean Delmas collection)

BELOW *Photographed during the buildup of the French 'îlôts aéroterrestres" at Diên Biên Phu, these two DC-3s belonged respectively to Autrex (F-OAMU, and ex C-47A-70-DL, in the foreground) and CTAC (F-OAIF, an ex C-53D-DO).* (DR, Stéphane Nicolaou collection)

ABOVE *This* Dakota, *probably an ex-C-53, was among the first aircraft of the* Bhartiya Vayu Sena *following the partition of India in 1947.* (USAF)

reactivated and was used by C-47s and impressed DC-3s to land supplies and reinforcements and to evacuate wounded soldiers. In addition, detachments of French fighters (mostly Grumman *Bearcats*) were based on that strip. The battle itself commenced in March 1954 and ended in defeat, in spite of the almost universal gallantry and particularly that of the crews of the C-47s who kept landing under fire until nearly the last week. On 7 May 1954 the last French and non-Communist Vietnamese troops surrendered to the Communist forces led by Vo Nguyên Giáp. This defeat was followed by the partition of Vietnam and the creation of the independent states of Cambodia and Laos.

While the main French transport units were re-equipped with the Nord 2501 *Noratlas*, C-47s remained in service with the *armée de l'Air* and the *Aéronautique navale* to serve in another colonial war, that which ended in 1962 when independence was granted to Algeria.

BELOW *In the postwar period, the USAAF/USAF had to operate under major budgetary constraints, hence the 'blotched' appearance of this Air Transport Command C-47 photographed at Coraopolis, Pennsylvania, in 1946.* (William Balogh, David W. Menard collection)

France, however, was not the only nation to use C-47s and *Dakotas* in support of combat operations in their colonies while other nations operated theirs when trying to secure their newly-acquired independence. In Africa and Asia, this was notably the case of the:

* *Bharatiya Vayu Sena* (Indian Air Force) and *Pakistan Fiza'ya* (Pakistan Air Force) after the partition of India in 1947;
* *Força Aérea Portuguesa* (Portuguese Air Force) in Angola, Portuguese Guinea (now Guinea-Bissau), and Mozambique between 1961 and 1975;
* *Force aérienne belge* (Belgian Air Force) to evacuate Belgian nationals from the Congo (now the Democratic Republic of Congo) in 1960;
* *Militaire Luchtvaart van het Koninklijk Nederlands-Indisch Leger* (Military Aviation-Royal Netherlands East Indies Army) in the Dutch East Indies (now Indonesia) between 1946 and the end of 1948;
* Royal Air Force in Malaya (along with *Dakotas* of the RAAF and RNZAF) between 1948 and 1960, and in Kenya between 1952 and 1956; and
* Royal Rhodesian Air Force (Rhodesian Air Force after 1970) in Southern Rhodesia (now Zimbabwe) between 1965 and 1979; and
* South African Air Force/*Suid-Afrikaanse Lugmag* during the Border and Bush Wars in Angola, Botswana, Mozambique, Namibia, Zambia, and Zimbabwe between 1966 and 1989.

Cold War

The first open conflict in the four-decade long confrontation between the Western Nations and the Communist World broke out in Greece a few months after George Orwell first used the term 'Cold War' in an October 1945 article. Support for the Greek government came from the United Kingdom and the United States which began supplying armament, aircraft, and other forms of assistance beginning in 1947. Twenty-two ex-RAF Dakotas and 20 ex-USAF C-47s were included in the initial deliveries of aircraft to the *Ellinikí Vasilikí Aeroporía* (Royal Hellenic Air Force). Most went to *335 Mira Metaforon* (335 Transport Squadron) which operated them not only in the transport role but also for offensive missions with 250lb and 500lb bombs carried beneath the fuselage.

While fighting was taking place in Greece, the confrontation between the Cold War nemeses took another form. In March 1948, displeased with measures taken by the other three occupying forces (Great Britain, the United States, and France), the Soviet Union began limiting access by land and water to West Berlin (then a Western 'island' in the mist of the Soviet zone). When the blockade became total on 24 June 1948, the Western Allies had to find an alternative to bring the minimum of 4,700 tons of food, fuel, and other necessities needed every day by their garrisons and by West Berliners. This led to the implementation of the justly famous Berlin Airlift *Operation Vittles* for the United States and, successively *Operations Knicker*, *Carter Paterson*, and *Plainfare* for the United Kingdom. The first USAF C-47s landed at Berlin-Tempelhof on 26 June and were followed two days later by the first RAF *Dakotas* at Berlin-Gatow. During the first months of the airlift, the Douglas twin-engined transports were by far the most numerous in use. However, when larger aircraft were added by the USAF and USN (mainly Douglas C-54s and R5Ds), the US C-47s were no longer used for *Operation Vittles* after September 1948. Even though supplemented by other aircraft (including some from British companies), the RAF *Dakotas* remained in use until the last day of the airlift.

Between 24 June 1948 and 30 September 1949, military and civilian aircrews from Australia, Britain, Canada, France, New Zealand, South Africa, and the United States made 278,228 flights to Berlin to deliver over 2.8 million tons of supplies (with a 24hr record of 12,941 tons being set on 15–16 April 1949). In the process, 101 lives and 25 aircraft (including five C-47s and three *Dakotas*) were lost. But the West Berliners had been fed and kept warm by the Western flyers while the Soviets lost the propaganda war and were forced to back down.

On 25 June 1950, almost nine months after the Berlin Airlift had ended, war broke out in Korea. Once again C-47s and *Dakotas* were called to duty. During this 37-month conflict, C-47s from seven air forces (Australian, Greek, South Korean, Thai, USAF, USMC, and USN) served in Korea with the United Nations while Chinese, North Korean, and Russian Li-2s flew for the other side. With the UN, the C-47s, R4Ds, and *Dakotas* were used extensively during the first months of the war to bring in supplies and ammunition. Thereafter, they were replaced in troop carrier squadrons by C-46s, C-54s, C-119s, and C-124s but remained in use for liaison and transport support as well as for electronic reconnaissance (*Bluesky*)[23] and flare dropping (*Firefly*) sorties.

Even when operating away from open conflict areas, C-47s and *Dakotas* were not out of harm's way during the Cold War. At first, it was Yugoslav pilots that proved the most aggressive. The following Douglas twins were either forced down or shot down:

- [unknown] 1946 - RAF *Dakota* forced down by a Yugoslav Yak-3;
- 9 August 1946 - USAAF C-47 shot down by a Yugoslav Yak-3;
- 19 August 1946 - USAAF C-47 shot down by a Yugoslav Yak-3;
- 18 November 1951 - USAF C-57 forced down in Romania by Soviet MiG-15;
- 13 June 1952 - Swedish Tp79 (an ex-USAAF C-47-DL purchased from SAS and modified as an ELINT platform) shot down by a Soviet MiG-15 over the Baltic;
- 29 November 1952 - CIA-operated C-47 of China Air Transport shot down by Chinese fighters in the PRC;
- 3 June 1954 - Belgian 'transport aircraft' (probably a C-47) shot down by an unidentified MiG over Yugoslavia;
- 11 November 1957 - Jordanian C-47 forced down in Israel by *Mystère IV A*s;
- 30 May 1959 - UN-operated C-47 forced down in Israel by *Mystère IV A*s; and
- 25 May 1960 - USAF C-47 forced down in East Germany by Soviet MiGs.

More peaceful uses of C-47s and related Douglas twins were also made during the Cold War years. This was particularly the case during the first two *Deep Freeze* operations in Antarctica. In 1947,

---

23 For this mission 10 RC-47Ds were specially modified and, beginning at the end of 1952, were flown along the North Korean coasts and forward of the battlefields to record enemy transmissions. Recording tapes were air dropped on Cho-do, a small island on the East Coast of North Korea, near Wonsan, where American forces had established a forward post. *Bluesky* sorties continued for 10 years after combat in Korea had ceased.

ABOVE *43-48579, one of the first AC-47D gunships of the Fourth Air Commando Squadron at Bien Hoa AB in February 1966.* (David W. Menard)

six R4D-5s fitted with retractable skis on either side of the main and tail wheels were loaded aboard the carrier USS *Philippine Sea* (CV 47) to take part in Operation *Highjump*. On 29 January 1947, while the carrier was steaming 660 nautical miles from Antarctica, the first pair of R4D-5s was boosted aloft by JATO (Jet-Assisted Take-Off) bottles enabling them to use less than 400ft of the flight deck to get airborne. The two aircraft then proceeded to McMurdo Station where they landed on the ice and snow-packed surface to support the first US permanent research station on the frozen continent. Two days later, they were joined by the four other R4D-5s with which they then compiled the first full photographic survey of the coast of Antarctica as well as quite a bit of the inland area.

Even more impressive results were achieved during *Deep Freeze II* in the southern summer of 1956. This time, six ski-equipped R4D-5Ls and R4D-6Ls were ferried by air to Dunedin in New Zealand. From there, they proceeded to *Little America IV* at McMurdo Station in October 1956. On the 31st of that month, BuNo12418, an R4D-5L named *Que Sera Sera* and carrying a crew of seven made a round-trip flight from McMurdo to the South Pole where they made an ice landing at the South Pole (the first ever at the southernmost point on Earth). On take-off, 11 JATO bottles were required to get the R4D-5L off the unprepared surface on which the skis had frozen. A few days later, BuNo 17274 *Charlene*, an R4D-6L, took 11 members of the Seabees (construction battalions of the US Navy), their sled dogs, supplies, and equipment to begin construction of the first permanent station at the South Pole.

Vietnam ops

For the third time in 20 years, US C-47s were sent back to a war zone when four aircraft from Det. 2 of the 4400th Combat Crew Training Squadron[24] were ferried from Eglin AFB, Florida, to

Bien-Hoa, South Vietnam, in September 1961. Designated SC-47s, without a suffix letter, they were fitted with strengthened undercarriage and attachment points for JATO bottles to facilitate operations from short fields with rough surfaces. In addition, their modifications included the installation of additional tanks to double disposable fuel, flare and leaflet dispensers, and loudspeakers for use in psychological warfare operations. The first USAF aircraft lost in Vietnam was an SC-47 (43-15732, an ex-C-47A-90-DL) which went down on 11 February 1962 near Bao Loc, some 70 miles north of Saigon, during a leaflet drop sortie. All nine on board were killed. Another SC-47 was shot down on 24 March 1962 while flying a photo-reconnaissance sortie in Laos. Many more C-47s, whether bearing pseudo-US markings, full USAAF markings, VNAF markings, or those of CIA covert airlines (principally Air America) were lost in Vietnam, Cambodia, and Laos during 14 years of fighting ending with the fall of Saigon in April 1975.

With the USAF, the SC-47s of the 4400th CCTS were followed by two other variants bearing different mission prefixes as befitted their use for special operations. The best known of these Vietnam-era versions was the 'gunship' AC-47 (where the prefix A, previously identifying aircraft modified for airways checking, stood for 'armed'). The gunship had already seen limited use in this theatre of operations during the French war in Indochina as a Grumman JRF-5 *Goose* of the *Aéronautique navale* had been fitted with a 12.7mm machine gun mounted in the entrance door to fire downward at a fixed angle while the aircraft was circling the target. The concept was next tested in 1964 at Eglin AFB, Florida, where a C-131B was equipped with a SUU-11A 7.62mm gun pod on the left side of the cargo compartment. This was quickly followed by the initial installation of three SUU-11A pods in a C-47 which then was designated FC-47 (with F for fighter). Once again, tests proved more than encouraging and a modification crew was sent from Eglin AFB to Bien Hoa to modify two C-47s into FC-47s and to train crews from the 1st Air Commando Squadron (the ex 4400th CCTS) in their use. The first combat use of these 'in country' modified FC-47s was made on 15 December 1964 and was followed by the first night operations on 23 and 24 December. Almost immediately, it was decided to have four more aircraft modified locally, but to have them armed with 10 single-barrel AN/M-2 machine guns as SUU-11A pods were in short supply. At the same time, an initial batch of 26 AC-47Ds (the new gunship designation adopted at the end of 1965) was to be modified to full specifications in the United States.

24 The 4400th Combat Crew Training Squadron was activated at Hurlburt Field, Florida, on 14 April 1961 as a counterinsurgency unit and was manned by 'Jungle Jim' volunteers. When ordered to Vietnam in September 1961, its Detachment 2 (Det. 2) was initially composed of 155 officers and airmen with four Douglas SC-47s, eight armed North American T-28s and four Douglas B-26Bs. Under the cover of providing training to the fledgling Vietnamese Air Force (VNAF), *Operation Farmgate* saw American aircrews commence flying covert combat missions in Vietnam (the first without a Vietnamese officer on board being made on 26 December 1961).

The fully modified AC-47Ds were armed with three MXU-470/A pods, each housing a six-barrel 7.62mm gun. They carried 48 flares and had a crew of seven (pilot, co-pilot, navigator, flight engineer, loadmaster and two gunners). At the target, AC-47Ds flew at 3,000ft in 5,000ft circles, banking at 30° and cruising at 120mph. The first four were sent to Forbes AFB, Kansas, where crew training took place with the others being ferried across the Pacific to equip the 4th Air Commando Squadron and then also the 3rd ACS. Proving very effective as long as AAA and shoulder-fired missiles were not deployed by the Viet Cong or the North Vietnamese Army, the AC-47S were referred to by the affectionate names of 'Spooky' and 'Puff the Magic Dragon' (inspired by a then very popular song by Peter, Paul, and Mary). Nineteen of the 53 AC-47Ds eventually obtained by the USAF were shot down during the war with the others going to the Laotian and South Vietnamese air forces after being replaced in USAF service by more potent and better performing gunships. By the end of April 1975, the last AC-47Ds of the VNAF and the Royal Lao Air Force had either been destroyed or captured, or were no longer serviceable.

Less well-known than the gunships, the EC-47 electronic reconnaissance versions played an equally important role during the war in Southeast Asia. In January 1966, seeking ways to identify, locate, and record various types of transmission from Viet Cong units, the USAF asked the industry to submit proposals for Airborne Radio Direction Finding (ARDF) equipment capable of working even when transmitters were under deep jungle cover. Air International, a specialized firm in Florida, got the contract to modify 69 C-47s into three EC-47 configurations with distinct electronic gathering equipment and slightly different cabin configurations. Twenty-five EC-47Ns were fitted for locating/recording only Morse code transmitters, 28 EC-47Qs also gathered voice transmissions, and 16 EC-47Qs added jamming equipment and had their R-1830-90D engines replaced by R-2000-4s. EC-47s entered service in April 1966 and were initially operated by the 360th, 361st, and 362nd Tactical Electronic Warfare Squadrons (with aircraft respectively coded AJ, AL, and AN) of the 460th Tactical

Reconnaissance Wing. In all cases, the basic crew members were provided by those three squadrons while 'back-ender' electronic specialists were from the 6994th Security Squadron. In eight years of operations ending on 15 May 1974, eight EC-47s were shot down and one was destroyed on the ground. The remaining 60 then went to the air forces of Cambodia, Laos, and South Vietnam.

Into the sunset

In 1975, after combat operations in Southeast Asia had ended and as the aviation community was celebrating the 40th anniversary of the first flight of the DST, military versions of the DC-3 remained in operation with 68 air forces: 23 in Africa, 16 in Asia and the Pacific, 10 in Europe, 17 in Latin America, and two in North America. Fifteen years later, in 1990, only 38 air forces still flew military DC-3s: 12 in Africa, nine in Asia and the Pacific, two in Europe, and 15 in Latin America.

Even though the entry into service during the 1990s of modernized variants with PT6A turbines slowed down the ageing process for venerable military DC-3s (with even the 6th Special Operations Squadron, USAF, using a leased BT-67 to train foreign aircrews between 2002 and 2008), the number of operators has kept decreasing. In the middle of 2011, only 10 air forces (those of Colombia, El Salvador, Greece, Honduras, Mali, Mauritania, Mexico, Serbia, South Africa, and Thailand) still operated DC-3 military derivatives, including some fitted as gunships. The last recorded losses of piston-engined and turboprop-powered military DC-3s were those of a C-47A-80-DL of the *armée de l'Air malgache* (Madagascar Air Force) on 18 July 2005 and a BT-67 of the *Fuerza Aérea Colombiana* (Colombian Air Force) on 18 February 2009.

BELOW *This EC-47Q of the* Không Quân Việt Nam *(VNAF, Vietnamese Air Force) has been re-engined with R-2000 radials as evidenced by the location of the propeller further ahead of the cowling than was that of standard R-1830 powered aircraft.* (David W. Menard)

ABOVE *Belonging to the Fuerza Aérea Ecuatoriana (FAE, Ecuadorian Air Force) but regularly operated on commercial flights on behalf of* Transportes Aéreos Militares Ecuatorianos *(TAME, Ecuatorian Military Air Transport), this C-47-DL in military markings also carries a civil registration, HC-AUZ.* (René J. Francillon)

LEFT *A line-up of three C-47s of the Air Academy,* Tûrk Hava Kuvvetleri *(Turkish Air Force), is shown at Istanbul-Yesilkoy on 22 August 1994. They were the last military C-47s based in Europe.* (Benoit Colin)

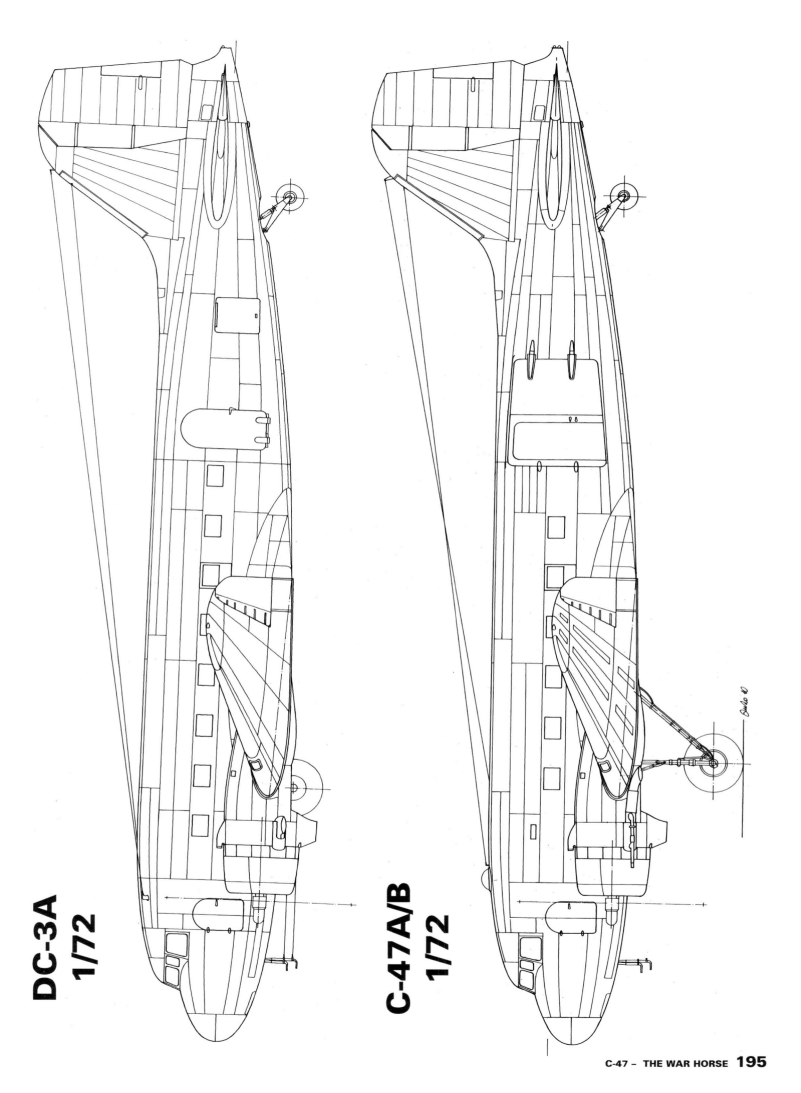

DC-3A
1/72

C-47A/B
1/72

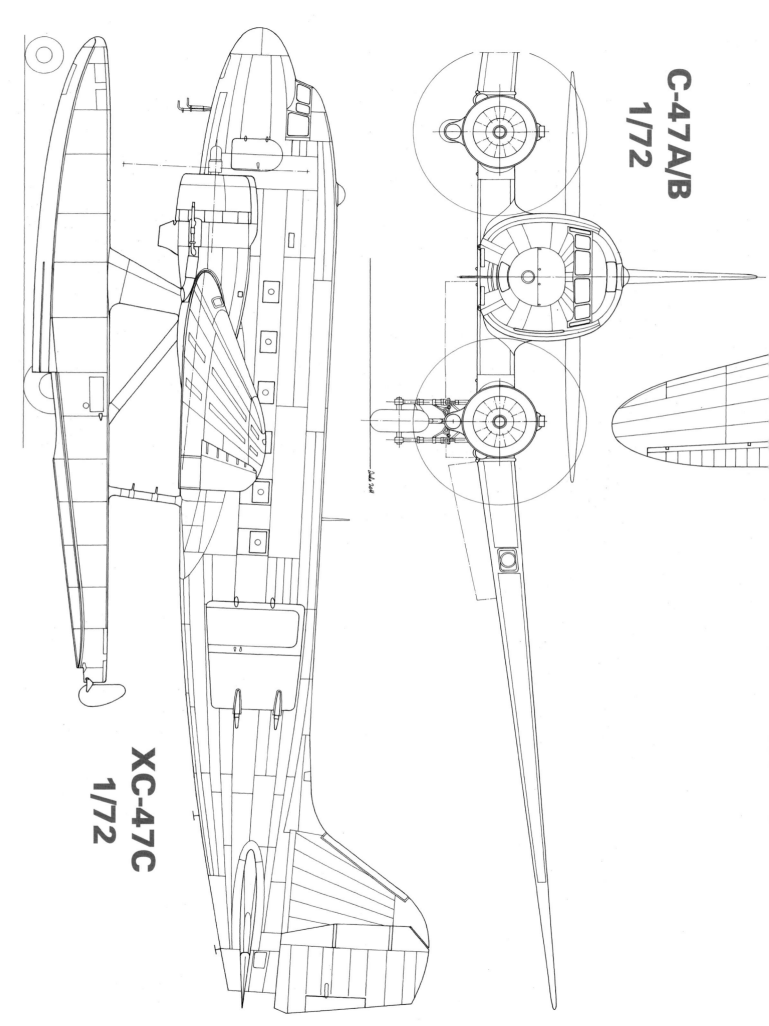

C-47A/B
1/72

XC-47C
1/72

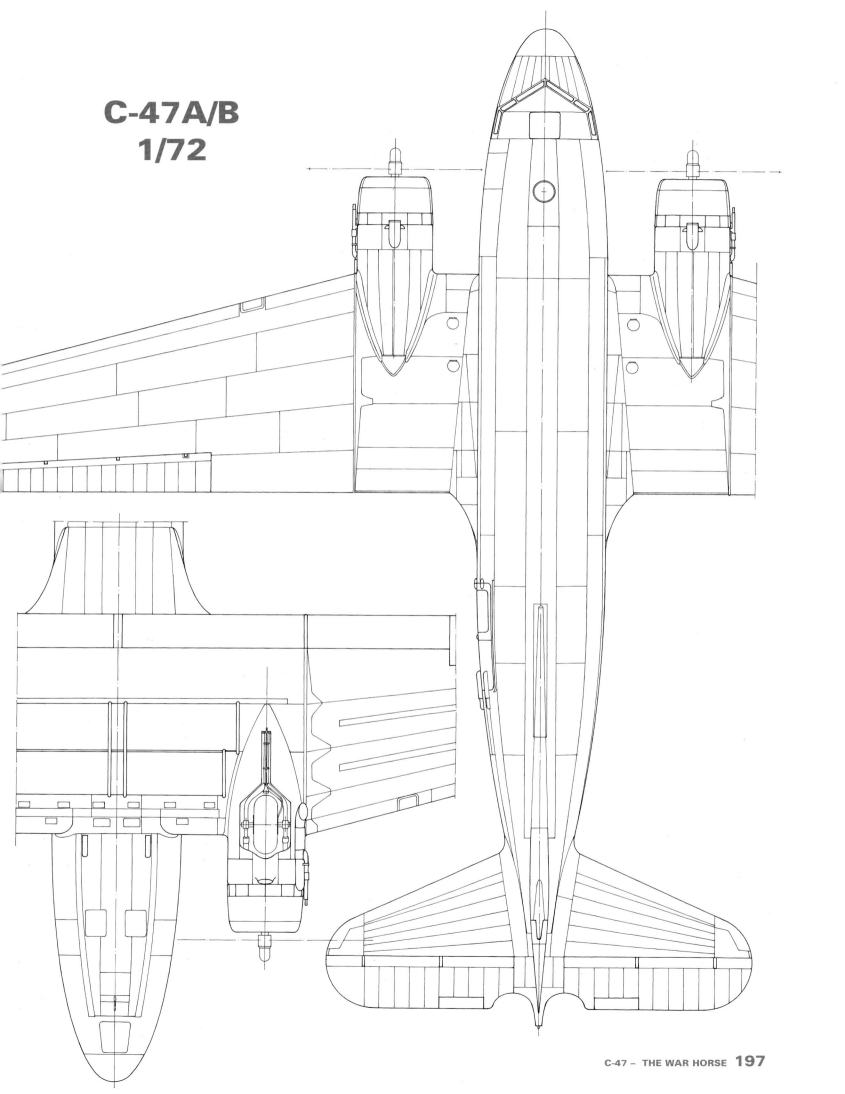

C-47A/B
1/72

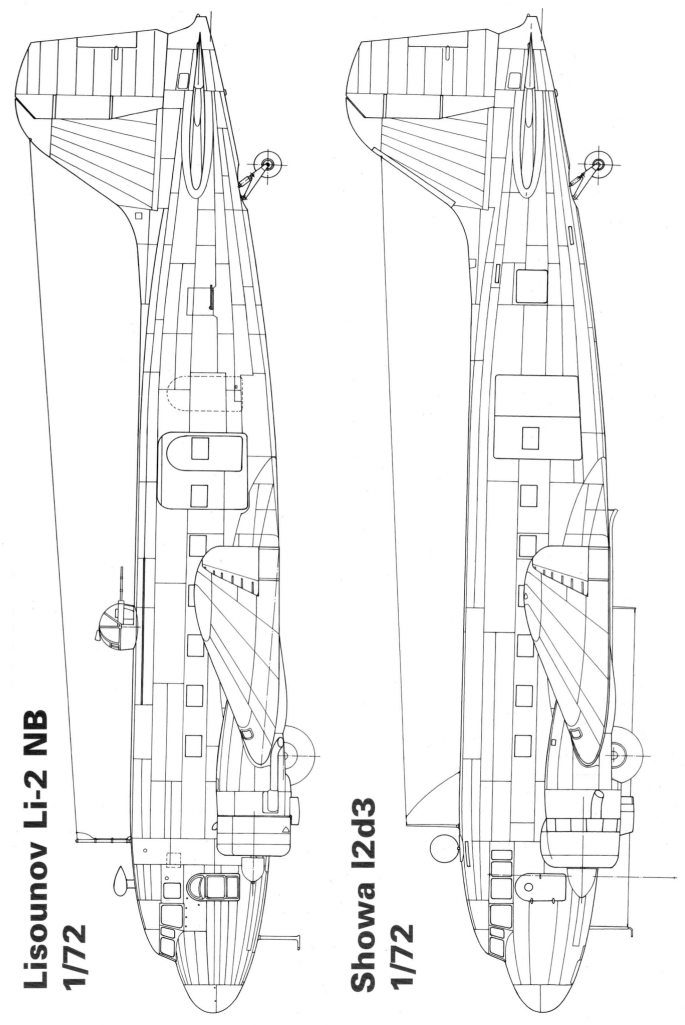

Lisounov Li-2 NB
1/72

Showa l2d3
1/72

C-47 on operations

ABOVE *Although officially named Skytroopers, C-53s, such as this aircraft of the 10th Transport Group at Wright Field in 1941, were better known to GIs as 'Gooney Birds' like the other military versions of the DC-3.* (USAAF)

RIGHT *When America was drawn into World War Two, it was rapidly called to operate in unfamiliar territory, such as the middle of Papua New Guinea, a yet relatively uncharted territory where natives had not yet been close to aircraft.* (USAAF)

RIGHT *Paratroopers line up to board a Skytrain during a postwar exercise, after this C-47A-90-DL had received the 'buzz number' CE-074.* (USAF)

ABOVE *A C-47 of the 1st Air Commando Group in the CBI theatre has just got a CG-4 glider up in the air.* (USAAF)

LEFT *Another major role for C-47s of troop carrier units was the evacuation of wounded personnel as demonstrated by litter patients being transferred from a Dodge WC54 ambulance.* (USAAF)

BELOW *A spare wing is mounted beneath the centre fuselage of this C-47 during operations in New Guinea.* (USAAF)

ABOVE *This C-47A-10-DK, 42-92577, has been modified into a C-47C by installation of amphibian floats. When operating from land bases, the loading was complicated by the height of the cargo deck above the tarmac.* (Douglas)

BELOW *Built as a TC-47B-20DK in January 1945, this 'Gooney Bird' had been modified into a C-47B by the time it was operated in Vietnam to drop propaganda leaflets as part of the 'psy-war'.* (USAF)

US military C-47s and derivatives

LEFT *A C-47A-90-DL is having its wartime camouflage paint stripped.* (USAAF, David W. Menard collection)

BELOW The Speaker *was a C-47B that was fitted with a battery of loudspeakers in the aft fuselage for 'psy-war' operations in Korea.* (NMUSAF)

LEFT *The last USAF piston-engined 'Gooney Bird' was this C-47B-15-DK which was sent to the Museum at Wright-Patterson AFB on 1 July 1975. At least one turboprop-powered BT-67 was operated by the 6th Special Operations Squadron, USAF, between 2002 and 2008.* (David W. Menard)

RIGHT *Wearing the badge of the Tactical Air Command on its fin, this C-47D was photographed at Nellis AFB, Nevada, on 15 March 1967.* (Peter B. Lewis)

BELOW *An EN-coded AC-47D of the 4th Air Commando Squadron at Tan Son Nhut AB, Vietnam, in December 1967.* (Jacques Guillem collection)

BOTTOM *A C-47H (ex-R4D-5) of H&MS-24 at MCAS Yuma on 11 March 1967.* (Peter B. Lewis)

TOP *Used at China Lake, California, for missile guidance tests, this C-47J was fitted with specialized equipment in a nose radome.* (Peter B. Lewis)

ABOVE *This ex-Navy R4D-6Q had become an Army EC-47J by the time it was photographed at the San Francisco International Airport.* (David W. Menard collection)

LEFT *An Army C-47K at NAS Lakehurst, New Jersey, on 9 September 1971.* (Steve Miller, David W. Menard collection)

TOP *An EC-47N of the 360th Tactical Electronic Warfare Squadron was photographed in front of the 460th Tactical Reconnaissance Wing HQ at Tan Son Nhut AB in May 1968.* (Jacques Guillem collection)

ABOVE *Photographed in July 1966, this C-117B bears the markings of the USAF headquarters.* (David W. Menard)

RIGHT *Even space flights required support from the venerable 'Gooney Bird' such as this NASA R4D-5.* (NASA)

Foreign military C-47s and derivatives

TOP *The South African Air Force got its first* Dakotas *in June 1943. The SAAF still operates turbine-engined C-47s 78 years later. These* Twin Wasp-*engined C-47s of the SAAF were photographed in December 1987.* (Cyril Avinens)

ABOVE *This ex-C-47A-40-DL was modified for use in the maritime patrol role by 35 Squadron, SAAF.* (Martin E. Siegrist)

LEFT *A C-47 of the* Force aérienne belge *(Belgian Air Force) modified as an F-104G radar trainer.* (David W. Menard collection)

TOP *TJ-XAL, a C-47B of the armée de l'Air du Cameroun (Cameroon Air Force), at Douala in November 1975.* (Jacques Guillem)

ABOVE *A Dakota IV of the Canadian Armed Forces at Travis AFB, California, on 12 August 1984.* (Peter B. Lewis)

RIGHT *Fitted with a CF-104 radar in its nose, this Canadian Dakota was photographed at Abbotsford, British Columbia on 7 June 1986.* (Jim Dunn)

ABOVE *A C-47B-1-DK of the ROKAF (Republic of Korea Air Force) bringing officials to Chinhae (K-10) in July 1952.* (David W. Menard collection)

LEFT *The* Kongelige Danske Flyvevåbnet *(Royal Danish Air Force) was a late C-47 operator. Its first C-47 was not put in service until September 1953.* (George Pennick, David W. Menard collection)

BELOW *FAES 116, a Basler BT-67 (ex-C-47B-35-DK) of the* Fuerza Aérea de El Salvador *(El Salvador Air Force).* (M. J. Delgado)

ABOVE *This C-47B-35-DK of the* Fuerza Aérea Ecuatoriana *was photographed at Quito in October 1974 just prior to taking paratroopers for a demonstration on the occasion of the FAE Day.* (René J. Francillon)

RIGHT *The last C-47s in French military service were those of the* Aéronautique navale *which were in use until August 1984. This pair of French 'Gooney Birds' was photographed in October 1980.* (Michel Fournier)

BELOW *Thirty C-47s were refurbished in 1949 by Aviation Maintenance Corporation in Van Nuys, California, for the Royal Hellenic Air Force. This RHAF aircraft was operating in Korea in 1951.* (J. Corrigan)

TOP *FAG 535 (ex-43-16266, a C-47B1-DL) of the* Fuerza Aérea Guatemalteca *was photographed at McGuire AFB, New Jersey, on 19 May 1973.* (David Ostrowski)

ABOVE *Festooned with antennae, this Barvaz (Mallard) was a C-47 of the Heyl Ha'Avir modified to serve in the ELINT (electronic intelligence) gathering role.* (Simon Watson)

LEFT *MM61815 (ex 43-49539) entered service with the Aeronautica Militare Italiana in October 1952. It was later modified for navaids calibration, a role in which it served until 1986 with the 14º Stormo at Pratica di Mare.* (DR)

TOP *Photographed in March 1979, this C-47 was one of six donated by Israel to the Uganda Air Force, apparently in compensation for damage at the Entebbe airport caused during* Operation Thunderbolt, *the Israeli rescue of passengers from the hijacked Air France Flight 139 on 4 July 1976.* (Cyril Avinens collection)

ABOVE *This unidentified C-47 was still in service with the* Transporte Aéreo Militar, Fuerza Aérea del Paraguay *(Military Air Transport, Paraguayan Air Force) in January 1996.* (g.g.j. Kamp)

RIGHT *A C-47A-90-DL of the Philippine Air Force at Clark AB in 1964.* (David W. Menard)

LEFT *6W-SAD (ex-44-76746) of the* armée de l'Air du Sénégal *(Senegal Air Force) at Paris-Le Bourget in 1974.* (Jacques Guillem)

BELOW *A C-47A-35-DL of the* Escadrille nationale tchadienne *(Chad National Flight) at N'Djamena in January 1988.* (Jacques Guillem)

BOTTOM *This C-47A-35-DL (ex-42-23941) of the* force aérienne togolaise *(Togo Air Force), crashed at Lama Kara, north-eastern Togo, on 24 January 1974.* (Jacques Guillem collection)

RIGHT *This C-47 of the Turk Hava Küvvetleri (Turkish Air Force) was operated by the base flight at Mürted in July 1992.* (Benoit Colin)

BELOW *Photographed on 28 July 1973, this Turkish military C-47 had been modified into a mineral resource survey aircraft.* (Steve Miller, David W. Menard collection)

BOTTOM *In April 1975, 13 months after this photograph had been taken at Clark AB, the Philippines, this EC-47D of the Vietnamese Air Force (VNAF) was among the aircraft that succeeded in fleeing Saigon ahead of North Vietnamese troops.* (David W. Menard)

Chapter 9

DC-4 & C-54 – The world within reach

Flying across the Atlantic at nearly 600mph and 35,000ft has become so common that the vast majority of passengers sitting in warm and pressurized comfort are unlikely to give much thought to those who pioneered the crossing of this ocean. Many of these spoiled passengers are so busy complaining about the food or the attitude of cabin attendants that they fail to give thanks to those who gave their lives making such travel possible. Some of those giving a thought to what it was like to cross the North Atlantic 'back then' will remember the 'Lone Eagle,' Charles Lindbergh and

his non-stop crossing from New York to Paris. Fewer will be those who know about the Pan American and Imperial Airways flying boats that inaugurated trans-Atlantic air service just before World War Two. But hardly any of today's fortunate travelers are likely to remember, or care, that it was mostly land-based aircraft and their military crews which turned daring into routine during the war. It was Douglas C-54s that accomplished the most over the Atlantic and elsewhere around the globe, after Consolidated LB-30As of the Atlantic Ferry Organisation of the Ministry of Aircraft Production had shown the way in May 1941. In early postwar years, many airlines then turned to the DC-4, the civil version of the C-54, to start their transoceanic operations.

As related in Chapter 6, before the original DC-4 had flown in June 1938, two of the five original sponsors of its development (Pan American Airways and Transcontinental & Western Airlines) had jumped ship to ask Boeing to develop a simpler and less

BELOW *The Berlin Airlift Historical Foundation keeps this C-54-E-15-DO, 44-9100 (aka R5D-4 BuNo 90414) in flying condition in remembrance for one of the key events during the Cold War. It was photographed at dawn at MacDill AFB, Florida, on 25 March 2008. (USAF)*

expensive to operate four-engined transport, the 307 *Stratoliner*. The remaining sponsors (American Airlines, Eastern Air Lines, and United Air Lines) then sought to recover part of their investment by asking Douglas to come up with a new four-engined design with less complex systems and lower weight. Acquisition and operating costs were also to be lower than those for the first DC-4 prototype. By resetting the clock to zero, Douglas and its three faithful customers managed to turn failure into success.

Keep it simple

When prodding Douglas into a new direction, away from the 'Rube Goldberg' design of the triple-tailed DC-4, American, Eastern, and United urged the manufacturer to follow the old KISS principle – keep it simple, stupid – much touted in American industries. Those working on the Santa Monica design team led by Arthur E. Raymond and Edward F. Burton were already well aware that their first four-engined airliner had been overly engineered. Consequently, they set their sights a bit lower while retaining the goal of coming up with an aircraft capable of carrying 40 passengers across the United States with only two stops. A smaller, lighter aircraft resulted from this new approach.

To make fabrication easier, a fuselage of constant cross-section – 138in high and 125in wide – was adopted giving internal cabin dimensions of 118.5in x 93in (versus 129in x 90in for the cabin of the original triple-tailed design). Passenger baggage was to be carried in 259cu ft compartments on the main deck while two under-floor holds with a combined volume of 266cu ft were reserved for cargo and mail.

An entirely new wing was designed with span and area of 117ft 6in and 1,457sq ft, versus 138ft 3in and 2,155sq ft for the DC-4E. It retained the proven three-spar 'Northrop-Douglas' multi-cellular construction for the center-section which incorporated the engine nacelles, the main gear housing, and the fuel tanks. Of similar construction, the outboard panels only had one spar. The new wing had a revised geometry with straight leading and trailing edges and chord progressively reduced from the roots to the tips. Finally, the new design differed externally as the result of the adoption of single vertical surfaces when the need for triple tails to reduce height was no longer justified as larger hangars were being built by the airlines.

Having incurred heavy losses with its first four-engined airliner, Douglas returned to a more conservative approach. With the support of the sponsoring airlines, its design team eschewed all propensity to use unproven or complex systems, such as the two auxiliary power units and power-boosted ailerons of the earlier aircraft. Conversely, airlines and manufacturer agreed that the new design would have a tricycle undercarriage as that had been the most liked feature of the triple-tailed prototype.

To power the new aircraft, Douglas suggested using four radial engines rated at around 1,000hp on take-off, with the airlines being given a choice between the 9-cylinder *Wright Cyclone* SGR-1820-G205A and the 14-cylinder Pratt & Whitney *Twin Wasp* S1C3-G. The fuselage was designed so that later production aircraft could be built with a pressurized cabin. Among other decisions taken during the early design phase was that concerning the main cabin which was to receive 40 seats (10 rows of 2 + 2) convertible into beds,

BELOW *The geometry of the DC-4 wings is well illustrated by this photograph of a C-54B-1-DC of the Air Transport Command flying near Kunming, China, on 5 June 1945. (USAAF)*

Twin Wasp 2SD1-G (a *Twin Wasp* development with increased bore and displacement) was adopted. Once the power plant installation had been agreed to, the three sponsoring airlines and Douglas worked on finalizing contracts covering a total of 61 of the new four-engined airliners, by then designated DC-4 as the earlier triple-tailed design had become the DC-4E. In anticipation of final contract signature, Douglas began building an initial lot of nine aircraft.

While this was taking place, the world situation became increasingly tense. Most of continental Europe was in the hands of the Nazis and fear of a war with Japan was growing. In response to this state of affairs, the US government instructed manufacturers to give priority to military aircraft production. In the case of the Douglas plant in Santa Monica, this meant that work would soon be centered on production of A-20 light bombers and military DC-3 derivatives. In March 1941, the War Department also began planning to take over the nine DC-4s then entering production. This was finalized with the award on 28 June 1941 of contract W-935 AC 19411. The first Douglas four-engined airliners would first serve in uniform.

Call of duty

The Air Corps Ferrying Command started its six monthly round trips between Washington D.C. and Scotland with modified Consolidated B-24As[1] in July 1941. As ACFC then planned to expand its overwater activities by having later models of the B-24 completed as C-87 transports, it did not anticipate having much use for the DC-4s about to be completed as C-54-DOs and Douglas was instructed not to rush completion of these orphaned military transport aircraft.

The first C-54-DO – fsn 3050, serial 41020137 – came off the Santa Monica line in February 1942. Finished in military markings and wearing camouflage paint, it made its first flight at Clover Field on 14 February with John F. Martin in command of the test crew. Uneventful manufacturer trials in California were followed by military testing at Wright Field, Ohio. The USAAF then realized that C-54s would be better performing and more reliable than C-87s. Suddenly, the C-54 program gained urgency and, with additional aircraft being rapidly ordered, production was to take

ABOVE *The battle of Los Angeles, 24/25 February 1942: After a Japanese submarine shelled an oil field installation at Ellwood, north of Los Angeles, during the evening of 23 February 1942, a panic alert resulted in heavy anti-aircraft fire in Los Angeles during the following night. This was followed by the release of 'patriotic' photographs, such as this one showing vigilant gunners protecting the first C-54 on the ramp at Clover Field.* (Douglas)

night-time accommodation being reduced to 28 with lower-double and upper-single berths.

American, Eastern, and United liked what they saw but did request that more powerful engines be installed. In response, a new 14-cylinder, double-row radial from Pratt & Whitney, the 1,450hp

BELOW *America having been thrown into the war two months earlier, the first C-54 received a coat of camouflage paint before being rolled out at Santa Monica in February 1942.* (Douglas)

---

1 Generally similar to the RAF's *Liberator I*s, nine B-24As were not considered battle-ready by the Army Air Corps. With bombing equipment removed and fitted with bucket seats in a Spartan accommodation, eight of those became the first 'long-range' of the Air Corps Ferrying Command.

place not only in the Santa Monica plant (DO) but also in the new government-owned plant (DC) that was being built for Douglas at Elk Grove in the suburbs of Chicago, Illinois.

Military production

Production of C-54 *Skymasters*[2] began with the completion of the nine aircraft taken over from the initial batch for the airline and the assembly of 15 additional aircraft for which Douglas had already ordered material and equipment. These 24 C-54-DOs were followed by 1,141 other aircraft built under military contracts in the following models with C-54 and R5D designations.

C-54-DO: Built at the Santa Monica plant, the 24 C-54-DOs had started as airliners but were completed to partial military configuration. They were powered by four R-2000-3 radials (military designation of the Pratt & Whitney *Twin Wasp* 2SD1-Gs) delivering 1,350hp on take-off, 1,100hp at 6,900ft, and 1,000hp at 14,000ft. Having been designed to transport 40 passengers across the United States with two refueling stops, these aircraft lacked the payload/range capability required by the Air Transport Command.[3] Consequently, provision was made for installing four auxiliary tanks in the cabin to increase fuel capacity from the built-in 1,675 Imp. gallons to 2,980 Imp. gallons. When the cabin tanks were installed, seating was reduced from 40 to 16 but the C-54 still retained airline-style galley and lavatory. When the standard airline seats were replaced by military web seats the number of passengers went up to 26 with all cabin tanks in place.

It had been planned to deliver the last 15 C-54-DOs to Britain where they were to be given serials FL996/FL999 and FR100/FR110. Instead, they went to the USAAF as 42-32936 to 42-32950.

C-54A-DO & -DC: Built in Santa Monica (97 C-54A-DOs) and Chicago (252 C-54A-DCs), the first variant intended from the onset for military use differed from the C-54-DOs in having reinforced cabin flooring with cargo handling (including a twin-boom hoist for loads of up to 4,000lb) and tie-down fittings. Cargo loading/unloading was accomplished through a 94in x 67in double cargo door on the left side of the rear fuselage (in place of the passenger access door) with provisions for attaching a platform and ramp for loading wheeled vehicles. Maximum cargo load was 32,500lb with alternative load consisting of either up to 50 troops on folding canvas seats or 36 stretchers.

The first C-54A-DO was delivered on 14 January 1943 and was followed on 1 October by the first C-54A-DC. Fifty-six of the 349 C-54As were transferred to the USN with which they became R5D-1s.

C-54B-DO: With auxiliary fuel tanks in the cabin, the first two variants were endowed with adequate range for transoceanic operations. This installation, however, limited available space in the cabin too much, reducing useful loads on long sectors. Accordingly, the fuel system of 100 C-54B-DOs and 120 C-54B-DCs was modified by replacing two of the four cabin tanks by integral tanks in the wing outer panels, to obtain a maximum fuel capacity of 3,115 Imp. gallons. This enabled C-54Bs to transport 41 military passengers and five crewmembers between California and Hawaii. Thirty-two C-54B-DCs went to the Navy as R5D-2s and one went to the Royal Air Force for use by Prime Minister Winston Churchill.

VC-54C-DO: A C-54A-5-DO (41-37295, fsn 3086, which was nicknamed *Sacred Cow*)[4] was modified during construction to become the first US presidential aircraft. A hatch beneath the fuselage was fitted with an electrically-operated lift for the wheelchair of President Roosevelt. The sound-proofed cabin was fitted with a presidential state-room, a conference room, seating for 15, and sleeping accommodation for six. Additional wing tanks were fitted to raise fuel capacity to 3,755 Imp. gallons. It is best remembered for being used to take President Roosevelt to the Soviet Union on the occasion of the Yalta Conference in February 1945.

C-54D-DC: This version, which differed from the C-54B

4 The aircraft was first dubbed the 'Sacred Cow' by the Washington press corps. This irreverent name was never approved but has stuck as an unofficial nickname.

---

2 The name *Skymaster* was almost exclusively used by the manufacturer while military personnel almost universally referred to these aircraft by their C-54 designation (or R5D in the case of the USN).
3 The Air Corps Ferrying Command had been reorganized into the larger Air Transport Command on 20 June 1942.

BELOW *After World War Two had ended, this C-54A-15-DC (42-73304) was acquired by American Airlines (as N90435) before becoming F-BBDQ with Air France in August 1949. It was photographed 37 years later at N'Djamena in the markings of the* Escadrille nationale tchadienne *(Chad National Flight).* (A. Arrieumeres, Cyril Avinens collection)

TOP *Nicknamed* Sacred Cow *by the Washington press corps, the presidential VC-54C has been restored by the National Museum of the USAF at Wright-Patterson AFB, Ohio.* (NMUSAF)

ABOVE *Wearing the insignia of the Air Transport Command on its rear fuselage, 42-72628 is a C-54D-5-DC. The cabin floor level with the ground and the large double door made for easy loading and unloading of the aircraft.* (Douglas)

essentially in being powered by 1,350hp R-2000-11s, was built in the largest number, 380 coming off the Chicago lines. After the last C-54D-15-DC (fsn 22203, 43-17523) was delivered to the USAAF on 20 August 1945, the Chicago plant was closed; 86 went to the USN as R5D-3s and 22 to the RAF as *Skymaster* Mk. Is.

C-54E-DO: The 125 aircraft built in Santa Monica (including 20 diverted to the USN as R5D-4s) had a new fuel arrangement with collapsible bag-type tanks in the inner wings bringing total capacity up to 2,931 Imp. gallons and eliminating the need for auxiliary tanks in the fuselage. The cabin arrangement was modified to permit rapid conversion from cargo (up to 32,500lb) to troop carriers (50 on bucket canvas seats) or to staff transport (44 airline-type-seats).

XC-54F-DC: One C-54B-1-DC (fsn 10426, 42-73221) was fitted with jump doors on both sides of the rear fuselage to serve as the prototype for a planned paratroop transport version. Production

Data for the Douglas C-54D-DC

Dimensions: Span, 117ft 6in; length, 93ft 10in; height, 27ft 6in; wing area, 1,460sq ft.

Weights: Empty, 38,000lb; loaded, 62,000lb; maximum, 73,000lb; wing loading, 42.5lb/sq ft; power loading, 11.5lb/hp.

Crew: Two pilots, a flight engineer, a radio operator, a navigator, and two relief crewmembers.

Accommodation: 40 military passengers on troop seats or 36 litter patients and four medical attendants; maximum cargo load, 32,500lb.

Power plant: Four Pratt & Whitney R-2000-11 14-cylinder radials rated at 1,350hp on take-off, 1,100hp at 7,000ft, and 1,000hp at 16,500ft, and driving three-blade constant-speed propellers. Fuel tank capacity, 2,365 Imp. gallons or 3,114 Imp. gallons with auxiliary tanks.

Performance: Max speed, 275mph at 20,000ft; cruising speed, 203mph; climb to 10,000ft in 14.6min; service ceiling, 22,300ft; range with 14,100lb payload, 3,100 miles.

C-54F-DCs for the Troop Carrier Command were to be based on the C-54G airframes but none were built.

C-54G-DO: The last mass-produced model, 162 C-54Gs were built in Santa Monica to be used primarily as troop transports. They had the double cargo door replaced by a smaller single door and were powered by R-2000-9s, but did not have either auxiliary tanks in the cabin or bag-type tanks in the wing center-section. Thirteen became R5D-5s in USN service. The last C-54 built for the military – C-54G-15-DO, 45-636 – was delivered on 22 January 1946.

C-54H-DO: Planned but not built, this was to have been a paratrooper transport model with fuel tank arrangement similar to that of the C-54E.

C-54J-DO: Projected personnel/staff transport model without the reinforced cabin floor or double cargo door.

C-54L-DO: One C-54A-DO was modified to test a new fuel system, but no production was undertaken.

R5D-1: Eighteen C-54A-DOs and 38 C-54A-DCs were transferred to the USN and became R5D-1s with BuNos, 39137, 39139, 39141/39181, 50840/50849, 57988/57989, and 91105.

R5D-2: Thirty-nine C-54B-DCs went to the Navy straight from the Chicago plant as R5D-2s (BuNos 50850/50868 and 90385/90395).

R5D-3: BuNos 50869/50878, 56484/56549, and 91994/92003 were given to 86 C-54D-DCs when they went to the Navy as R5D-3s.

R5D-4: Taken from the C-54E-DO production, 20 R5D4s were assigned BuNos 90396/90415.

R5D-5: The transfer of 13 C-54G-DOs to the USN was planned but none were delivered. Later the R5D-5 designation was used to identify 60 R5D-2s and R5D-3s which were brought to a common standard and re-engined with more reliable R-2000-9s.

R5D-6: This designation was planned for the USN equivalent of the C-54J-DOs but none were built.

Skymaster: The name favored by Douglas was retained by the Royal Air Force for its 23 Lend-Lease C-54s even though it was not a geographical name as usually bestowed on British military transports. The first to reach Britain was a C-54B-1DO (fsn 18326, 43-17126) which was rolled out at Santa Monica in June 1944, just before D-Day. It was then ferried to England where its bare cabin was to be fitted with a plush interior (said to have been more luxurious than that of the US presidential VC-54C)[5] by Armstrong Whitworth Aircraft with additional contributions by the General Electric Company, and L.A. Rumbold, an aircraft furnishing firm. After modifications, and now bearing the British serial EW999 but no special markings, it was taken on charge by the newly formed 'Metropolitan Communications Squadron' on 19 November 1944.[6] This unique aircraft was followed in early 1945 by 22 Lend-Lease

ABOVE *Retrofitted with a weather radar in the nose, this C-54G-5-DO was used as VC-54G staff transport when photographed at McClellan AFB, California, on 28 October 1967.* (Peter B. Lewis)

C-54Ds which were operated by 232 and 246 Squadrons, as well as other smaller units mostly in Southeast Asia. At war's end, all 23 Lend-Lease *Skymasters* were returned to the United States. The former Prime Minister's transport was then used by General George C. Marshall, a special presidential envoy, for a trip to China during which it was damaged beyond economical repair in a taxying accident at Tai Chiao Chang on 13 October 1946.

During the postwar years and well into the 1960s, many C-54s and R5Ds were modified to be used in various roles. The table on page 222 identifies these modified versions.

BELOW *During World War Two, the principal R5D base on the US East Coast was at NAS Norfolk, Virginia. The second aircraft in this line up is BuNo 39137, an R5D-1. Built as a C-54-DO (41-37275), this aircraft was retrofitted with the double door on the rear fuselage.* (NNAM)

---

5   It has been reported that Prime Minister Churchill gave a clear directive 'Make it Look British'.
6   The Prime Minister first used EW999 when he went to Athens, Greece, in December 1944. The aircraft left from RAF Northolt on 25 December, refueled in Naples, Italy, and arrived at the Kalamaki Airport near Athens on the 26th. The return trip left Greece on 28 December and, after an overnight stop in Naples, landed at RAF Bovington the next afternoon.

Projected re-engined models

For Douglas, the first flight of the Lockheed C-69 – the militarized version of the four-engined *Constellation* – at Burbank, California, on 9 January 1943 was an unwelcome warning shot. It was clear that, after the war, the rival manufacturer from across the Hollywood Hills would be in a strong position to provide civil operators with four-engined airliners which would not only have a pressurized cabin (a feature not incorporated in C-54s then in production and only planned for later models of the DC-4) but would also be faster and longer-ranged than DC-4s. Douglas did have the engineering talent to come up with a worthy commercial competitor to the *Constellation* but was prevented from doing so by the wartime obligation under which all aircraft manufacturers had to give priority to building and developing military aircraft. Fortunately, after C-54s proved to lack the altitude performance required for the safe crossing of the Himalayas, Douglas was authorized by the War Department to undertake design studies for transport aircraft powered by new and more powerful engines and, in some instances, fitted with a pressurized cabin. This resulted in the following projects.

XC-54K: This minimum change version of the C-54 was proposed with 1,425hp Wright *Cyclone* R-1820-HDs. However, this would not have improved the altitude performance of USAAF C-54s. From the Douglas point of view, this power plant installation had the distinct advantage of being likely to attract the interest of airlines seeking an engine commonality with their other *Cyclone*-powered aircraft. The existence

of a XC-54K prototype – 42-72176, a re-engined C-54A-1-DC – has long been rumored. If a *Cyclone*-powered XC-54K flew, it was likely modified by some firm other than Douglas – possibly Rohr Aircraft in San Diego, California, which did re-engine five C-54s for Chicago & Southern Airlines after the war (see photo on page 228).

XC-112: Powered by a Pratt & Whitney R-2800-22Ws and fitted with a pressurized cabin, aircraft 45-873 became the prototype for the DC-6 (see Chapter 10). It first flew on 15 February 1946.

XC-114: A prototype for this model to be powered by 1,620hp Allison V-1710-131 12-cylinder air cooled radials was under construction for the USAAF when the war ended. It used the airframe of an aircraft ordered as a C-54E (fsn 36327, 45-874) but fitted with a pressurized cabin while under construction. The uncompleted XC-114 was purchased back by Douglas and was re-engined with Pratt & Whitney *Double Wasp* radials to become a DC-6 prototype (NX 90809, see insert on page 253).

XC-115: Like the XC-114, this aircraft was to have a pressurized cabin and was to be powered by liquid-cooled engines: 1,650hp Packard V-1650-209s (a US development of the Rolls-Royce *Merlin*). It was not built, but the drawings for its power plant installation were useful to Canadair (see page 229).

XC-116: Also to be powered by Allison V-1710-131s, this prototype was to differ from the XC-114 in having the pneumatic boots replaced by thermal de-icing equipment. A prototype (fsn 36328, 45-875) was under construction when the war ended but was not completed.

ABOVE *Photographed at Elmendorf AFB, Alaska, in July 1964, this colorful aircraft was an RC-54V (ex-C-54D-1-DC, 42-72486) of the US Coast Guard.* (Lionel Paul)

OPPOSITE *This USN R5D3 (BuNo 56540), assigned to the Atlantic Division of the Military Air Transport Service, has been fitted with a radome beneath the forward fuselage, aft of the nose gear.* (Brian Jones, David W. Menard collection)

MIDDLE AND RIGHT *TC-54D trainers were used in at least two configurations. The aircraft at the top was used to train navigators and had a row of astrodomes atop the fuselage; that at the bottom was a radar-navigator trainer and had a row of radomes beneath the fuselage.* (C. Hinton, David W. Menard and Peter B. Lewis collection)

Designations given by the USAAF/USAF, the US Army, and the USN to modified C-47s and R5Ds

Military designations before/after September 1962	Original version	Remarks
JZC-54A / —	C-54A	One aircraft modified for temporary use as a test bed; the second prefix, Z, indicated that the aircraft was considered to be obsolete.
AC-54B / EC-54D	C-54D	C-54Ds modified for navaids calibration.
JC-54D / —	C-54D	Nine C-54Ds fitted with equipment to snatch small space capsules parachuting down to earth.
SC-54D / HC-54D	C-54D	Thirty-six C-54Ds equipped for maritime search and rescue.
TC-54D / TC-54D	C-54D	C-54Ds modified for navigator and bombardier training.
VC-54D / VC-54D	C-54D	C-54Ds with upgraded accommodations for staff/VIP transport.
WC-54D / —	C-54D	C-54Ds fitted for weather reconnaissance.
AC-54E / —	C-54E	C-54Es modified for navaids calibration.
JC-54G / —	C-54G	C-54Gs modified for temporary use as test beds.
VC-54G / VC-54G	C-54G	C-54Gs with upgraded accommodations for staff/VIP transport.
C-54GM / —	—	US designation for *Merlin*-powered aircraft built by Canadair.
C-54M / C-54M	C-54E	Thirty-eight C-54s with cabin stripped down to carry coal during Berlin Airlift.
MC-54M / MC-54M	C-54E	Thirty C-54Es modified for aeromedical evacuation.
VC-54M / VC-54M	C-54E	C-54Ds with upgraded accommodations for staff/VIP transport.
— / C-54P	R5D-2	Post September 1962 designation for R5D-2s.
— / C-54Q	R5D-3	Post September 1962 designation for R5D-3s.
— / C-54R	R5D-4	Post September 1962 designation for R5D-4s.
— / C-54S	R5D-5	Post September 1962 designation for R5D-5s.
— / EC-54U	R5D-4	Postwar modification for the USCG with new electronic equipment.
— / RC-54V	R5D-3	Postwar modification for the USCG with a large observation window on each side of the rear fuselage plus photography equipment.
R5D-1C / —	R5D-1	R5D-1s fitted with same fuel tanks as C-54Bs.
R5D-1Z / VC-54N	R5D-1	R5D-1s with upgraded accommodations for staff/VIP transport.
R5D-2Z / VC-54P	R5D-2	R5D-2s with upgraded accommodations for staff/VIP transport.
R5D-3Z / VC-54Q	R5D-3	R5D-3s with upgraded accommodations for staff/VIP transport.
R5D-4R / C-54R	R5D-4	R5D-4s with upgraded accommodations for personnel transport.
R5D-5Z / VC-54	R5D-5	R5D-5s with upgraded accommodations for staff/VIP transport.
R5D-5R / C-54T	R5D-5	R5D-5s with upgraded accommodations for personnel transport.

Aircraft 41-20145, an early C-54-DO, was damaged in a landing accident in November 1942. After being rebuilt and having its camouflage removed, it was returned to service in June 1943. It is shown here in Brisbane, Queensland, in 1944. (USAAF)

World War Two operations

When the first C-54A-DO (fsn 3060, 41-20138) was handed over to the USAAF in March 1942, service testing began at Wright Field, Ohio. Then, after eight other C-54As were delivered before the end of July, the new four-engined transport, wearing camouflage paint and the national markings then in use (a white star on a blue circle), was declared ready for operations. At the time, however, the USAAF was experiencing a shortage of experienced flight crews with those who were fully qualified being assigned in priority to combat units, thus creating a critical crewing problem for the Air Transport Command. This was solved by having the new transport aircraft flown by crews of airlines operating under military contracts.

Pan American Airways, which was under contract to operate a route from Florida to Brazil and onward across the South Atlantic for the US government, was provided with four C-54As in August 1942. The airline began by operating them between Florida and Brazil before extending operations to West Africa.[7] Other C-54s were then handed over to TWA and American for contract operations between the US Northeast and Scotland, a route on which TWA had begun flying with C-75s (military designation given to impressed Boeing 307 *Stratoliners*) in April 1942. As flying conditions over the North Atlantic were not favorable during the winter months, TWA switched its C-54 service to the UK via a southern route beginning in January 1943.[8] When weather conditions improved, direct routing over the North Atlantic was resumed by both airlines while TWA continued providing regular service between Scotland and French Morocco.

TWA operations over the South Atlantic increased in importance as preparations were made for the Casablanca Conference between President Roosevelt and Prime Minister Churchill (plus French generals de Gaulle and Giraud) in January 1944. On 15 January, the second day of the conference, a TWA C-54 (fsn 3114, 42-42939) crashed in Dutch Guiana, some 30 miles from Paramaribo, while on its way to Morocco. All 35 persons on board were killed in this crash, the first for the new Douglas four-engined airliner.[9]

The first C-54A-DC was handed over to the USAAF in October 1943 and, thereafter, deliveries of improved models gained tempo rapidly. From 23 of these aircraft in service in December 1942, the fleet of the Air Transport Command grew to 76 C-54s in December 1943, 347 in December 1944, and 839 in August 1945. By then, C-54s accounted for more than one in five aircraft in the ATC fleet and were outnumbered only by Curtiss C-46s (with 1,341 in service at war's end). With more and better C-54s (a majority fitted with reinforced cabin floor, cargo handling equipment, double loading/unloading door, and increased fuel capacity), both the Air Transport Command and the airlines operating under contract were able to open many transoceanic and other demanding routes.

Across the Dark Continent, C-54s were operated not only along the west coast (and onward to Great Britain) as indicated earlier, but also to Oran in Algeria, between Algiers and Cairo, and on the transcontinental route from West Africa to Khartoum and Cairo with continuation to Iran and India. In the New World,

ABOVE *With the cabin floor of the C-54 being 8ft 10in above the tarmac, loading required appropriate equipment. The USAAF found it convenient to have General Motors CCKW trucks fitted with a bed on a scissor lift.* (USAAF)

C-54s boosted capabilities on flights to the Territory of Alaska as they could carry greater loads than twin-engined C-46s and C-47s and could operate on the more direct coastal route from Seattle to Anchorage instead of having to follow the treacherous airways across the Yukon Territory.

In the Pacific, C-54s were first used on 23 September 1942 by United Air Lines on its contract route between California and Hawaii. Flights across the Pacific were then extended to Canton Island, Fiji, New Caledonia, Australia, New Guinea, the Philippines, the Marianas, and Okinawa. The Japanese defeat then created new needs and opened new destinations. On 19 August 1945, a C-54E-1-DO (44-9045) transported the Japanese surrender delegation from the island of Ie Shima to the Philippines and back. Then, between 28 August and 12 September, 185 C-54s and R5Ds airlifted the first 23,456 occupation troops to Japan, as well as General Douglas MacArthur and his staff. Moreover, after the signing of the surrender on 2 September 1945 aboard the USS *Missouri* (BB 63) anchored in the Bay of Tokyo, a C-54 flew to the American capital in 31hr 25min to deliver still photos and motion pictures of the ceremony ending the Second World War.

C-54s were first operated over the 'Hump,' from India to China, in February 1944 but did not prove as successful on this difficult run as they lacked the altitude performance to cross the Himalayas over the most direct route which entailed going over much higher average elevations. C-54s thus had to be restricted to flying to Kunming in China from Kurmitola-Tezgaon in Burma, on a longer but lower route. On this route, C-54s soon built up a strong reputation and, by war's end, 131 of the 640 aircraft with the ATC India-China Wing were Douglas four-engined transports.

In Europe, the fall of Rome on 4 June 1944, followed two days later by D-Day, and then in August by landings in Provence and the liberation of Paris, created new air transport needs. Beginning on 4 October 1944, C-54s flew daily, and then three times daily, between New York and Orly (via Newfoundland and the Azores), the new military transport hub just south of Paris. Typical loads were made up of critically-needed parts for aircraft and other weaponries, mail,

---

7   The initial route was from Morrison Field, Florida, to Natal, in the Brazilian state of Rio Grande do Norte, via Borinquen Field, Puerto Rico; Waller Field, Trinidad; Atkinson Field, British Guiana; and Belém, in the Brazilian state of Pará. When the route was extended to West Africa, C-54s first flew from Natal to Roberts Field, Liberia. After Senegal joined the Free French in November 1942, an airfield for the C-54s and other large aircraft was built by the US at Rufisque, near Dakar (with two 6,000ft runways with Marsden Matting – PSP, pierced steel planking). Next, a permanent field at Dakar-Yoff was opened in June 1944.
8   From Washington, D.C., the C-54s flew to Accra (in the Gold Coast, now Ghana) via the South Atlantic and then proceeded to Marrakech, in French Morocco, and onward to Prestwick, Scotland. Weekly flights on this route soon gave place to two flights a week.
9   For a long time, authors, including myself, kept repeating the wartime propaganda that 'C-54s made 79,642 transoceanic crossings during the war without a single one being lost.' As a matter of fact, 29 C-54s crashed during the war, two in 1943, 11 in 1944 (including the C-54A-5-DO 42-107740 accidentally shot down over the Atlantic by a RAF fighter on 26 July), and 16 in 1945. However, there is no denying that by the standards of the time, and during pioneering operations, C-54s proved highly reliable and remarkably safe.

The Yalta Conference

The three major Allied leaders in World War Two – President Franklin Roosevelt, Prime Minister Winston Churchill, and Secretary General Joseph Stalin – had first met in November/December 1943 at Tehran, Iran. Their next conference was to be held in February 1945 at Yalta, Crimea, with resulting long travels for the American president and the British prime minister. Both ended up using the new Douglas four-engined aircraft. Among the 32 other transports of the American and British delegations, most were DC-4s, others being Avro *Yorks* and Consolidated C-87s.

President Roosevelt left the United States on 23 January 1945 aboard the heavy cruiser USS *Quincy* (CA 71) bound for Malta. On 3 February, he boarded the VC-54C (which, for the occasion, bore the

serial number 42-72252 of another C-54 which had been lost off Hawaii less than three months earlier) for the 1,360-mile circuitous flight to avoid 'hot spots' between Malta and Saki, Crimea. The VC-54C then took him to Egypt on 12 February for more diplomatic meetings before returning home aboard the *Quincy*.

Prime Minister Churchill left from RAF Northolt on 29 January 1945 aboard his specially appointed *Skymaster* to join with President Roosevelt in Malta and onward to Crimea. Churchill left Crimea aboard EW999 on 14 February and, after an overnight stop in Athens, rejoined Roosevelt in Cairo. The Prime Minister flew back from Cairo to RAF Lyneham non-stop on 19 February.

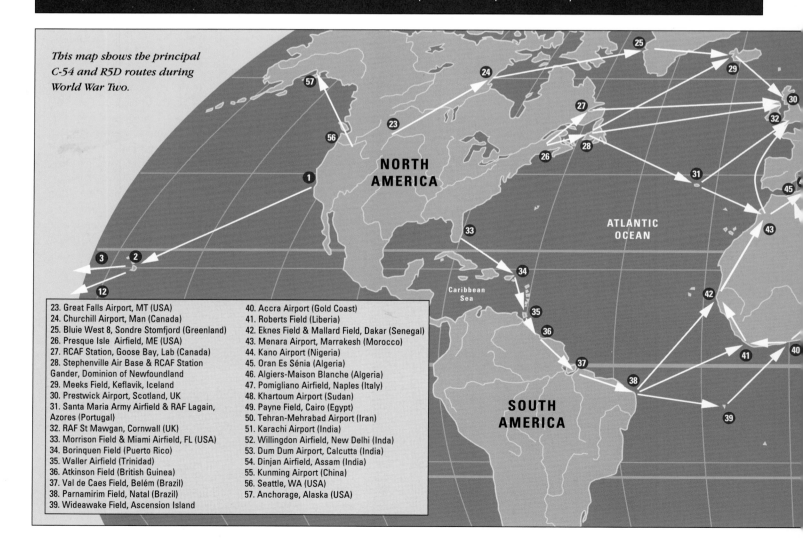

This map shows the principal C-54 and R5D routes during World War Two.

23. Great Falls Airport, MT (USA)
24. Churchill Airport, Man (Canada)
25. Bluie West 8, Sondre Stomfjord (Greenland)
26. Presque Isle Airfield, ME (USA)
27. RCAF Station, Goose Bay, Lab (Canada)
28. Stephenville Air Base & RCAF Station Gander, Dominion of Newfoundland
29. Meeks Field, Keflavik, Iceland
30. Prestwick Airport, Scotland, UK
31. Santa Maria Army Airfield & RAF Lagain, Azores (Portugal)
32. RAF St Mawgan, Cornwall (UK)
33. Morrison Field & Miami Airfield, FL (USA)
34. Borinquen Field (Puerto Rico)
35. Waller Airfield (Trinidad)
36. Atkinson Field (British Guinea)
37. Val de Caes Field, Belém (Brazil)
38. Parnamirim Field, Natal (Brazil)
39. Wideawake Field, Ascension Island

40. Accra Airport (Gold Coast)
41. Roberts Field (Liberia)
42. Eknes Field & Mallard Field, Dakar (Senegal)
43. Menara Airport, Marrakesh (Morocco)
44. Kano Airport (Nigeria)
45. Oran Es Sénia (Algeria)
46. Algiers-Maison Blanche (Algeria)
47. Pomigliano Airfield, Naples (Italy)
48. Khartoum Airport (Sudan)
49. Payne Field, Cairo (Egypt)
50. Tehran-Mehrabad Airport (Iran)
51. Karachi Airport (India)
52. Willingdon Airfield, New Delhi (Inda)
53. Dum Dum Airport, Calcutta (India)
54. Dinjan Airfield, Assam (India)
55. Kunming Airport (China)
56. Seattle, WA (USA)
57. Anchorage, Alaska (USA)

OPPOSITE *This R5D-1 of Transport Squadron One (VR-1), USN, was in transit at Lajes Field, in the Azores, when photographed on 27 January 1944.* (NNAM)

RIGHT *Bearing the markings of the Air Transport Command, this C-54B-15-DC flies over Angel Island with the Golden Gate Bridge seen above its tail.* (Douglas)

and medical supplies (including a daily supply of 3,750lb of whole blood flown from New York). Even fresh food was included when space was available. In the Mediterranean Theatre of Operations, new C-54 destinations were Naples and Athens.

The United States Navy obtained its first R5D-1 – BuNo 39137, which had started down the Santa Monica line as a C-54A-DO (fsn 3065, 41-37275) – in February 1943 and sent it to NAS Norfolk, Virginia, to be operated by Transport Squadron One (VR-1). R5Ds were then assigned to VR-2 at NAS Olathe, Kansas; VR-3 at NAAS Oakland, California; VR-5 at NAS Seattle, Washington; and VR-11 at NAS Honolulu, Territory of Hawaii. This last squadron became the largest R5D operator with no fewer than 89 aircraft on strength at the time of the Japanese surrender. In late 1944, two other naval squadrons were equipped with Douglas four-engined transport aircraft. Based at NAS Honolulu and then at NAS Guam, VRE-1 was used almost exclusively for aeromedical evacuations during the heavily fought battles on Iwo Jima and Okinawa. Also based at NAS Honolulu, VRJ-1 was assigned the task of transporting senior officers from the mainland and throughout the Pacific Theatre of Operations.

After the German and Japanese surrenders C-54 activities peaked for a few months. In May 1945, the Green Project was organized to return troops from Europe to the United States for 'rest & relaxation' before onward deployment to the Pacific for further fighting. In four months, from the middle of May to 15 September, C-54s brought 166,000 military passengers back from Europe, including 101,000 as part of the Green Project, 38,500 military and government officials, and 26,400 medical evacuees. For this time period, these numbers were indeed quite remarkable, especially if one remembers that in 1939–1940, Pan American and Imperial Airways had barely managed to fly 1,000 passengers in their Boeing 314 and Short *Empire* flying boats.

The era of attention-getting pioneers and route developers was truly over. Now it was time for anonymous crews to fly across the oceans and around the globe without attracting much interest.

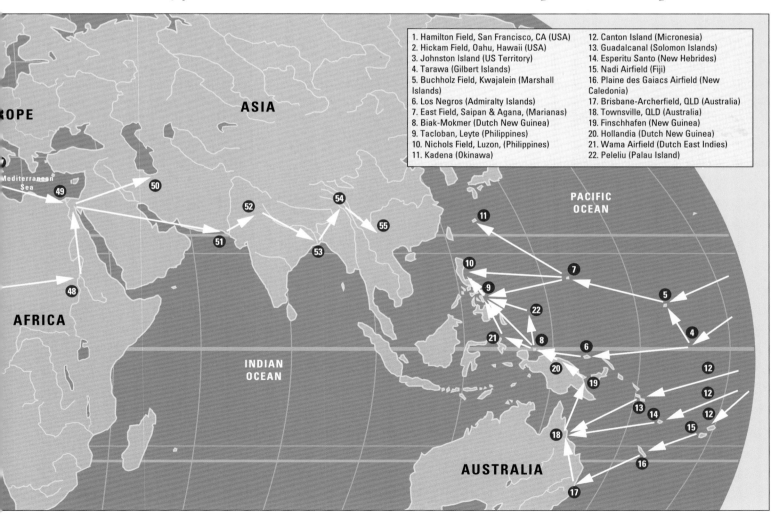

1. Hamilton Field, San Francisco, CA (USA)
2. Hickam Field, Oahu, Hawaii (USA)
3. Johnston Island (US Territory)
4. Tarawa (Gilbert Islands)
5. Buchholz Field, Kwajalein (Marshall Islands)
6. Los Negros (Admiralty Islands)
7. East Field, Saipan & Agana, (Marianas)
8. Biak-Mokmer (Dutch New Guinea)
9. Tacloban, Leyte (Philippines)
10. Nichols Field, Luzon, (Philippines)
11. Kadena (Okinawa)
12. Canton Island (Micronesia)
13. Guadalcanal (Solomon Islands)
14. Esperitu Santo (New Hebrides)
15. Nadi Airfield (Fiji)
16. Plaine des Gaiacs Airfield (New Caledonia)
17. Brisbane-Archerfield, QLD (Australia)
18. Townsville, QLD (Australia)
19. Finschhafen (New Guinea)
20. Hollandia (Dutch New Guinea)
21. Wama Airfield (Dutch East Indies)
22. Peleliu (Palau Island)

ABOVE Clipper Argonaut, *a DC-4 of Pan American World Airways, was an ex-C-54A-1-DC.* (DR)

Postwar airline operations

Notwithstanding the quasi certainty that the Boeing *Stratocruiser* and Lockheed *Constellation* were likely to be formidable postwar competitors, Douglas had ample reasons to be optimistic as the war was drawing to its end. The Santa Monica firm not only was offering two strong competitors of its own – the DC-6 and the Model 415 respectively described in Chapters 10 and 12 – but it also had an ace up its sleeve which its competitors did not possess. The C-54 was in full production, and the switch to its DC-4 airliner could be quickly achieved. Therefore during the summer of 1944 Douglas began aggressively marketing two DC-4 models: the Model 1009 passenger airliner and the Model 1037 optimized as a freighter. The Model 1009, with or without a

BELOW *NC6403, a DC-4-1009, was delivered to Northwest Airlines on 18 March 1946.* (Douglas, Alain Pelletier collection)

pressurized cabin, was to have a single-panel passenger access door on the left side of the rear fuselage and, to reduce empty weight and improve economic performance, an unreinforced main deck floor. Conversely, the unpressurized Model 1037 was offered with the strengthened cabin floor and double cargo door as first fitted to C-54As.

United Air Lines was the first to choose the DC-4-1009 and ordered 15 of these aircraft on 11 September 1944. Other orders were confidently expected but Douglas did not take sufficiently into consideration the fact that the USAAF would dispose of its early C-54s as soon as the war ended, thus flooding the market with relatively cheap aircraft. Indeed, this was what happened in 1946 when the War Assets Administration offered C-54s and C-54As at a unit price of $75,000 (±$830,000 today), C-54Bs and C-54Ds for $90,000 (±$994,000 today), and C-54Es and C-54Gs for $100,000 (±$1.1million today). Douglas was then asking $385,000 (±$4.3 million today) for a brand new DC-4-1009 without cabin pressurization and $595,000 (±$6.6 million today) for a pressurized DC-6. United Air Lines canceled its order for DC-4-1009s, acquired surplus C-54s for conversion into DC-4s, and ordered DC-6s to compete more effectively against the Lockheed *Constellations* of TWA.

Douglas did not sell a single DC-4-1037 and only managed the sale of 79 DC-4-1009s. The main customer for these all-new airliners was the provisional French government which ordered 15 DC-4-1009s for Air France on 26 June 1945. Ranked in decreasing order of the number of aircraft ordered, the DC-4-1009 customers in the United States were National Airlines (for seven aircraft), Western Airlines (five), Northwest Airlines (three), and Waterman Airlines (one). Foreign DC-4-1009 customers were SILA, soon to become a founding member of SAS (ten); Sabena (nine); KLM and South African Airways (six each); Swissair and Trans-Australia Airlines (four each); Iberia (three); and Aramco (one). The first DC-4-1009 (fsn 42904, NC10201) was delivered to Western Airlines on 18 January 1946 and the last (fsn 43157, ZS-BMH) went to South African Airways on 9 August 1947, thus bringing to an end the production of C-54s and DC-4s. This strictly commercial version of the Douglas four-engined transport was powered by Pratt & Whitney *Twin Wasp* 2SD13-Gs delivering 1,450hp on take-off and producing 1,200hp at 5,000ft and 1,100hp at 14,000ft.

Most airlines, whether in the United States or abroad, opted to acquire surplus C-54s which were modified to civil requirements by

either Douglas, other specialized firms, or the airlines themselves.[10] DC-4s and C-54s modified for civil use were covered by ATC No A-762 dated 6 June 1946.

The DC-4, or more precisely the C-54 modified for airline use, made its début on 24 October 1945 when American Export Airlines[11] began operating between New York and RAF Hurn (then the temporary transatlantic terminal in Dorset) with refueling stops in Gander and Shannon. On the North Atlantic route, the DC-4s of this airline were successively joined by those of Pan American, TWA,[12] KLM, Air France, Sabena, and Swissair. In November 1945, KLM also began using DC-4s/C-54s on its route between Amsterdam and Batavia. Across the Pacific, the first DC-4 operators were Pan American and Australian National Airways (the latter providing crews and aircraft to British Commonwealth Pacific Airlines which was yet to get the DC-6s it had ordered). On routes across the South Atlantic, the first were DC-4s from *Flota Aérea Mercantile Argentina* in September 1946. In South Africa, SAA began DC-4 service in 1946, on 1 May between Johannesburg and Cape Town, and on 8 July to London (via Nairobi, Khartoum, and Tripoli).

However, on these long and prestigious routes, DC-4s soon had a difficult time competing against newer, faster, and pressurized Lockheed *Constellations*. For example, in 1946 TWA offered flights from New York to Paris with both DC-4s and *Constellations*. Eastbound, the Douglas airliners linked those two points in 22 hours via Boston, Gander, and Shannon, whereas the Constellations did so in 17 hours and without the need for a stop in Boston.

Britain and the DC-4

At war's end, the Royal Air Force had returned all 23 Lend-Lease *Skymasters* (including that specially fitted out for the Prime Minister) to the United States. In the immediate postwar years, British airlines could not acquire DC-4s or C-54s due to restrictions on dollar purchases. Hence, the first of these aircraft were four civilian

ABOVE *Air France became the main customer for DC-4-1009s, the new aircraft built after C-54 production had ended.* (Douglas)

C-54s acquired in September 1947 by Skyways Ltd (mostly for use on trooping flights) from KLM as the Netherlands was then in the sterling zone. A fifth followed during the following year. More were acquired after British import restrictions were eased in 1955.

Whereas Douglas sales in Britain were impeded by currency regulations, British Overseas Airways Corporation was authorized to acquire the DC-4's main competitor, the Lockheed *Constellation* (including an ex-USAAF C-69 and four Model 049s ordered in April 1946). This proved fortuitous for BOAC as the Avro *Tudor 1*, which was developed as an interim type under the Brabazon program, was repeatedly delayed and never entered service over the North Atlantic.

BELOW *In September 1946, TWA and the US Post Office experimented with mail casing aboard specially fitted DC-4s. Shades of the Wild West and the days of stagecoach robbers, one of the postal officers is 'packing' a holstered gun!* (TWA)

---

10 The modifications to civil standard consisted mainly of replacing folding military seats with more comfortable passenger seats arranged in a 2 + 2 configuration, the addition of thermal and sound-proofing wall blankets, and the replacement of the military windows with a hole for gun-firing in their centre (as had first been adopted for C-47s and were standard on most military C-54s) with conventional passenger portholes.

11 This air carrier, a subsidiary of the shipping firm American Export Lines, is not to be confused with the better known American Airlines. Within one month of starting its DC-4 service to England, American Export Lines merged with the transatlantic division of American Airlines to become American Overseas Airlines Inc. In turn, this carrier was absorbed by Pan American in September 1950.

12 Faced with foreign competitors with limited experience on transoceanic operations, TWA boasted about the knowledge gained by its crews during the war. Its February 1948 timetable carried this proud commentary: 'TWA crews of men long seasoned in transatlantic flying, with a combined experience of more than 40,000,000 miles of international operations, including more than 9,000 overocean flights.'

ABOVE *Double oddity at Lambert Field, St Louis, Missouri: the sole McDonnell XHJD-1* Whirlaway *hovers in front of NC54361* City of San Juan, *one of only five DC-4s re-engined with Wright* Cyclone *736C9HD1 radials.* (McDonnell)

BELOW *With their inline Rolls-Royce* Merlin *engines, the Canadair North Stars were the sharpest-looking aircraft in the DC-4 family. This is CF-TEN-X, the Canadian prototype, photographed at Montreal-Dorval.* (Canadair)

BOTTOM *17501, the first C-54GM for the RCAF, was delivered on 29 August 1947. It crashed at Rockliffe, Ontario, on 4 August 1954.* (Canadair)

Whereas Douglas-built DC-4s/C-54s only saw limited service in Britain, Canadair-built, *Merlin*-powered aircraft found a ready market in the United Kingdom. Next, the Douglas four-engined transports got a new lease on life in British skies when Aviation Traders (Engineering) Ltd rebuilt C-54s into *Carvair* vehicle-ferry aircraft (see pages 229 and 235).

On the US transcontinental routes, the rivals both débuted on 1 March 1946, a United Air Lines DC-4 flying from New York to San Francisco and a TWA *Constellation* from New York to Los Angeles. Other US DC-4 (and ex C-54) operators in the immediate postwar period were American Airlines, Braniff Airways, Capital Airlines, Chicago and Southern Air Lines, Colonial Airlines, Delta Air Lines, Northwest Airlines (including flights to Japan), Pan American (exclusively outside the US), TWA (including all-cargo flights, first over the North Atlantic on 30 January 1947, and also experimental mail flights), and Western Airlines. In most instances, the cabin of DC-4s had between 40 and 44 seats (in 2 + 2 rows) arranged in a single-class (what must be regarded as the equivalent of today's first class as far as fares and clientele are concerned). Then, in November 1948, Capital Airlines introduced 'coach' class service between New York and Chicago, its DC-4 being fitted with 60 seats (2 + 3) and fares being two-thirds of standard (first) class fare. Coach service was universally offered soon afterwards.

Among airlines flying DC-4s in the United States, Chicago and Southern deserves a special mention as it was the only one with aircraft powered by nine-cylinder Wright engines. As its primary routes were in the Midwest and to the South, and did not cross high ranges as was the case in the West, this airline found it advantageous to have two ex C-54As and three ex C-54Bs re-engined with *Cyclone* 736C9HD1s rated at 1,425hp on take-off and 1,125hp at 10,500ft, thus benefitting from the commonality with its *Cyclone*-powered DC-3s. The lighter Wright engines were fitted to the C&S DC-4s by Rohr Aircraft in San Diego, California.

Major airlines which had not ordered Lockheed *Constellations* or Boeing *Stratocruisers* found it difficult to compete with their unpressurized DC-4s until they could place their DC-6s in service. First in the United States, and then slowly elsewhere, DC-4s were progressively downgraded for operations by lower-tier carriers over lesser routes. That process, however, took many years, and, today, worldwide there are still some 40 DC-4s/C-54s in service or undergoing overhaul.

Even in scheduled airline operations, DC-4s were not immune to attack from trigger-happy fighter pilots from unfriendly air forces. This was notably the case of a DC-4 from Air France which, on 29 April 1952, was shot up by Soviet MiG-15s while on approach to Berlin, three passengers being wounded. Then, on 22 July 1954, a DC-4 (VR-HEU, ex C-54A-10-DC) of Cathay Pacific Airways was

forced down in the South China Sea by Chinese Lavochkin La-9 fighters while flying from Bangkok to Hong Kong; 10 of the 18 occupants were killed.

Canadian-built versions

The concept of replacing the radial engines of the DC-4 with 12 cylinder Rolls-Royce *Merlin* liquid-cooled engines was suggested in 1943 by the engineering department of Trans-Canada Air Lines. During the following year, Douglas picked up the idea and suggested to the USAAF that a developed version of the C-54, the XC-115, could be powered by V-1650-209s (Rolls-Royce *Merlins* built under license in the United States by the Packard Motor Car Company in Detroit, Michigan).

Even though Canada only had a population of around 14 million in 1944 and a relatively limited economic base, the federal dominion contributed significantly to Allied aircraft production. As the war was drawing to a close, the government of the dominion became desirous of maintaining this newly gained industrial capability. To this end, the government bought up Canadian Vickers, a subsidiary of Vickers Limited in Britain, which among others had built 422 *Lancaster X* bombers during the war. This company was then reorganized into Canadair Limited with its main activities situated at the large Cartierville plant on the outskirts of Montreal. In 1944, the government of Prime Minister Mackenzie King secured license rights for the Douglas DC-4s and its planned derivatives and, when the war ended and Douglas was closing the Chicago plant, it purchased the C-54 tooling and uncompleted parts at that US government site. When this was done, the Canadians decided that the Cartierville plant would build

TOP *Looking much like a DC-6, the C-5 (RCAF 10000) was the only radial-engined aircraft in the series built by Canadair.* (Harry S. Gann)

ABOVE *Confusingly, Canadair* North Stars *with four-blade propellers were DC-4M-2/3s while those with three-blade props were DC-4M-2/4s.* (Air Canada)

BELOW *This ex-BOAC Canadair C-4 is shown after it was acquired by British Midland in October 1964. It crashed at Stockport, Cheshire, on 4 April 1967.* (Jacques Guillem collection)

ABOVE *During* Operation Vittles, *the US contribution to the Berlin Airlift, USAF C-54s and USN R5Ds operated out of Frankfurt-Rhein Main, Celle, Fassberg, and Wiesbaden.* (USAF, David W. Menard collection)

a version of the DC-4 powered by Rolls-Royce *Merlins*, the choice of this British power plant being dictated by the fact that, being a Commonwealth product, it would be exempt from customs duties.[13]

The expected availability of Canadian-built, British-powered, DC-4 derivatives was greeted with much interest by both the Royal Canadian Air Force and Trans-Canada Air Lines. The RCAF ordered 24 C-54GMs with unpressurized fuselage fitted out for troop and cargo transport while TCA opted for 20 passenger transport DC-4M-2s with pressurized cabins. The DC-4M-X prototype for these two models was assembled mostly from Chicago-built parts and components, and was fitted with four *Merlin* 620s rated at 1,760hp on take-off, 1,175hp at 12,800ft, and 1,160hp at 23,600ft. Registered CF-TEN-X, it was first flown at Cartierville on 15 July 1946 by a Douglas test pilot, Robert J. Brush, and a Canadair pilot, Alexander J. Lilly. After testing was completed, this aircraft went to the RCAF in November 1952 and, designated C-54GM, was assigned the Canadian military serial 17525.

Production of an initial batch of six aircraft for the RCAF had been initiated without waiting for the DC-4M-X test results. After acceptance trials, these six unpressurized DC-4M-1s were leased to TCA for a three-year period and were registered CF-TEK/CF-TEM and CF-TEO/CF-TEQ. One was destroyed in a ground fire but the other five went to the RCAF as *North Star* Mk 1 STs and were given serials 17518 and 17519/17523. In military service, they were joined by 17 C-54GM *North Star* Mk 1s (17501/17517) with gross weight increased from 73,000 to 78,000lb. In RCAF service, *North Stars* saw much use not only in support of the UN 'police action' in Korea[14] but more so to provide logistic and personnel support to RCAF fighter units which were based in Great Britain, France, and Germany beginning in November 1951.

Before being withdrawn from use by the RCAF, *North Stars* also took part in numerous humanitarian relief operations. One of the ex-Canadian Military aircraft, 17507, was sold in El Salvador where it was operated briefly by TACA (*Transportes Aéreos Centro-*

Americanos) with the registration YS-27C before serving with the *Fuerza Aérea Salvadoreña* between 1968 and 1972.

In addition to its *Merlin*-powered *North Stars*, the RCAF obtained a hybrid. Bearing the Canadair C5 designation and the RCAF serial 17524 (later changed to 17000), this aircraft had a pressurized fuselage similar to that of the Douglas DC-6 and was powered by four 2,400hp Pratt & Whitney *Double Wasp* CA5 radial engines. It was primarily operated to fly VIPs, including members of the Royal family. Seventy-first and last Canadair built derivative of the DC-4, the RCAF C-5 was withdrawn from use in 1967.

Three Canadair models with pressurized cabin and rectangular windows (instead of the portholes of the C-54s, DC-4s, and *North Stars*) were built for airline customers. These *Merlin*-powered aircraft incorporated some DC-6 elements (including wing outboard panels with two, instead of one, spars) and reinforced undercarriage. Twenty were operated by Trans-Canada Air Lines between 1947 and 1961, some as DC-4M-2/3s with *Merlin* 622s or 722s with four-blade propellers, the others being DC-4M-2/4s with Merlin 624s or 724s and three-blade propellers. Take-off weight was increased to 79,600lb, and fuel tank capacity to 3,226 Imp. gallons (versus only 1,991 gallons for the Douglas-built DC-4-1009s). In 1955, three TCA DC-4M-2s were modified to carry cargo and were redesignated DC-4M-2/4Cs.

When the Avro *Tudor* proved unsatisfactory, British Overseas Airways Corporation found itself without suitable aircraft for its Empire routes and those to South America. This led BOAC to order 22 Canadair C-4s (G-ALHC/G-ALHP and G-ALHR/G-LHY) as its *Argonaut* class. They differed from the TCA DC-4M-2s in having their gross weight brought up to 82,300lb and a number of instruments and systems replaced by British-produced items. They entered service in March 1949 and remained in use with BOAC until 1960 before being operated by British Midland Airways and the Royal Rhodesian Air Force among others. Next came four Canadair C-4-1s (CF-CPI, -CPJ, -CPP, and -CPR) for Canadian Pacific Airlines. They were essentially similar to the BOAC aircraft except for their Canadian and US equipment. The last two were retired by CPA in 1962.

With its pressurized cabin and more powerful engines, the DC-4M flew higher and faster than the DC-4-1009. Conversely, its cabin proved exceptionally noisy, even after TCA had the engine exhaust diverted away from the fuselage. Consequently, the DC-4M was retired much before the radial-engined DC-4 and none remain in service.

---

13 For a while, the Canadians had contemplated using *Twin Wasp* D-9 engines which were to have been built under license by Canadian Pratt & Whitney in Longueuil, Quebec.

14 During this conflict, No 426 Transport Squadron was attached to the US Military Air Transport Service, transporting more than 13,000 military passengers and 3,000 tons of cargo in the course of 599 transpacific crossings.

Postwar military operations

After American prisoners of war had been returned home and the major demobilisation tasks had been accomplished during the second half of 1945, the USAAF no longer needed as many C-54s as it then had in service. On the other hand, as large occupation forces were to be kept and supplied in Austria, Germany, and Japan, the Air Transport Command would still have to maintain its overwater transport capability. Accordingly, only initial C-54 production models would be declared surplus and sold by the War Assets Administration while the majority of the C-54D/E/Gs would be retained by the USAAF (that also being the case for the Navy R5Ds). The wisdom of retaining these four-engined transport aircraft was soon proven as the Soviets blockaded Berlin in 1948 and the North Koreans invaded the South two years later.

When the Western Allies decided to respond to the blockade of Berlin by setting up a large scale airlift in June 1948, the United States Air Force in Europe had less than 100 C-47s and only two C-54s. The USAFE commander, Maj. Gen. Curtiss LeMay, immediately asked the USAF headquarters to have all available C-54s and R5Ds transferred from other commands as each of these four-engined aircraft could carry nearly three times as much cargo as could the C-47s. Moreover, even when carrying heavier loads, C-54s could be loaded and unloaded faster than C-47s as their cabin floor was level to the ground.

As early as July 1948, within a few weeks of the start of operations on the Berlin Airlift, the Douglas four-engined

ABOVE *Photographed in April 1970, this C-54D-15-DC was used by the US Army in support of its operations at the Kwajalein Missile Range in the Pacific. Black paint around the portholes makes it look as if rectangular windows 'à la DC-6' have been fitted.* (David W. Menard collection)

transports began supplementing C-47s as the Military Air Transport Service[15] kept sending USAF C-54s and USN R5Ds to Germany. Thereafter, with the exception of a single Boeing YC-97A, a single Douglas C-74, and a handful of Fairchild C-82s, the American fleet on the Berlin Airlift[16] was made up of 225 C-54s and R5Ds.

On the three air corridors between West Germany and the Berlin airports (Tempelhof, Gatow, and Tegel, respectively in the American, British, and French sectors), aircraft were stacked up between 4,000ft and 6,000ft, with a 1,000ft vertical separation and followed each other every three minutes, day and night. Aircraft remained on the ground in Berlin only long enough to be

15 The Military Air Transport Service, a USAF command, had just been organized on 1 June 1948. It was composed of the former Air Transport Command and four squadrons of the Naval Air Transport Service. MATS also absorbed the Air Rescue Service, the Air Weather Service, and the Airways and Air Communications Service.
16 All operations on the Berlin Airlift came under a joint US-British command, the Combined Airlift Task Force. Its American component was organized on 29 June 1948 as the Berlin Airlift Task Force. It became the Airlift Task Force Provisional on 31 July and the 1st Airlift Task Force on 28 October 1948.

BELOW *This C-54D was operated by the* Escuadrón Aéreo de Transporte Pesado 302 *(302nd Heavy Transport Squadron) of the* Fuerza Aérea Mexicana. (Norm Taylor, David W. Menard collection)

ABOVE *For quick identification when taxying during the Berlin Airlift, C-54s and R5Ds had three-digit numbers applied on their tail and, often also, on the nose cone.* (J.J. Tarsitano collection and David W. Menard collection)

LEFT *This R5D-3 of Marine Transport Squadron 152 (VMR-152) is being loaded by hand at Chunchon, Korea, in 1950.* (USMC)

BELOW *A stretcher patient is being brought aboard a C-54D-10-DC of the 374th Troop Carrier Wing at Taegu (K-2) in 1951.* (Jackson, David W. Menard collection)

ABOVE *Registered D6-CAA, this ex-C-54A-15-DC was operated by Air Comores.* (Jacques Guillem collection)

unloaded, with crewmembers quickly eating a sandwich or gulping a hot beverage, before setting back to their departure bases in West Germany. There the aircraft were on the ground for 1hr 40min to be serviced, refueled, and loaded.

Even though the Soviets threw in the towel on 12 May 1949, operations on the airlift continued until the end of September as the Allies wanted to build up stock in West Berlin as a precautionary measure in the event of a new blockade. The financial price for the Berlin Airlift was $224 million (±$2 billion today) for the US alone, costs to British and other Allied taxpayers remaining unreported.

Less than ten months after the end of Berlin Airlift operations, C-54s had to go back to war. At 4:00 AM on 25 July 1950, another fateful Sunday morning for American forces, North Korean troops crossed the 38th parallel and ran over outnumbered and outgunned South Korean defenders. The so-called UN 'police action' that ensued lasted until the signing of an armistice at Panmunjom on 27 July 1953. Incredibly, peace has yet to return officially to Korea.

Just 24 hours after the North Korean invasion had begun, a C-54 of the 374th Troop Carrier Wing landed at Kimpo, the main airfield for the South Korean capital, to begin airlifting US nationals out of harm's way. It took less than 24 additional hours for two C-54s and 10 C-47s to evacuate 748 people. However, one of the four-engined transports – 45-518, a C-54G-1-DO – was destroyed on the ground when North Korean Yak-9 fighters strafed Kimpo. The next day,

another C-54 was destroyed at the Suwon airfield. However, a third, intercepted by North Korean fighters, managed to escape.

As the front moved up and down the Korean Peninsula before settling down near the original 38th parallel boundary lines, USAF C-54s and USMC R5Ds were kept busy, increasingly for aeromedical evacuation of wounded personnel to Japan. For this role, 30 C-54Es were fitted with improved accommodations for better medical care, the modified aircraft becoming MC-54Ms.

Following operations in Korea, C-54s were withdrawn from troop carrier squadrons but they remained in USAF service for staff transport and other ancillary duties (notably with the headquarters units of the Air National Guard). Likewise, the USN and USMC R5Ds (which were given new C-54 designations in September 1952) did not disappear until the 1970s. The last C-54 in US military service was BuNo 56501, a C-54Q at the Naval Test Pilot School, NAS Patuxent River, Maryland, which was retired on 2 April 1974.

The United States Coast Guard, another component of US

BELOW *This ex-R5D-1 (BuNo 50845) ended up being used by Air France on its night postal service.* (Jacques Guillem collection)

ABOVE *This DC-4-1009 was delivered to Ansett Australia Airlines in July 1946 as VH-ANE. It later became 5R-MCO with Air Madagascar as shown in this March 1977 photograph taken at Tananarive.* (Jacques Guillem collection)

Naval Aviation (which, in peacetime, reported to the Department of the Treasury), first obtained six R5D-3s in 1945. Nine other R5Ds were later transferred to the USCG to be used for maritime search and rescue, ice patrol, mapping, and electronic testing. Their replacement by Lockheed HC-130s was initiated in 1962 and completed three years later. Another US military operator of the Douglas four-engined transport was the US Army which obtained the transfer of four C-54Ds to support testing of the *Nike-Zeus* anti-ballistic missile at Kwajalein Atoll, in the Marshall Islands, during the early sixties. At least another eight of these four-engined aircraft (one C-54B, five C-54Ds, and two C-54Gs) were in USA service in the mid- to late 1960s.

Not to be outdone, the National Air and Space Administration obtained three C-54G-DOs during the 1960s primarily to provide logistic support between its various research centers. One of these aircraft – then numbered NASA 438, the ex-45-578 of the USAAF – was experimentally fitted in 1973 with wingtip vortex attenuating devices (called wingtip splines). Tests were conducted by the NASA Langley Research Center in Virginia with an instrumented Piper

BELOW *This* Carvair *of British United Air Ferries was the ex-42-72206, a C-54A-10-DO.* (British United)

PA-28 being flown anywhere up to five nautical miles behind the modified C-54. Two ex-NASA aircraft are still active, one with Brooks Air Fuel in Alaska and the other with Buffalo Airways in Canada.

During World War Two, C-54s were not included in Lend-Lease deliveries with the exception of the United Kingdom (23 *Skymasters*) and France (one C-54B-1-DO, 43-17126, delivered in November 1944, for use by Gen de Gaulle, the president of the French provisional government).[17] Postwar, and particularly several years later when airlines began disposing of their ageing DC-4s and C-54s, Douglas four-engined transports went into service with the air forces of at least 22 other countries: Argentina, Belgium, Brazil, Chad, Colombia, Denmark, Ethiopia, Honduras, Mexico, the Netherlands, Nigeria, Peru, Portugal, El Salvador, Spain, Saudi Arabia, South Africa, Taiwan, Tanzania, Thailand, Turkey, and Zaire. None made it to the new millennium in military service. The last operational use was made at the end of 1992 by the South African Air Force. The last of the SAAF aircraft – serial 6905, a DC-4-1009 built as fsn 42984 – is now operated in civilian markings by the South African Airways Historic Flight with the registration ZS-AUB.

Not quite ready for retirement

By the end of the 1940s, major airlines were no longer operating DC-4s on their main routes. These well-built aircraft, however, still had long lives in front of them. The principal US and European airlines reallocated their DC-4s progressively to less dense and shorter sectors. Then, even on those routes, DC-4s were replaced by twin-engined aircraft with pressurized cabins (Convair 240/340/440) or four-turbine Vickers *Viscounts* and were sold to less demanding operators. For example, in the United States, Eastern and United disposed of their last DC-4s respectively in 1955 and 1961. Likewise in Europe, Alitalia last operated DC-4s in 1954 while KLM used them six years longer. In France, after being taken out of passenger service, the old work horses were used for night mail operations by the *Center d'exploitation postale métropolitain d'Air France* until 1973 on the route between Paris–Lyon–Marseilles–Nice–Ajaccio–Bastia.

With smaller airlines in North America and Europe, but more so with operators in what was then referred to as the 'Third World' (the preferred term now being 'less economically developed countries'), mostly in Africa and Latin America, DC-4s still had long careers either transporting passengers in more confined accommodations[18] or as freight carriers. In that role, even though

17 This aircraft eventually went to France's *Aéronautique navale*, with this service then acquiring two more C54s in 1961–62, the last being withdrawn in March 1969.
18 Some airlines went as far as fitting up to 86 seats – more than twice the original number – in their 'cattle car' DC-4s/C-54s. Seats were arranged five abreast (2 + 3) and pitch was drastically reduced.

ABOVE *After being modified as a* Carvair, *this ex-C-54A-1-DC became G-ASDC* Pont du Rhin *with British United Air Ferries. It later became N103, first with Pacific Air Express as illustrated, and then with Great Southern Airways (with which it crashed at Venetie, Alaska, on 28 June 1997).* (David W. Menard)

RIGHT *A DC-4 with a difference: 9Q-CBG of Air Congo (the ex 42-72347) was the only one modified with a swing-tail by Sabena.* (Jean Delmas collecion)

the double door on the rear fuselage of ex C-54s was already quite satisfactory, some operators had more demanding loading/unloading requirements for which major airframe modifications were needed.

In July 1948, Silver City Airways began offering a car ferry service between Lympne, Kent, and Le Touquet, Pas-de-Calais. Channel Air Bridge entered into competition with Silver City in April 1955 with

a route from Southend-on-Sea, Essex, to Calais, Pas-de-Calais. The two carriers operated Bristol *Freighters*, in both standard Mk 31 and long-nosed Mk 32 versions, the latter transporting two large motor cars (or three medium-sized vehicles) and 16 passengers across the Channel. However, as the *Freighters* lacked the range to operate over longer, more direct routes to other points on the Continent, Channel Air Bridge requested its sister company, Aviation Traders

Data for civil DC-4 and derivatives

	DC-4-1009 (*Twin Wasp* 2SD13-G)	Canadair C-4 (Merlin 626-1)	AT(E)L 98 Carvair (R-2000-7)
Dimensions:			
Span, ft in	117 6	117 6	117 6
Length, ft in	93 10	93 7½	102 7
Height, ft in	27 6	27 6⁵⁄₁₆	29 10
Wing area, sq ft	1,460	1,460	1,462
Weights:			
Empty, lb	43,300	46,832	41,365
Loaded, lb	63,500	70,000	73,800
Maximum, lb	73,000	82,300	—
Wing loading, lb/sq ft	48.5	47.9	50.5
Power loading, lb/hp	10.9	9.9	12.7
Performance:			
Max speed, mph/ft	280/14,000	325/25,200	184/10,000
Cruising speed, mph	227	289	—
Range, miles/lb	2,500/11,440	—	3,330/8,000

OPPOSITE TOP *Photographed at the Chester Fire Base in California on 18 August 1985, the air tanker N4989P was an ex-C-54G (45-629). On 21 June 1995, when returning from a retardant drop in Southern California, it collided with the lead aircraft, a Beech* Baron. *Both aircraft crashed and the pilots (two in the C-54 and one in the* Baron*) were killed.* (René J. Francillon)

OPPOSITE MIDDLE AND BOTTOM *This C-54D-1-DC, 42-72442, has had a long career and is still active in 2011. It successively was a* Skymaster *Mk 1 (RAF serial KL977) and an USN R5D3 (BuNo 91994) before being acquired by Aero Union and modified as an air tanker. It is shown at Chico, California, in 1976 (above as N76AU) and at Lancaster, California, on 26 October 2003 (below as N3054V of Aero-Flite). Still registered N3054V, but returned to standard cargo configuration, it is currently operated by Brooks Air Fuel in Alaska.* (Carl E. Porter and Jim Dunn)

RIGHT AND BOTTOM *Seventy-nine DC-4-1009s were built in 1945–46. These photographs show the cockpit of one of these aircraft (right) and the assembly line at the Santa Monica plant (below).* (Douglas)

(Engineering) Ltd, to study the feasibility of converting C-54s into specialized car transport aircraft. Nose loading was considered essential. The result was the AT(E)L 98 *Carvair*.

Modifications devised by Aviation Traders included: (1) the raising of the cockpit 6ft 10in above the fuselage and the relocation of the nosewheel in an external fairing, both features enabling straight-through loading; (2) the lengthening of the forward fuselage by 8ft 8in; (3) the incorporation in the lengthened nose of a hydraulically-operated swing door opening to the left; and (4) the enlarging of vertical tail surfaces, increasing overall height on the ground to 29ft 10in versus 27ft 6in for the C-54. The revised fuselage design resulted in an increase in cabin length from 49ft 10in to 80ft 2in, and in usable volume from 3,691 to 4,350cu ft. Space would thus be available for carrying five motorcars and 23 passengers while payload-range would be sufficient for direct service from England to Holland. As C-54s with good remaining potential were available for around $110,000 (±$800,000 today), the conversion was forecast to be financially feasible even if the number of *Carvairs* remained small.

The first AT(E)L 98 *Carvair* was obtained by modifying fsn 10528, G-ANYB, an ex-C-54B-1-DC (42-72423) then owned by British United Airways. First flown at Southend-on-Sea on 21 June 1961, this aircraft obtained ARB and FAA certification on 31 January 1962. Channel Air Bridge put the ATL into service between Southend and Rotterdam on 1 March 1962, and 20 other C-54B/E and DC-4-1009s were converted into Carvairs for Aer Lingus, Ansett Australia, Aviaco, British United Air Ferries, and Intercontinental US Inc. The last AT(E)L 98 was first flown on 12 July 1968 and, 43 years later, two[19] were in storage, possibly to be returned to flying status.

The next cargo conversion, realized by Sabena's Engineering Department at the request of Air Congo, was equally unusual. Needing an aircraft to carry unusually large items that could not be loaded through the double door of a C-54, this African operator asked the Belgian airline to have an aircraft (fsn 10452, a C-54B-1-DC) modified to have straight-through loading. Sabena engineers chose to have the rear fuselage and tail surfaces swing out to the right of the rear fuselage. After modifications, 9Q-CBG flew again on 16 December 1967. It then was operated by Air Congo

(redesignated Air Zaire in October 1971) before passing on to Zaire Aero Service and then to Kinair Cargo. Registered 9Q-CBK with this last carrier, the swing-tail DC-4 crashed in the Zaire River on 23 August 1988.

Toward the end of their careers, DC-4s and C-54s found a new lease on life when they were modified as air tankers for use in fighting forest fires. Additional windows were provided in the cockpit roof and a 1,665-Imp. gallon retardant tank was fitted beneath the center fuselage. At least one was re-engined with 1,600hp Wright *Duplex-Cyclones* and had an enlarged under fuselage tank for 1,832 Imp. gallons of retardant. Cruising speed was increased from 205 to 230mph. DC-4 air tankers were last used in the United States in 2003 but are still operated by Buffalo Airways in Canada.

In July 2011, AeroTransport Data Bank (http://aerotransport.org) was reporting that 20 DC-4s/C-54s remained in operation while 20 more (possibly including two *Carvairs*) were being overhauled/ modified before being returned to service. The largest operator then was Buffalo Airways which had nine Canadian-registered aircraft in service.

---

19 In 2011, N89FA (fsn 27249) belonged to Custom Air Services and 9J-PAA (fsn 27314) to Phoebus Apollo Zambia.

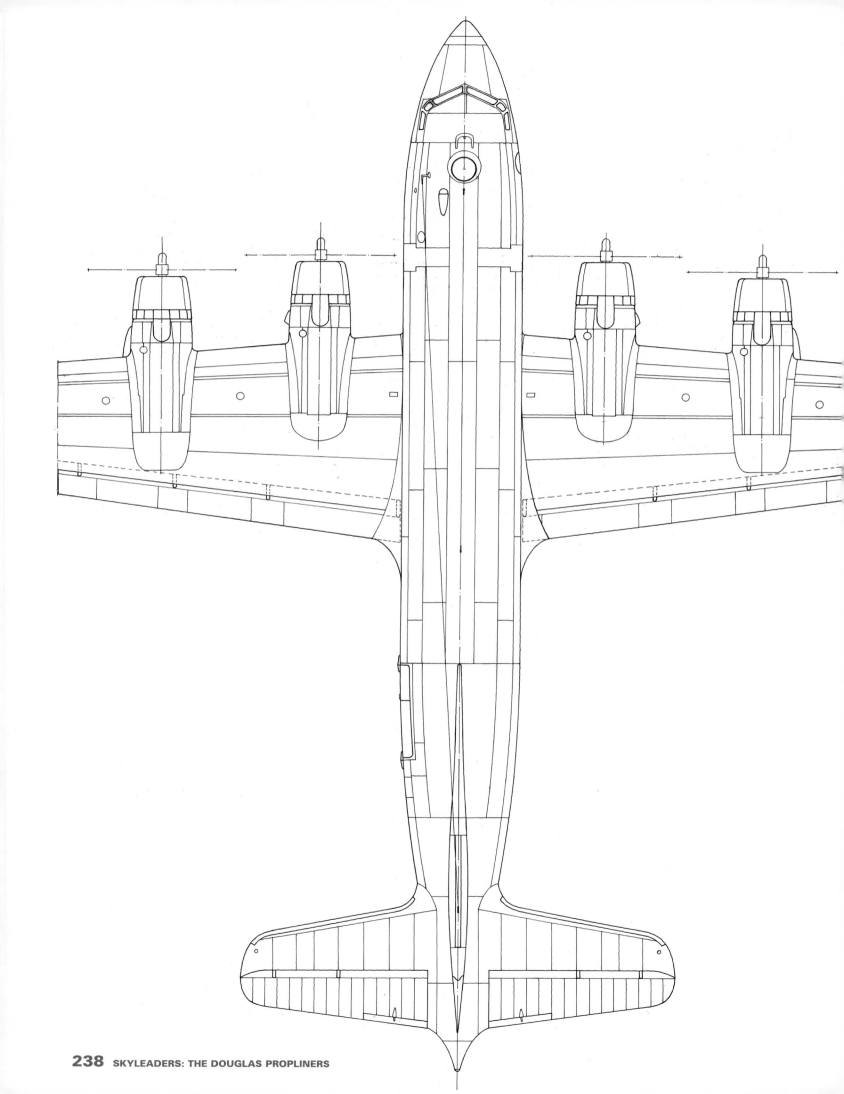

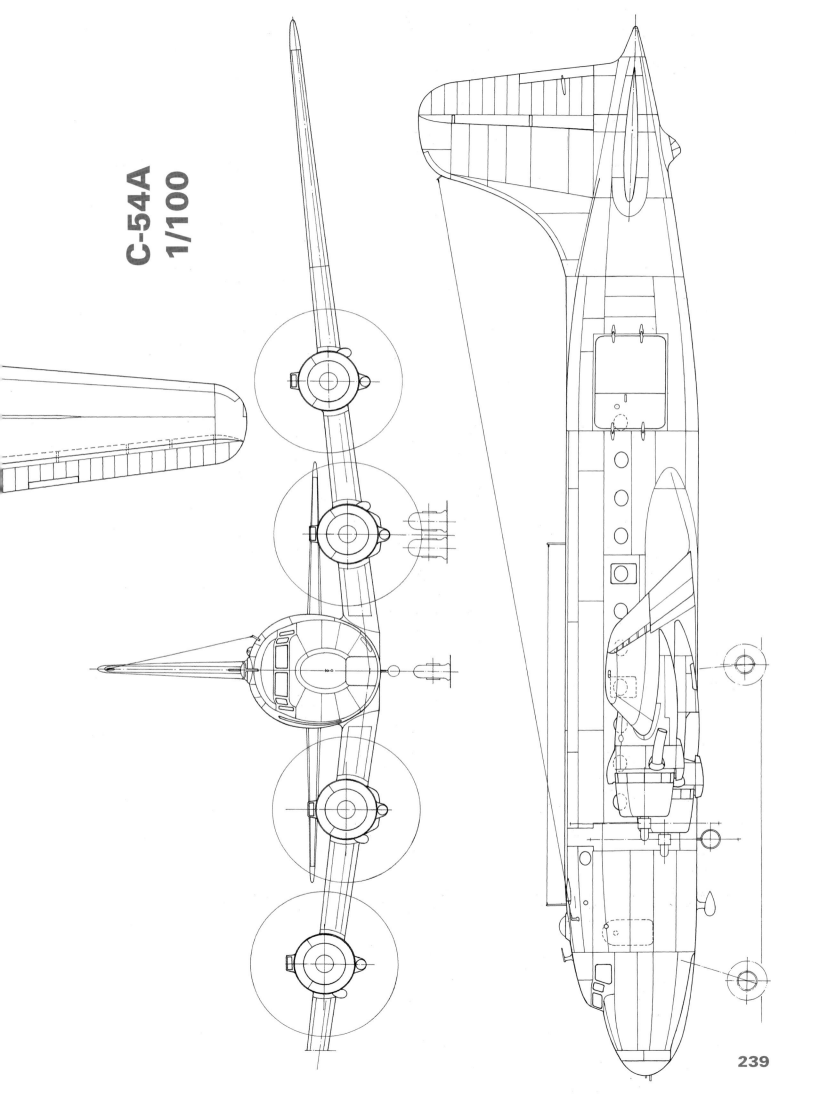

C-54A
1/100

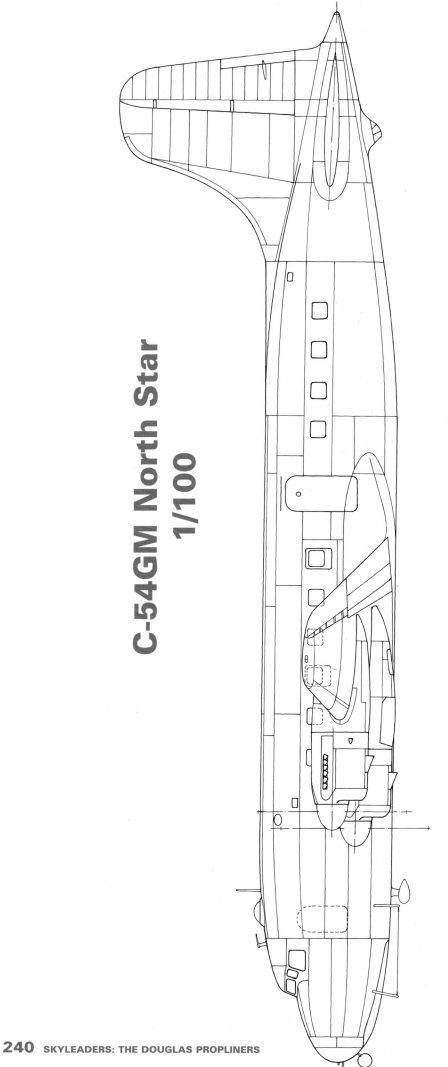

C-54GM North Star 1/100

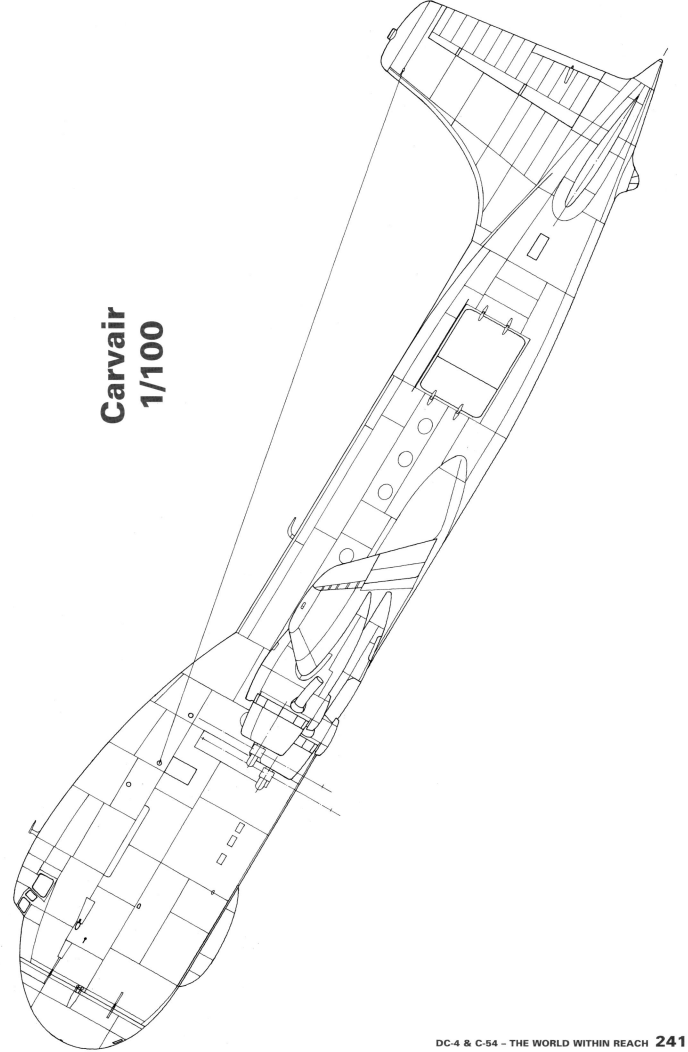

Carvair
1/100

C-54 in military service

LEFT *A C-54-DO at Hollandia, Dutch New Guinea, in June 1944.* (USAAF)

BELOW *These two* Skymasters *of the Air Transport Command are 43-17274, a C-54-D-15-DC, and 42-72569, a C-54D-5-DC.* (Douglas)

BOTTOM *This C-54D-1-DC of the 374th Troop Carrier Wing was photographed at Tachikawa AB in 1957, a few weeks before the wing was inactivated in Japan.* (Roger Thompson, David W. Menard collection)

RIGHT *43-17237, a C-54D-15-DC in the markings of the US Army.* (David W. Menard collection)

BELOW *A C-54G-15-DO assigned to the headquarters of the Iowa Air National Guard. The two squadrons of the Iowa ANG were then equipped with Northrop F-89Js (124th FIS at Des Moines) and North American F-100Cs (174th TFS at Sioux City).* (Peter B. Lewis)

BOTTOM *45-613, a C-54G-10-DO of the New Mexico Air National Guard at Kirtland AFB on 28 September 1967.* (David W. Menard collection)

LEFT *During the Korean War, some 30 C-54Es were modified for use in the aeromedical evacuation role and were redesignated MC-54Ms; one of these aircraft is shown here at Santa Rosa, California, in January 1957.* (Harrison Rued, David W. Menard collection)

LEFT AND BELOW *Over the years the* Blue Angels, *the Navy Flight Demonstration Squadron, has used several R5Ds to transport maintenance personnel and spare parts when operating away from its home base. BuNo 50868, an R5D-2, was photographed at NAS Pensacola, Florida, in July 1960 (above) while BuNo 91666, a C-54Q, was at NAS Los Alamitos, California, in July 1967 (below).* (William Balogh, David W. Menard collection and René J. Francillon)

RIGHT *Photographed at Travis AFB, California, on 20 April 1966, this VC-54M (44-9055, an ex-C-54E-5-DO) had a two-star flag painted aft of the cockpit, indicating that it was assigned to a Major General.* (Peter B. Lewis)

BELOW *This ROKAF (Republic of Korea Air Force) C-54D-15-DC was photographed at Osan AB in August 1991.* (Bill Curry)

BOTTOM *FAB 2406 (ex-C-54G-10-DO, 45-601) of the* Força Aérea Brasileira. *The 1º/2º GT (2nd Squadron of the 1st Transport Group) of the Brazilian Air Force operated 12 C-54s between 1959 and 1970.* (R. Carson Seely, David W. Menard collection)

Civilian DC-4s

TOP *United Air Lines had been about to firm up an order for DC-4s in 1941. When the war was ending, it ordered, but soon cancelled, DC-4-1009s in 1944. It ended up operating a large fleet of ex-C-54s.* (DR)

ABOVE *The first DC-4-1009, fsn 42904, was delivered to Waterman Airlines in January 1946. In the early 1960s it was with TACA International Airlines in El Salvador as YS-O2C.* (DR)

LEFT *The second DC-4-1009, fsn 42905, was ordered by AB Aerotransport (aka Swedish Airlines) but went into service with SAS.* (Alain Pelletier collection)

RIGHT *Named* Villes de Bruxelles, *the third DC-4-1009 was delivered to* Sabena *in February 1946.* (Douglas)

BELOW *Delivered in July 1946 to Iberia, this DC-4-1009 (fsn 42952) was with Delta Air Transport (a Belgian airline not to be confused with Delta Air Lines in the US) when photographed at Antwerp in 1974 bearing a US registration.* (Jacques Guillem collection)

BOTTOM *The last DC-4-1009, fsn 43157 was delivered to South African Airways in August 1947. Repainted in SAA colours, it is shown landing at Fairford on 24 July 1998.* (Richard Gennis)

ABOVE *HK-172 of* Taxi Aéreo El Venado *was an ex-C-54A-5-DC that crashed into a mountain top during a flight from Bogota to Lamacareña on 15 January 1976.* (DR)

LEFT *OB-R-248 (ex-42-72180, C-54A-5-DC) of* Compañia de Aviación Faucett *at Lima in May 1977 is shown on start of its No 1 engine.* (René J. Francillon)

BELOW *N60115, an ex-C-54B-1-DC of Transocean Air Lines, at Oakland, California.* (J. Noah)

ABOVE *With* Suid-Afrikaanse-Lugdiens *written on the right side of the fuselage and South African Airways on the left, this is the last DC-4-1009 during a recent photo flight in South Africa.* (Frédéric Lert)

RIGHT *NC37472 of Delta Air Lines was an ex-C-54B-1-DC (fsn 10444) which was operated by that airline between 1946 and 1953.* (Douglas)

RIGHT *TJ-CCA of Cameroon Airlines was an ex-C-54B-15-DO.* (Jacques Guillem collection)

RIGHT *In the early 1960s, Lloyd International Airways operated two DC-4s, including G-ARWI, an ex-C-54B-10-DO.* (Jacques Guillem collection)

ABOVE *Photographed in June 1973 at Juba (now the capital of the Republic of South Sudan), EI-ARS was an ex-C-54E belonging to Aer Turas which was chartered to the United Nations Commissioner for Refugees.* (René J. Francillon)

LEFT *N8812 of Eastern Air Lines was an ex-R5D-2 (BuNo 39117).* (Douglas)

LEFT *G-ASDC, an ATL 98 Carvair of BAF Cargo, was the ex-42-72418 (C-54A-1-DC).* (DR)

BELOW *Recently withdrawn from use by NASA, this was the last-built C-54 (45-637).* (Peter B. Lewis)

ABOVE *Air Tanker 02, an ex-C-54-DO (fsn 3088), at Ryan Field, Hemet, California, in October 1989.* (Peter B. Lewis)

RIGHT *Air Tanker 15, an ex-C-54G-15-DO, on the ramp of Aero Union in Chico, California, in 1985.* (Carl E. Porter)

BELOW *In 2011, Buffalo Airways was still operating this ex-C-54G-15-DO (45-635, now registered C-FIQM).* (DR)

Chapter 10

DC-6 – Top of the line

To be ready to meet the postwar needs of airlines, Douglas smartly manoeuvred the War Department and obtained authorization in 1944 to develop derivatives of the DC-4 with new engines and/or pressurized cabins (see insert on page 220). Whereas the XC-114 with Allison V-1710 and XC-115 with Packard V-1650 (a US development of the Rolls-Royce *Merlin*) never reached flight status as American air carriers did not want the complexity of liquid-cooled engines, the XC-112A (fsn 36326) powered by four 18-cylinder, twin row radials flew on 15 February 1946, exactly six months after the war had ended. On that occasion, the test crew was captained by John F. Martin.

Although it was a military prototype, the XC-112A flew without national markings or its USAAF serial number (45-873), thus hinting about its impending commercial use. Its airframe was derived from that of the C-54E but differed in having cabin length increase by 81 inches aft of the wings and in incorporating cabin pressurization (the first for a Douglas aircraft).[1] It was powered by four 2,100hp Pratt & Whitney R-2800-22Ws driving constant-speed three-blade propellers with reversible pitch. To allow for operations at higher weights, the undercarriage was beefed up and the structure was locally strengthened.[2] Finally, in order to minimize field length

BELOW *A family portrait at the* Aeropuerto Internacional Jorge Chávez *in Lima, Peru, in May 1977: OB-R-846 was a DC-6B (in the foreground) and OB-R-248 was an ex-C-54A-5-DC, both belonging then to* Compañia de Aviación Faucett. *(René J. Francillon)*

---

1 Compressors were fitted in engines Nos 2 and 3 to provide for a cabin altitude of 8,000ft while the aircraft was cruising at an altitude of 20,000ft.
2 In particular, a second spar was added to the wing outboard panels thus also providing space in between the spars for more fuel.

ABOVE *Devoid of markings, serial number, or registration number, this is the XC-112, the prototype of the DC-6 series, flying along the Malibu coast, just north of Santa Monica.* (Douglas)

requirements in spite of increased operating weights, the single slot NACA flaps of the C-54 were replaced by Douglas-designed double slotted flaps.

Although the USAAF lost further interest in the XC-112A at war's end, airlines which had not ordered Lockheed *Constellations* found this new design well-suited to filling their need for a pressurized airliner. American Airlines and United Air Lines thus became the launch customers for the DC-6 which went on to be built in three major civil variants.

DC-6: With the exception of full cabin furnishing and the fitting of civil instruments and systems, the DC-6 was essentially identical

to the XC-112A military prototype. The Santa Monica plant built 175 of these aircraft. They were powered by various models of the Pratt & Whitney *Double Wasp* (R-2800) radials with take-off rating ranging between 2,100hp and 2,500hp, the higher rating being obtained by injecting water-methanol on take-off. (See engine listing table on page 256.) According to customers' specifications,

The enigmatic NX90809

Among the C-54E derivatives ordered by the USAAF in January 1945 was fsn 36327, 45-874, which was to be powered by four 1,620hp Allison V-1710-131s and fitted with a pressurized cabin as the XC-114 prototype. Later, it was planned to become an XC-112A with R-2800-85 radials. The incomplete airframe was then re-purchased by the manufacturer, and fitted with Pratt & Whitney *Double Wasp* radials, became the second prototype of the DC-6. Its fsn was changed to 43061 and the aircraft was registered NX90809.

On 27 November 1947, after completion of flight tests, the aircraft was leased to United Air Lines to be used for DC-6 crew training. It was

then returned to the manufacturer to have test equipment removed and its cabin brought up to commercial standard before being sold to United. Registered N37536 and named *Mainliner Mesa Verde*, it was operated by this airline for 14 years before being traded off to Sud-Aviation when United ordered *Caravelle VI R* jetliners. N37356 remained in California where it was broken up in 1962.

BELOW *NX90809, the second prototype for the DC-6, flies with feathered propellers on its Nos 3 and 4 engines.* (Douglas)

ABOVE *The first DC-6, shown here with temporary test registration NX90701, was flown on 29 June 1946 and delivered to American Airlines on 20 April 1947. Named* Flagship New York *it was used for the first DC-6 revenue flight on 27 April between New York and Chicago.* (Douglas)

maximum weight ranged between 87,900kg and 98,800kg and fuel tank capacity between 2,766 Imp. gallons (in eight tanks) and 4,107gal (in 10 tanks).

In their initial delivery configuration, most DC-6s had their cabin fitted with 50 seats (in 2 +2 arrangement); a three-seat sofa was provided at the rear of the cabin but could not be occupied during take-offs or landings. Some of the early American Airlines DC-6s were fitted with seats convertible into bunks but that arrangement was no longer favored by passengers. Later, seating was increased

BELOW *The DC-6A freighters had two large, upward-opening, cargo doors on the main deck. The opening of the rear door was even larger (124in × 78in vs 91in × 67in) as the forward-opening passenger door could be opened to supplement the upward-opening cargo door.* (KLM)

to 68, and then to 86, by fitting five seats abreast (2 + 3) and reducing pitch. Finally, some DC-6s were converted into cargo aircraft by removal of their cabin fittings and installation of both reinforced flooring and a large main deck cargo door (on the left of the rear fuselage).

The first genuine DC-6 (fsn 42854, NX90701) flew on 29 June 1946. Simultaneous deliveries to American and United commenced on 20 November, and the aircraft was certificated on 23 June 1947. The 175th and last DC-6 was delivered to Braniff Airways on 2 November 1951.

DC-6A: The availability of more powerful versions of the *Double Wasp* engine with water-methanol injection, together with encouraging results from structural analyses, led Douglas to offer new DC-6 models with a 5ft longer and more capacious fuselage, increased maximum gross weights (up to a 107,000lb) and fuel tank capacity (3,547 to 4,600 Imp. gallons), and improved performance. The first of the new model was optimized as a freighter with a reinforced cabin floor and two 79in x 126in upward- and outward-opening cargo doors on the left side of the fuselage, one forward and one aft of the wings. A powered-loading elevator with a 4,000lb capacity could be attached to either cargo door and stored aboard the aircraft when not in use. A passenger access door, opening forward and outward, was also provided ahead of the rear cargo

door. The 4,431cu ft main deck and two underfloor holds (244 and 265cu ft) could accommodate a maximum cargo load of 30,000lb.

The initial DC-6A (fsn 42901, N30006) first flew on 29 September 1949 but was not certificated until 17 April 1951. The 74th and last DC-6A (fsn 45530, PP-LFD) was delivered to the Brazilian carrier *Lóide Aéreo Nacional* on 10 February 1959. Most DC-6As had the cabin windows covered with metal plugs which could be removed to convert this freighter aircraft back to passenger transport. Some aircraft, sometimes designated DC-6Cs, had standard windows and could be used either in cargo or passenger configuration.

DC-6B: Dimensionally identical to the DC-6A, this model was optimized for passenger transport, thus dispensing with the reinforced flooring and two cargo doors of the freighter. Customers were offered a similar range of options as for the DC-6A: *Double Wasp* engines rated at 2,400hp or 2,500hp with water-methanol injection, gross weight of up 107,000lb, and fuel tank capacity

ABOVE *The first DC-6B – fsn43257, N37547* Mainliner Newark *– first flew on 2 February 1951 and was delivered to United Air Lines on 27 April 1951.* (Douglas)

of up to 4,590 Imp. gallons. Seating was initially provided for 52 passengers (in 2 + 2 rows) but was increased to 82 (in 2 + 3) in coach class or 102 (in 2 + 3 rows with reduced pitch) for charter operations.

After being taken out of service by the major air carriers, many DC-6Bs were converted into freighters by replacement of the

BELOW *The engineering department of* Sabena *modified two DC-6Bs (including fsn 45202, OH-KDA, of* Kar-Air O/Y*) and fitted them with a swing-tail.* (Kar-Air O/Y)

original cabin floor with a reinforced floor with tie-downs and installation of either one (forward of the wings) or two (fore and aft) cargo doors on the left side of the fuselage. Even though these modified aircraft have been referred to as DC-6AB, DC-6AC, DC-6A(C), DC-6BF, and DC-6B(F), none of these designations appear in official Douglas and Federal Aviation Administration documentation. In the Type Certificate Data Sheet, the FAA refers to DC-6Bs modified as freighters by the single appellation of DC-6B (Cargo). Two other DC-6Bs (fsn 44434 and 45202) were more extensively modified by the Engineering Department of Sabena which fitted them with a swing tail (rear fuselage and tail surfaces) hinged to the right. One went to Spantax in Spain and the other to Kar-Air O/Y in Finland.

The first DC-6B (fsn 43257 for United Air Lines), delivered on 2 February 1951, was certificated on 11 April of that year. The 288th and last DC-6B (fsn 45564) went to JAT (*Jugoslovenski Aerotransport*) on 17 November 1958.

Engineering studies for DC-6 derivatives did not end with the design of the DC-6A and DC-6B as, during the late 1940s and early 1950s, Douglas relentlessly searched for ways to keep its DC-6 in demand. That search led Santa Monica engineers to study various developments powered by either turboprop or turbojet engines. To illustrate some of the more interesting preliminary studies, manufacturer's drawings for three models, all retaining the basic fuselage design of the DC-6, are reproduced on these two pages. That below would have retained the wings (suitably strengthened to allow the use of tip tanks) and tail surfaces (slightly enlarged) of the DC-6B and would have been powered by four 3,000shp General Electric TG-110 turboprops. Those on the opposite page were more extensively redesigned and would have had swept wing and tail surfaces. Power was to be provided by four 5,000lb st Rolls-Royce *Nene* turbojets which were to be mounted, one above the other, in wing nacelles (plan view drawing) or side-by-side in underslung nacelles (side-view).

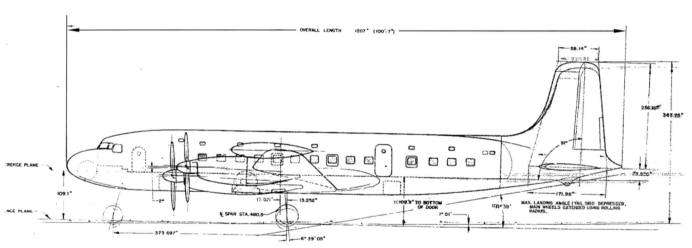

Pratt & Whitney engines for the DC-6

Engine models	Take-off rating (with/without water injection)	Maximum rating	Aircraft models
R-2800-34	2,100hp/—	2,100hp @ 3,000ft, 1,700hp @ 16,000ft	DC-6
R-2800-52W	2,200hp/2,500hp	2,300hp @ 3,500ft	DC-6A, DC-6B, C-118A & R6D-1
R-2800-83A	2,100hp/—	2,100hp @ 3,000ft, 1,700hp @ 16,000ft	DC-6
R-2800-83AM3	2,100hp/2,400hp	1,800hp @ 6,000ft, 1,600hp @ 16,000ft	DC-6 & DC-6B
R-2800-83AM4	2,100hp/2,400hp	1,800hp @ 6,000ft, 1,600hp @ 16,000ft	DC-6
R-2800-83AM5	2,100hp/2,400hp	1,800hp @ 6,000ft, 1,600hp @ 16,000ft	DC-6A & DC-6B
R-2800-83AM7	2,200hp/2,500hp	1,900hp @ 10,000ft, 1,750hp @ 15,000ft	DC-6A & DC-6B
R-2800-85XA	2,100hp/—	2,100hp @ 3,000ft, 1,700hp @ 16,000ft	XC-112A
R-2800-95	2,100hp/2,400hp	1,600hp @ 10,000ft, 1,600hp @ 14,500ft	C-118
Double Wasp CA15	2,100hp/2,400hp	1,900hp @ 6,000ft, 1,600hp @ 16,000ft	DC-6 & DC-6B
Double Wasp CA18	2,100hp/2,400hp	1,900hp @ 4,000ft, 1,675hp @ 13,500ft	DC-6
Double Wasp CB3	2,050hp/2,400hp	1,800hp @ 8,500ft	DC-6A & DC-6B
Double Wasp CB4	2,200hp/2,500hp	1,900hp @ 7,000ft	DC-6A & DC-6B
Double Wasp CB16	2,050hp/2,400hp	1,800hp @ 8,500ft, 1,700hp @ 14,500ft	DC-6A & DC-6B
Double Wasp CB17	2,200hp/2,500hp	1,900hp @ 7,000ft, 1,750hp @ 13,500ft	DC-6, DC-6A & DC-6B

Sources: Federal Aviation Administration, Aircraft Specifications Nos A781, 6A3 & 6A4
Pratt & Whitney Aircraft, Engine Listings Manual, March 1967

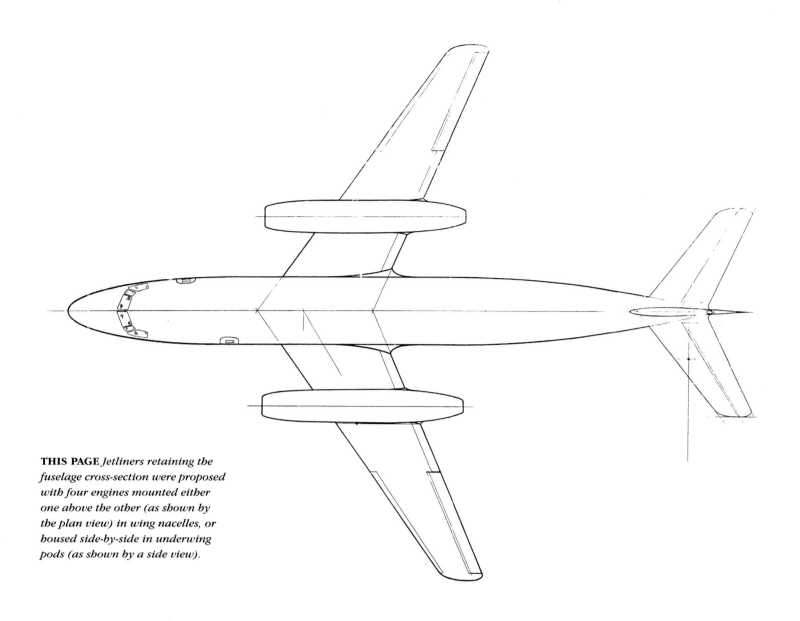

THIS PAGE *Jetliners retaining the
fuselage cross-section were proposed
with four engines mounted either
one above the other (as shown by
the plan view) in wing nacelles, or
housed side-by-side in underwing
pods (as shown by a side view).*

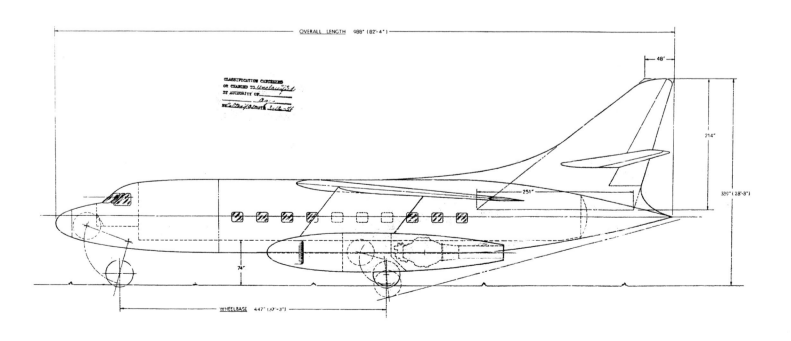

ABOVE *The first two DC-6s – fsn 42855, N90702* Flagship New Jersey *for American Airlines and fsn 42866, N37501* Mainliner Bonneville *for United Air Lines – were handed over to their customers during a joint ceremony at Clover Field on Sunday 24 November 1946.* (Douglas)

Down the West Coast of South America

The longest leg on Panagra's run down the South American Coast was between Lima, Peru, and Santiago, Chile. The 1,520 miles between these two points were flown non-stop with DC-6s and DC-6Bs, scheduled time being 6hr 25min when flying south. Except for a few minutes after take-off and before landing, the flight was almost entirely over the Pacific. The passengers could always sleep to pass the time more quickly, but that was not the case for the flight crew, at least under established procedures.

In the 1950s, as the story is told, Panagra had a captain and a co-pilot reputed for frequently leaving the cockpit to get some rest aft. On one particular flight, when crew scheduling had managed to get them aboard together, these two pilots lived up to their reputations. They left their seats and entrusted the aircraft to 'George' (the automatic pilot), with monitoring left to a relatively junior second officer. At the risk of endangering his career with the airline, the young pilot decided to 'teach a thing or two' to his wandering seniors. He set out to work immediately after they left the cockpit.

First he set the clock on the instrument panel one hour ahead. Then, while keeping up with his normal duties, he kept an ear on the cockpit door. When he realized that the captain was about to return to his post, the daring second officer turned the aircraft westward… toward the vast open Pacific. Rubbing sleep out of his eyes, the captain first thought he had overslept. OK, no big deal except… 'Just, a minute, why is the compass pointing west when, en route to Santiago, we should be flying on a SSE track? How long have we been flying in that direction? Will we have enough fuel to make it to Santiago from that far at sea?'

The young second officer survived the ire of his seniors and, as they could not report the incident for fear of attracting attention to their own improper action, he was able to stay with Panagra. In 1967, when that airline was merged with Braniff, the no-longer-so-young pilot became chief pilot. He did have quite a glee in his eyes when telling this story!

Worrisome beginnings

In the immediate postwar period, the US Civil Aeronautics Administration (CAA) found itself overloaded with work as new safety and certification regulations were being devised and implemented. At the same time, quite a variety of surplus military aircraft was finding its way into the hands of civil operators, and all of these types needed to be certificated. As a result of this work overload, aircraft certification was not obtained as quickly as in the past. In the case of the DC-6, Type Certificate A-781 was only delivered on 23 June 1947, 16 months after the first flight of its military prototype, the XC-112A. Urged on by its customers who needed their DC-6s as soon as possible to compete with carriers flying Lockheed *Constellations*, Douglas began delivering its pressurized transport before it was certificated. The first two DC-6s were handed over to American Airlines and United Air Lines during a joint ceremony at Clover Field, Santa Monica, on 24 November 1946. Without type certificate, the new aircraft could only be used by the two airlines for crew training. However, Douglas and the two carriers obtained a special dispensation from the CAA and were thus able to begin service simultaneously on 27 April 1946, with American and United first using their DC-6s on service from New York respectively to Los Angeles (with only one refueling stop in Lincoln, Nebraska) and to Chicago. Once certification was on hand, other carriers quickly offered DC-6 flights: Panagra, between Panama and Buenos Aires, and National Airlines between New York and Miami on 16 May 1947;[3] and Sabena between Brussels and New York in July and later from Brussels to Leopoldville. All appeared promising and the list of DC-6 customers grew rapidly. Unfortunately, two accidents led to the temporary grounding of DC-6s.

The first accident, in which 47 passengers, three cockpit crew members, and two stewardesses perished, originated in Los Angeles on 24 October 1947 as a United Air Lines flight bound for Chicago. While over Utah, the crew reported a cabin fire and attempted to make an emergency landing before crashing. A little over two weeks later, on 11 November, an American Airlines DC-6 also reported an in-flight fire; fortunately it landed safely in New Mexico. In both instances, it was determined that improper venting of a fuel tank resulted in an explosive accumulation of gas fumes in the belly compartment housing the cabin heater. A simple fix was devised and the DC-6 was returned to flight status on 21 March 1948. In the meantime, however, no fewer than 146 DC-6s were left on the ground. All were modified at the manufacturer's expense.

TWA had begun US transcontinental service with the *Constellation* on 15 February 1946, a full 15 months before American could provide comparable service with its pressurized DC-6s. However, some of Lockheed's lead time was lost when the *Constellation* had to be grounded in July and August 1946, in the midst of the busy summer travel season. Getting the *Constellation* back into service was not all that expensive for Lockheed, whether financially or in terms of negative publicity, as its four-engined airliner was kept grounded for 43 days. For Douglas, however, it was a different story as DC-6s were kept on the ground for 140 days.

Parries and counter-parries

Today, most of those who did not live through the years of rivalry between Lockheed and Douglas tend to express considerably more interest in the *Constellation* than in its rival. Undoubtedly, the Lockheed four-engined airliner was gifted with an exceptionally clean appearance. Its dolphin-like fuselage, dainty triple-tail surfaces, and clean engine cowlings made it look to be a thoroughbred

3 Using a Panagra DC-6, the flight originated in New York; its first leg, to Miami, was undertaken in the name of National Airlines. The same aircraft continued to Panagra as a Pan American flight. The true Panagra flight commenced in Panama, went down the West Coast of South America, and then across the Andes to its final destination, Buenos Aires.

filly. And yet, in spite of its plainer looks, the DC-6 and the other Douglas four-engined transports were not sloths. On New York to Los Angeles flights, they crossed the country in 11 hours, cutting 20 to 30 minutes off the scheduled *Constellation* time. However, looks and speed are not the most important attributes of successful airliners. Reliability and dependability generally come in first, and the DC-6 had what it took to be successful in these key areas. Its proven airframe was strong and easily maintained, it was easier and quicker to manufacture as it had a fuselage of almost constant cross-section whereas the *Constellation*'s attractive fuselage lines made it more time-consuming to assemble. Finally, and what became a key factor in the success and longevity of the DC-6 family, was the extreme reliability of its *Double Wasp* engines. Not only were they better than the proven R-2000s powering DC-4s but they were also less temperamental than the *Duplex-Cyclones* of the *Constellations* and the *Turbo-Compounds* of *Super Constellations* and DC-7s.[4] Thus, to put it simply, the DC-6 ended up being more like a dependable plow horse, not winning beauty contests but earning profits and attracting customers. In the very competitive airline business such considerations are far more important than pleasing the spotters' gallery.

Obviously after the early success of its *Constellation*, Lockheed did not intend resting on its laurels. Neither did its rival from across town. Consequently, over a period of ten years, these two manufacturers fought fierce competitive battles. Douglas having responded to the threat posed by the *Constellation* by developing the DC-6, Lockheed forged ahead once more with the first version of its *Super Constellation*. Retaining the *Duplex-Cyclones* of the *Constellation*, the first L-1049s carried 66 passengers in first class versus only 50 for the DC-6. In coach configuration, the L-1049 had a greater lead: 99 seats instead of 66. That gave the initial version of the *Super Constellation* an edge in terms of seat-mile costs. Conversely, as installed power had not been increased from the L-749 to the L-1049, *Super Constellations* proved even slower but, nevertheless,

ABOVE *When DC-6s were grounded between 12 November 1947 and 21 March 1948, undelivered aircraft were stored in Long Beach. Except for the VC-54C at the lower left corner of this photograph, all four-engined aircraft in this view are DC-6s (for American, CMA, FAMA, Panagra, SAS/ABA, DAS/DNL, and United).* (Douglas)

Douglas and its customers were forced to seek improvements in the performance of the DC-6. The results were the DC-6A and DC-6B with more powerful engines and increased seating capacity. As DC-6Bs became the new benchmark in the air transportation industry, Lockheed had again to do better than Douglas.

BELOW *Although ordered by the* Aktiebolaget Aerotransport *(Swedish Airline) and photographed with the registration SE-ABA, fsn 43125 was not taken up by SAS and instead went to British Commonwealth Pacific Airlines as VH-BPE. It crashed during an instrument landing at San Francisco on 29 October 1953.* (Douglas)

4   In the mid-1950s typical engine overhaul life was 1,600 hours for the *Turbo-Compound*, 2,000 hours for the *Duplex-Cyclone*, 2,100 hours for the R-2000, and 2,300 to 2,500 hours for the *Double Wasp*. Mean time between failures was also significantly less for the trusty R-2800.

ABOVE *Having acquired five DC-6s,* Sabena *then added two DC-6As and nine DC-6Bs, including OO-CTN photographed at Bruxelles-National late in its career with the Belgian carrier.* (DR)

Having gained experience with the new *Turbo-Compounds* as first fitted to its P2V-4 *Neptune* maritime patrol aircraft, Lockheed did not hesitate to use these new engines as soon as they became available for commercial operations. Mounting *Turbo-Compounds* on the longer airframes of *Super Constellations* resulted in the L-1049C through L-1049G series of four-engined transport. In the competitive battle between major airlines on the US transcontinental routes, the L-1049C gave a new edge to TWA by enabling that airline to begin offering non-stop transcontinental service in the eastbound direction on 19 October 1953. American Airlines and its supplier, Douglas, picked up the gauntlet and came up with the *Turbo-Compound* powered DC-7 capable of flying across the United States, non-stop in either direction and regardless of weather. Next, Douglas took advantage of its investment in *Turbo-Compounds* airliners to offer an even longer-range version, the DC-7 *Seven Seas*, which could have been rather successful with international carriers had it not been for

the appearance on the scene of the first jetliners. Lockheed made one more move to get ahead of Douglas by offering the L-1649 *Starliner*, a L-1049G with new, high aspect-ratio wings. But that was late, way too late. The jet era had begun and was there to stay.

In full glory

Douglas produced 78 DC-6As (including the prototype which was eventually sold to Slick Airways) for 11 American customers, eight foreign airlines, and the Belgian Air Force. After Slick Airways introduced the type into service on 16 April 1951, competition became fierce in the United States between specialized carriers (such as Slick and Flying Tigers) and larger all-purpose airlines (notably American and United) and resulted in a rapid and drastic reduction in ton-mile rates. On international routes, DC-6As were operated not only by US airlines (Pan American, primarily over the North Atlantic, and Northwest across the Pacific) but also by Brazilian, Canadian, and European carriers.

Once major passenger airlines began disposing of their DC-6s and DC-6Bs, the number of freighters increased significantly as the DC-6As were joined by a growing number of the formerly passenger-configured aircraft versions now fitted with either one or two cargo loading doors, reinforced cabin floor, and cargo handling and tie-down equipment. These freighters rapidly found takers not only with established airlines in the industrialized world but also with new operators which placed them in service in developing

BELOW *N90884, a DC-6 of Braniff Airways in 1950, was sold to Aviateca Guatemala in February 1966.* (Douglas)

nations with growing economies where the surface transportation infrastructure was still relatively limited. In fact, this situation prevails to this day with the last freighters of the DC-6 family being operated in Alaska by Everts Air Cargo and Everts Air Fuel, and in the Northwest Territories by Buffalo Airways.

Five days after Slick Airways had placed the DC-6A into service, Western Airlines became the first DC-6B operator when it initiated operations with the new airliner on its California routes. Then, on 29 April 1951, American Airlines replaced its DC-6s with DC-6Bs on the transcontinental route. Stopping in each direction in Chicago, American's DC-6Bs had a scheduled time of 8hr 55min eastbound and 9hr 45min westbound. Altogether, 287 DC-6Bs were delivered to nine US airlines, 20 non-US airlines, and one Saudi-American oil company (Aramco). In almost all instances, these airliners proved to be 'money-printing' machines, mainly on account of their exceptional reliability and longevity. They enabled operators to obtain good results not only when in use over well-established and heavily traveled routes (across the US and over the Pacific and the North Atlantic) but also when offering new services. For example, when International Air Transport Association mandated that its member airlines not fly first class and coach passengers in the same aircraft, Pan American chose to use specially-acquired DC-6Bs to initiate coach service across the North Atlantic on 1 May 1952, while continuing to use *Stratocruisers* and *Constellations* for its first-class service.

Proving to be exceptionally reliable by the standards of the day, DC-6Bs enabled other airlines to initiate service over more challenging routes. Notably, this was the case of Scandinavian Airlines System (SAS) which took advantage of the delivery flight of its first DC-6B in June 1952 to verify the feasibility of operating between the US West Coast and Europe by flying over a so-called 'polar route' (in fact, this route remained well south of the North Pole). Then, on 15/16 November 1954, SAS initiated scheduled service on this route with DC-6B OY-KMI *Helge Viking* flying from Copenhagen to Los Angeles with intermediate stops in Söndre Stromfjord, Greenland, and Winnipeg, Manitoba. Including stops, Denmark and California were linked in 27hr 15min with airborne time being 24hr 25min. On the same day and night, service in the opposite direction was provided by LN-LMP *Leif Viking* with the same two fuelling stops. DC-6Bs of Canadian Pacific followed on this 'polar route' beginning on 3/4 June 1955, stopping in Edmonton and Söndre Stromfjord.

Then, over the years, DC-6As and DC-6Bs – like their Lockheed competitors and their immediate derivatives from Santa Monica and Burbank – were pushed out of the glamour routes by the

arrival of jetliners. Moving further and further down the operational scale, aircraft that had once dominated long over-water operations ended their lives with large airlines on shorter and shorter routes (such as the intra-California routes on which United Air Lines last operated DC-6Bs). Elsewhere in the world, all DC-6 versions still had a long useful life, often for uses far from those for which they had been designed.

Military variants

Ordered by the War Department on 15 January 1945, the XC-112A was a military prototype. Yet it is best remembered as the first in the civil DC-6 family. Taken on charge by the Army Air Forces, the XC-112A was little used after completing military trials at Wright Field, Ohio. Then, being covered by an addendum to the DC-6 Type Certificate, it was acquired by Conner Airlines in August 1956 and registered N6166G. This 'DC-6' passed through the hands of various operators before being destroyed on 8 February 1976 in a crash landing at Van Nuys Airport, on the outskirts of Los Angeles, while being operated by Mercer Airlines.

Early in its military life, the XC-112A was followed by a closely related derivative ordered by the War Department to replaced the unpressurized presidential VC-54C. The airframe selected to become the VC-118 for President Truman was fsn 42881, the 26th in the DC-6 line. Assigned military serial number 46-505 and named *Independence*, after the Missouri hometown of President Truman, the new presidential aircraft was officially commissioned into the USAAF on 4 July 1947. The forward portion of the cabin had 24 seats, convertible into 12 beds, for members of the presidential staff. The aft cabin was fitted as a presidential suite with a sofa convertible into a bed, a fully reclining seat, and a conference table.

The VC-118, for which the call-sign 'Air Force One' was not used, remained in use as the presidential aircraft until May 1953. It then was used by the Military Air Transport Service as one of its VIP transports, with accommodation progressively becoming more Spartan. Now in the collection of the National Museum of the United States Air Force, at Wright-Patterson AFB, the VC-118 has been restored to its full presidential splendor.

It was the Korean War which, in 1951, finally led the Department of Defense to adopt a derivative of the DC-6A as the standard military transport for both the USAF and the USN. The USAF ordered 101

TOP AND ABOVE *Two views of the VC-118: that at the top was taken in 1954 when it no longer was the presidential aircraft; that at the bottom shows it in 1978 at the Air Force Museum after it had been restored to its original splendor.* (William Balogh and David W. Menard)

aircraft as C-118As while the Navy got 65 R6D-1s (which became C-118Bs in September 1962; 40 of these aircraft exchanged their Navy BuNos for Air Force serials when they were transferred to the USAF). Most C-118As and R6D-1s were fitted out to transport either 74 military passengers in relatively modest comfort or 27,000lb of cargo. Many, however, had the cabin arranged to carry fewer passengers in a comfort-level approaching that found in civil airliners. Thirty-five of these aircraft with plusher accommodation were designated VC-118As by the USAF while four were R6D-1Zs (later VC-118Bs) with the USN. Finally, revised designations were given to C-118As modified for medical evacuation (with 60 litters plus medical attendants) as MC-118As and photomapping as RC-118As.

As is generally the case with military transports, the C-118As and the R6D-1s were used mostly for unglamorous, but most necessary, activities often referred to disparagingly in the military as 'trash hauling.' There were, however, exceptions which attracted the interest of the media such as the large inter-service exercises that took place in the Caribbean (*Big Slam/Puerto Rico*) in March 1960 and in the Pacific (*Long Pass*) in February 1961. Then, during the mid-sixties, increasing US military activities in Southeast Asia brought the C-118s to the forefront, initially to ferry troops but increasingly to bring the wounded to military hospitals close to the war zone or to transport them between specialized facilities within the Continental United States.

Far more discrete, and hence less well known, is the role played by C-118s in covert operations in Tibet starting in 1957. A few C-118As (possibly including 51-3820 and 51-3822) from a mysterious 'Detachment 2, 313th Air Division, USAF' were provided to Air America, an 'airline' controlled by the Special Activities Division of the Central Intelligence Agency. In 1958–59, to supply Tibetan freedom fighters with 'untraceable' weaponries, the aircraft were loaded in Okinawa with guns and ammunition of Soviet origin. The unmarked aircraft were flown by the USAF to Kurmitola in East Pakistan (now Bangladesh) from whence Air America crews took them to airdrop the weapons in Tibet. The C-118As, however, lacked the required high altitude performance (being able to carry only one-third of their design loads) and were soon replaced by Lockheed C-130As.

Among other unusual modifications, mention must be made of 53-3273 and 53-3283 which were modified as command posts by Temco in Texas and were operated by the 7110th Airborne Command and Control Squadron out of Wiesbaden, Germany. Another C-118A, 53-3245, became an EC-118A testbed for electronic equipment. Finally, C-118As retaining their standard designation were occasionally flown along and across the Iron Curtain. One of them, 51-3822 was shot down by a pair of MiG-17s while flying over Armenia on 27 June 1958.

During the late fifties and early sixties, USAF C-118As were replaced by Lockheed C-130s and C-141s, and its MC-118As by McDonnell Douglas C-9As. The Navy C-118Bs, which progressively gave way to McDonnell Douglas C-9Bs, remained operational quite a bit longer, the last being those of a reserve squadron, VR-3, which were withdrawn from use in October 1983.

The only foreign military operator to acquire a new DC-6 was the

ABOVE *At least two USAF C-118As were modified as RC-118As. Bearing the markings of the 1370th Photo Mapping Squadron, 53-3264 was photographed while in transit at Beirut in 1966.* (Jacques Guillem collection)

Force aérienne belge which took over a DC-6A (fsn 45458) ordered by, but not delivered to Slick Airways. It then added three second-hand DC-6As, all remaining in service with *21 Smaldeel* until 1976.

Other operators of previously-owned DC-6s and C-118s were the armed forces of Argentina, Bolivia, Chile, Colombia, Denmark, Ecuador, France, Germany, Guatemala, Honduras, Italy, Mexico, New Zealand, Paraguay, Peru, Portugal, El Salvador, South Korea, Taiwan, South Vietnam, Yugoslavia, and Zambia.

The golden years

The arrival of jetliners rapidly pushed out propliners from the fleet of major airlines, thus making a large number of DC-6s – reliable, easy to maintain, and requiring only modest support – available at reasonable price to operators with less demanding clientele. This proved to be a real bonanza for carriers offering specialized services or operating in less developed areas. It also enabled American, Canadian, and French firms to obtain aircraft with strong airframes and adequate performance for modification into forest fire fighting aircraft, a task for which they were fitted with a 2,040-Imp. gallon fire retardant tank beneath the fuselage. In 2011, the last of these air tankers remained in use with Conair Aviation in Abbotsford, British Columbia.

A small number of aircraft were modified for even more unusual uses. Notably, this was the case of two DC-6s modified into airborne television relay stations and operated by Purdue Airlines to transmit educational programs to schools in sparsely populated areas of the US Midwest. Two DC-6As (fsn 45227 and 45368) were modified in 1961 for the National Oceanographic and Atmospheric Administration (NOAA) of the US Weather Bureau of the Department of Commerce as 'hurricane hunters' with radar, radiosondes, and other specialized equipment.

According to AeroTransport Data Bank (http://aerotransport.org), 21 aircraft in the DC-6 family remained in service at the end of July 2011. All were civil-registered with 17 in the United States (four DC-6As, five DC-6Bs, six C-118As, and two C-118Bs), three were in Canada (two DC-6As and one DC-6B) and one C-118B in Venezuela.

BELOW *BuNo 131601, one of the last C-118Bs of Reserve Transport Squadron 52 (VR-52), was about to touch down at Dobbins AFB, Georgia, when it was photographed on 19 October 1982.* (Carl E. Porter)

Data for civil DC-6 models

	DC-6	DC-6A	DC-6B
Dimensions:			
Span, ft in	117 6	117 6	117 6
Length, ft in	100 7	105 7	105 7
Height, ft in	29 1	28 8	28 8
Wing area, sq ft	1,463	1,463	1,463
Weights:			
Empty, lb	53,623	49,767	55,357
Loaded, lb	97,200	107,000	107,000
Performance:			
Max speed, mph/ft	356/19,600	360/18,100	—
Cruising speed, mph	328	315	315
Climb rate, ft/min	900/1	1,010/1	1,120/1
Service ceiling, ft	29,000	—	—
Range, miles/lb	3,340/21,300	2,925/28,188	3,005/24,565
Ferry range, miles	3,915	4,720	4,720

TOP Pélican 64, *was one of the five DC-6 air tankers operated by France's Sécurité Civile between 1980 and 1990.* (Humbert Charvé)

ABOVE *In July 2011, the fleet of the two Everts companies in Alaska (Everts Air Cargo and Everts Air Fuel) still included 10 DC-6 series aircraft: four DC-6As, one DC-6B, three DC-6B(F)s, and two ex-C-118As.* (Jacques Guillem collection)

OPPOSITE *The cockpit of a DC-6B.* (Swissair)

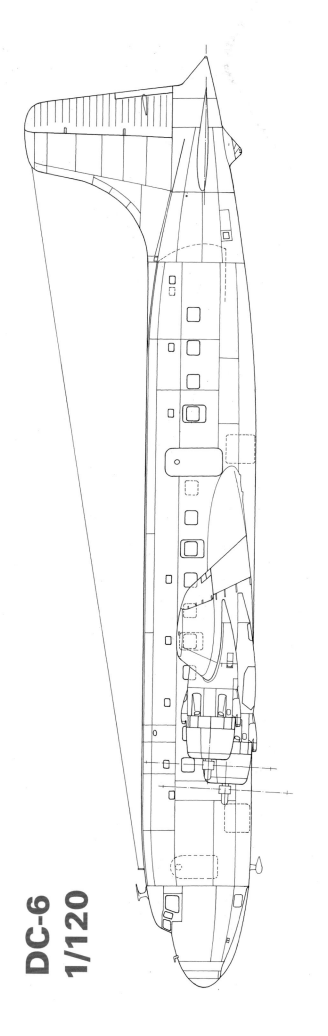

DC-6
1/120

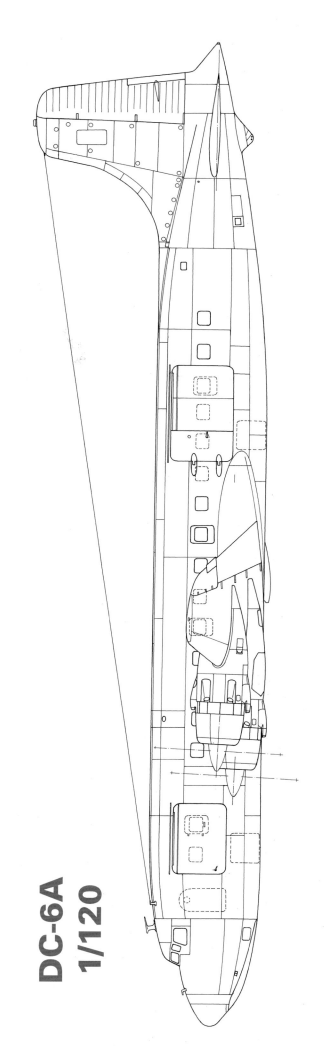

DC-6A
1/120

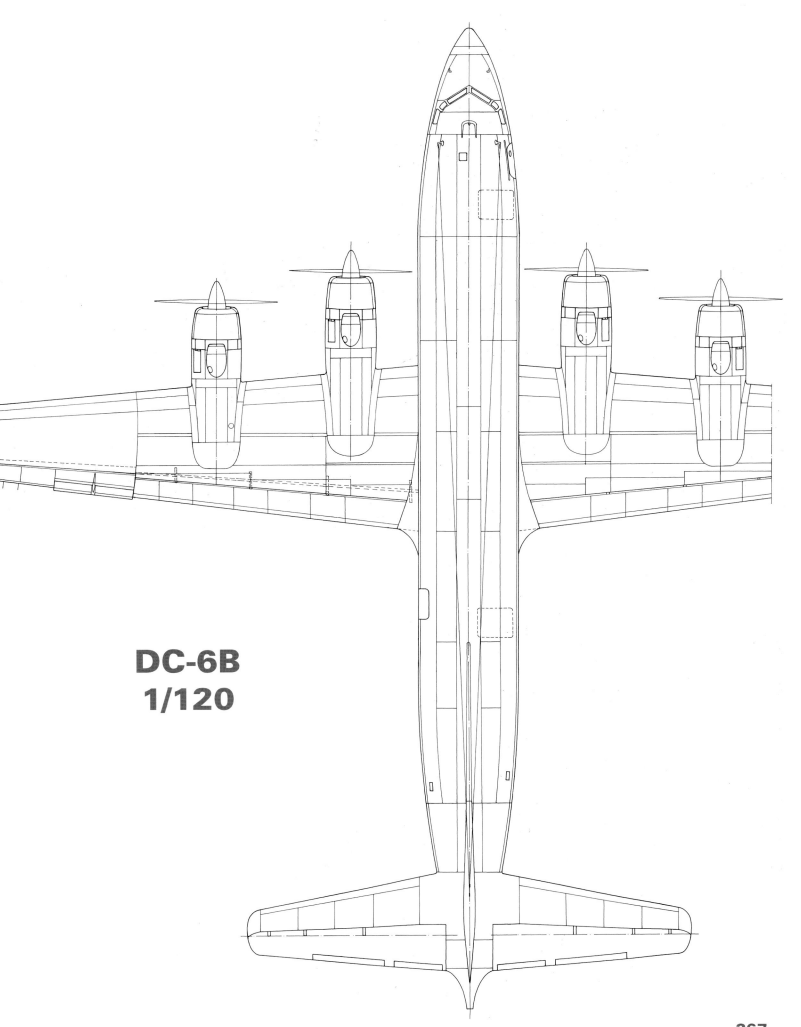

DC-6B
1/120

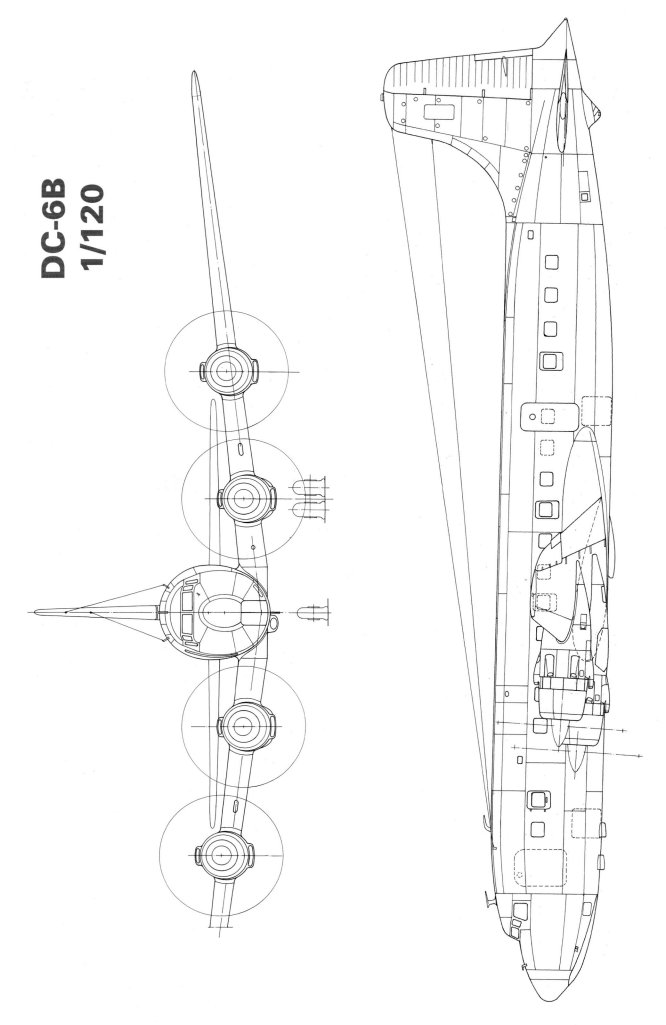

DC-6B
1/120

Military C-118s & DC-6s

RIGHT *Named after the Missouri hometown of President Harry S. Truman, the VC-118 remains the most colourful of the US presidential aircraft.* (David W. Menard)

BELOW *53-3245, an anonymous C-118A, at McClellan AFB, California, on 27 November 1972.* (Peter B. Lewis)

BOTTOM *A MC-118A of the 375th Aeromedical Airlift Wing at Travis AFB, California, on 30 April 1966.* (Peter B. Lewis)

LEFT *BuNo 131600, a C-118B of VR-54, taking off from Dobbins AFB, Georgia, on 19 October 1982.* (Carl E. Porter)

BELOW *BuNo 128427, a VC-118B, was the transport aircraft assigned to the Commandant of the US Marine Corps.* (Cloud 9 Photography)

BOTTOM *France's* Aéronautique navale *only had one DC-6A, fsn 44063, shown in this February 1982 photograph.* (DR)

RIGHT *The* Força Aérea Brasileira *(Brazilian Air Force) acquired five DC-6Bs from* VARIG *in 1968. Two crashed and the other three went to the* Fuerza Aérea del Paraguay *(Paraguayan Air Force) in 1980.* (Jacques Guillem collection)

BELOW *FAG 926, the only DC-6B of the* Escuadrón de Transporte, Fuerza Aérea Guatemalteca *(Transport Squadron of the Guatemala Air Force) at Dobbins AFB, Georgia, in April 1981.* (Robert E. Kling)

BOTTOM *The* Luftwaffe *acquired two DC-6Bs from Western Airlines in 1962 and two from* Sabena *in 1965. They were operated by its* Flugbereitschaftstaffel *(VIP Flight) until 1969.* (Jacques Guillem collection)

Civilian DC-6s

ABOVE *This pre-delivery photograph of fsn 43111, a DC-6 of KLM, was taken at Santa Monica in March 1948. It was then incorrectly marked as PH-TDI instead of the proper PH-TPI. On the Dutch civil register, this aircraft then appeared as PH-DPI and, finally, as PH-DPE before being sold in January 1964 to Linn Aeronautica S.A. in Panama.* (Douglas)

LEFT *XA-JOT (the DC-6 fsn 43213), was delivered to Mexicana (*Compañía Mexicana de Aviación, S.A.*) in November 1950.* (Jacques Guillem collection)

LEFT *N37590 Cargoliner New York, a DC-6A, was delivered to United Air Lines in May 1956 and remained with that carrier until February 1968.* (Douglas)

ABOVE *Clearly, this photograph of SU-ANO, a DC-6B of United Arab Airlines on a snow-covered field, was not taken in Egypt.* (Jacques Guillem collection)

RIGHT *This DC-6B registered VH-INS was operated by Ansett-ANA between August 1956 and July 1968.* (Jacques Guillem collection)

RIGHT *Even though control of Civil Air Transport was acquired by the Central Intelligence Agency in 1950, this airline based in Taiwan (Republic of China), maintained a civilian appearance by flying scheduled passenger flights with brightly marked aircraft such as this DC-6B. Its CIA activities relied on more discretely marked aircraft.* (Jacques Guillem collection)

ABOVE *Delivered to Philippines Air Lines on 31 July 1952, this DC-6B was operated by* Aigle Azur *for just over a year in 1954–55.* (DR)

LEFT *Photographed at Paris-Orly in April 1976, this DC-6B was with Air Djibouti between 1974 and 1977.* (Jacques Guillem collection)

LEFT *As its name* Transportes Aéreos Militares Ecuatorianos *indicates, TAME was an airline run by the* Fuerza Aérea Ecuatoriana. *Over the years, its fleet included a variety of aircraft including this clean looking DC-6B photographed in front of the terminal at the* Aeropuerto Internacional Mariscal Sucre *in Quito.* (Jacques Guillem collection)

ABOVE *This DC-6B (fsn 45560) originally went to the oil company ARAMCO in September 1952. As PH-TRC it was operated by Transavia Holland after this company was organized in 1966.* (Jacques Guillem collection)

RIGHT *On landing at its home base, the Ostend-Bruges International Airport, this DC-6B of Delta Air Transport suffered a nose gear failure on 6 April 1972.* (Jacques Guillem collection)

RIGHT Air Afrique, *a Pan-African airlines operating primarily to/from/within francophone West and Central Africa, was organized in 1961. Among its early aircraft was this DC-6B registered TU-TCH in Ivory Coast.* (Jacques Guillem collection)

RIGHT *AHK-1700, a DC-6B of* Aeronorte Colombia *is about to touch down at the* Aeropuerto Internacional de Palonegro *in Bucaramanga, Colombia.* (Jacques Guillem collection)

ABOVE *Modified into a freighter, fsn 43524 became a DC-6B(F) as shown here in the markings of* Inair Panama *on a stop in Cali, Colombia, in 1975.* (René J. Francillon)

LEFT *Fire retardant demonstration by fsn 43044 at the Lancaster Airport, California, on 26 October 2003.* (Jim Dunn)

BELOW *N90MA, photographed at the Santa Rosa Airport, California on 8 February 1986, was a DC-6 modified as an air tanker for Sis-Q Flying Services.* (René J. Francillon)

ABOVE Pélican 61, *a brightly painted air tanker of France's Sécurité Civile was photographed at Marseille-Marignane on 4 April 1986.* (Humbert Charvé)

RIGHT *Air Tanker CF-PWA, a DC-6B of Conair, drops retardant at Abbotsford, British Columbia, on 10 August 1973.* (Peter B. Lewis)

BELOW *Belonging to Conair and registered C-GHLY, this air tanker DC-6B is about to land at Kingsley Field, in Klamath Falls, Oregon on 15 August 2003.* (Jim Dunn)

Chapter 11

DC-3S – Too little, too late

As World War Two was drawing to a close, Donald Douglas and his close collaborators spent more and more time planning a strategy for the company's postwar operations. It was expected that the end of combat operations would result in massive cancellations of military contracts. Conversely, US airlines would then be freed of the controls imposed during the war and could be expected to expand rapidly. Abroad, airlines were predicted to grow even more rapidly as they would take up the slack in the transportation system created by massive destruction of road and rail infrastructure and heavy shipping losses. For Douglas, this presented broad opportunities as, in many ways, its existing and planned product line was better suited to the impending needs of commercial operators than were those of most of its industry rivals which had concentrated their wartime activities on the production of combat aircraft and trainers. The Santa Monica firm also had ample financial reserves as, in spite of a lower profit margin, wartime contracts had boosted net revenues. Conversely, Douglas trailed behind some of its rivals when it came to adopting new technologies, including jet power and cabin pressurization (the first Douglas with a pressurized cabin, the XC-112, only flew six months after the war had ended).

The strategy adopted by Donald Douglas and his advisors called for beginning by modifying surplus C-47s and C-54s to secure a foothold with as many airlines as possible. Next, as some customers were expected to want new-built aircraft as quickly as possible, DC-3Ds and DC-4-1009s would be produced by making full use of the trained manpower, tooling, and spare part inventory left by the cancellation of military contracts. For customers wanting better performing aircraft with pressurized cabin, Douglas would then begin producing four-engined DC-6s in 1946 and would follow by offering the Model 415A, a DC-7 derived from the C-74 ordered by the USAAF (at the instigation of Pan American Airways). Left out of this ambitious program was a new short- to medium range aircraft to compete with twin-engined airliners known to be under development at Convair and Martin. Hoping to limit market inroads by these two rivals, Douglas intended to offer DC-3s (new or rebuilt) at competitive price while working on a more ambitious aircraft, the Model 1004 (see Chapter 12).

Even though Pan American Airways cancelled its order for Model 415As (DC-7s), the Douglas strategy in the four-engined segment of the market succeeded and the Santa Monica manufacturer went on to outsell both of its main competitors.[1] Conversely, Douglas did not do well with its twin-engined propliners, rebuilding only

BELOW *Delivered as an R4D-5 (fsn 13226) in May 1944, BuNo 17216 was rebuilt as an R4D-8 in 1952, became a C-117D in 1962, and was withdrawn from use by the USMC in 1972.* (Carl E. Porter)

---

1 Postwar, Douglas built 1,161 four-engined propliners (including the C-118 and R6D military variants of the DC-6): 79 DC-4-1009s, 704 DC-6s, and 338 DC-7s. Again including military versions of their four-engined transports, Boeing came in second place with 872 aircraft (816 military C/KC-97s but only 56 civil *Stratocruisers*) just ahead of Lockheed with 856 four-engined airliners and military transports (233 *Constellations*, 579 *Super Constellations*, and 44 *Starliners*).

21 aircraft into DC-3Cs, producing 28 DC-3Ds, and canceling development of the Model 1004 without even building a prototype. And that in spite of the fact that its competitors did not manage to have their twin-engined airliners in service until 5 October 1947 for the unpressurized Martin 2-0-2, 1 June 1948 for the Convair 240 with pressurized cabin, and 1 September 1950 for the pressurized Martin 4-0-4.[2]

The Douglas strategy for the short-range airliner market had two flaws. Firstly, it did not take into sufficient consideration the fact that customers would not need the manufacturer to convert C-47s into airliners as they could do so themselves or could rely on specialized conversion companies with lower costs than Douglas. Indeed, DC-3s/C-47s became the most used transports well into the 1950s. Secondly, Douglas erred in offering the overly complex and costly Model 1004 as a successor to the DC-3, causing airlines to turn primarily to Convair and its Model 240/440 series.

For Douglas, there was another consideration. New and more stringent certification requirements were developed by the Civil Aeronautics Administration after the war. Although they were initially intended to apply to new aircraft being submitted for certification, the CAA announced its intent to have the new requirements apply to older aircraft if they were to retain their approved type certificate. Concerns were expressed that DC-3s (and related models) would no longer be certificated as their take-off and climb performance on one engine were not up to the new standards. That fear combined with its decision to discontinue work on the Model 1004, brought Douglas to assign the task of modernising the DC-3 and upgrading it to meet all CAA certification requirements to a project team led by Mel K. Oleson.

The Super DC-3

As it set out to 'make old into new,' the Oleson team received the following instructions from the leadership of the Santa Monica engineering department:

- Upgrade single-engined performance and handling characteristics to meet CAA certification requirements;
- Increase overall performance to reduce the gap with the new Convair and Martin twins;

2 The big winner in this market segment was Convair which, including military versions, built 1,077 of its twin-engined transports (one Model 110, 566 Model 240s, 311 Model 340s, and 199 Model 440s) whereas Martin only built 47 Model 2-0-2s and 103 Model 4-0-4s.

ABOVE *NC30000 was the first DC-3C; it was rebuilt in 1946 from 43-30674, a C-47A-DL. When it was brought up to civil standard, its fsn was changed from 13825 to 43073.* (Douglas)

- Reduce operating costs, particularly on short flights, below those of the DC-3;
- Keep development costs as low as possible as Douglas was facing heavy expenditures due to the five-month grounding of the DC-6 fleet and the resultant need to bear the costs for the required modifications; and
- Price the aircraft substantially below that asked by competitors in order to offset the fact that it would have lower performance and would not be pressurized.

In many ways, these requirements were stringent and, in some cases, conflicting.

BELOW *Dotted lines have been added to this photograph of a Super DC-3 to show the outline of the original DC-3.* (Douglas)

ABOVE *The registration N30000, which had been that of the first DC-3C, was used again for the first DC-3S.* (Douglas)

The last of these demands could only be met by retaining a maximum of the airframe of existing DC-3s (or military derivatives) when building the Super DC-3. Operating costs could be reduced by increasing the fuselage length by 3ft 3in to make room for additional seating (in the standard configuration this meant an increase from 21 to 30 seats). Other requirements could only be met if more significant, and hence costly, changes were made. This led to:

- Increasing installed horsepower by replacing the 1,200hp Pratt & Whitney R-1830s as used for most DC-3 models by either a pair of Pratt & Whitney R-2000-7 double-row radials or Wright R-1820-C9HEs single-row radials driving three-blade, constant-speed, auto-feathering propellers. Both types of engine would be enclosed in revised nacelles in which the main undercarriage legs and their single wheel would be fully enclosed. The tailwheel was also to retract fully in the rear fuselage.
- Retaining the center section of the wings but replacing the outer sections with panels with squared tips and 15.5° sweep on the leading edge and 4° sweep on the trailing edge. This reduced span from 95ft to 90ft and wing area from 986sq ft to 969sq ft.
- Fitting vertical and horizontal tail surfaces with squared tips and increased area. A dorsal fin of greater area was added to improve single-engined handling.

To serve as prototypes for the Super DC-3 (or *Super Three*) Douglas re-acquired two aircraft: a C-47-DL (fsn 6017, ex-41-18656) and a DC-3-277D (fsn 4122 which had been taken over by the USAAF before delivery and had become a C-50-DO with serial 41-7700). The former was given a new factory serial number (fsn 43158, N30000) and, powered by two 1,475hp Cyclone 968C9HE radials, was first flown at Clover Field on 23 June 1949 by John F. Martin. The latter, which became fsn 43159, N15579, was powered by two 1,450hp R-2000-7 radials.

Tests and certification proceeded uneventfully and the Super DC-3 was given ATC No 6A2 on 24 July 1950. Unfortunately for the manufacturer, the Super DC-3 was 'too little, too late' and

only attracted a single airline customer. Capital Airlines did order five DC-3Ss but cancelled two of them before taking delivery. Its three Super DC-3s were delivered by Douglas between July and September 1950 but were withdrawn from use by the airline less than two years later, in April 1952. These three Super DC-3s were then acquired by United States Steel Corporation which used them to transport staff members between its headquarters in Pittsburgh, Pennsylvania, and its various plants and foundries around the country.

R4D-8 and C-117D

In 1950, still hoping to rescue its Super DC-3 program, Douglas offered the first test aircraft to the USAF at a bargain price. With the budgetary constraints existing before the outbreak of the Korean War, the USAF had to husband limited funding to acquire bombers for the Strategic Air Command and interceptors for the Air Defense Command. Other funding, however, was available for 'black programs,' thus leading to the acquisition of the Super DC-3 prototype as the YC-129 (see boxed text on page 282). Even though they were successful, tests with the YC-129 did not lead to a production order and the aircraft, serial 51-3817, was 'demodified' into the YC-47F by replacement of its dual wheel main undercarriage with a conventional C-47 gear and removal of the provision for a landing chute. Still, the USAF had no need for a 'warmed-up' C-47 and the aircraft was transferred to the Navy as the R4D-8X BuNo 138659.

Pleased with results from its evaluation of the R4D-8X, US Naval Aviation became the long sought after prime customer for the Super DC-3 as it opted to have 100 of its R4Ds rebuilt by the manufacturer to R4D-8 standards. The work to be accomplished was sufficiently important for the rebuilt aircraft to receive new constructor's numbers (fsn 43301 to 43400) while retaining their original naval BuNos. Toward the end of 1951, the majority of the 'new' R4D-8s, which were powered by 1,475hp Wright R-1820-80s, were distributed among the support flights at Naval Air Stations and Marine Corps Air Stations. Many were further modified to become R4D-8T multi-engine and navigator trainers for assignment to the Navy's VT-29 squadron and to VMTGR-20 of the USMC. Still

others were fitted out as R4D-8Z staff transports with upgraded accommodations (16 airline-type seats instead of folding troop seats). The three R4D-8 designations were changed to C-117D, TC-117D, and VC-117D in September 1962. The last C-117Ds served at the Naval Weapons Center China Lake, California, until 1982.

Once more into civvies

After the USN and USMC withdrew their C-117Ds from service, the type finally gained some acceptance with civil operators as they were available at favorable prices and had enough potential use left in them. Quite a number of these aircraft were then acquired by small operators in the United States, Canada, and Latin America. By July 2011, AeroTransport Data Bank (http://aerotransport.org), reported five Super DC-3s registered in the United States and one in Bolivia as being currently in service; 14 more were in storage (ten in the US, two in Canada, and one each in Peru and the Philippines).

Mention must be made of the fate of fsn 43193, one of the three Super DC-3s acquired by Capital Airlines. It had started as fsn 1548, the fourth DC-3-178 delivered to American Airlines in September

ABOVE *Bearing the markings of the Naval Air Training Center at NAS Lakehurst, New Jersey, BuNo 12419 was fsn 43116. Originally, it had been fsn 9359, a C-47A-5-DL which was delivered to the USN in April 1943 as an R4D-5.* (Steve Miller, David W. Menard collection)

1936. It remained with this airline until May 1949 when it was acquired back by Douglas for conversion into a DC-3S. It was then operated as N16012 by Capital Airlines between September 1950 and April 1952. After passing through the hands of four other operators, it was re-engined in 1974 with Rolls-Royce *Dart* propeller turbines as the sole *Super Turbo Three*, being registered as N156WC. On 24 February 1984 it was damaged beyond economical repair in a ground collision in New London, Connecticut.

BOTTOM *Photographed in 1971 on arrival at the Military Aircraft Storage and Disposition Center (MASDC), Davis-Monthan AFB, Arizona, BuNo 12443 had last been used by Training Squadron 29 (VT-29) at NAS Corpus Christi, Texas.* (Peter B. Lewis)

The covert YC-129

During the Cold War, the Western Allies experienced considerable difficulties in acquiring reliable military and industrial information from across the Iron Curtain. This led to a series of then highly classified intelligence gathering programs. Some have now become quite well-known such as secret overflights by RAF *Canberras* and leased B-45As, by USAF RB-57s, and by CIA U-2s. Other programs were even more esoteric such as those which saw the US send camera-carrying weather balloons eastward when wind conditions were favorable (Weapons systems WS-119L *Genetrix* and WS-461L *Melting Pot*). But the most reliable information could only be obtained through HUMINT (human intelligence), which presented the problem of how to bring across and recover agents.

It was to perform that risky task that the Air Force undertook in the late 1940s to acquire aircraft capable of getting airborne in 500ft during operations from unprepared or plowed fields when recovering agents from the other side of the Iron and Bamboo Curtains. Alternatively, these aircraft were to be used for combat rescue of downed crews. The USAF then funded the development of a specialized aircraft, the Northrop N-32 *Raider* (of which 13 were ordered as 'troop carrier' YC-125As and ten as 'Arctic rescue' YC-125Bs) while Douglas proposed a cheaper modification of its Super DC-3. The result was the YC-129, a designation which has long remained unsatisfactorily explained.

In his self-published biography *The Inside Story: The Rise & Fall of Douglas Aircraft* which came out in December 2000, Harold W. Adams,

a former Douglas chief designer, revealed that half a century earlier the modification of a Super DC-3 into the YC-129 had entailed: (1) replacing the single-wheel main gear legs with modified twin-wheel C-54 units in order to better distribute the weight of the aircraft on soft ground; (2) drastically reducing operating weight by eliminating all non-essential equipment and limiting onboard fuel; (3) adding a 100ft diameter braking chute attached to the existing glider towing hook; and (4) fitting up JATO bottles beneath the fuselage to reduce take-off length. Modification of the first Super DC-3, fsn 43158, was undertaken in secrecy. Those in the know now refer to it as the 'E and E' (for Escape and Evacuation).

Discretely flown to Edwards AFB, the 'E and E' (by then wearing the USAF serial number 51-3817) went through the first trial phase devoted to take-off performance without a hitch as, with the boost of JATO bottles, it easily got airborne in 500ft or less from a variety of surfaces. The first short landing attempt almost ended in catastrophe. The landing chute had been designed to open first to a diameter of just 10ft while on approach before blossoming to a full 100ft once the main wheels were on the ground. On the first of the short landing tests, the chute diameter grew to 30ft while the aircraft was still airborne. Only the quick release of the chute and a masterfully-controlled hard landing by John Martin saved aircraft and crew from a fiery crash. After the chute was modified to limit its inflight opening to not more than 5ft, testing was completed without further ado.

LEFT *Fumes from JATO bottles billowing aft and below, the YC-129 (51-3817) climbs sharply during a short-field test at Edwards AFB. Note the twin-wheel main undercarriage, a dead-giveaway to identify the sole YC-129.* (AFFTC, Peter M. Bowers collection)

Data for the DC-3S

Dimensions: Span, 90ft; length, 67ft 9in; height, 18ft 3in; wing area, 969sq ft.

Weights: Empty, 19,537lb; maximum, 31,000lb; wing loading, 32lb/sq ft; power loading, 10.5lb/hp.

Crew: Two pilots and a cabin attendant.

Accommodation: 30 to 38 seats.

Power plant: Two 1,475hp Wright *Cyclone* 968C9HE nine-cylinder radials driving three-blade, constant-speed, auto-feathering propellers. Fuel tanks in the wing center section and outer panels with a total capacity of 1,354 Imp. gallons.

Performance: Max speed, 270mph at 5,900ft; cruising speed, 251mph; initial climb rate, 1,300ft/min; max range, 2,500 miles.

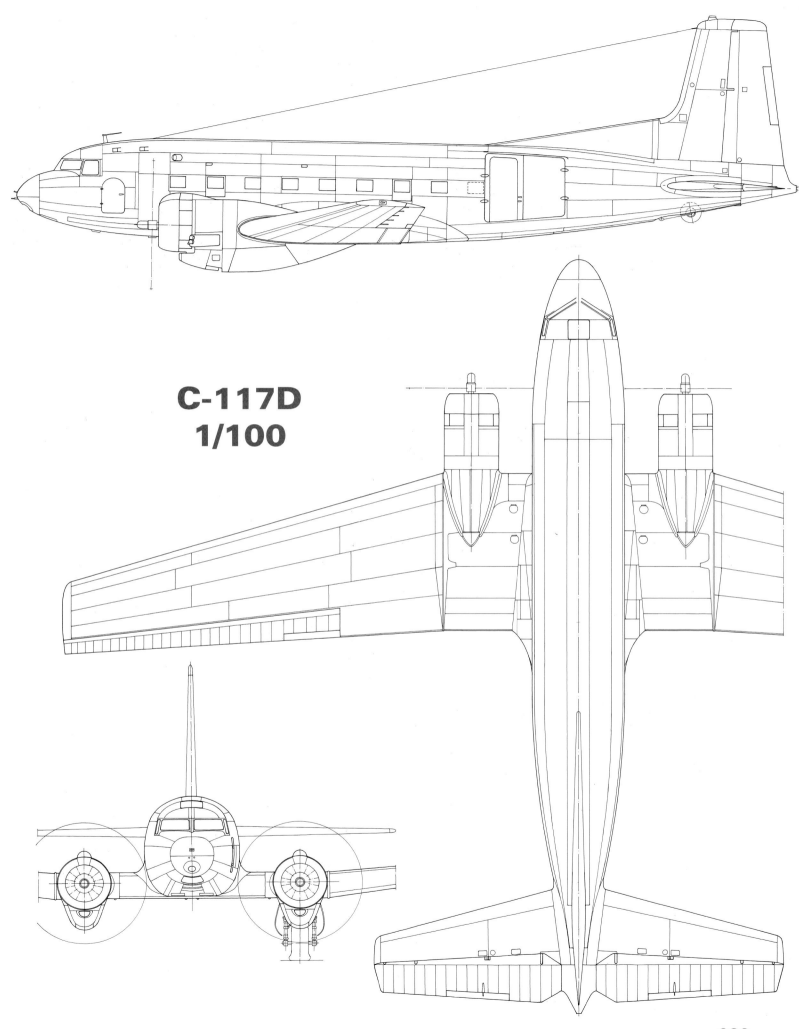

C-117D
1/100

Chapter 12

Model 415 and Model 1004

The unborn DC-7 and DC-8

Before America was drawn into World War Two, Pan American Airways had full wind in its sails. Its *Clippers* had opened the trans-Pacific route with Martin 130s flying between San Francisco (Alameda), Honolulu, Midway, Wake, and Manila in October 1936 with continuing service to Hong Kong with Sikorsky S-42Bs starting in May 1937. Keeping up with their fast-paced development venture, Pan American *Clippers* began flying to Bermuda in June 1937 with S-42Bs, to Lisbon and Marseille in June 1939 with Boeing 314s, and to Southampton in July 1939 with 314s. The outbreak of war in Europe hardly put a dent in Pan American's expansion plans as it nevertheless became the first to place pressurized Boeing 307 *Stratoliner* landplanes in operation

on 4 July 1940, initially between Miami and Baranquilla, Colombia, and as its Boeing 314s started flying to New Zealand in September 1940. Although not in any official manner, Pan American had become the de facto 'flag carrier' of the United States.

Juan Trippe, airline entrepreneur and founder of Pan American Airways, entertained good relations with several members of the Roosevelt administration. These connections eased the way for his airline to receive the first government contract to build airfields in the Caribbean and South America[1] on 2 November 1940. During the war, Pan American obtained numerous additional contracts (see chapter 8).

---

1   The project had been under consideration by the Army and Navy since the previous year as they recognized that, in the event of war, airfields between the United States and the easternmost point on the Brazilian coast would be needed for antisubmarine operations, troop and materiel transport, and aircraft ferrying onward to West Africa. For Pan American, the July 1940 start of its Latin American service with four-engined Boeing 307s also gave the company an interest in airfield improvements for purely commercial reasons. The combination of military needs and commercial desirability eventually led to Pan American building, improving, and maintaining no fewer than 40 airfields and seaplane bases from Cuba all the way south to Paraguay under the US government-funded $100 million (±$1.3 billion today) 'Airport Development Program.'

BELOW *The Model 415A, which Pan American Airways ordered at the end of 1945, was to be derived from the C-74 Globemaster. Had it been built, the airliner version would have been the DC-7; however, the contract for Model 415As was never finalised.* (Douglas)

Certainly, the British and US governments benefitted from Pan American's airfield construction and aircraft ferrying activities. But it is equally certain that the airline also derived considerable direct and indirect benefits from its wartime pursuits. Among the indirect gains for Pan American were those which came from being in a position to influence the development of new transport aircraft without having to contribute to their financing. In this manner, large four-engined and six-engined aircraft, all of which were likely to prove of interest to the airline after the war, were begun as military transport projects with funding by the War Department and the Navy Department. Boeing obtained a development contract for its XC-97 *Stratofreighter* in January 1942. Next came contracts for the Douglas XC-74 *Globemaster* in June 1942, the Lockheed XR6O-1 *Constitution* in June 1942, the six-engined Convair XC-99 in December 1942, and the Republic XF-12 in March 1944.

Having provided key inputs when requirements for these aircraft were drawn up, Pan American was able to follow their developments. As the war came to an end, only the XC-97 had flown while the XC-74 was just about to enter flight trials. Meanwhile, Pan American had concluded that projected civil derivatives of the Convair XC-99 (the six-engined Model 37 designed to transport 204 passengers on two decks between New York and London with two technical stops) and the Lockheed XR6O-1 (the four-engined Model 89 offered to Pan American with 109 seats on two decks) would be too large for its needs. The airline still saw merits to the three other four-engined aircraft. Orders were placed for six Republic RC-2 *Rainbow* high-speed airliners (derived from the XF-12 long-range photo-reconnaissance aircraft) with accommodation for 46 premium service passengers to be carried at higher cruising speeds; 20 Boeing 377 *Stratocruisers* with 66 seats on the main deck and a seven-seat lounge on the lower deck which could only be used in flight; and 26 Douglas Model 415As with 108 seats. In the end, however, Pan American only confirmed its order for the 20 *Stratocruisers* (later adding eight ex-American Export Airlines aircraft).

The Douglas Model 415A

In 1940, after studying a range of 24-cylinder H-type sleeve-valve engines, Pratt & Whitney concluded that liquid-cooled engines had reached the end of their potential development and that its 2,650hp H-3130 was unlikely to be developed into a reliable power plant. Instead, Pratt & Whitney undertook to develop a 28-cylinder, four-row, air-cooled radial to obtain engines developing 3,000hp or more on take-off. As the war was drawing to a close, it was this new R-4360 that was selected by the manufacturers of all five new airliners in which Pan American was interested.

The prototype for the R-4360 series was first run on the bench on 28 April 1941 and flight tests were initiated during the spring of 1942 after one of these 28-cylinder engines was fitted to a specially-modified Vultee *Vengeance*. By then, all major US airframe manufacturers had received preliminary information on this new and powerful radial engine.

While the development of the R-4360 engine was underway in Connecticut, on the opposite coast Douglas had become convinced that, once at war, the USAF and the USN would need transport aircraft carrying more and farther than the C-54 could. As the forthcoming availability of the R-4360 engine to power such a large aircraft made its development feasible, responsibility for the Model 415 design was entrusted to the Santa Monica engineering department.

Prodded along the way by Pan American, the Air Materiel Command, USAAF, was instructed by the War Department to order an initial batch of Douglas Model 415s. Given serials 42-65402 to 42-

BELOW *During the war, Pan American had used its influence to have the military order prototypes of large transport aircraft from Boeing, Convair, Douglas, and Lockheed. The Boeing 377* Stratocruiser *was the only one of these aircraft to be built for Pan American (and other civil customers)*. (Boeing)

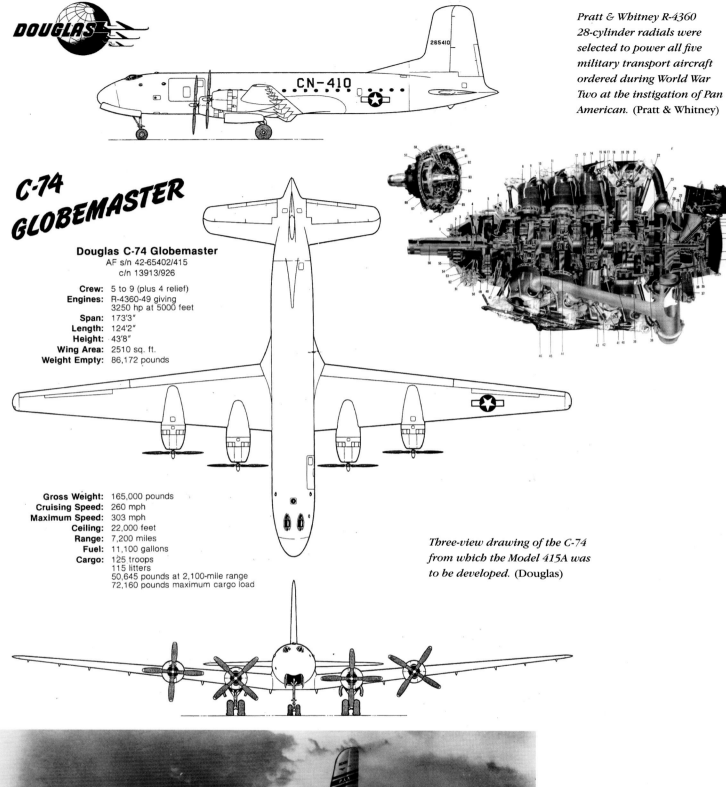

DOUGLAS

Pratt & Whitney R-4360 28-cylinder radials were selected to power all five military transport aircraft ordered during World War Two at the instigation of Pan American. (Pratt & Whitney)

C-74 GLOBEMASTER

Douglas C-74 Globemaster
AF s/n 42-65402/415
c/n 13913/926

Crew:	5 to 9 (plus 4 relief)
Engines:	R-4360-49 giving 3250 hp at 5000 feet
Span:	173'3"
Length:	124'2"
Height:	43'8"
Wing Area:	2510 sq. ft.
Weight Empty:	86,172 pounds

Gross Weight:	165,000 pounds
Cruising Speed:	260 mph
Maximum Speed:	303 mph
Ceiling:	22,000 feet
Range:	7,200 miles
Fuel:	11,100 gallons
Cargo:	125 troops
	115 litters
	50,645 pounds at 2,100-mile range
	72,160 pounds maximum cargo load

Three-view drawing of the C-74 from which the Model 415A was to be developed. (Douglas)

LEFT Artist's rendering of the Model 415A in the markings of Pan American World Airways. (Douglas)

65451, the 50 aircraft were to be built in the new Long Beach plant. Contract W535-AC-27402 covering these C-74-DLs was signed on 25 June 1942. The USAAF, however, instructed the Long Beach team to give priority to building C-47s, B-17s, and A-26s, and therefore work on the C-74 was slowed down repeatedly. Hence, it was only three weeks after the Japanese surrender, on 5 September 1945, that the first *Globemaster*, aircraft 42-65402, was flown at Long Beach. With the war having just ended and the need for large military transport aircraft disappearing, the number of aircraft to be built was reduced from 50 to 13.

While design and construction of the C-74 proceeded slowly, Pan American had been kept fully appraised of its calculated performance and other technical details. The airline was thus able to firm up its interest in the new Douglas transport aircraft. The proposed airliner version, the Model 415A, was to differ from the USAAF C-74 (Model 415) in: (1) having a fully pressurized cabin with a new window arrangement and either 108 seats for daytime operations or 76 seats and beds for night flights, plus room for separate lounge and dining areas; (2) dispensing with both the main deck cargo loading door forward of the wing on the left side and the trap door-and-lift beneath the rear fuselage; and (3) installing Pratt & Whitney *Wasp Major* engines (civil version of the R-4360s) driving three-blade propellers (as planned for the C-124 double-deck derivative of the C-74) instead of 4-blade units as in the C-74. Had the Model 415A actually been built, it would have become the DC-7 and would have featured wings of typical Douglas/Northrop multi-cellular design but with only two main spars. Their entire trailing edge was to have consisted of Fowler-type flaps, the outer sections doubling up as ailerons.

Starting in late 1944, Pan American was sufficiently pleased with the Douglas design to indicate that it was prepared to order 26 Model 415As (aka DC-7s), as many as the combined orders it was planning for Republic RC-2s and Boeing 377s. The postwar reduction in the C-74 order from 50 to 13 brought an increase in unit cost, leading Pan American to lose interest and not firm up its planned order. The designation DC-7 would remain available for a later development of the DC-6 (see Chapter 13).

(Data for the Model 415/C-74, which are similar to those for the Model 415A/DC-7, are provided on the opposite page on the edge of the manufacturer's drawing for that aircraft.)

The Douglas Model 1004

Distances in the Pacific Theatre of Operations being longer than those in the European and Mediterranean Theatres, the Santa

ABOVE *Had the Model 415A been built as the DC-7 for Pan American, it would have received a conventional cockpit as fitted to 42-65408, the seventh C-74-DL.* (Douglas)

Monica engineering department had, by the first quarter of 1943, become increasingly conscious that a substantially better performing attack aircraft/light bomber would be needed before operations ended in that theatre. Not only would this new combat aircraft have to be longer ranged than the company's A-20 *Havoc* and A-26 *Invader*, respectively in service and entering production, but it would need to be faster and to carry a heavier load. As no suitably-sized engine of adequate power was expected to become available, increased performance would have to come almost entirely from improved aerodynamic cleanliness. The challenging requirement was taken up by a team led by chief engineer Ed F. Burton and chief aerodynamicist Carlos C. Wood who came up with the revolutionary Model 459 bomber.

To achieve the hoped for performance, the advanced concept

BELOW *The clean lines of the Douglas Model 459 (military designation XA-42 and then XB-42) are shown to advantage in this photograph taken at Palm Springs, California.* (Douglas)

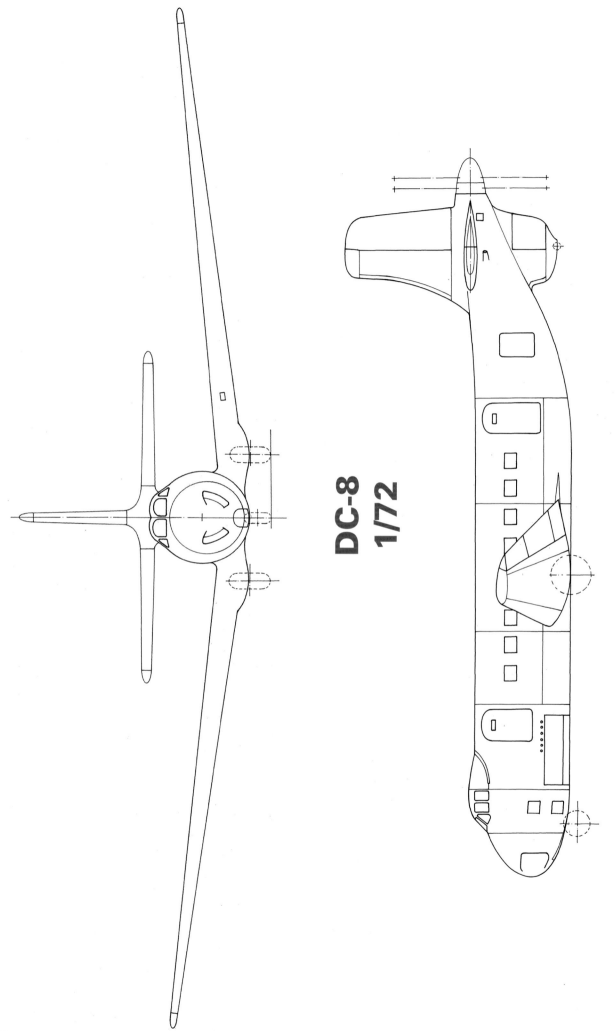

DC-8
1/72

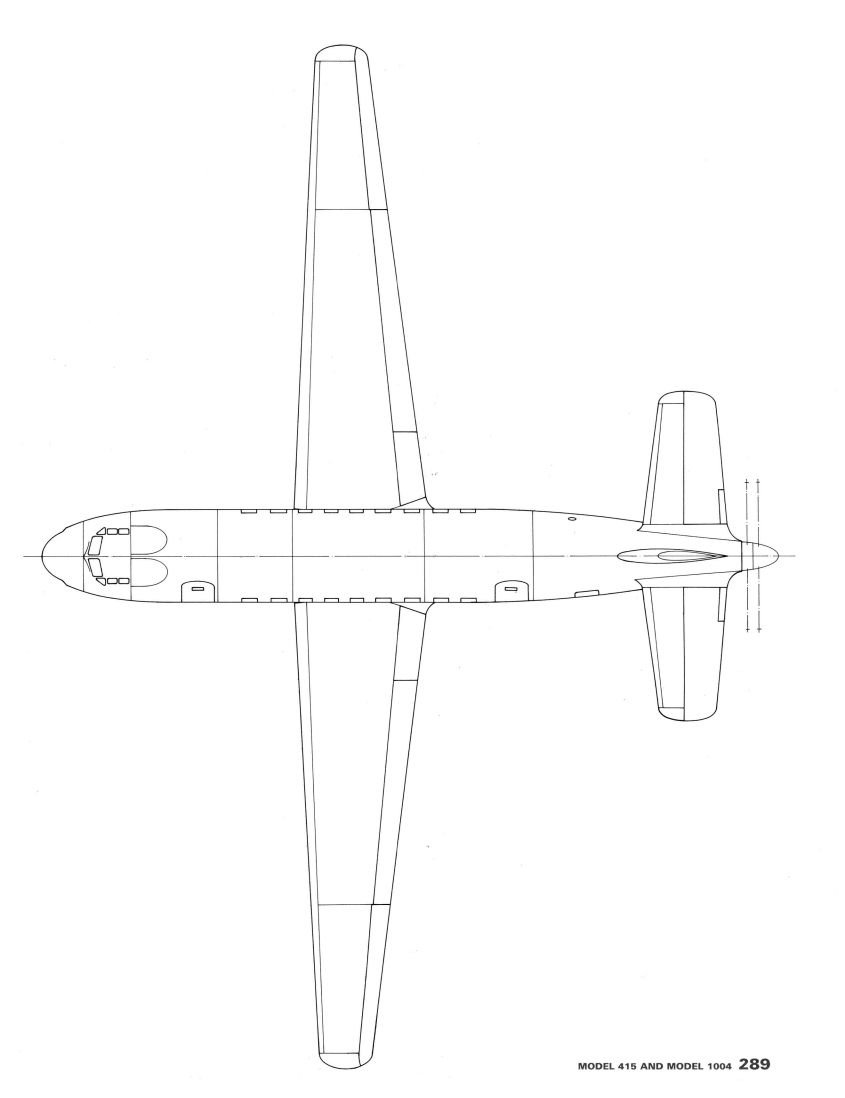

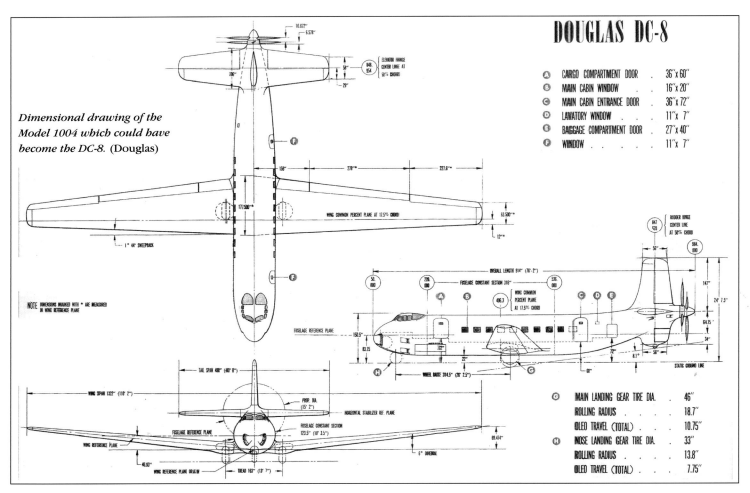

DOUGLAS DC-8

Ⓐ	CARGO COMPARTMENT DOOR	36" x 60"
Ⓑ	MAIN CABIN WINDOW	16" x 20"
Ⓒ	MAIN CABIN ENTRANCE DOOR	36" x 72"
Ⓓ	LAVATORY WINDOW	11" x 7"
Ⓔ	BAGGAGE COMPARTMENT DOOR	27" x 40"
Ⓕ	WINDOW	11" x 7"

Dimensional drawing of the Model 1004 which could have become the DC-8. (Douglas)

Ⓖ	MAIN LANDING GEAR TIRE DIA.	46"
	ROLLING RADIUS	18.7"
	OLEO TRAVEL (TOTAL)	10.75"
Ⓗ	NOSE LANDING GEAR TIRE DIA.	33"
	ROLLING RADIUS	13.8"
	OLEO TRAVEL (TOTAL)	7.75"

team chose to rely on a laminar-flow wing design with no protuberance or excrescence other than those caused by the intake for oil and Prestone cooling radiator on the leading edge of the wing root and by gaps in the control surfaces. In turn, that required finding ways to locate both a pair of 1,345hp Allison V-1710 liquid-cooled inline engines and the retracted tricycle undercarriage entirely within the fuselage. Power was transmitted by five lengths of shafting to the gear reduction for contra-rotating propellers, aft of the cruciform empennage.

Calculated performance was such that an unsolicited proposal sent in April 1943 to the Air Materiel Command was received with much enthusiasm. Negotiations rapidly led to the award of a $3.1

million (±$38.1 million today) contract covering final design, a static test airframe, and construction and testing of two prototypes. Initially designated XA-42 in the attack category, the two prototypes became XB-42 in the bomber category in February 1944. The first flight was made at Clover Field, Santa Monica, on 6 May 1944, a full seven weeks ahead of schedule. Flight trials proceeded as smoothly as could be expected with such an innovative design and a contract for 13 pre-production aircraft was being finalized when the Japanese surrender terminated the need for B-42s.

As was already the case with other development projects at Douglas, as well as at all major manufacturers, government controls over the time devoted to other than strictly military programs were

relaxed before war's end, making it possible to commence work on a Model 1004 airliner of similar concept as the XB-42. Initially planned to transport between 30 and 40 passengers, the new airliner would have its side-side mounted inline engines moved further down the forward fuselage than was the case for those of the XB-42.[2] The laminar wings, still unencumbered, were also to be moved down the fuselage from the mid to a low-mounting, thus avoiding the need for having their spars cross through the cabin. Moreover, the low position of the wings together with the high mounting of the contra-rotating propellers resulted in a shorter main undercarriage (now retracting in the wings inboard section). The cabin floor was thus going to be only 5ft above the tarmac, easing cabin access and baggage/cargo handling. Generally, the Model 1004 was to be larger and heavier than the Model 459 bomber, with span of 110.2ft (vs 70.5ft), wing area of 1,104sq ft (vs 555sq ft), and gross weight of 39,500lb (vs 35,700lb). Conversely, as the Model 1004 was offered as the short-range 'Skybus', fuel tank capacity was reduced from 1,457 Imp. gallons to 833gal.

At the customer's option, the Model 1004 was to be supplied with or without cabin pressurization, a rather odd choice at a time when the end of unpressurized airliners was predicted. The two pilots were to sit side-by-side under a conventional cockpit rising above the fuselage top (instead of under separate tear drop canopies as they did in the XB-42) and located above and slightly ahead of the engine bay. Standard seating in the main cabin was provided for 37 passengers: one row with three seats followed by eight rows of 2 + 2, and a last row with just two seats on one side of the aisle across from the main entrance door with built-in steps. The cabin also had room for either two lavatories or a galley and a lavatory. A baggage compartment accessible in flight was located at the rear of the cabin, while cargo and mail were to be carried in a compartment situated between the cockpit and the cabin. Alternatively, the cabin could be arranged with 34 seats (by eliminating the row of three forward and increasing seat pitch from 36in to 40in) or with 48 seats (by adding folding seats which, when occupied, would block the center aisle – something that would never be considered today). Finally, Douglas proposed a 'combi' version with an enlarged cargo compartment followed by 22 seats.

In spite of a major marketing effort and its excellent reputation with airlines, the Douglas Aircraft Company totally failed to gain

---

2   The engines had to be relocated so that the drive shafts could now be located beneath the cabin floor. This lower location, however, meant that the straight drive shafts of the XB-42 had to be replaced with shafts having two angle joints to reach up to the reduction gear for the propellers.

Data for the Model 1004 (aka, DC-8)

Dimensions: Span, 110.2ft; length, 77ft 2in; height, 26ft 9½in; wing area, 1,104sq ft.

Weights: Empty, 23,915lb; maximum, 39,500lb.

Crew: Two pilots and two cabin attendants.

Accommodation: standard seating for 37; alternate arrangements with 22 to 48 seats.

Power plant: Two 1,600hp Allison V-1710-G4R and -G4L (respectively with right-hand and left-hand turning propeller shafts) 12-cyliner liquid-cooled engines driving contra-rotating three-blade, constant-speed, auto-feathering propellers (with 15ft 2in diameter for the forward propeller set and 15ft for the rear set).

Performance: Max speed, 292mph at 15,800ft; cruising speed, 275mph; service ceiling, 30,000ft; initial climb rate, 950ft/min; range with full payload, 300 miles; ferry range, 2,370 miles.

acceptance for its Model 1004. More expensive to buy and operate than either the Convair 240 or Martin 404 and powered by more complex inline engines requiring the use of long shafts to drive propellers (two features looked on suspiciously by the airline engineering departments), the Model 1004 was considered too much of a gamble for carriers having an aversion to risk.

As if this was not already enough complexity, Douglas offered an even more convoluted derivative. It was to be powered by four, instead of two, Allison V-1710s. Two of the engines were to be in the usual location but were to drive contra-rotating propellers in the nose of the aircraft. The other two were to be housed beneath the main cabin floor, aft of the wings, and to drive the usual contra-rotating propellers aft of the empennage. Not surprisingly, no one was interested in this 'Rube Goldberg' contraption.

The Model 1004 and its derivative remained on the drawing board and DC-8, which would have been their designation if they had been built, was left to be used in October 1955 when Pan American ordered the first Douglas jetliners.

OPPOSITE *The Model 1004 was planned to have passenger boarding/deplaning and cargo loading/unloading eased by having a cabin floor that was only five feet above the tarmac.* (Douglas)

RIGHT *A larger derivative of the Model 1004 was projected. It would have had four fuselage-mounted engines as shown in this manufacturer drawing.* (Douglas)

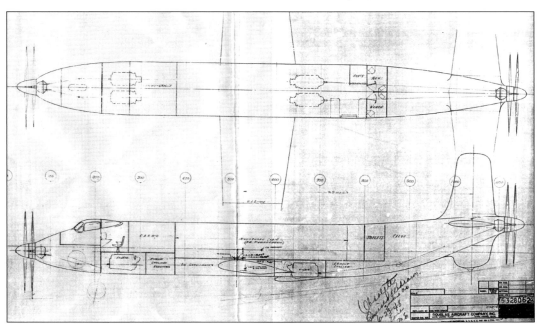

Chapter 13

DC-7 – The end of an era

Since before World War Two, transcontinental air services between New York and the West Coast had been provided by three airlines. United Air Lines was alone to fly to and from San Francisco while both American Airlines and Transcontinental & Western Air operated to/from Los Angeles with TWA benefitting from a more direct routing. In 1947, the competition grew in intensity after the Civil Aeronautics Board authorized all three to fly from New York to both Los Angeles and San Francisco by whatever routing they chose.[1] Offering the faster, shorter service became vital for the airlines and also fueled the competition between their two aircraft suppliers. As their *Constellations* and DC-6Bs had to make at least one-stop in either direction, the rival airlines sought to become the first to offer non-stop transcontinental service. Eastbound, TWA took the lead on 19 October 1953 when its L-1049C *Super Constellations* began flying non-stop between Los Angeles and New York; westbound, against the prevailing winds, the L-1049C still had to make a stop. Travel time to New York was reduced to just eight hours (one hour less than for American DC-6Bs stopping in Dallas, Texas). Moreover, the *Super Constellation* provided first class seating for 66 versus only 54 in the case of the DC-6B.

Nearly two years before the entry into service of the L-1049C, Cyrus R. Smith, the president of American Airlines, had asked Douglas to come up with an improved version of the DC-6B capable of flying between New York and Los Angeles non-stop in both directions, regardless of weather conditions. In addition, Smith stipulated that the revised airliner would need to be fast enough to allow scheduling westbound flights (*ie* those slowed down by flying against prevailing winds) for less than eight hours, thus avoiding the need for a relief cockpit crew as stipulated by the pilots' union for flights of eight hours or more.

Donald Douglas discussed the American request with vice-president of engineering Art Raymond and chief engineer Ed

---

1 This was pursuant to a CAB decision of 23 October 1947 to grant nonstop privileges between any two points.

BELOW *The first DC-7 flew on 18 May 1953 and was delivered to American Airlines on 30 April 1954. It remained with this trunk carrier for only 61 months as jetliners pushed it out from the first team.* (Douglas)

Burton. None of them showed much enthusiasm as they felt that few airlines could use an aircraft with similar performance, especially as such performance could only be achieved by substantially increasing power, thus rendering the aircraft more expensive to operate. Nevertheless, with C.R. Smith remaining adamant, Douglas agreed to build 25 DC-7s to American's specifications but priced this aircraft on the basis of no additional production. Once again, Douglas proved overly conservative as it ended by building 338 DC-7s for 21 customers. All were able to acquire their aircraft at a lower unit price than had been paid by American Airlines when the manufacturer refused to reduce its original pricing demand. The long friendship between Donald Douglas and C.R. Smith did not survive the resulting discord. When acquiring jetliners, American Airlines turned to Boeing, and then also to Convair and BAC. This long, and for Douglas, costly spat lasted until after the California firm was merged with McDonnell in 1967; only then did American return to the fold when it became the first customer for the DC-10 trijet.

Convinced that American would be the only customer for the DC-7, Douglas did everything to minimize development and production costs. The airframe of the new model was to be that of the DC-6B with only a 40in increase in fuselage length to add a single row of seats and some local strengthening as required to cope with higher weights and operating speeds. Installed power was to be boosted 30% by substituting 3,250hp Wright *Turbo-Compound*[2] engines for

the 2,500hp Pratt & Whitney *Double Wasps* of the DC-6B. Satisfied with the calculated performance, American Airlines ordered 25 DC-7s in January 1952 (with a follow-on order for nine more DC-7s and 24 DC-7Bs). Then, United Air Lines also ordered DC-7s as it could not compete with American and TWA with slower DC-6Bs and without offering non-stop transcontinental service.

The DC-7 and DC-7B

The *Turbo-Compound* engines powering DC-7s were either Wright 972TC18DA2s or 972TC18DA4s rated at 3,250hp on take-off, 2,650hp at 6,000ft, and 2,450hp at 15,000ft. They drove four-blade propellers (whereas DC-4s and DC-6s had three-blade props). Up to eight wing tanks were provided with fuel capacity ranging between 3,757 and 4,590 Imp. gallons at customers' option. Maximum gross weight was between 114,600 and 122,420lb. The principal structural modifications consisted of using titanium in the engine nacelles and fitting stronger main undercarriage units so that they could be lowered at higher speeds and used to reduce descent speeds.

The first flight of fsn 44122, N301AA, was made at Santa Monica on 18 May 1953 by a crew captained by John F. Martin. American Airlines accepted its first DC-7 on 10 October, the Type Certificate 4A10 was obtained on 12 November, and commercial operations on the New York–Los Angeles route commenced 17 days later.

---

2 The *Turbo-Compound* was derived from the *Duplex-Cyclone* by adding three 'blow-down' turbines, one to each group of six cylinders, to recover about one-fifth of the exhaust energy. Maximum rating was increased by up to 30% while specific fuel consumption was reduced by 20%. Reliability, however, suffered. This led to DC-7s and *Super Constellations* powered by *Turbo-Compound* engines earning the dubious soubriquet of 'world's best three-engined aircraft' due to the frequency with which they completed long flights with one engine shut-down.

ABOVE *Based at Cincinatti, Ohio* Travel a Go Go Club *was in operation between 1966 and 1970. This ex-United Airlines DC-7, N6357C, was photographed in the markings of this charter organization at Long Beach, California, in August 1967.* (René J. Francillon)

Upon entering service, the DC-7 fully met American Airlines' requirements as it could be scheduled for non-stop flights of 7hr 15min eastbound and 7hr 50min westbound, becoming the first airliner to fly westward across the North American continent without the need for refueling stops. The distance between New York and Los Angeles being only 2,475miles, this feat may not appear very impressive to a generation of travelers used to flights

between points nearly four times farther apart (*ie* 9,537miles between Singapore and New York). However, that was indeed quite an achievement and brought to an end an old quest. Having received its first DC-7 on 21 November 1953, National Airlines was next to put the type into service, first between New York and Miami. Next, DC-7s went into operations with Delta Air Lines in February 1954 and United Air Lines two months later.

Differing externally from DC-7s in having elongated engine nacelles in which saddle tanks could be installed to increase maximum fuel capacity to 5,390 Imp. gallons, the DC-7Bs were powered by Wright 972TC18DA4s, 988TC18EA-1s, or 988TC18EA4s with ratings similar to those powering DC-7s. Take-off gross weights ranged between 116,900 and 126,000lb while maximum landing weight was increased from 97,000lb for DC-7s to 102,000lb for DC-7Bs.

The DC-7B was first flown in October 1954 and, from 25 May 1955, was covered by an amendment to the original Type Certificate. Built in the Santa Monica plant, the 112 DC-7Bs went to

BELOW *ZS-DKF, a DC-7B was operated by South African Airways between 1956 and 1957. It was named* Goede Hoop, *Dutch for Good Hope.* (SAA)

eight customers (American, Continental, Delta, Eastern, National, Panagra, Pan American, and South African Airways). Pan American commenced operating DC-7Bs on 13 June 1955 when it began flying non-stop between New York and London (but a refueling stop was still required in the opposite direction). SAA, which was the only customer beside Pan American and Panagra to have saddle tanks fitted, used its DC-7Bs on long flights from Johannesburg to London (via East Africa and Rome) and to Perth (via the Cocos Island Airport).

The airlines and their passengers appreciated the shorter travel time made possible by the faster operating speeds of the DC-7s (with typical cruising speed of 359mph vs 315mph for the DC-6B) and longer range (making non-stop transcontinental flights possible). Conversely, passengers complained about the higher cabin noise level resulting from the proximity of the inboard *Turbo-Compound* engines while the carriers found these engines less reliable and more expensive to maintain than the *Double Wasps* of the DC-6s. Also for the airlines, the DC-7s and competing models

of the *Super Constellation*, had one serious economic weakness: they entered service only five years before the first generation of jetliners. The entry into service of Boeing 707s in October 1958 rapidly rendered obsolete both the DC-7 and the *Super Constellation*. With their operating costs being higher than those of DC-6As and DC-6Bs, DC-7s and DC-7Bs did not attract a lasting interest from second-tier airlines, even when modified as freighters.

ABOVE *Another DC-7C(F) operated by Riddle Airlines was N301G, the ex-HB-IBL of Swissair. Riddle Airlines became Airlift Inc. in November 1963.* (Jacques Guillem collection)

In spite of the poorer reliability of their power plants, the DC-7s proved to be safe airliners. As a matter of fact, the first airframe losses resulted not from design deficiencies but from mid-air and ground collisions. On 30 June 1956, a United DC-7 and a TWA L-1049C collided over the Grand Canyon with the loss of 128 lives; on 31 January 1957, a DC-7 on a manufacturer's test flight over the Mojave Desert collided with a Northrop F-89D *Scorpion* of the USAF (four fatalities); and on 28 June 1957 two Eastern Air Lines aircraft were destroyed on the ground in Miami (no fatalities) when a taxying DC-7B collided with a parked L-1049.

BELOW *Yet another example of a freighter conversion is provided by this photograph of N337AA, a DC-7B which American Airlines had modified into a DC-7B(F) in 1960 after using it for only 27 months to transport passengers.* (DR)

Seven Seas

Over the North Atlantic, competition was not just between commercial airlines as most of the non-US operators were flag carriers (and often owned or controlled by their governments). As far as aircraft type was concerned, competition was not just between Douglas and Lockheed as aircraft from other manufacturers (notably Boeing and Canadair) were used on scheduled passenger service. Nevertheless, the competitive battle was soon dominated by the rivalry between DC-6B and *Constellation/Super Constellation* operators (see page 303). Again, being able to provide non-stop service became the focus of attention for airlines and aircraft manufacturers. This led Douglas to develop the DC-7C, the first aircraft with sufficient range to operate non-stop in either direction between New York and London or Paris regardless of atmospheric conditions.

The DC-7C, which was designed at the request of Pan American, differed from the DC-7B most significantly in having a 5ft section added to the wing center panel between the fuselage and the inboard engine nacelles. This not only provided room for additional tanks (total fuel capacity increasing to

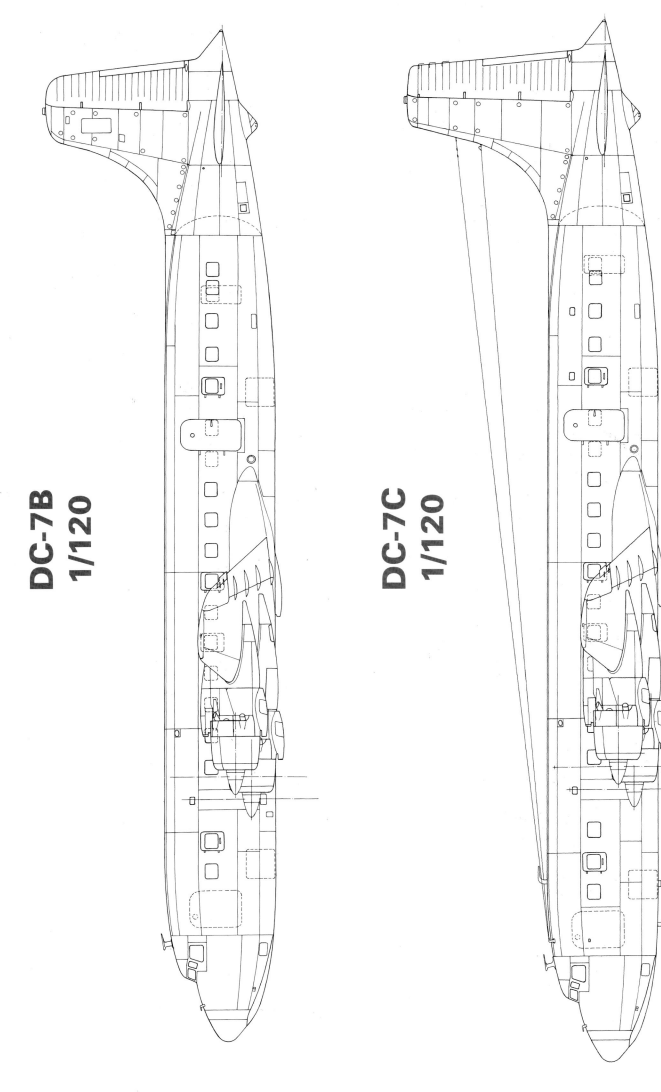

DC-7B
1/120

DC-7C
1/120

297

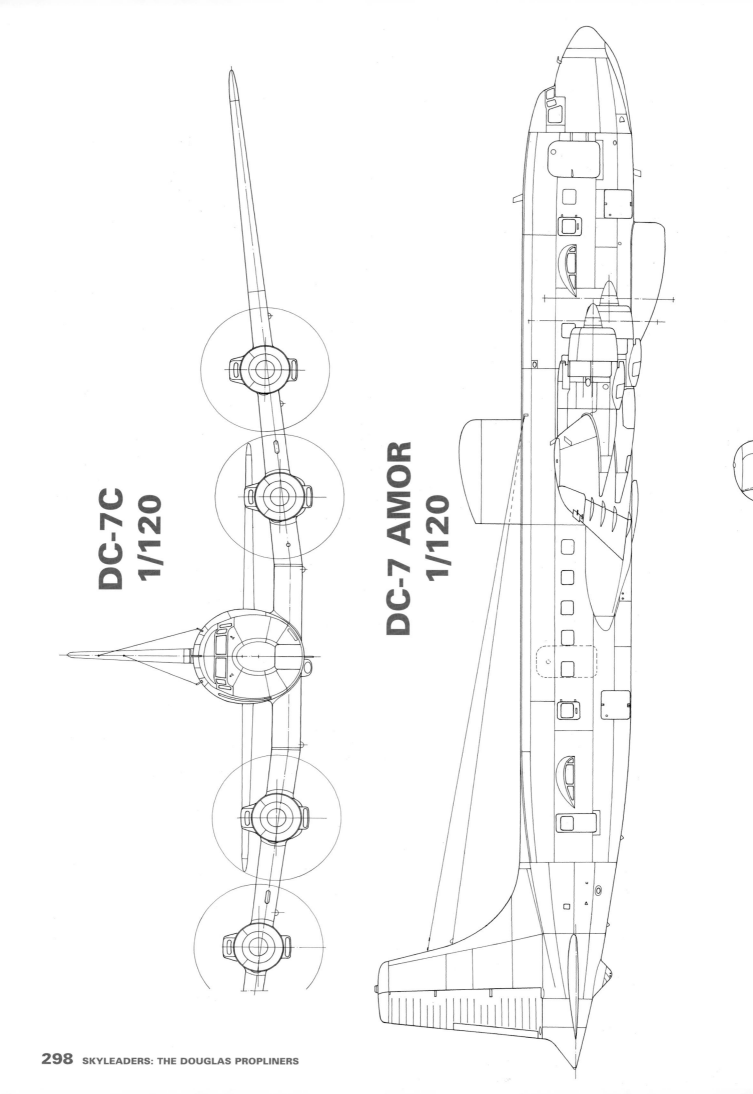

DC-7C
1/120

DC-7 AMOR
1/120

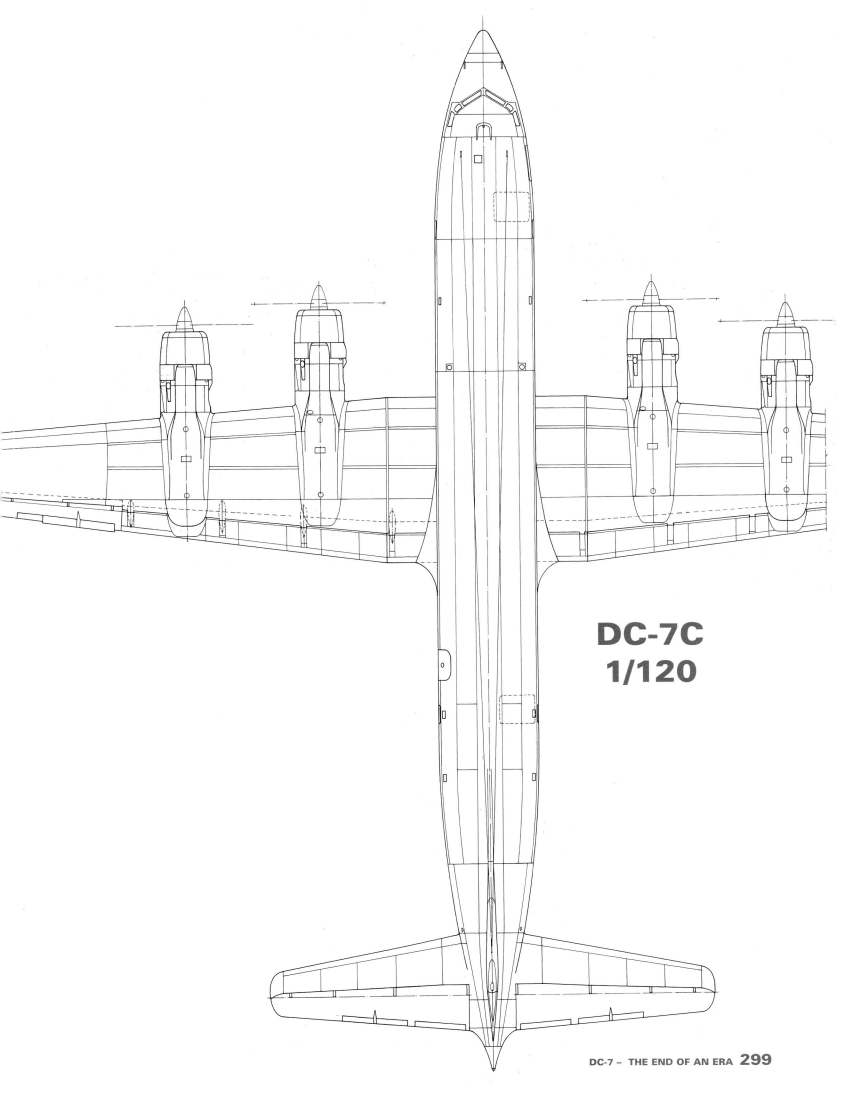

DC-7C
1/120

6,515 Imp. gallons) but also improved the aerodynamic efficiency of the wings. Moreover, by moving the engines (3,400hp Wright *Turbo-Compound* 988TC18EA1s or EA4s) further outboard noise level in the cabin was reduced. In addition, a 42in section was added to the fuselage increasing seating on the main deck and cargo/mail volume in the belly holds. Maximum gross weight rose to 143,000lb.

Appropriately named *Seven Seas*, the first DC-7C (fsn 44872) flew on 20 December 1955 and was covered by a revision of the Type Certificate approved on 15 May 1956. Two weeks later Pan American put the DC-7C into service on its first non-stop scheduled flights between London and New York. The long-range capability of DC-7Cs was also put to good use in other markets; SAS used its *Seven Seas* for 'polar' service between Copenhagen and Tokyo (via Anchorage) beginning on 24 February 1957. Seven months later, Pan American began operating non-stop between London and San Francisco with continuation to Los Angeles. In turn, Northwest Airlines started flying between New York and Tokyo with a single refueling stop in Edmonton, Canada.

Douglas built 121 DC-7Cs for 13 customers, delivering the last (fsn 45553) to Swissair on 4 November 1958. By then, however, Boeing 707s and de Havilland *Comet 4s* were in service over the North Atlantic and were soon to be joined by Douglas DC-8s. Although a number of DC-7Cs were modified as freighters while others went to charter airlines, their second life was not all that long and did not compare to that of its grandfather, the DC-4.

BELOW *This ex-Eastern Air Lines DC-7B (N848D, fsn 45454) was Air Tanker 61 of TBM Inc. when photographed at Klamath Falls, Oregon, on 9 August 1992. It crashed while helping fight a forest fire near Union Valley, California, on 1 October 1992. (René J. Francillon)*

Water bombers and AMOR

Once pushed out from the fleet of the major airlines, the various DC-7 versions had difficulty finding long-term homes with other carriers. Those modified to cargo configurations by the addition of reinforced flooring and main deck cargo doors did better, but only marginally, as they were more expensive to operate and less reliable than cargo variants of the DC-6, whether built as DC-6As or modified from DC-6s or, more frequently, DC-6Bs. On the other hand, their abundant power made standard-sized DC-7s and DC-7Bs, which retained the notably strong airframe of earlier Douglas four-engined airliners, ideal as water bombers for fighting forest fires. For this role, they were fitted with a 2,498 Imp. gallon water or water/retardant tank beneath the center fuselage and had additional windows cut in the cockpit roof for additional visibility when manoeuvring in tight canyons. In this role, they were used for many years with conspicuous success in the United States and Canada. However, in 2010, DC-7s were withdrawn from the fleet of air tankers approved by Fire & Aviation Management of the US Forestry Service for contract operations in the United States, the last two on the US register now being limited to operations under contracts from local agencies.

Three others of the last DC propliners had an interesting second career after being acquired by France's *armée de l'Air* for conversion as airborne stations for detection of re-entering space objects (AMOR, Avion de Mesure et d'Observation au Réceptacle). For that purpose, three DC-7Cs (fsn 45367 and 45446, ex-F-BIAQ and F-BIAR of TAI/UTA, and fsn 45061, ex-HB-IBK of Swissair) were modified in 1963–64 by UTA Industries. In the process, they were fitted with a large radome above the fuselage, another radome beneath the fuselage, a Doppler radar at the rear of the fuselage,

Data for DC-7s

	DC-7	DC-7B	DC-7C
Dimensions:			
Span, ft in	6	117 6	127 6
Length, ft in	11	108 11	112 3
Height, ft in	7	28 7	31 10
Wing area, sq ft	1,463	1,463	1,637
Weights:			
Operating empty, lb	66,306	67,995	72,763
Max Take-off, lb	122,200	126,000	143,000
Performance:			
Cruising speed, mph	359	360	355
Initial climb rate, ft/min	1,760/1	—	—
Service ceiling, ft	27,900	—	21,700
Range with payload, miles/lb	2,850/20,000	3,280/21,516	4,605/23,350
Ferry range, miles	4,340	4,920	5,640

observation blisters on the forward fuselage sides, and provision for direction and distance measuring instrumentation in removable wingtip pods. Operated from the *Center d'Essais des Landes* (one of the French test centers situated at Biscarosse) during missile re-entry tests, mostly in the gulf of Biscay, they were later operated by GAM-85 in the Pacific to detect intruders during French nuclear testing at Mururoa. The last went to the *musée de l'Air* at Le Bourget in 1979.

According to AeroTransport Data Bank (http://aerotransport. org), four aircraft were still US registered in July 2011: two DC-7 water bombers with Butler Aviation (only available for use by non-federal agencies), one DC-7B belonging to Legendary Airliners and recently repainted in authentic Eastern Air lines markings, and one DC-7B(F) with Turks Air Cargo. Five more DC-7s in various configurations were in storage. The end of the last of the DC propliners was looming. On the other hand, the last DC propliners were likely to outlast the first generation of wide-bodied jetliners. And, whereas the supersonic *Concorde* last carried paying passengers on 24 October 2003, the decidedly subsonic DC-3 is still in revenue service.

Douglas forever!

BELOW *F-ZBCA was one of three DC-7Cs modified in France to the* ***distinctive AMOR*** (Avion de mesure et d'Observation au Réceptacle) *configuration. It had been delivered to Swissair as HB-IBK.* (Jean Cuny collection)

Turbines or turbojets?

The Vickers *Viscount*, the world's first airliner designed to be powered by propeller turbines, first flew on 16 July 1948. Next, on 27 July 1949, the world's first turbojet-power airliner, the de Havilland *Comet*, made its maiden flight. These epochal flights were noted by American transport aircraft manufacturers which had been contemplating designing similarly-powered airliners albeit without much enthusiasm. In the United States, few then believed that the time had come for such aircraft, as available turbine engines, particularly turbojets, were neither powerful nor economical enough.

As early as 1946, Douglas had studied the feasibility of developing a turboprop- or turbojet airliner using as much of the DC-6 airframe as possible. Lots of drawings were prepared but none gained support in the front office. Even the first flight of the *Comet* and the interest it generated in some US airlines failed to have Douglas respond to this challenge. At most, this situation led Arthur Raymond and Ed Burton to champion the development of minimum change derivatives of the DC-6 and DC-7 to be powered by Allison or Bristol turboprop engines, as both felt that the real challenge to their four-engined propliners would come not from the *Comet* but from the four-turboprop Bristol *Britannia* then under construction in England and which was expected to fly in 1952. Airlines, however, did not show much interest in the Douglas turboprop proposals, forcing the Santa Monica manufacturer to announce in August 1952 its intent to develop a jetliner. This resulted in the DC-8 which did not fly until May 1958.

Beginning in October 1955, the world's airlines rushed to order Douglas DC-8 and Boeing 707 jetliners. However, this did not end turboprop studies at Douglas as airlines were still required to fly first class and economy passengers on different aircraft. As Hawaii had become a major vacation destination for Americans, the demand for economy class service from the mainland was growing rapidly.

To meet this need, Douglas proposed its DC-7T which, with 3 + 2 seating, would be able to transport 135 passengers to/from Hawaii at seat-mile costs significantly lower than those of DC-8s and 707s. Powered by four 4,450shp Bristol *Tynes*, the DC-7T was expected to cruise at between 425 and 435mph. During the gestation of this proposal, airlines finally agreed that mixed-class seating would be allowed aboard their aircraft. Thus, United Air Lines, to which the DC-7T was aimed, lost all interest. For Douglas, there would be no further DC propliner developments.

RIGHT *General arrangement drawing of the DC-7T.* (Douglas)

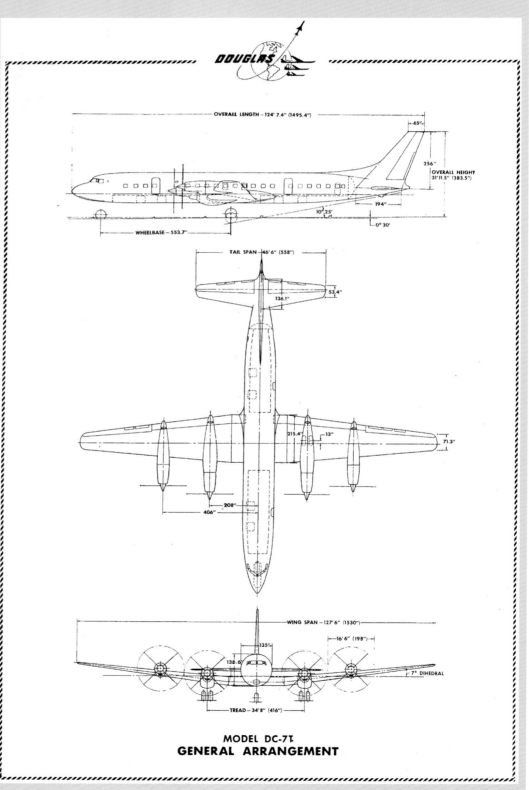

MODEL DC-7T
GENERAL ARRANGEMENT

Blue Ribbon Service

DCs and Connies battle it out over the North Atlantic

Commercial operations over the North Atlantic resumed in the fall of 1945 when American Export Airlines made the first scheduled transatlantic flight by landplane on 23–24 October. The aircraft, a Douglas DC-4, flew from New York to Hurn, via Gander and Shannon, in 23hr 48min.

Over the next 13 years, that is to say until jetliners were introduced by BOAC (de Havilland *Comet 4* between London and New York on 4 October 1958) and by Pan American World Airways (Boeing 707-121 between New York and Paris on 26 October 1958), 15 other airlines began operating on the North Atlantic routes on the following dates:

- 14 January 1946: Pan American Airways from New York to London with the Lockheed 049, this being the *Constellation*'s first commercial use over the North Atlantic;
- 5 February 1946: Transcontinental & Western Air from New York to Paris with the 049 *Constellation*;
- 21 May 1946: KLM from Amsterdam to New York with the DC-4;
- 24 June 1946: Air France from Paris to New York with the 049 *Constellation*;
- 1 July 1946: BOAC from London to New York with the 049 *Constellation*;
- 16 September 1946: SAS from Stockholm and Copenhagen to New York with the DC-4;
- 1 May 1947: Trans-Canada Air Lines from Montreal to London with the Canadair DC-4M (first use of this airliner on the North Atlantic);
- 4 June 1947: *Sabena* from Brussels to New York with the DC-4;
- 25 August 1948: *Loftleidir* between Copenhagen, Reykjavik, and New York with the DC-4;
- 29 April 1949: *Swissair* between Zurich, Geneva, and New York with the DC-4;
- 13 July 1950: *Linee Aeree Italiane* between Rome and New York with the Douglas DC-6 (initial use of the DC-6 on the North Atlantic);
- 16 May 1951: *El Al* between Tel Aviv and New York with the 749 *Constellation*;
- 2 September 1954: *Iberia* between Madrid and New York with the Lockheed 1049E (first *Super Constellation* service over the North Atlantic);
- 8 June 1955: *Lufthansa* between Hamburg, Dusseldorf, and New York with the 1049G *Super Constellation*; and
- 28 April 1958: *Aerlinte Eireann* between Shannon and New York with the 1049H *Super Constellation*.

During those years, new aircraft (other than noted above) came on line and improved services were started on the following dates:

- 2 June 1949: Boeing *Stratocruiser* put into service to London by Pan American;
- 1 May 1952: First all-coach service over the North Atlantic (Pan American with the DC-6B and TWA with the with matching *Constellation*);
- 1 October 1953: First mixed-class service (first and coach in the same aircraft) over the North Atlantic;
- 15 November 1954: First non-stop eastbound service to

BELOW *When entering service in June 1956, the DC-7C enabled Pan American to commence non-stop service in either direction between London and New York.* (Douglas)

London by Pan American *Stratocruiser* operating with increased fuel capacity and reduced seating (westbound service still required a minimum of one-stop);
- 1 June 1956: Douglas DC-7C put into service by Pan American making possible the first regular transatlantic service on a non-stop basis in both directions;
- 1 June 1957: Lockheed 1649 *Starliner* put into service by TWA;
- 19 December 1957: BOAC placed the turbine-engined Bristol *Britannia 312* on non-stop service between London and New York: and
- 1 April 1958: Economy class service began.

Douglas and Lockheed four-engined aircraft accounted for the vast majority of operations and carried the most passengers over the North Atlantic between 1945 and 1958. The 'Connies' won the beauty contest but the DCs did better with profitability and, consequently, the DC-6B ought to be remembered as the winner of the transatlantic competition in the years of piston-powered aircraft. At the end of that period, although Douglas DC-7Cs and Lockheed 1649 *Starliners* did offer the best service, they never matched the economy of operations or reliability provided by the older DC-6Bs.

At this time, long before the days of airline deregulation and free competition, transatlantic fares were set for all carriers (with the notable exception of *Loftleidir*) by the International Air Transport Association (IATA). One-way first-class fare between New York and London had started at $375 (±$4,340 today) in 1946 and gone to $400 in 1958; however, when taking inflation into account, fares had actually dropped 28% (from ±$4,340 to ±$3,125 in today's money). During the summer of 1958, just before jetliners came into the picture, the one-way economy class fare between New York and London was $252 (±$1,970 today). For comparison purposes, it is worth noting that in July 2011, three airlines were offering one-way tickets between those two cities for just $802.

Throughout this period, the number of passengers carried over the North Atlantic had risen from 240,000 in 1948 (all first class) to 1.2 million in 1958 (21.4% first, 23.0% coach, and 55.6% economy).

Appendix 1

Production summary DC-1 through DC-7

Douglas propliners were built in California (Santa Monica, El Segundo, and Long Beach), Illinois (Chicago), and Oklahoma (Oklahoma City). DC-2s were assembled in Japan, and DC-3s built in Japan and the Soviet Union. The following tables summarize their production in Douglas plants.

BELOW *Family portrait in front of the final assembly building at Long Beach in 1958: from left to right, behind the first DC-8, a NACA DC-3, a DC-4 from PSA, a USAF C-118A, and a United DC-7.* (Douglas)

Douglas DC-1

Model	Santa Monica (DO)	El Segundo (DE)	Long Beach (DL)	Chicago (DC)	Oklahoma City (DK)	Total
DC-1	1					1
Total	1					1

RIGHT *The DC-1 at Clover Field, Santa Monica, before its first flight on 1 July 1933.* (Douglas)

Douglas DC-2 and derivatives

Model	Santa Monica (DO)	El Segundo (DE)	Long Beach (DL)	Chicago (DC)	Oklahoma City (DK)	Total
DC-2	125					125
DC-2A	3					3
DC-2B	2					2
R2D-1	5					5
XC-32	1					1
C-33	18					18
YC-34	2					2
C-39	35					35
C-42	1					1
Total	**192**					**192**

RIGHT *HB-ITI, a DC-2-115B of Swissair flying over the Pre-Alps.* (Swissair)

Douglas DC-3 and derivatives						
Model	**Santa Monica (DO)**	**El Segundo (DE)**	**Long Beach (DL)**	**Chicago (DC)**	**Oklahoma City (DK)**	**Total**
DST	21					21
DST-A	19					19
DC-3	265					265
DC-3A	127					127
DC-3B	10					10
DC-3D	28					28
C-41	2					2
C-47			965			965
C-47A			2,954		2,299	5,253
C-47B			300		2,932	3,232
TC-47B					133	133
C-48	11					11
C-49	75					75
C-50	14					14
C-51	1					1
C-52	5					5
C-53	397					397
C-68	2					2
C-117					17	17
R4D	12		66			78
Total	**989**		**4,285**		**5,381**	**10,655**

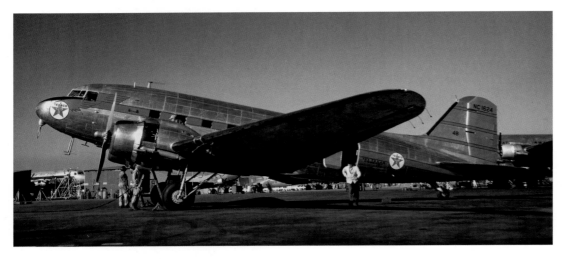

LEFT *NC1624, a DC-3D belonging to Texaco, at Clover Field, Santa Monica, in April 1946.* (Douglas)

Douglas DF						
Model	**Santa Monica (DO)**	**El Segundo (DE)**	**Long Beach (DL)**	**Chicago (DC)**	**Oklahoma City (DK)**	**Total**
DF-151	2					2
DF-195	2					2
Total	**4**					**4**

LEFT *One of the two DF-191s at Santa Monica in September 1936.* (Douglas)

Douglas DC-4E						
Model	Santa Monica (DO)	El Segundo (DE)	Long Beach (DL)	Chicago (DC)	Oklahoma City (DK)	Total
DC-4E	1					1
Total	1					1

RIGHT *The DC-4E flying over the Signal Hill oil field in Long Beach.* (Douglas)

BELOW *PJ-AIW* Wakago *of KLM (West Indies).* (Douglas)

Douglas DC-5 and derivatives						
Model	Santa Monica (DO)	El Segundo (DE)	Long Beach (DL)	Chicago (DC)	Oklahoma City (DK)	Total
DC-5		5				5
R3D-1		3				3
R3D-2		4				4
Total		12				12

Douglas DC-4 and derivatives						
Model	Santa Monica (DO)	El Segundo (DE)	Long Beach (DL)	Chicago (DC)	Oklahoma City (DK)	Total
C-54	24					24
C-54A	97			155		252
C-54B	100			120		220
C-54D	55			325		380
C-54E	125					125
C-54G	162					162
XC-114	1					1
YC-116	1					1
DC-4	79					79
Total	**644**			**600**		**1,244**

LEFT *N62297 (ex-C-54E-15-DO, 44-9102), a fire-fighting tanker of Aero Union, at Klamath Falls, Oregon, on 7 September 2003.* (Jim Dunn)

Douglas DC-6 and derivatives						
Model	Santa Monica (DO)	El Segundo (DE)	Long Beach (DL)	Chicago (DC)	Oklahoma City (DK)	Total
DC-6	171					171
DC-6A	78					78
DC-6B	287					287
XC-112A	1					1
VC-118	1					1
C-118A	101					101
R6D-1	65					65
Total	**704**					**704**

LEFT *Last of the DC propliners, fsn 45564 was delivered to JAT on 17 November 1958. In January 2008, when photographed at Swakopmund, Namibia, it was registered V5-NCG and belonged to Springbok Classic Air.* (Jean-Marie Gall)

Douglas DC-7						
Model	Santa Monica (DO)	El Segundo (DE)	Long Beach (DL)	Chicago (DC)	Oklahoma City (DK)	Total
DC-7	105					105
DC-7B	112					112
DC-7C	121					121
Total	338					338

RIGHT *N51700* 'Los Inter Americano', *a DC-7B, was delivered to Panagra in June 1955.* (Douglas)

TOTAL: Douglas DC-1 through DC-7 and derivatives						
Model	Santa Monica (DO)	El Segundo (DE)	Long Beach (DL)	Chicago (DC)	Oklahoma City (DK)	Total
DC-1 and derivatives	1					1
DC-2 and derivatives	192					192
DC-3 and derivatives	989		4,285		5,381	10,655
DF	4					4
DC-4E	1					1
DC-5 and derivatives		12				12
DC-4 and derivatives	644			600		1,244
DC-6 and derivatives	704					704
DC-7	338					338
Total	2,873	12	4,285	600	5,381	13,151

Appendix 2

Factory serial numbers (fsn) DC-1 through DC-7

Entire volumes listing the factory serial numbers, civil registrations and military serial numbers for aircraft in the Douglas DC-1 through DC-7 families have been published over the years. For readers keenly interested in such details, we heartily recommend *DC-1, DC-2, DC-3 – The first seventy years*, a two-volume publication compiled by Jennifer Gradidge and a team from AIR-BRITAIN Publication. It never was our intent to duplicate their thorough work.

In this appendix, we present relevant data in five columns with, from left to right, factory serial numbers (fsn), model and variant designations, customers, original civil registrations or military serial numbers, and the number of aircraft built.

We chose to use the abbreviation fsn (factory serial numbers) as used in most Douglas documents instead of c/n (constructor number) as commonly used in the United Kingdom.

BELOW *Bearing the factory serial number (fsn) 45437, this DC-7B was delivered to Eastern Air Lines on 10 February 1958. Later, it was modified as a forestry fire-fighting bomber and, then belonging to Butler Aviation, is seen landing at Klamath Falls, Oregon, on 15 October 2003.* (Jim Dunn)

DOUGLAS DC-1
(Number built: 1)

fsn	Model	Client		No
1137	DC-1	TWA	X223Y	1

DOUGLAS DC-2 and derivatives
(Number built: 192 by Douglas plus 5 assembled in Japan by Nakajima)

fsn	Model	Client		No
1237/1256	DC-2-112	TWA	NC13711/NC13730	20
1257/1260	DC-2-112	General AL	NC13731/NC13734	4
1261	DC-2-112	Eastern	NC13735	1
1286/1290	DC-2-112	Eastern	NC13736/NC13740	5
1291/1292	DC-2-112	Eastern	NC13781 & NC13782	2
1293/1300	DC-2-112	TWA	NC13783/NC13790	8
1301/1306	DC-2-118A/B	PAA/PAA Grace	NC14268/NC14273	6
1307/1316	DC-2-120	American	NC14274/NC14283	10
1317	DC-2-115A	Fokker	NC14284	1
1318	DC-2-115D	Fokker	PH-AKF	1
1320	DC-2-115D	Austrian Government	A-500	1
1321/1322	DC-2-115B	Swissair	HB-ITI & HB-ITE	2
1323	DC-2-123	Nakajima	NC14284	1
1324	DC-2-124	Swiftlite Corp	NC1000	1
1329	DC-2-115B	Swissair	HB-ITA	1
1330	DC-2-115D	LAPE	EC-XAX	1
1331/1332	DC-2-115D/F	Swissair	HB-ISI & HB-ITO	2
1333	DC-2-115B	French Government	F-AKHD	1
1334	DC-2-115B	LAPE	EC-AAY	1
1335	DC-2-115E	KLM	PH-AKG	1
1350/1352	DC-2-118B/A	PAA/PAA Grace	NC14290/NC14292	3
1354/1365	DC-2-115E	KLM	PH-AKH/PH-AKS	12
1367/1370	DC-2-118B/A	PAA/PAA Grace	NC14295/NC14298	4
1371	DC-2-118B	PAA	NC14950	1
1372/1373	DC-2-171	Eastern	NC14969 & NC14970	2
1374/1376	DC-2-115G	KNILM	PK-AFJ/PK-AFL	3
1401/1403	DC-2-120	American	NC14921/NC14923	3
1406	DC-2-120	American	NC14966	1
1407	DC-2	American	Spare parts only	–
1408/1409	DC-2-172	TWA	NC14978 & NC14979	2
1410/1411	DC-2-120	American	NC14924 & NC14925	2
1412	DC-2	American	Spare parts only	–
1413	DC-2-152	Amtorg (USSR)	NC14949 (URSS-M25)	1
1417	DC-2-115J	LAPE	EC-EBB	1
1418/1422	DC-2	Nakajima	Assembled by Nakajima	–
1521	DC-2-115J	LAPE	EC-BFF	1
1527	DC-2-115M	LAPE	EC-BBE	1
1560	DC-2-192	China	–	1
1561	DC-2-199	Holymanís AW	VH-UXJ	1
1562	DC-2-200	CLS	OK-AIC	1
1563	DC-2-210	ANA	VH-UYB	1
1564	DC-2-211	Fokker	PH-ALZ	1
1565	DC-2-211	CLS	OK-AID	1
1566	DC-2-210	ANA	VH-UYC	1
1567/1568	DC-2-221	CNAC	–	2
1580	DC-2-185	Holymanís AW	VH-USY	1
1581/1582	DC-2-115K	CLS	OK-AIA & OK-AIB	2
1583/1585	DC-2-115L	KLM	PH-ALD/PH-ALF	3
1586	DC-2-190	Capt G Whittell	NC16048	1
1598	DC-2-193	Canton Airways	–	1
1599	DC-2-172	TWA	NC16049	1
1600	DC-2	CNAC	Spare parts only	–
			Subtotal DC-2	125
1319	DC-2-115B (DC-2A)	Avio Linee Ital	I-EROS	1
1328	DC-2A-127 (DC-2A)	Standard Oil	NC14285	1
1366	DC-2-115H (DC-2A)	KLM	PH-AKT	1
			Subtotal DC-2A	3
1377/1378	DC-2-115F (DC-2B)	LOT	SP-ASK & SP-ASL	2
			Subtotal DC-2B	2
1325/1327	R2D-1 (DC-2-125)	USN	9620/9622	3
1404/1405	R2D-1 (DC-2-142)	USN	9993 & 9994	2
			Subtotal for the US Navy	5
1414	XC-32 (DC-2-153)	USAAC	36-1	1
1503/1520	C-33 (DC-2-145)	USAAC	36-70/36-87	18
1415	YC-34 (DC-2-173)	USAAC	36-345	1
1416	YC-34 (DC-2-346)	USAAC	36-346	1
2057/2059	C-39 (DC-2-243)	USAAC	38-499/38-501	3
2061/2092	C-39 (DC-2-243)	USAAC	38-504/38-535	32
2060	C-42 (DC-2-267)	USAAC	38-503	1
			Subtotal for the USAAC	57

The DC-1 received the fsn 1137 while it was being built. This photograph shows the aircraft after its second transcontinental record flight in April 1935. (TWA)

DOUGLAS DC-3 and derivatives
(Number built: 10,655 by Douglas, 472 in Japan, and 4,989 in the Soviet Union)

fsn	Model	Client		No
1494	DST-144	American	NX14988	1
1495/1500	DST-144	American	NC16001/NC16006	6
1549	DST-144	American	NC16007	1
1976	DST-217	American	NC18144	1
2149	DST-217A	American	NC21769	1
2165	DST-217A	American	NC21752	1
2216/2217	DST-217B	American	NC25685 & NC25686	2
2224/2226	DST-318	Eastern	NC25649/NC25651	3
2263/2264	DST-217A	American	NC28325 & NC28350	2
3250/3251	DST-318A	Eastern	NC28394 & NC28393	2
4129	DST-406	Eastern	NC33643	1
			Subtotal DST	21
1951/1958	DST-A-207	United	NC18103/NC18110	8
1959/1960	DST-A-207	Western	NC18101 & NC18102	2
1977/1978	DST-A-207A	United	NC18145 & NC18146	2
2222/2223	DST-A-207B	United	NC25682 & NC25683	2
3263/3264	DST-A-207C	United	NC25619 & NC25620	2
3265	DST-A-207D	United	NC25621	1
4113/4114	DST-A-207D	United	NC33641 & NC33642	2
			Subtotal DST-A	19

KLM acquired 19 DC-2s, all but one powered by Wright engines. The exception was this DC-2-115H – fsn 1366, PH-AKT 'Toekan' – which had Pratt & Whitney Hornet engines. (KLM)

Delivered to Northwest in June 1939, fsn 2131 was a DC-3A. It was initially registered as NC21716 but had become N21716, without the C, before being reduced to components in 1973. (Northwest)

fsn	Model	Client		No
1545/1548	DC-3-178	American	NC16009, NC16030, NC16011 & NC16012	4
1551/1557	DC-3-178	American	NC16013/NC16019	7
1588	DC-3-178	American	NC16008	1
1589	DC-3-196	URSS	–	1
1590	DC-3-194	KLM	PH-ALI	1
1915/1916	DC-3-201	Eastern	NC16094 & NC16095	2
1917/1921	DC-3-178	American	NC17331/NC17335	5
1935/1944	DC-3-194B	KLM	PH-ALH, -ALN, -ALO & -ALR/-ALW	10
1945/1946	DC-3-216	Swissair	HB-IRA & HB-IRI	2
1948/1949	DC-3-201	Eastern	NC16081 & NC16082	2
1961/1964	DC-3-208	American	NC17326/NC17329	4
1965	DC-3-194B	KLM	PH-ALP	1
1966/1970	DC-3-209	TWA	NC17320/NC17324	5
1971	DC-3-201	Eastern	NC16083	1
1973	DC-3-220	CLS	OK-AIH	1
1974	DC-3-227	URSS	–	1
1979	DC-3-237A	Mitsui	–	1
1980/1982	DC-3-194C	KLM	PH-ARB, -ARE, -ARG	3
1985/1986	DC-3-227	Lares	YR-PIF & YR-PAF	2
1987/1988	DC-3-227	URSS	–	2
1989/1994	DC-3-228	Pan American	NC18113/NC18118	6
1995	DC-3-229	Panagra	NC18119	1
1996/2000	DC-3-201	Eastern	NC18120/NC18124	5
2002/2003	DC-3-232	AL of Australia	VH-UZJ & VH-UZK	2
2011	DC-3-229	Panagra	NC18936	1
2012	DC-3-228	Pan American	NC18937	1
2013/2016	DC-3-209A	TWA	NC18949/NC18952	4
2019/2022	DC-3-194B	KLM	PH-ARW/-ARZ	4
2023/2024	DC-3-220A	CLS	OK-AIE & OK-AIF	2
2025/2026	DC-3-237A	Mitsui	–	2
2029/2030	DC-3-232A	AL of Australia	VH-ABR & VH-ACB	2
2031/2035	DC-3-196A	URSS	–	5
2036	DC-3-194E	KLM	PH-ASK	1
2042/2047	DC-3-196A	URSS	–	6
2049/2052	DC-3-237C	Mitsui	–	4
2054	DC-3-227A	Swissair	HB-IRO	1
2093/2094	DC-3-227B	Sabena	OO-AUH & OO-AUI	2
2095	DC-3-220B	CLS	OK-AIG	1
2096/2101	DC-3-260	Nakajima	–	6
2102	DC-3-201A	Eastern	NC21743	1
2103/2107	DC-3-208A	American	NC21745/NC21749	5
2108	DC-3-201A	Eastern	NC21744	1
2109/2111	DC-3-194F	KLM	PH-ASP, -ASR & -AST	3
2112/2117	DC-3-196B	URSS	–	6
2118/2120	DC-3-209B	TWA	NC14931/NC14933	3
2121	DC-3-276	Swissair	HB-IRE	1
2122	DC-3-294	Air France	F-ARQJ	1
2126/2127	DC-3-270	Can Colonial	NC21750 & NC21751	2
2128	DC-3-228A	Pan American	NC21717	1
2132	DC-3-268	Swissair	HB-IRU	1
2133	DC-3-268	ABA	SE-BAF	1
2134	DC-3-279	Panagra	NC21718	1
2135	DC-3-228B	CNAC	–	1
2136/2140	DC-3-277	American	NC16096, NC18141/ NC18143, NC17340	5
2141	DC-3-201B	Eastern	NC21729	1

fsn	Model	Client		No
2142	DC-3-194G	KLM	PH-ASM	1
2143/2144	DC-3-201B	Eastern	NC21727 & NC21728	2
2147	DC-3A	United	NC25765	1
2148	DC-3-294A	CNAC	–	1
2166/2167	DC-3-277A	American	NC21767 & NC21768	2
2168/2173	DC-3-313	Penn Central	NC21780/NC21785	6
2178	DC-3-268B	Aer Lingus	EI-ACA	1
2179/2182	DC-3-314	Braniff	NC21773/NC21776	4
2186/2189	DC-3-313	Penn Central	NC21787/NC21790	4
2198/2215	DC-3-277B	American	NC21793/NC21795, NC21797/NC21799, NC25658, NC25660/NC25661, NC25663/NC25665, NC25670/NC25673, NC25676 & NC25684	18
2218/2220	DC-3-322	Chicago & So	NC25625/NC25627	3
2233	DC-3-322	Chicago & So	NC25628	1
2234/2236	DC-3-201C	Eastern	NC25646/NC25648	3
2237/2238	DC-3-270A	Can Colonial	NC21758/NC21759	2
2239/2242	DC-3-314A	Braniff	NC25666/NC25669	4
2243/2245	DC-3-277C	American	NC15589/NC15591	3
2246/2247	DC-3-201D	Eastern	NC15595 & NC15596	2
2248/2254	DC-3-277C	American	NC15592, NC15629, NC19974, NC28310, NC28321, NC28323 & NC28324	7
2255	DC-3-322A	Chicago & So	NC19977	1
2256	DC-3-313A	Penn Central	NC25691	1
2257/2260	DC-3-201D	Eastern	NC15597/NC15599 & NC19963	4
2261	DC-3-268C	Aer Lingus	EI-ACB	1
2262	DC-3-313A	Penn Central	NC25692	1
2266/2267	DC-3-313A	Penn Central	NC25693 & NC28343	2
2268/2269	DC-3-201E	Eastern	NC28391 & NC28392	2
2271/2272	DC-3-270B	Can Colonial	NC28360 & NC25694	2
3252/3254	DC-3-201E	Eastern	NC19968/NC19970	3
3266/3269	DC-3-362	TWA	NC1941/NC1944	4
3277/3279	DC-3-357	Delta	NC28340/NC28342	3
3281	DC-3-357	Delta	NC28344	1
3285	DC-3-322B	Chicago & So	NC28378	1
3294/3296	DC-3-362	TWA	NC1945/NC1947	3
3298/3299	DC-3-362	TWA	NC1948 & NC1949	2
4081/4082	DC-3-313B	Penn Central	NC25696 & NC25697	2
4089/4093	DC-3-201F	Eastern	NC28381/NC28385	5
4099	DC-3-313C	Penn Central	NC25689	1
4106/4108	DC-3-314B	Braniff	NC28362/NC28364	3
4115/4118	DC-3-277D	American	NC33651 & NC33653/ NC33655	4
4130	DC-3-313D	Penn Central	NC33675	1
4132/4133	DC-3-313D	Penn Central	NC33677 & NC33678	2
4137/4140	DC-3-201G	Eastern	NC33631/NC33635	4
4802/4803	DC-3-277D	American	NC33656 & NC33657	2
			Subtotal DC-3	266
1900/1909	DC-3A-191	United	NC16060/NC16069	10
1910/1914	DC-3A-197	United	NC16070/NC16074	5
1925/1929	DC-3A-197	United	NC16086/NC16090	5
1947	DC-3A-214	ABA	SE-BAA	1
1972	DC-3A-214	ABA	SE-BAB	1
1975	DC-3A-214	ABA	SE-BAC	1
1983/1984	DC-3A-197	United	NC18611 & NC18612	2
2004/2008	DC-3A-197B	United	NC18938/NC18942	5
2009	DC-3A-237A	Mitsui	–	1
2010	DC-3A-197B	United	NC18943	1
2017	DC-3A-197B	United	NC18944	1
2018	DC-3A-191B	United	NC18945	1
2037/2041	DC-3A-237B	Mitsui	–	5
2048	DC-3A-237D	Mitsui	–	1
2055/2056	DC-3A-237D	Mitsui	–	2
2123/2125	DC-3A-269	Northwest	NC21711/NC21713	3
2129/2131	DC-3A-269	Northwest	NC21714/NC21716	3
2146	DC-3A-253A	Northwest	NC21777	1
2174/2177	DC-3A-197C	United	NC25677/NC25680	4
2183/2185	DC-3A-269B	Northwest	NC25608/NC25610	3
2190/2192	DC-3A-279A	Panagra	NC14967, NC14996 & NC25652	3
2193/2197	DC-3A-228C	Pan American	NC25653/NC25657	5
2221	DC-3A-197C	United	NC25681	1
2227	DC-3A-269B	Northwest	NC25621	1
2228/2232	DC-3A-228C	Pan American	NC25641/NC25645	5
2265	DC-3A-343	Western	NC19964	1
2270	DC-3A-269C	Northwest	NC25622	1
3255	DC-3A-197D	United	NC25611	1
3257/3262	DC-3A-197D	United	NC25613/NC25618	6
3275	DC-3A-363	Swiftlite	NC1000	1
3276	DC-3A-269C	Northwest	NC25623	1
3283	DC-3A-343A	Western	NC28379	1

fsn	Model	Client		No
3284	DC-3A-393	Panagra	NC28380	1
3286/3288	DC-3A-367	Northeast	NC33621/NC33623	3
3290/3293	DC-3A-228D	Pan American	NC28301/NC28304	4
4080	DC-3A-348	CAA	NC14	1
4085/4088	DC-3A-228D	Pan American	NC28305/NC28308	4
4100/4105	DC-3A-228F	Pan American	NC33609/NC33614	6
4123	DC-3A-197E	United	NC33644	1
4124	DC-3A-399	Panagra	NC33645	1
4125/4126	DC-3A-197E	United	NC33646 & NC33647	2
4800/4801	DC-3A-279B	Panagra	NC28334 & NC28335	2
4806/4808	DC-3A-375	Inter Island AL	NC33606/NC33608	3
4809	DC-3A-408	Douglas	NC30000	1
4811/4812	DC-3A-343B	Western	NC33670 & NC33671	2
4957	DC-3A-345	DSC	NC34925	1
4958	DC-3A-438	DSC	NC34947	1
4959	DC-3A-414A	DSC	NC34948	1
4963	DC-3A-414A	DSC	NC33684	1
4968	DC-3A-414A	DSC	NC33689	1
4977	DC-3A-414A	DSC	NC30024	1
4981	DC-3A-414A	DSC	NC33659	1
4177	DC-3A-414	DSC	NC30008	1
4179/4181	DC-3A-414	DSC	NC30010/NC30012	3
4183	DC-3A-414	DSC	NC30014	1
			Subtotal DC-3A	126
1922/1924	DC-3B-202	TWA	NC17312/NC17314	3
1930/1934	DC-3B-202	TWA	NC17315/NC17319	5
2027/2028	DC-3B-202A	TWA	NC18953 & NC18954	2
			Subtotal DC-3B	10
43073	DC-3C	W. W. West	N27W	(1)
43074	DC-3C	Pacific Northern	N33676	(1)
43075	DC-3C	Tenn. Gas	N33692	(1)
43076	DC-3C	–	N355M	(1)
43077/43079	DC-3C	TACA Venezuela	YV-C-AZY, -AZF & -AZA	(3)
43080	DC-3C	Seaboard Oil	N1822	(1)
43081	DC-3C	United Aircraft	N13300	(1)
43082	DC-3C	Johns Manville	N34916	(1)
43083	DC-3C	–	–	(1)
43084	DC-3C	Gulf Oil	N37497	(1)
43085	DC-3C	Creole Petroleum	N37499	(1)
43086	DC-3C	Chase Natíl Bk	N67125	(1)
43087/43092	DC-3C	Sabena	OO-AUV, -AUX, -AUZ, -AWG & -CBJ	(6)
43154	DC-3C	Sabena	OO-AWH	(1)
			Subtotal DC-3C	(21)
42954	DC-3D	Dutch Air Force	DT993	1
42955	DC-3D	Pacific Northern	N37465	1
42956/42957	DC-3D	–	N37466 & N37467	2
42958	DC-3D	Colonial AL	N37468	1
42959/42960	DC-3D	Pacific Northern	N37469 & N37470	2
42961	DC-3D	Swiftlite	NC3000	1
42962/42963	DC-3D	SAS	OY-DCO & OY-DCU	2
42964	DC-3D	Colonial AL	N34968	1
42965	DC-3D	–	NC34969	1
42966	DC-3D	Pacific Northern	N34970	1
42967	DC-3D	Braniff	N34971	1
42968	DC-3D	Sabena	OO-UAL	1
42969	DC-3D	Swissair	HB-IRB	1
42970/42972	DC-3D	Air France	F-BAXA/F-BAXC	3
42973	DC-3D	Sabena	OO-AUM	1
42974	DC-3D	Piedmont	N34978	1
42975	DC-3D	Air France	F-BAXD	1
42976	DC-3D	SAS	OY-DCY	1
42977	DC-3D	Sabena	OO-AUN	1
42978	DC-3D	Swissair	HB-IRC	1
42979/42980	DC-3D	Navigação Aérea	PP-NAL & PP-NAM	2
42981	DC-3D	Texas Co.	N1624	1
			Subtotal DC-3D	28
2053	C-41 (DC-3-253)	USAAC	38-502	1
2145	C-41A-DO	USAAC	40-70	1
			Subtotal C-41	2
4200/4203	C-47-DL	USAAF	41-7722/41-7725	4
4205/4221	C-47-DL	USAAF	41-7726/41-7742	17
4230/4279	C-47-DL	USAAF	41-7743/41-7792	50
4285/4299	C-47-DL	USAAF	41-7793/41-7807	15
4307/4359	C-47-DL	USAAF	41-7808/41-7860	53
4369/4374	C-47-DL	USAAF	41-7861/41-7866	6
4375/4432	C-47-DL	USAAF	41-18337/41-18394	53
4442/4444	C-47-DL	USAAF	41-18395/41-18397	3

This early C-47-DL, fsn 7365, bore the military serial number 42-5671. After being fitted with amphibious floats to become the XC-47C-DL, it flew in July 1942. It crashed in Jamaica Bay, New York, on 13 November 1943. (Douglas)

fsn	Model	Client		No
4445/4459	C-47-DL	USAAF	41-38564/41-38578	15
4460/4527	C-47-DL	USAAF	41-18398/41-18465	68
4528/4549	C-47-DL	USAAF	41-38579/41-38600	22
4558/4628	C-47-DL	USAAF	41-18466/41-18536	71
4629/4653	C-47-DL	USAAF	41-38601/41-38625	25
4662/4728	C-47-DL	USAAF	41-18537/41-18603	67
4729/4753	C-47-DL	USAAF	41-38626/41-38650	25
4765/4799	C-47-DL	USAAF	41-18604/41-18638	35
6000/6033	C-47-DL	USAAF	41-18639/41-18672	34
6034/6058	C-47-DL	USAAF	41-38651/41-38675	25
6059/6070	C-47-DL	USAAF	43-30628/43-30639	12
6071/6078	C-47-DL	USAAF	41-38676/41-38683	8
6078/6105	C-47-DL	USAAF	41-18673/41-18699	27
6106/6142	C-47-DL	USAAF	41-19463/41-19499	37
6143/6222	C-47-DL	USAAF	41-38684/41-38763	80
6223/6258	C-47-DL	USAAF	42-5635/42-5670	36
7365/7386	C-47-DL	USAAF	42-5671/42-5692	22
9000/9011	C-47-DL	USAAF	42-5693/42-5704	12
9012/9149	C-47-DL	USAAF	42-32786/42-32923	138
			Subtotal C-47-DL	965
9150/9161	C-47A-DL	USAAF	42-32924/42-32935	12
9162/9208	C-47A-1-DL	USAAF	42-23300/42-23346	47
9209/9217	C-47A-5-DL	USAAF	42-23347/42-23355	9
9218/9241	C-47A-10-DL	USAAF	42-23356/42-23379	24
9242/9274	C-47A-15-DL	USAAF	42-23380/42-23412	33
9275/9399	C-47A-20-DL	USAAF	42-23413/42-23537	125
9400/9442	C-47A-25-DL	USAAF	42-23538/42-23580	43
9443/9649	C-47A-30-DL	USAAF	42-23581/42-23787	207
9650/9824	C-47A-35-DL	USAAF	42-23788/42-23962	175
9825/9947	C-47A-40-DL	USAAF	42-23963/42-24085	123
9948/9999	C-47A-45-DL	USAAF	42-24086/42-24137	52
10000/10183	C-47A-50-DL	USAAF	42-24138/42-24321	184
10184/10199	C-47A-55-DL	USAAF	42-24322/42-24337	16
10200/10269	C-47A-60-DL	USAAF	42-24338/42-24407	70
13779/13790	C-47A-60-DL	USAAF	42-24408/42-24419	12
13791/13912	C-47A-DL	USAAF	43-30640/43-30761	122
18899/19098	C-47A-65-DL	USAAF	42-100436/42-100635	200
19099/19298	C-47A-70-DL	USAAF	42-100636/42-100835	200
19299/19498	C-47A-75-DL	USAAF	42-100836/42-101035	200
19499/19898	C-47A-80-DL	USAAF	43-15033/43-15432	400
19899/20098	C-47A-85-DL	USAAF	43-15433/43-15632	200
20099/20598	C-47A-90-DL	USAAF	43-15633/43-16132	500
			Subtotal C-47A-DL	2,954
11779/11846	C-47A-DK	USAAF	42-92024/42-92091	68
11847/12170	C-47A-1-DK	USAAF	42-92092/42-92415	324
12171/12327	C-47A-5-DK	USAAF	42-92416/42-92572	157
12328/12498	C-47A-10-DK	USAAF	42-92573/42-92743	171
12499/12678	C-47A-15-DK	USAAF	42-92744/42-92923	180
12679/12913	C-47A-20-DK	USAAF	42-92924/42-93158	235
12914/12920	C-47A-DK	USAAF	42-108794/42-108800	7
12921/12956	C-47A-1-DK	USAAF	42-108801/42-108836	36
12957/12974	C-47A-5-DK	USAAF	42-108837/42-108854	18
12975/12993	C-47A-10-DK	USAAF	42-108855/42-108873	19

fsn	Model	Client		No
12994/13013	C-47A-15-DK	USAAF	42-108874/42-108893	20
13014/13039	C-47A-20-DK	USAAF	42-108894/42-108919	26
13041/13164	C-47A-20-DK	USAAF	42-93160/42-93283	124
13165/13704	C-47A-25-DK	USAAF	42-93284/42-93823	540
13705/13718	C-47A-20-DK	USAAF	42-108920/42-108933	14
13719/13778	C-47A-25-DK	USAAF	42-108934/42-108993	60
25224/25532	C-47A-30-DK	USAAF	43-47963/43-48262	300
			Subtotal C-47A-DK	2,299
20599/20898	C-47B-1-DL	USAAF	43-16133/43-16432	300
			Subtotal C-47B-DL	300
25524/25639	C-47B-1-DK	USAAF	43-48263/43-48378	116
25640	C-47B-2-DK	USAAF	43-48379	1
25641/25766	C-47B-1-DK	USAAF	43-48380/43-48505	126
25767	C-47B-2-DK	USAAF	43-48506	1
25768/25823	C-47B-1-DK	USAAF	43-48507/43-48562	56
25824/25866	C-47B-5-DK	USAAF	43-48563/43-48605	43
25867	C-47B-7-DK	USAAF	43-48606	1
25868/25896	C-47B-5-DK	USAAF	43-48607/43-48635	29
25897	C-47B-7-DK	USAAF	43-48636	1
25898/25901	C-47B-5-DK	USAAF	43-48637/43-48640	4
25903/25946	C-47B-5-DK	USAAF	43-48642/43-48685	44
25947	C-47B-6-DK	USAAF	43-48686	1
25948/25958	C-47B-5-DK	USAAF	43-48687/43-48697	11
25959/25963	C-47B-9-DK	USAAF	43-48698/43-48702	5
25964/25996	C-47B-5-DK	USAAF	43-48703/43-48735	33
25997	C-47B-6-DK	USAAF	43-48736	1
25998/26018	C-47B-5-DK	USAAF	43-48737/43-48757	21
26019	C-47B-8-DK	USAAF	43-48758	1
26020/26066	C-47B-5-DK	USAAF	43-48759/43-48805	47
26067	C-47B-7-DK	USAAF	43-48806	1
26068/26076	C-47B-5-DK	USAAF	43-48807/43-48815	9
26077	C-47B-6-DK	USAAF	43-48816	1
26078/26146	C-47B-5-DK	USAAF	43-48817/43-48885	69
26147	C-47B-7-DK	USAAF	43-48886	1
26148/26166	C-47B-5-DK	USAAF	43-48887/43-48905	19
26167	C-47B-6-DK	USAAF	43-48906	1
26168/26173	C-47B-5-DK	USAAF	43-48907/43-48912	6
26174/26182	C-47B-10-DK	USAAF	43-48913/43-48921	9
26183	C-47B-13-DK	USAAF	43-48922	1
26184/26192	C-47B-10-DK	USAAF	43-48923/43-48931	9
26193	C-47B-13-DK	USAAF	43-48932	1
26194/26212	C-47B-10-DK	USAAF	43-48933/43-48951	19
26213	C-47B-13-DK	USAAF	43-48952	1
26214/26266	C-47B-10-DK	USAAF	43-48953/43-49005	53
26267	C-47B-13-DK	USAAF	43-49006	1
26268/26276	C-47B-10-DK	USAAF	43-49007/43-49015	9
26277	C-47B-13-DK	USAAF	43-49016	1
26278	C-47B-10-DK	USAAF	43-94017	1
26279	C-47B-11-DK	USAAF	43-49018	1
26280/26283	C-47B-10-DK	USAAF	43-49019/43-49022	4
26284	C-47B-11-DK	USAAF	43-49023	1
26285/26288	C-47B-10-DK	USAAF	43-49024/43-49027	4
26289	C-47B-11-DK	USAAF	43-49028	1
26290/26293	C-47B-10-DK	USAAF	43-49029/43-49032	4
26295/26337	C-47B-10-DK	USAAF	43-49034/43-49076	43
26338	C-47B-11-DK	USAAF	43-49077	1
26339	C-47B-10-DK	USAAF	43-49078	1
26340	C-47B-14-DK	USAAF	43-49079	1
26341/26342	C-47B-10-DK	USAAF	43-49080 & 43-49081	2
26343	C-47B-11-DK	USAAF	43-49082	1
26344/26347	C-47B-10-DK	USAAF	43-49083/43-49086	4
26348	C-47B-11-DK	USAAF	43-49087	1
26349/26358	C-47B-10-DK	USAAF	43-49088/43-49097	10
26359	C-47B-11-DK	USAAF	43-49098	1
26360/26368	C-47B-10-DK	USAAF	43-49099/43-49107	9
26369	C-47B-11-DK	USAAF	43-49108	1
26370/26378	C-47B-10-DK	USAAF	43-49109/43-49117	9
26379	C-47B-11-DK	USAAF	43-49118	1
26380/26388	C-47B-10-DK	USAAF	43-49119/43-49127	9
26389	C-47B-11-DK	USAAF	43-49128	1
26390/26398	C-47B-10-DK	USAAF	43-49129/43-49137	9
26399	C-47B-11-DK	USAAF	43-49138	1
26400/26406	C-47B-10-DK	USAAF	43-49139/43-49145	7
26407	C-47B-13-DK	USAAF	43-49146	1
26408/26442	C-47B-10-DK	USAAF	43-49147/43-49181	35
26443	C-47B-11-DK	USAAF	43-49182	1
26444	C-47B-10-DK	USAAF	43-49183/43-49191	9
26453	C-47B-11-DK	USAAF	43-49192	1
26454/26462	C-47B-10-DK	USAAF	43-49193/43-49201	9
26463	C-47B-11-DK	USAAF	43-49202	1
26464/26472	C-47B-10-DK	USAAF	43-49203/43-49211	9
26473	C-47B-11-DK	USAAF	43-49212	1
26474/26482	C-47B-10-DK	USAAF	43-49213/43-49221	9
26483	C-47B-11-DK	USAAF	43-49222	1
26484/26486	C-47B-10-DK	USAAF	43-49223/43-49225	3
26487	C-47B-13-DK	USAAF	43-49226	1
26488	C-47B-11-DK	USAAF	43-49227	1
26489/26492	C-47B-10-DK	USAAF	43-49228/43-49231	4
26493	C-47B-11-DK	USAAF	43-49232	1
26494/26497	C-47B-10-DK	USAAF	43-49233/43-49236	4
26498	C-47B-11-DK	USAAF	43-49237	1
26499/26502	C-47B-10-DK	USAAF	43-49238/43-49241	4
26503	C-47B-11-DK	USAAF	43-49242	1
26504/25507	C-47B-10-DK	USAAF	43-49243/43-49246	4
26508	C-47B-11-DK	USAAF	43-49247	1
26509/26512	C-47B-10-DK	USAAF	43-49248/43-49251	4
26513	C-47B-11-DK	USAAF	43-49252	1
26514/26516	C-47B-10-DK	USAAF	43-49253/43-49255	3
26517	C-47B-13-DK	USAAF	43-49256	1
26518	C-47B-11-DK	USAAF	43-49257	1
26519/26522	C-47B-10-DK	USAAF	43-49258/43-49261	4
26523	C-47B-11-DK	USAAF	43-49262	1
26524/26528	C-47B-15-DK	USAAF	43-49263/43-49267	5
26530	C-47B-16-DK	USAAF	43-49269	1
26531/26532	C-47B-15-DK	USAAF	43-49270 & 43-49271	2
26533/26534	C-47B-16-DK	USAAF	43-49272 & 43-49273	2
26535	C-47B-15-DK	USAAF	43-49274	1
26536/26537	C-47B-18-DK	USAAF	43-49275 & 43-49276	2
26538/26589	C-47B-15-DK	USAAF	43-49277/43-49328	52
26590	C-47B-16-DK	USAAF	43-49329	1
26591/26593	C-47B-15-DK	USAAF	43-49330/43-49332	3
26594	C-47B-18-DK	USAAF	43-49333	1
26595/26596	C-47B-15-DK	USAAF	43-49334 & 43-49335	2
26597	C-47B-16-DK	USAAF	43-49336	1
26598	C-47B-15-DK	USAAF	43-49337/43-49339	3
26601	C-47B-18-DK	USAAF	43-49340	1
26602/26604	C-47B-15-DK	USAAF	43-49341/43-49343	3
26605	C-47B-16-DK	USAAF	43-49344	1
26606/26608	C-47B-15-DK	USAAF	43-49345/43-49347	3
26610/26611	C-47B-15-DK	USAAF	43-49349 & 43-49350	2
26613/26615	C-47B-15-DK	USAAF	43-49352/43-49354	3
26616	C-47B-16-DK	USAAF	43-49355	1
26617/26619	C-47B-15-DK	USAAF	43-49356/43-49358	3
26620	C-47B-18-DK	USAAF	43-49359	1
26621/26622	C-47B-15-DK	USAAF	43-49360 & 43-49361	2
26623	C-47B-16-DK	USAAF	43-49362	1
26624/26626	C-47B-15-DK	USAAF	43-49363/43-49365	3
26627	C-47B-18-DK	USAAF	43-49366	1
26628/26629	C-47B-15-DK	USAAF	43-49367 & 43-49368	2
26630	C-47B-16-DK	USAAF	43-49369	1
26631/26632	C-47B-15-DK	USAAF	43-49370 & 43-49371	2
26633	C-47B-16-DK	USAAF	43-49372	1
26634/26635	C-47B-15-DK	USAAF	43-49373 & 43-49374	2
26637/26668	C-47B-15-DK	USAAF	43-49376/43-49407	32
26669	C-47B-16-DK	USAAF	43-49408	1
26670/26671	C-47B-15-DK	USAAF	43-49409 & 43-49410	2
26672	C-47B-16-DK	USAAF	43-49411	1
26673	C-47B-15-DK	USAAF	43-49412/43-49415	4
26677	C-47B-16-DK	USAAF	43-49416	1
26678/26873	C-47B-15-DK	USAAF	43-49417/43-49612	196
26874/26900	C-47B-20-DK	USAAF	43-49613/43-49639	27
26901	C-47B-23-DK	USAAF	43-49640	1
26902/26963	C-47B-20-DK	USAAF	43-49641/43-49702	62
26965/27005	C-47B-20-DK	USAAF	43-49704/43-49744	41
27006	C-47B-23-DK	USAAF	43-49745	1
27007/27020	C-47B-20-DK	USAAF	43-49746/43-49759	14
27022/27035	C-47B-20-DK	USAAF	43-49761/43-49774	14
27036	C-47B-23-DK	USAAF	43-49775	1
27037/27050	C-47B-20-DK	USAAF	43-49776/43-49789	14
27052/27062	C-47B-20-DK	USAAF	43-49791/43-49801	11
27063	C-47B-23-DK	USAAF	43-49802	1
27064/27068	C-47B-20-DK	USAAF	43-49803/43-49087	5
27070/27074	C-47B-20-DK	USAAF	43-49809/43-49813	5
27076/27086	C-47B-20-DK	USAAF	43-49815/43-49825	11
27087	C-47B-23-DK	USAAF	43-49826	1
27088/27092	C-47B-20-DK	USAAF	43-49827/43-49831	5
27094/27105	C-47B-20-DK	USAAF	43-49833/43-49844	12
27106	C-47B-23-DK	USAAF	43-49845	1
27107/27112	C-47B-20-DK	USAAF	43-49846/43-49851	6
27114/27119	C-47B-20-DK	USAAF	43-49853/43-49858	6
27120	C-47B-23-DK	USAAF	43-49859	1
27121/27133	C-47B-20-DK	USAAF	43-49860/43-49872	13
27134	C-47B-23-DK	USAAF	43-49873	1
27135/27140	C-47B-20-DK	USAAF	43-49874/43-49879	6
27143/27147	C-47B-20-DK	USAAF	43-49881/43-49886	6
27148	C-47B-23-DK	USAAF	43-49887	1
27149/27158	C-47B-20-DK	USAAF	43-49888/43-49897	10
27159	C-47B-23-DK	USAAF	43-49898	1
27160/27163	C-47B-20-DK	USAAF	43-49899/43-49902	4
27165/27167	C-47B-20-DK	USAAF	43-49904/43-49906	3
27168	C-47B-23-DK	USAAF	43-49907	1

fsn	Model	Client		No
27169/27176	C-47B-20-DK	USAAF	43-49908/43-49915	8
27177	C-47B-23-DK	USAAF	43-49916	1
27178/27181	C-47B-20-DK	USAAF	43-49917/43-49920	4
27183/27185	C-47B-20-DK	USAAF	43-49922/43-49924	3
27186	C-47B-23-DK	USAAF	43-49925	1
27187/27194	C-47B-20-DK	USAAF	43-49926/43-49933	8
27195	C-47B-23-DK	USAAF	43-49934	1
27196	C-47B-20-DK	USAAF	43-49935/43-49938	4
27201/27203	C-47B-20-DK	USAAF	43-49940/43-49942	3
27204	C-47B-23-DK	USAAF	43-49943	1
27205/27212	C-47B-20-DK	USAAF	43-49944/43-49951	8
27213	C-47B-23-DK	USAAF	43-49952	1
27214/27216	C-47B-20-DK	USAAF	43-49953/43-49955	3
27218/27221	C-47B-20-DK	USAAF	43-49957/43-49960	4
27222	C-47B-23-DK	USAAF	43-49961	1
27223	C-47B-20-DK	USAAF	43-49962	1
32527	C-47B-25-DK	USAAF	44-76195	1
32528/32529	C-47B-27-DK	USAAF	44-76196 & 44-76197	2
32530/32534	C-47B-25-DK	USAAF	44-76198/44-76202	5
32535	C-47B-28-DK	USAAF	44-76203	1
32536/32537	C-47B-25-DK	USAAF	44-76204 & 44-76205	2
32539/32541	C-47B-25-DK	USAAF	44-76207/44-76209	3
32542	C-47B-28-DK	USAAF	44-76210	1
32543/32545	C-47B-25-DK	USAAF	44-76211/44-76213	3
32547/32550	C-47B-25-DK	USAAF	44-76215/44-76218	4
32551	C-47B-28-DK	USAAF	44-76219	1
32552/32554	C-47B-25-DK	USAAF	44-76220/44-76222	3
32556/32558	C-47B-25-DK	USAAF	44-76224/44-76226	3
32559	C-47B-28-DK	USAAF	44-76227	1
32560/32567	C-47B-25-DK	USAAF	44-76228/44-76235	8
32568	C-47B-28-DK	USAAF	44-76236	1
32569/32571	C-47B-25-DK	USAAF	44-76237/44-76239	3
32573/32575	C-47B-25-DK	USAAF	44-76241/44-76243	3
32576	C-47B-28-DK	USAAF	44-76244	1
32577/32579	C-47B-25-DK	USAAF	44-76245/44-76247	3
32581/32583	C-47B-25-DK	USAAF	44-76249/44-76251	3
32584	C-47B-28-DK	USAAF	44-76252	1
32585	C-47B-25-DK	USAAF	44-76253	1
32586	C-47B-27-DK	USAAF	44-76254	1
32587/32588	C-47B-25-DK	USAAF	44-76255 & 44-76256	2
32590/32592	C-47B-25-DK	USAAF	44-76258/44-76260	3
32593	C-47B-28-DK	USAAF	44-76261	1
32594/32596	C-47B-25-DK	USAAF	44-76262/44-76264	3
32598/32600	C-47B-25-DK	USAAF	44-76266/44-76268	3
32601	C-47B-28-DK	USAAF	44-76269	1
32602/32604	C-47B-25-DK	USAAF	44-76270/44-76272	3
32606/32608	C-47B-25-DK	USAAF	44-76274/44-76276	3
32609	C-47B-28-DK	USAAF	44-76277	1
32610/32613	C-47B-25-DK	USAAF	44-76278/44-76281	4
32615/32617	C-47B-25-DK	USAAF	44-76283/44-76285	3
32618	C-47B-28-DK	USAAF	44-76286	1
32619/32621	C-47B-25-DK	USAAF	44-76287/44-76289	3
32623	C-47B-25-DK	USAAF	44-76291	1
32624	C-47B-27-DK	USAAF	44-76292	1
32625	C-47B-25-DK	USAAF	44-76293	1
32626	C-47B-28-DK	USAAF	44-76294	1
32627/32629	C-47B-25-DK	USAAF	44-76295/44-76297	3
32631/32633	C-47B-25-DK	USAAF	44-76299/44-76301	3
32634	C-47B-28-DK	USAAF	44-76302	1
32635/32637	C-47B-25-DK	USAAF	44-76303/44-76305	3
32639/32641	C-47B-25-DK	USAAF	44-76307/44-76309	3
32642	C-47B-28-DK	USAAF	44-76310	1
32643/32645	C-47B-25-DK	USAAF	44-76311/44-76313	3
32647/32649	C-47B-25-DK	USAAF	44-76315/44-76317	3
32650	C-47B-28-DK	USAAF	44-76318	1
32651/32653	C-47B-25-DK	USAAF	44-76319/44-76321	3
32655/32657	C-47B-25-DK	USAAF	44-76323/44-76325	3
32658	C-47B-28-DK	USAAF	44-76326	1
32659/32661	C-47B-25-DK	USAAF	44-76327/44-76329	3
32663/32665	C-47B-25-DK	USAAF	44-76331/44-76333	3
32666	C-47B-28-DK	USAAF	44-76334	1
32667/32669	C-47B-25-DK	USAAF	44-76335/44-76337	3
32671/32673	C-47B-25-DK	USAAF	44-76339/44-76341	3
32674	C-47B-28-DK	USAAF	44-76342	1
32675	C-47B-25-DK	USAAF	44-76343	1
32676	C-47B-27-DK	USAAF	44-76344	1
32677	C-47B-25-DK	USAAF	44-76345	1
32679/32681	C-47B-25-DK	USAAF	44-76347/44-76349	3
32682	C-47B-28-DK	USAAF	44-76350	1
32683/32685	C-47B-25-DK	USAAF	44-76351/44-76353	3
32687/32689	C-47B-25-DK	USAAF	44-76355/44-76357	3
32690	C-47B-28-DK	USAAF	44-76358	1
32691/32693	C-47B-25-DK	USAAF	44-76359/44-76361	3
32695/32697	C-47B-25-DK	USAAF	44-76363/44-76365	3
32698	C-47B-25-DK	USAAF	44-76366	1
32699/32701	C-47B-25-DK	USAAF	44-76367/44-76369	3
32703/32705	C-47B-25-DK	USAAF	44-76371/44-76373	3
32706	C-47B-28-DK	USAAF	44-76374	1

fsn	Model	Client		No
32707/32709	C-47B-25-DK	USAAF	44-76375/44-76377	3
32711/32713	C-47B-25-DK	USAAF	44-76379/44-76381	3
32714	C-47B-28-DK	USAAF	44-76382	1
32715/32717	C-47B-25-DK	USAAF	44-76383/44-76385	3
32719/32721	C-47B-25-DK	USAAF	44-76387/44-76389	3
32722	C-47B-28-DK	USAAF	44-76390	1
32723/32725	C-47B-25-DK	USAAF	44-76391/44-76393	3
32727	C-47B-27-DK	USAAF	44-76395	1
32728/32729	C-47B-25-DK	USAAF	44-76396 & 44-76397	2
32730	C-27B-28-DK	USAAF	44-76398	1
32731/32733	C-47B-25-DK	USAAF	44-76399/44-76401	3
32735/32737	C-47B-25-DK	USAAF	44-76403/44-76405	3
32738	C-47B-28-DK	USAAF	44-76406	1
32739/32741	C-47B-25-DK	USAAF	44-76407/44-76409	3
32743/32745	C-47B-25-DK	USAAF	44-76411/44-76413	3
32746	C-47B-28-DK	USAAF	44-76414	1
32747/32749	C-47B-25-DK	USAAF	44-76415/44-76417	3
32751/32753	C-47B-25-DK	USAAF	44-76419/44-76421	3
32754	C-47B-28-DK	USAAF	44-76422	1
32755/32761	C-47B-25-DK	USAAF	44-76423/44-76429	7
32763/32769	C-47B-25-DK	USAAF	44-76431/44-76437	7
32771/32777	C-47B-25-DK	USAAF	44-76439/44-76445	7
32779/32780	C-47B-25-DK	USAAF	44-76447 & 44-76448	2
32781	C-47B-27-DK	USAAF	44-76449	1
32782/32785	C-47B-25-DK	USAAF	44-76450/44-76453	4
32787/32793	C-47B-25-DK	USAAF	44-76455/44-76461	7
32795/32801	C-47B-25-DK	USAAF	44-76463/44-76469	7
32803/32809	C-47B-25-DK	USAAF	44-76471/44-76477	7
32811/32817	C-47B-25-DK	USAAF	44-76479/44-76485	7
32819/32825	C-47B-25-DK	USAAF	44-76487/44-76493	7
32827/32833	C-47B-25-DK	USAAF	44-76495/44-76501	7
32835/32841	C-47B-25-DK	USAAF	44-76503/44-76509	7
32843/32849	C-47B-25-DK	USAAF	44-76511/44-76517	7
32851/32855	C-47B-25-DK	USAAF	44-76519/44-76523	5
32857/32865	C-47B-30-DK	USAAF	44-76525/44-76533	9
32867/32873	C-47B-30-DK	USAAF	44-76535/44-76541	7
32875/32881	C-47B-30-DK	USAAF	44-76543/44-76549	7
32883/32884	C-47B-30-DK	USAAF	44-76551 & 44-76552	2
32886/32889	C-47B-30-DK	USAAF	44-76554/44-76557	4
32891/32897	C-47B-30-DK	USAAF	44-76559/44-76565	7
32899/32905	C-47B-30-DK	USAAF	44-76567/44-76573	7
32907/32909	C-47B-30-DK	USAAF	44-76575/44-76577	3
32911/32913	C-47B-30-DK	USAAF	44-76579/44-76581	3
32915/32919	C-47B-30-DK	USAAF	44-76583/44-76587	5
32921/32924	C-47B-30-DK	USAAF	44-76589/44-76592	4
32926/32929	C-47B-30-DK	USAAF	44-76594/44-76597	4
32931/32937	C-47B-30-DK	USAAF	44-76599/44-76605	7
32939/32943	C-47B-30-DK	USAAF	44-76607/44-76611	5
32945/32949	C-47B-30-DK	USAAF	44-76613/44-76617	5
32951/32956	C-47B-30-DK	USAAF	44-76619/44-76624	6
32958/32963	C-47B-30-DK	USAAF	44-76626/44-76631	6
32965/32969	C-47B-30-DK	USAAF	44-76633/44-76637	5
32971/32976	C-47B-30-DK	USAAF	44-76639/44-76644	6
32978/32983	C-47B-30-DK	USAAF	44-76646/44-76651	6
32985/32989	C-47B-30-DK	USAAF	44-76653/44-76657	5
32991/32994	C-47B-30-DK	USAAF	44-76659/44-76662	4
32996/32999	C-47B-30-DK	USAAF	44-76664/44-76667	4
33001/33006	C-47B-30-DK	USAAF	44-76669/44-76674	6
33008/33011	C-47B-30-DK	USAAF	44-76676/44-76679	4
33013/33017	C-47B-30-DK	USAAF	44-76681/44-76685	5
33019/33022	C-47B-30-DK	USAAF	44-76687/44-76690	4
33024/33027	C-47B-30-DK	USAAF	44-76692/44-76695	4
33029/33031	C-47B-30-DK	USAAF	44-76697/44-76699	3
33033/33036	C-47B-30-DK	USAAF	44-76701/44-76704	4
33038/33042	C-47B-30-DK	USAAF	44-76706/44-76710	5
33044/33047	C-47B-30-DK	USAAF	44-76712/44-76715	4
33049/33053	C-47B-30-DK	USAAF	44-76717/44-76721	5
33055/33060	C-47B-30-DK	USAAF	44-76723/44-76728	6
33062/33065	C-47B-30-DK	USAAF	44-76730/44-76733	4
33067/33070	C-47B-30-DK	USAAF	44-76735/44-76738	4
33072/33075	C-47B-30-DK	USAAF	44-76740/44-76743	4
33077/33079	C-47B-30-DK	USAAF	44-76745/44-76747	3
33081/33084	C-47B-30-DK	USAAF	44-76749/44-76752	4
33086/33089	C-47B-30-DK	USAAF	44-76754/44-76757	4
33091/33094	C-47B-30-DK	USAAF	44-76759/44-76762	4
33096/33099	C-47B-30-DK	USAAF	44-76764/44-76767	4
33101/33104	C-47B-30-DK	USAAF	44-76769/44-76772	4
33106/33109	C-47B-30-DK	USAAF	44-76774/44-76777	4
33111/33120	C-47B-30-DK	USAAF	44-76779/44-76788	10
33122/33125	C-47B-30-DK	USAAF	44-76790/44-76793	4
33127/33132	C-47B-30-DK	USAAF	44-76795/44-76800	6
33134/33143	C-47B-30-DK	USAAF	44-76802/44-76811	10
33145/33154	C-47B-30-DK	USAAF	44-76813/44-76822	10
33156/33159	C-47B-30-DK	USAAF	44-76824/44-76827	4
33161/33169	C-47B-30-DK	USAAF	44-76829/44-76837	9
33171/33179	C-47B-30-DK	USAAF	44-76839/44-76847	9
33181/33185	C-47B-30-DK	USAAF	44-76849/44-76853	5
33187/33191	C-47B-35-DK	USAAF	44-76855/44-76859	5

fsn	Model	Client		No
33193/33200	C-47B-35-DK	USAAF	44-76861/44-76868	8
33202/33205	C-47B-35-DK	USAAF	44-76870/44-76873	4
33207/33215	C-47B-35-DK	USAAF	44-76875/44-76883	9
33217/33229	C-47B-35-DK	USAAF	44-76885/44-76894	10
33228/33231	C-47B-35-DK	USAAF	44-76896/44-76899	4
33233/33240	C-47B-35-DK	USAAF	44-76901/44-76908	8
33242/33250	C-47B-35-DK	USAAF	44-76910/44-76918	9
33252/33255	C-47B-35-DK	USAAF	44-76920/44-76923	4
33257/33266	C-47B-35-DK	USAAF	44-76925/44-76934	10
33268/32274	C-47B-35-DK	USAAF	44-76936/44-76942	7
33276/33282	C-47B-35-DK	USAAF	44-76944/44-76950	7
33284/33290	C-47B-35-DK	USAAF	44-76952/44-76958	7
33292/33298	C-47B-35-DK	USAAF	44-76960/44-76966	7
33300/33304	C-47B-35-DK	USAAF	44-76968/44-76972	5
33306/33313	C-47B-35-DK	USAAF	44-76974/44-76981	8
33315/33321	C-47B-35-DK	USAAF	44-76983/44-76989	7
33323/33328	C-47B-35-DK	USAAF	44-76991/44-76996	6
33330/33336	C-47B-35-DK	USAAF	44-76998/44-77004	7
33338/33344	C-47B-35-DK	USAAF	44-77006/44-77012	7
33346/33350	C-47B-35-DK	USAAF	44-77014/44-77018	5
33352/33358	C-47B-35-DK	USAAF	44-77020/44-77026	7
33360/33366	C-47B-35-DK	USAAF	44-77028/44-77034	7
33368/33516	C-47B-35-DK	USAAF	44-77036/44-77184	149
33517/33626	C-47B-40-DK	USAAF	44-77185/44-77294	110
34134/34135	C-47B-45-DK	USAAF	45-876 & 45-877	2
34137/34144	C-47B-45-DK	USAAF	45-878/45-885	8
34146/34167	C-47B-45-DK	USAAF	45-886/45-907	22
34169/34190	C-47B-45-DK	USAAF	45-908/45-929	22
34192/34211	C-47B-45-DK	USAAF	45-930/45-949	20
34213/34233	C-47B-45-DK	USAAF	45-950/45-970	21
34235/34249	C-47B-45-DK	USAAF	45-971/45-985	15
34251/34263	C-47B-45-DK	USAAF	45-986/45-998	13
34265/34277	C-47B-45-DK	USAAF	45-999/45-1011	13
34279/34290	C-47B-45-DK	USAAF	45-1012/45-1023	12
34292/34304	C-47B-45-DK	USAAF	45-1024/45-1036	13
34306/34317	C-47B-45-DK	USAAF	45-1037/45-1048	12
34319/34325	C-47B-45-DK	USAAF	45-1049/45-1055	7
34326/34409	C-47B-50-DK	USAAF	45-1056/45-1139	84
			Subtotal C-47B-DK	2,932
25902	TC-47B-5-DK	USAAF	43-48641	1
26294	TC-47B-10-DK	USAAF	43-49033	1
26529	TC-47B-15-DK	USAAF	43-49268	1
26609	TC-47B-15-DK	USAAF	43-49348	1
26612	TC-47B-15-DK	USAAF	43-49351	1
26636	TC-47B-15-DK	USAAF	43-49375	1
26964	TC-47B-20-DK	USAAF	43-49703	1
27021	TC-47B-20-DK	USAAF	43-49760	1
27051	TC-47B-20-DK	USAAF	43-49790	1
27069	TC-47B-20-DK	USAAF	43-49808	1
27075	TC-47B-20-DK	USAAF	43-49814	1
27093	TC-47B-20-DK	USAAF	43-49832	1
27113	TC-47B-20-DK	USAAF	43-49852	1
27141	TC-47B-20-DK	USAAF	43-49880	1
27164	TC-47B-20-DK	USAAF	43-49903	1
27182	TC-47B-20-DK	USAAF	43-49921	1
27200	TC-47B-20-DK	USAAF	43-49939	1
27217	TC-47B-20-DK	USAAF	43-49956	1
32538	TC-47B-25-DK	USAAF	44-76206	1
32546	TC-47B-25-DK	USAAF	44-76214	1
32555	TC-47B-25-DK	USAAF	44-76223	1
32572	TC-47B-25-DK	USAAF	44-76240	1
32580	TC-47B-25-DK	USAAF	44-76248	1
32589	TC-47B-25-DK	USAAF	44-76257	1
32597	TC-47B-25-DK	USAAF	44-76265	1
32605	TC-47B-25-DK	USAAF	44-76273	1
32614	TC-47B-25-DK	USAAF	44-76282	1
32622	TC-47B-25-DK	USAAF	44-76290	1
32630	TC-47B-25-DK	USAAF	44-76298	1
32638	TC-47B-25-DK	USAAF	44-76306	1
32646	TC-47B-25-DK	USAAF	44-76314	1
32654	TC-47B-25-DK	USAAF	44-76322	1
32662	TC-47B-25-DK	USAAF	44-76330	1
32670	TC-47B-25-DK	USAAF	44-76338	1
32678	TC-47B-25-DK	USAAF	44-76346	1
32686	TC-47B-25-DK	USAAF	44-76354	1
32694	TC-47B-25-DK	USAAF	44-76362	1
32702	TC-47B-25-DK	USAAF	44-76370	1
32710	TC-47B-25-DK	USAAF	44-76378	1
32718	TC-47B-25-DK	USAAF	44-76386	1
32726	TC-47B-25-DK	USAAF	44-76394	1
32734	TC-47B-25-DK	USAAF	44-76402	1
32742	TC-47B-25-DK	USAAF	44-76410	1
32750	TC-47B-25-DK	USAAF	44-76418	1
32762	TC-47B-25-DK	USAAF	44-76430	1
32770	TC-47B-25-DK	USAAF	44-76438	1
32778	TC-47B-25-DK	USAAF	44-76446	1
32786	TC-47B-25-DK	USAAF	44-76454	1
32794	TC-47B-25-DK	USAAF	44-76462	1
32802	TC-47B-25-DK	USAAF	44-76470	1
32810	TC-47B-25-DK	USAAF	44-76478	1
32818	TC-47B-25-DK	USAAF	44-76486	1
32826	TC-47B-25-DK	USAAF	44-76494	1
32834	TC-47B-25-DK	USAAF	44-76502	1
32842	TC-47B-25-DK	USAAF	44-76510	1
32850	TC-47B-25-DK	USAAF	44-76518	1
32856	TC-47B-25-DK	USAAF	44-76524	1
32866	TC-47B-30-DK	USAAF	44-76534	1
32874	TC-47B-30-DK	USAAF	44-76542	1
32882	TC-47B-30-DK	USAAF	44-76550	1
32885	TC-47B-30-DK	USAAF	44-76553	1
32890	TC-47B-30-DK	USAAF	44-76558	1
32898	TC-47B-30-DK	USAAF	44-76566	1
32906	TC-47B-30-DK	USAAF	44-76574	1
32910	TC-47B-30-DK	USAAF	44-76578	1
32914	TC-47B-30-DK	USAAF	44-76582	1
32920	TC-47B-30-DK	USAAF	44-76588	1
32925	TC-47B-30-DK	USAAF	44-76593	1
32930	TC-47B-30-DK	USAAF	44-76598	1
32938	TC-47B-30-DK	USAAF	44-76606	1
32944	TC-47B-30-DK	USAAF	44-76612	1
32950	TC-47B-30-DK	USAAF	44-76618	1
32957	TC-47B-30-DK	USAAF	44-76625	1
32964	TC-47B-30-DK	USAAF	44-76632	1
32970	TC-47B-30-DK	USAAF	44-76638	1
32977	TC-47B-30-DK	USAAF	44-76645	1
32984	TC-47B-30-DK	USAAF	44-76652	1
32990	TC-47B-30-DK	USAAF	44-76658	1
32995	TC-47B-30-DK	USAAF	44-76663	1
33000	TC-47B-30-DK	USAAF	44-76668	1
33007	TC-47B-30-DK	USAAF	44-76675	1
33012	TC-47B-30-DK	USAAF	44-76680	1
33018	TC-47B-30-DK	USAAF	44-76686	1
33023	TC-47B-30-DK	USAAF	44-76691	1
33028	TC-47B-30-DK	USAAF	44-76696	1
33032	TC-47B-30-DK	USAAF	44-76700	1
33037	TC-47B-30-DK	USAAF	44-76705	1
33043	TC-47B-30-DK	USAAF	44-76711	1
33048	TC-47B-30-DK	USAAF	44-76716	1
33054	TC-47B-30-DK	USAAF	44-76722	1
33061	TC-47B-30-DK	USAAF	44-76729	1
33066	TC-47B-30-DK	USAAF	44-76734	1
33071	TC-47B-30-DK	USAAF	44-76739	1
33076	TC-47B-30-DK	USAAF	44-76744	1
33080	TC-47B-30-DK	USAAF	44-76748	1
33085	TC-47B-30-DK	USAAF	44-76753	1
33090	TC-47B-30-DK	USAAF	44-76758	1
33095	TC-47B-30-DK	USAAF	44-76763	1
33100	TC-47B-30-DK	USAAF	44-76768	1
33105	TC-47B-30-DK	USAAF	44-76773	1
33110	TC-47B-30-DK	USAAF	44-76778	1
33121	TC-47B-30-DK	USAAF	44-76789	1
33126	TC-47B-30-DK	USAAF	44-76794	1
33133	TC-47B-30-DK	USAAF	44-76801	1
33144	TC-47B-30-DK	USAAF	44-76812	1
33155	TC-47B-30-DK	USAAF	44-76823	1
33160	TC-47B-30-DK	USAAF	44-76828	1
33170	TC-47B-30-DK	USAAF	44-76838	1
33180	TC-47B-30-DK	USAAF	44-76848	1
33186	TC-47B-30-DK	USAAF	44-76854	1
33192	TC-47B-30-DK	USAAF	44-76860	1
33201	TC-47B-35-DK	USAAF	44-76869	1
33206	TC-47B-35-DK	USAAF	44-76874	1
33216	TC-47B-35-DK	USAAF	44-76884	1
33227	TC-47B-35-DK	USAAF	44-76895	1
33232	TC-47B-35-DK	USAAF	44-76900	1
33241	TC-47B-35-DK	USAAF	44-76909	1
33251	TC-47B-35-DK	USAAF	44-76919	1
33256	TC-47B-35-DK	USAAF	44-76924	1
33267	TC-47B-35-DK	USAAF	44-76935	1
33275	TC-47B-35-DK	USAAF	44-76943	1
33283	TC-47B-35-DK	USAAF	44-76951	1
33291	TC-47B-35-DK	USAAF	44-76959	1
33299	TC-47B-35-DK	USAAF	44-76967	1
33305	TC-47B-35-DK	USAAF	44-76973	1
33314	TC-47B-35-DK	USAAF	44-76982	1
33322	TC-47B-35-DK	USAAF	44-76990	1
33329	TC-47B-35-DK	USAAF	44-76997	1
33337	TC-47B-35-DK	USAAF	44-77005	1
33345	TC-47B-35-DK	USAAF	44-77013	1
33351	TC-47B-35-DK	USAAF	44-77019	1
33359	TC-47B-35-DK	USAAF	44-77027	1
33367	TC-47B-35-DK	USAAF	44-77035	1
			Subtotal TC-47B-DK	133

fsn	Model	Client		No
3256	C-48-DO	USAAF	41-7681	1
4146/4148	C-48A-DO	USAAF	41-7682/41-7684	3
4170/4172	C-48C-DO	DSC	42-38332/42-38334	3
4175/4176	C-48C-DO	DSC	42-38335 & 42-38336	2
4178	C-48C-DO	DSC	42-38337	1
4182	C-48C-DO	DSC	42-38338	1
			Subtotal C-48	11
3270/3274	C-49-DO	USAAF	41-7685/41-7689	5
3297	C-49-DO	USAAF	41-7694	1
3282	C-49A-DO	USAAF	41-7690	1
4094/4096	C-49B-DO	USAAF	41-7691/41-7693	3
3280	C-49D-DO	USAAF	42-65584	1
4814/4815	C-49C-DO	USAAF	41-7715 & 41-7721	2
4141/4145	C-49D-DO	USAAF	41-7716/41-7720	5
4987/4992	C-49J-DO	USAAF	43-1962/43-1967	6
4993/4995	C-49J-DO	USAAF	43-1969/43-1971	3
4996	C-49J-DO	USAAF	43-1961	1
4997	C-49J-DO	USAAF	43-1968	1
4998	C-49J-DO	USAAF	43-1974	1
4999	C-49J-DO	USAAF	43-1979	1
5000	C-49J-DO	USAAF	43-1982	1
6259/6261	C-49J-DO	USAAF	43-1983/43-1985	3
6262	C-49J-DO	USAAF	43-1987	1
6263/6264	C-49J-DO	USAAF	43-1980 & 43-1981	2
6313/6314	C-49J-DO	USAAF	43-1972 & 43-1973	2
6315/6318	C-49J-DO	USAAF	43-1975/43-1978	4
6319/6323	C-49J-DO	USAAF	43-1990/43-1994	5
6342	C-49J-DO	USAAF	43-1986	1
6343/6344	C-49J-DO	USAAF	43-1988 & 43-1989	2
4982/4986	C-49K-DO	USAAF	43-1995/43-1999	5
6324	C-49K-DO	USAAF	43-2012	1
6325/6336	C-49K-DO	USAAF	43-2000/43-2011	12
6337/6341	C-49K-DO	USAAF	43-2013/43-2017	5
			Subtotal C-49	75
4119/4122	C-50-DO	USAAF	41-7697/41-7700	4
4804/4805	C-50A-DO	USAAF	41-7710 & 41-7711	2
4109/4111	C-50B-DO	USAAF	41-7703/41-7705	3
4083	C-50C-DO	USAAF	41-7695	1
4084	C-50D-DO	USAAF	41-7696	1
4131	C-50D-DO	USAAF	41-7709	1
4134/4135	C-50D-DO	USAAF	41-7712 & 41-7713	2
			Subtotal C-50	14
3289	C-51-DO	USAAF	41-7702	1
			Subtotal C-51	1
4112	C-52-DO	USAAF	41-7708	1
4813	C-52A-DO	USAAF	41-7714	1
4127/4128	C-52B-DO	USAAF	41-7706 & 41-7707	2
4136	C-52C-DO	USAAF	41-7701	1
			Subtotal C-52	5
4810	C-53-DO	USAAF	41-20045	1
4816/4906	C-53-DO	USAAF	41-20046/41-20136	91
4907/4956	C-53-DO	USAAF	42-6455/42-6504	50
4960/4961	C-53-DO	USAAF	43-14404 & 43-14405	2
7313/7324	C-53-DO	USAAF	42-47371/42-47382	12
7325/7364	C-53-DO	USAAF	42-15530/42-15569	40
7387/7411	C-53-DO	USAAF	42-15870/42-15894	25
4964/4967	C-53C-DO	USAAF	43-2018/43-2021	4
4969/4976	C-53C-DO	USAAF	43-2025/43-2032	8
4978/4980	C-53C-DO	USAAF	43-2022/43-2024	3
6346/6347	C-53C-DO	USAAF	43-2033 & 43-2034	2
11620/11778	C-53D-DO	USAAF	42-68693/42-68851	159
			Subtotal C-53	397
4173/4174	C-68-DO	USAAF	42-14297 & 42-14298	2
			Subtotal C-68	2
34129/34132	C-117A-1-DK	USAAF	45-2545/45-2548	4
34136	C-117A-1-DK	USAAF	45-2550	1
34133	C-117A-5-DK	USAAF	45-2549	1
34145	C-117A-1-DK	USAAF	45-2551	1
34168	C-117A-1-DK	USAAF	45-2552	1
34191	C-117A-1-DK	USAAF	45-2553	1
34212	C-117A-1-DK	USAAF	45-2554	1
34234	C-117A-1-DK	USAAF	45-2555	1
34250	C-117A-1-DK	USAAF	45-2556	1
34264	C-117A-1-DK	USAAF	45-2557	1

CCCP-H-205, the first DF-195, in Santa Monica Bay. (Douglas)

fsn	Model	Client		No
34278	C-117A-1-DK	USAAF	45-2558	1
34291	C-117A-1-DK	USAAF	45-2559	1
34305	C-117A-1-DK	USAAF	45-2560	1
34318	C-117A-1-DK	USAAF	45-2561	1
			Subtotal C-117	17
4204	R4D-1	USN	3131	1
4222/4229	R4D-1	USN	3132/3139	8
4280/4283	R4D-1	USN	3140/3143	4
4284	R4D-1	USN	4692	1
4300/4306	R4D-1	USN	4693/4699	7
4360/4366	R4D-1	USN	4700/4706	7
4367/4368	R4D-1	USN	01648 & 01649	2
4433/4441	R4D-1	USN	01977/01985	9
4550/4554	R4D-1	USN	01986/01990	5
4555/4557	R4D-1	USN	05051/05053	3
4654/4661	R4D-1	USN	05054/05061	8
4754/4764	R4D-1	USN	05062/05072	11
4097/4098	R4D-2	USN	4707 & 4708	2
4962	R4D-4	USN	07000	1
6345	R4D-4	USN	07001	1
6348/6349	R4D-4	USN	07002 & 07003	2
6350/6355	R4D-4	USN	33815/33820	6
			Subtotal R4D	78

DOUGLAS DF
(Number built: 4)

fsn	Model	Client		No
–	DF-151	Japan	J-ANES & J-ANET	2
–	DF-195	USSR	CCCP-H-205 & CCP-H-206	2
			Subtotal	4

DOUGLAS DC-4E
(Number built: 1)

fsn	Model	Client		No
1601	DC-4	Douglas	NX18100	1

The Pratt & Whitney Twin Hornet *engines of the DC-4E, NX18100, fsn 1601, are being warmed up before a night flight.* (Douglas)

The first DC-5, fsn 411, was built in the El Segundo plant. It is shown in its initial configuration without tailplane dihedral. (Douglas)

DOUGLAS DC-5 and derivatives
(Number built: 12)

fsn	Model	Client		No
* 411	DC-5	Douglas	NX21701	1
* 422/423	DC-5-518	Penn Central	Not completed	–
* 424	DC-5-510	KLM (West Indies)	PJ-AIW	1
* 425	DC-5-535	SCADTA (Colombia)	Not completed	–
* 426	DC-5-535	KLM (West Indies)	PJ-AIZ	1
* 427	DC-5-518	Penn Central	Not completed	–
* 428	DC-5-511	KNILM	PK-ADB	1
* 429	DC-5-518	Penn Central	Not completed	–
* 430	DC-5-511	KNILM	PK-ADA	1
			Subtotal DC-5	5
* 606/608	R3D-1	USN	1901/1903	3
* 609/612	R3D-2	USMC	1904/1907	4
			Subtotal R3D	7

Built in Santa Monica as a C-54B-10-DO (43-17149, fsn 18349), this DC-4 went directly to American Airlines in August 1944. It became G-ARWI of Lloyd International in January 1964. (Jacques Guillem collection)

DOUGLAS DC-4 SKYMASTER and derivatives
(Number built: 1,244 by Douglas and 71 under license by Canadair)

fsn	Model	Client		No
3050	C-54-DO	USAAF	41-20137	1
3051/3052	C-54-DO	USAAF	41-20139 & 42-20140	2
3053	C-54-DO	USAAF	41-20144	1
3060	C-54-DO	USAAF	41-20138	1
3061/3062	C-54-DO	USAAF	41-20141 & 41-20142	2
3063	C-54-DO	USAAF	41-20145	1
3075	C-54-DO	USAAF	41-20143	1
3111/3125	C-54-DO	USAAF	42-32936/42-32950	15
			Subtotal C-54-DO	24
3054/3059	C-54A-DO	USAAF	41-37268/41-37273	6
3064/3074	C-54A-DO	USAAF	41-37274/41-37284	11
3076/3110	C-54A-DO	USAAF	41-37285/41-37319	35
7445/7464	C-54A-1-DO	USAAF	42-107426/42-107445	20
7465/7489	C-54A-5-DO	USAAF	42-107446/42-107470	25
			Subtotal C-54A-DO	97
10270/10279	C-54A-1-DC	USAAF	42-72165/42-72174	10
10280/10304	C-54A-5-DC	USAAF	42-72175/42-72199	25
10305/10344	C-54A-10-DC	USAAF	42-72200/42-72239	40
10345/10424	C-54A-15-DC	USAAF	42-72240/42-72319	80
			Subtotal C-54A-DC	155
18324/18326	C-54B-1-DO	USAAF	43-17124/43-17126	3
18327/18348	C-54B-5-DO	USAAF	43-17127/43-17148	22
18349/18373	C-54B-10-DO	USAAF	43-17149/43-17173	25
18374/18398	C-54B-15-DO	USAAF	43-17174/43-17198	25
27227/27251	C-54B-20-DO	USAAF	44-9001/44-9025	25
			Subtotal C-54B-DO	100
10425/10544	C-54B-1-DC	USAAF	42-72320/42-72439	120
			Subtotal C-54B-DC	120
22149/22203	C-54D-15-DO	USAAF	43-17199/43-17253	55
			Subtotal C-54D-DO	55
10545/10644	C-54D-1-DC	USAAF	42-72440/42-72539	100
10645/10744	C-54D-5-DC	USAAF	42-72540/42-72639	100
10745/10844	C-54D-10-DC	USAAF	42-72640/42-72739	100
10845/10869	C-54D-15-DC	USAAF	42-72740/42-72764	25
			Subtotal C-54D-DC	325
27252/27276	C-54E-1-DO	USAAF	44-9026/44-9050	25
27277/27301	C-54E-5-DO	USAAF	44-9051/44-9075	25
27302/27326	C-54E-10-DO	USAAF	44-9076/44-9100	25

fsn	Model	Client		No
27327/27371	C-54E-15-DO	USAAF	44-9101/44-9145	45
27372/27376	C-54E-20-DO	USAAF	44-9146/44-9150	5
			Subtotal C-54E-DO	125
35929/35978	C-54G-1-DO	USAAF	45-476/45-525	50
35979/36028	C-54G-5-DO	USAAF	45-526/45-575	50
36029/36078	C-54G-10-DO	USAAF	45-576/45-625	50
36079/36090	C-54G-15-DO	USAAF	45-626/45-637	12
			Subtotal C-54G-DO	162
36327	XC-114-DO	USAAF	45-874	1
			Subtotal XC-114-DO	1
36328	YC-116-DO	USAAF	45-875	1
			Subtotal YC-116-DO	1
42904	DC-4-1009	Western	NC10201	1
42905	DC-4-1009	SILA	SE-BBA	1
42906	DC-4-1009	SABENA	OO-CBD	1
42907	DC-4-1009	National	NC33679	1
42908	DC-4-1009	KLM	PH-TAT	1
42909	DC-4-1009	Air France	F-BBDA	1
42910	DC-4-1009	ANA	VH-ANA	1
42911	DC-4-1009	Northwest	NC6402	1
42912	DC-4-1009	Air France	F-BBDB	1
42913/42914	DC-4-1009	Northwest	NC6403 & NC6404	2
42915	DC-4-1009	Waterman AL	NC33691	1
42916	DC-4-1009	ANA	VH-ANE	1
42917/42918	DC-4-1009	Western	NC10202 & NC10203	2
42919/42922	DC-4-1009	National	NC33680/NC33683	4
42923/42925	DC-4-1009	KLM	PH-TAR, -TAS, -TAP	3
42926/42927	DC-4-1009	SILA	SE-BBC & SE-BBD	2
42928/42930	DC-4-1009	ABA	SE-BBE/SE-BBG	3
42931	DC-4-1009	DDL	OY-DFI	1
42932/42933	DC-4-1009	SABENA	OO-CBE & OO-CBF	2
42934	DC-4-1009	SAA	ZS-AUA	1
42935/42943	DC-4-1009	Air France	F-BBDC/F-BBDK	9
42948/42950	DC-4-1009	ANA	VH-ANB/VH-AND	3
42951/42952	DC-4-1009	Iberia	EC-DAO & EC-DAP	2
42982/42983	DC-4-1009	Western	NC10204 & NC10205	2
42984/42985	DC-4-1009	SAA	ZS-AUB & ZS-AUC	2
42986	DC-4-1009	SABENA	OO-CBG	1
42987	DC-4-1009	DDL	OY-DFO	1
42988	DC-4-1009	Iberia	EC-DAQ	1
42989/42992	DC-4-1009	Air France	F-BBDL/F-BBDO	4
42993/42994	DC-4-1009	DNL	LN-IAD & LN-IAE	2
42995/42996	DC-4-1009	KLM	PH-TCE & PH-TCF	2
43065/43068	DC-4-1009	TAA	VH-TAA/VH-TAD	4
43071	DC-4-1009	National	NC37684	1
43072	DC-4-1009	Swissair	HB-ILA	1
43093	DC-4-1009	Swissair	HB-ILE	1
43094	DC-4-1009	Aramco	NC1625	1
43095/43096	DC-4-1009	SABENA	OO-CBH & OO-CBI	2
43097/43098	DC-4-1009	Swissair	HB-ILI & HB-ILO	2
43099/43101	DC-4-1009	SABENA	OO-CBP/OO-CBR	3
43102	DC-4-1009	National	NC74685	1
43155/43157	DC-4-1009	SAA	ZS-BMF/ZS-BMH	3
			Subtotal DC-4-1009	79

DOUGLAS DC-6 and derivatives

(Number built: 704)

fsn	Model	Client		No
36326	XC-112A-DO	USAAF	45-873	1
			Subtotal XC-112	1
42881	VC-118-DO	USAAF	46-505	1
			Subtotal VC-118	1
43565/43582	C-118A-DO	USAF	51-3818/51-3835	18
44594/44676	C-118A-DO	USAF	53-3223/53-3305	83
			Subtotal C-118A	101
43206/43210	R6D-1	USN	128423/128427	5
43401/43405	R6D-1	USN	128428/128432	5
43517	R6D-1	USN	128433	1
43670/43723	R6D-1	USN	131567/131620	54
			Subtotal R6D-1	65

fsn	Model	Client		No
42854/42865	DC-6	American	N90701/N90712	12
42866/42875	DC-6	United	N37501/N37510	10
42876/42878	DC-6	Panagra	N90876/N90878	3
42879/42880	DC-6	American	N90713/N90714	2
42882/42896	DC-6	American	N90715/N90729	15
42897/42899	DC-6	Delta	N1903M/N1905M	3
42900	DC-6	KLM	PH-TPW	1
42902/42903	DC-6	PAL	PI-C 293 & PI-C 294	2
43000/43024	DC-6	United	N37511/N37535	25
43025/43029	DC-6	United	N37537/N37541	5
43030/43034	DC-6	FAMA	LV-ADR/LV-ADV	5
43035/43054	DC-6	American	N90730/N90749	20
43055/43058	DC-6	National	N90891/N90894	4
43059/43060	DC-6	PAL	PI-C 290 & PI-C 291	2
43061	DC-6	United	N37536	1
43062/43064	DC-6	Sabena	OO-AWA/OO-AWC	3
43103/43104	DC-6	Panagra	N8103H & N8104H	2
43105/43110	DC-6	Braniff	N90881/N90886	6
43111/43112	DC-6	KLM	PH-TPJ & PH-TKW	2
43114/43118	DC-6	KLM	PH-TPJ, -TPM, -TPT, -TPB & -TPP	5
43119/43128	DC-6	ABA (SAS)	SE-BDA/SE-BDI	10
43129/43131	DC-6	SILA (SAS)	SE-BDL/SE-BDM & SE-BDO	3
43132/43133	DC-6	DDL (SAS)	OY-AAE & OY-AAF	2
43134/43135	DC-6	DNL (SAS)	LN-LAG & LN-LAH	2
43136	DC-6	FAMA	LV-ADW	1
43137	DC-6	American	N90750	1
43138	DC-6	PAL	PI-C 292	1
43139/43140	DC-6	Delta	N1901M & N1902M	2
43141	DC-6	Panagra	N6141C	1
43142	DC-6	Delta	N1906M	1
43143/43147	DC-6	United	N37542/N37546	5
43148/43149	DC-6	Sabena	OO-AWU & OO-AWW	2
43150/43151	DC-6	National	N90895 & N90896	2
43152	DC-6	LAI	I-LIKE	1
43211/43213	DC-6	Mexicana	XA-JOR/XA-JOT	3
43214	DC-6	National	N90897	1
43215/43217	DC-6	LAI	I-LUCK, -LADY & -LOVE	3
43218	DC-6	National	N90898	1
43219	DC-6	Delta	N1907M	1
			Subtotal DC-6	171
42901	DC-6A	Douglas	N30006	1
43296/43297	DC-6A	Slick	N90807 & N90808	2
43817/43819	DC-6A	Slick	N90809/N90811	3
43839/43841	DC-6A	American	N90776/N90778	3
43839/43841	DC-6A	American	N90776/N90778	3
44063/44064	DC-6A	Can Pacific	CF-CUS & CF-CUT	2
44069/44075	DC-6A	Flying Tiger	N34953/N34959	7
44076	DC-6A	KLM	PH-TGA	1
44257	DC-6A	KLM	PH-TGB	1
44258/44260	DC-6A	Pan American	N6258C/N6260C	3
44420/44421	DC-6A	Sabena	OO-CTO & OO-CTP	2
44677/44678	DC-6A	Flying Tiger	N34953 & N34954	2
44889	DC-6A	Airwork	G-AOFX	1
44890	DC-6A	Northwest	N571	1
44905/44909	DC-6A	United	N37590/N37594	5
44914/44917	DC-6A	American	N90779/N90782	4
45058	DC-6A	Airwork	G-AOFY	1
45110	DC-6A	Slick	N6815C	1
45226/45227	DC-6A	Trans Caribbean	N6538C & N6539C	2
45243	DC-6A	Slick	N6118C	1
45368/45369	DC-6A	Trans Caribbean	N6540C & N6541C	2
45372	DC-6A	Riddle	N7780B	1
45373/45375	DC-6A	American	N90783/N90785	3
45457	DC-6A	Slick	N7818C	1
45458	DC-6A	Belgian Air Force	OT-CDA	1
45474/45476	DC-6A	Overseas National	N630NA, N640NA & N650NA	3
45480/45481	DC-6A	Los Angeles Air Service	N6579C & N6580C	2
45497	DC-6A	Maritime Central	CF-MCK	1
45498/45500	DC-6A	Can Pacific	CF-CZZ, CF-CPB & CF-CPF	3
45503/45504	DC-6A	Nevada Aero Transport	N6575C & N6576C	2
45517/45520	DC-6A	Slick	N6119C & N7820C/N7822C	4
45521/45522	DC-6A	United	N37595 & N37596	2
45527/45530	DC-6A	Loide Aereo Nacional	PP-LFA/PP-LFD	4
45531/45532	DC-6A	Hunting Clan	G-APNO & G-APNP	2
45551	DC-6A	Swissair	HB-IBB	1
			Subtotal DC-6A	78
43257/43262	DC-6B	United	N37547/N37552	6
43263/43273	DC-6B	American	N90751/N90761	11
43274/43275	DC-6B	Swissair	HB-IBA & HB-IBE	2
43276	DC-6B	United	N37555	1
43291/43292	DC-6B	United	N37553 & N37554	2

Delivered to Japan Air Lines in September 1954, this DC-6B was sold to Faucett *12 years later. It was photographed at Lima in 1977 with its Peruvian registration, OB-R-846.* (René J. Francillon)

fsn	Model	Client		No
43298/43300	DC-6B	United	N37556/N37558	3
43518/43535	DC-6B	Pan American	N6518C/N6535C	18
43536/43537	DC-6B	Panagra	N6536C & N6537C	2
43538/43542	DC-6B	United	N37559/N37563	5
43543/43544	DC-6B	American	N90765 & N90766	2
43545/43547	DC-6B	American	N90762/N90764	3
43548/43549	DC-6B	SAS	OY-KMA & LN-LML	2
43550/43551	DC-6B	KLM	PH-TFH & PH-TFI	2
43552/43556	DC-6B	KLM	PH-TFK/PH-TFO	5
43557/43558	DC-6B	PAL	PI-C 295 & PI-C 296	2
43559/43560	DC-6B	Aramco	N708A & N709A	2
43561/43563	DC-6B	United	N37564/N37566	3
43564	DC-6B	American	N90767	1
43738/43743	DC-6B	National	N8221H/N8226H	6
43744/43749	DC-6B	SAS	OY-KME, LN-LMO, LN-LMP,	
			SE-BDP, SE-BDR, & SE-BDS	6
43750	DC-6B	Swissair	HB-IBI	1
43820/43821	DC-6B	National	N8227H & N8228H	2
43822/43826	DC-6B	Western	N91302/N91306	5

Built as a C-47B-15-DK, fsn 26668 was delivered to the USN as a R4D-6. It was rebuilt as an R4D-8 in 1952. (Norm Taylor)

fsn	Model	Client		No
43827/43832	DC-6B	Sabena	OO-SDF, OO-SDH, OO-CTH, OO-CTI, OO-CTK & OO-CTL	6
43833/43835	DC-6B	TAI	F-BGOB/F-BGOC	3
43836/43837	DC-6B	Mexicana	XA-KIQ & XA-KIR	2
43838	DC-6B	Pan American	N6538C	1
43842/43844	DC-6B	Can Pacific	CF-CUO/CF-CUQ	3
43845/43847	DC-6B	American	N90768/N90770	3
44056/44060	DC-6B	American	N90771/N90775	5
44061	DC-6B	Pan American	N4061K	1
44062	DC-6B	Can Pacific	CF-CUR	1
44080/44081	DC-6B	United	N37567 & N37568	2
44082/44083	DC-6B	Continental	N90960 & N90962	2
44087/44089	DC-6B	Swissair	HB-IBO, -IBU & -IBZ	3
44102	DC-6B	Pan American	N8102H	1
44103/44117	DC-6B	Pan American	N6103C/N6117C	15
44118/44121	DC-6B	Pan American	N5118V/N5121V	4
44165/44170	DC-6B	SAS	SE-BDT, OY-KMI, LN-LMS,	
			SE-BDU, OY-KMU & LN-LMT	6
44175/44176	DC-6B	Sabena	OO-CTM & OO-CTN	2
44251/44254	DC-6B	Alitalia	I-DIMA, -DIME, -DIMI & -DIMO	4
44255/44256	DC-6B	Panagra	N6255C & N6256C	2
44417/44419	DC-6B	LAI	I-LYNX, -LINE & -LAND	3
44424/44428	DC-6B	Pan American	N5024K/N5028K	5
44429/44431	DC-6B	Western	N91307/N91309	3
44432/44433	DC-6B	Japan AL	JA6205 & JA6206	2
44434	DC-6B	Western	N91310	1
44687/44688	DC-6B	Trans American	N6120C & N6121C	2
44689	DC-6B	Continental	N90961	1
44690/44692	DC-6B	LAN-Chile	CC-LDD/CC-LDF	3
44693/44694	DC-6B	ANA	VH-INH & VH-INU	2
44695	DC-6B	Sabena	OO-SDQ	1
44696/44697	DC-6B	TAI	F-BHEE & F-BHEF	2
44698/44699	DC-6B	Northwest	N569/N570	2
44871	DC-6B	UAT	F-BGSN	1
44888	DC-6B	Alitalia	I-DIMU	1
44891/44892	DC-6B	Can Pacific	CF-CZE & CF-CZF	2
44893/44902	DC-6B	United	N37569/N37578	10
44913	DC-6B	Alitalia	I-DIMB	1
45059	DC-6B	Aramco	N710A	1
45060	DC-6B	Western	N93117	1
45063/45067	DC-6B	Western	N93111/N93112 & N93114/N93116	5
45075	DC-6B	LAI	I-LEAD	1
45076/45077	DC-6B	ANA	VH-INS/VH-INT	2
45078/45079	DC-6B	Can Pacific	CF-CZQ & CF-CZR	2
45107/45109	DC-6B	Trans American	N3022C/N3024C	3
45131/45137	DC-6B	United	N37579/N37585	7
45173/45179	DC-6B	Western	N93118/N93124	7
45197/45202	DC-6B	Northwest	N572/N577	6
45216/45225	DC-6B	Northeast	N6580C/N6589C	10
45319/45320	DC-6B	Northwest	N578 & N579	2
45321/45324	DC-6B	Western	N93125/N93128	4
45326/45329	DC-6B	Can Pacific	CF-CZS/CF-CZV	4
45472/45473	DC-6B	Trans American	N3025C & N3026C	2
45478/45479	DC-6B	UAT	F-BIAM & F-BIAO	2
45491/45494	DC-6B	United	N37586/N37589	4
45496	DC-6B	Cathay Pacific	VR-HFK	1
45501/45502	DC-6B	Northwest	N581 & N582	2
45505	DC-6B	Can Pacific	CF-CZY	1
45506	DC-6B	Maritime Central	CF-MCL	1
45513/45516	DC-6B	LAN-Chile	CC-CCG/CC-CCJ	4
45523/45524	DC-6B	Ethiopian	ET-T-25 & ET-T-26	2
45533	DC-6B	Ethiopian	ET-T-27	1
45534/45538	DC-6B	Western	N93129/N93133	5
45539/45540	DC-6B	Olympic	SX-DAD & SX-DAE	2
45543	DC-6B	Olympic	SX-DAF	1
45544	DC-6B	Douglas	N6574C	1
45550	DC-6B	CAT	B-1006	1
45563/45564	DC-6B	JAT	YU-AFA & YU-AFB	2
			Subtotal DC-6B	287

DOUGLAS SUPER DC-3
(Number built: 105)

fsn	Model	Client		No
43158/43159	DC-3S	Douglas	N30000 & N15579	2
43191/43193	DC-3S	Capital	N16019, N16016 & N16012	3
			Subtotal DC-3S	5
43301/43400	R4D-8	USN	Retained their original BuNos	100
			Subtotal R4D-8	100

DOUGLAS DC-7

(Number built: 338)

fsn	Model	Client		No
44122/44146	DC-7	American	N301AA/N325AA	25
44171/44174	DC-7	National	N8205H/N8208H	4
44261/44264	DC-7	Delta	N4871C/N4874C	4
44265/44289	DC-7	United	N6301C/N6325C	25
44679/44684	DC-7	Delta	N4875C/64880C	6
44903/44904	DC-7	United	N6326C & N6327C	2
45098/45106	DC-7	American	N326AA/N334AA	9
45142/45156	DC-7	United	N6328C/N6342C	15
45356/45361	DC-7	United	N6343C/N6348C	6
45482/45490	DC-7	United	N6349C/N6357C	9
			Subtotal DC-7	105
44435	DC-7B	Douglas	N70D	1
44700/44704	DC-7B	Panagra	N51700/N51704	5
44852/44863	DC-7B	Eastern	N801D/N812D	12
44864/44870	DC-7B	Pan American	N771PA, N777PA & N772PA/N776PA	7
44910/44912	DC-7B	SAA	ZS-DKD/ZS-DKF	3
44921/44925	DC-7B	American	N381AA, N385AA, N387AA, N390AA & N394AA	5
45082/45089	DC-7B	Eastern	N813D/N820D	8
45192	DC-7B	Continental	N8210H	1
45193/45196	DC-7B	Continental	N8210H/N8213H	4
45232/45239	DC-7B	American	N335AA/N342AA	8
45244	DC-7B	Panagra	N51244	1
45311/45314	DC-7B	Delta	N4882C/N4885C	4
45330/45349	DC-7B	Eastern	N821D/N840D	20
45350/45355	DC-7B	Delta	N4886C/N4891D	6
45362/45365	DC-7B	National	N6201B/N6204B	4
45397/45407	DC-7B	American	N344AA/N350AA, N357AA, N359AA, N362AA & N365AA	11
45447/45456	DC-7B	Eastern	N841D/N850D	10
45477	DC-7B	SAA	ZS-DKG	1
45525	DC-7B	Continental	N8214H	1
			Subtotal DC-7B	112

fsn	Model	Client		No
44872	DC-7C	Douglas	N70C	1
44873/44887	DC-7C	Pan American	N731PA/N745PA	15
44926/44933	DC-7C	SAS	OY-KNA, LN-MOB, SE-CCA, OY-KNB, LN-MOD, SE-CCB, OY-KNC & LN-MOE	8
45061/45062	DC-7C	Swissair	HB-IBK & HB-IBL	2
45068/45074	DC-7C	Braniff	N5900/N5906	7
45090/45097	DC-7C	Pan American	N746PA/N753PA	8
45111/45120	DC-7C	BOAC	G-AOIA/G-AOIJ	10
45121	DC-7C	Pan American	N754PA	1
45122	DC-7C	Panair do Brasil	PP-PDL	1
45123	DC-7C	Pan American	N755PA	1
45124/45125	DC-7C	Panair do Brasil	PP-PDM & PP-PDN	2
45127/45130	DC-7C	Mexicana	XA-LOB/XA-LOE	4
45157/45162	DC-7C	Sabena	OO-SFA/OO-SFF	6
45180/45189	DC-7C	KLM	PH-DSA/PH-DSI & PH-DSK	10
45190/45191	DC-7C	Swissair	HB-IBM & HB-IBN	2
45203/45210	DC-7C	Northwest	N284/N291	8
45211/45215	DC-7C	SAS	OY-KND, LN-MOF & SE-CCD/SE-CCF	5
45228/45231	DC-7C	Alitalia	I-DUVA, -DUVE, -DUVI & -DUVO	4
45308/45310	DC-7C	Sabena	OO-SFG, -SFH & -SFJ	3
45325	DC-7C	SAS	SE-CCC	1
45366/45367	DC-7C	TAI	F-BIAP & F-BIAQ	2
45446	DC-7C	TAI	F-BIAR	1
45462/45467	DC-7C	Northwest	N292/N297	6
45468/45471	DC-7C	Japan Air Lines	JA6301/JA6303 & JA6305	4
45495	DC-7C	Sabena	OO-SFK	1
45541/45542	DC-7C	Alitalia	I-DUVU & I-DUVB	2
45545/45549	DC-7C	KLM	PH-DSM/PH-DSP & PH-DSR	5
45553	DC-7C	Swissair	HB-IBP	1
			Subtotal DC-7C	121

Registered F-BIAR and bearing fsn 45446, this DC-7C was delivered to Transports Aériens Intercontinentaux on 21 January 1953. TAI kept it in service for five years. (Paul Genest)

Douglas-built aircraft – Historical thumbnails

To complement the description and history of the Douglas piston-engined airliners found in the main text, brief details are given here on all the other types of aircraft built by the Douglas Aircraft Company, its forebears and its successors. In the case of aircraft built in numerous variants, the first flight dates quoted are those for the prototype of the first model.

Davis Douglas *Cloudster*

First flight: 24 February 1921, Goodyear Field, Los Angeles.
Number built: One by Davis-Douglas.
Type: Single-engined long-range record aircraft with fixed landing gear; later modified to transport passengers.
Background and significant events:
> The only aircraft built by the Davis-Douglas Company, *The Cloudster* had been planned to fly non-stop across the United States. After that attempt failed due to engine failure, it was modified to transport eight to ten passengers. It was destroyed in December 1926 after making an emergency landing on a beach near Enseñada, Mexico.

This overhead view of The Cloudster *shows the first Douglas in its original configuration.* (USN-NA)

Data for the aircraft as built

Dimensions: Span, 55ft 11in; length, 36ft 9in; height, 12ft.
Loaded weight: 9,600lb; power loading 24lb/hp.
Accommodation: Side-by-side seating for two in open cockpit.
Power Plant: One 400hp *Liberty* water-cooled engine driving a two-blade, fixed-pitch, wooden propeller.
Performance: Maximum speed at sea level, 120mph; cruising speed, 85mph; ceiling, 19,160ft; maximum range, 2,800 miles.

Douglas DT

First flight: November 1921, Goodyear Field, Los Angeles.
Number built: 46 by Douglas and 44 under license.
Type: Carrier-based or float-equipped torpedo-reconnaissance aircraft.

Background and significant events:

The single-seat DT-1 was followed at Douglas by 40 DT-2s for the US Navy, one DT-2B for Norway, and four DTBs for Peru. Six license-built DT-2Bs, re-engined with the 575hp Armstrong Siddeley *Panther II* radials, remained in Norwegian service until the German invasion in 1940.

Data for the DT-2 floatplane

Dimensions: Span, 50ft; length, 37ft 8in; height, 15ft 1in; wing area, 707sq ft.
Weights: Empty, 4,528lb; loaded, 7,293lb; wing loading, 10.3lb/sq ft; power loading, 16.2lb/hp.
Accommodation: Pilot and mechanic/gunner in tandem open cockpits.
Power Plant: One 400hp 12-cylinder *Liberty* water-cooled engine driving a two-blade, fixed-pitch wooden propeller.
Armament: One 1,835lb torpedo; provision for one flexible 0.30in machine gun in the rear cockpit.
Performance: Maximum speed at sea level, 99.5mph; service ceiling, 7,400ft; normal range, 274 miles.

The DT-1 was the first Douglas aircraft built for the USN. Intended to be embarked aboard the USS Langley (the first US carrier) or carried aboard seaplane tenders, it had manually-folded wings. (USN-NA)

Curtiss HS-2L modified by Douglas

Date: Modifications undertaken in 1922.
Number built: Two Boeing-built Curtiss HS-2L patrol flying boats modified by Douglas.
Type: Single-engine passenger transport flying boat.

Background and significant events:

At the request of Pacific Marine Airways, Douglas modified these two patrol flying boats into passenger transports. One had a six-seat open cabin in the forward portion of the hull, ahead of the cockpit; in the other, this passenger compartment was fully enclosed.

Data for the HS-2L as modified by Douglas

Dimensions: Span, 74ft 1in; length, 39ft; height, 14ft 7in; wing area, 803sq ft.
Weights: Take-off, 6,440lb; wing loading, 8.0lb/sqft; power loading, 18.4lb/hp.
Accommodation: Pilot and one passenger side-by-side in open cockpit; four passengers in an open (or enclosed) cabin forward of the cockpit.
Power Plant: One 350hp 12-cylinder *Liberty* water-cooled engine driving a four-blade, fixed-pitch wooden propeller.
Performance: Maximum speed at sea level, 82mph.

Two Boeing-built Curtiss HS-2Ls were modified by Douglas for Pacific Marine Airways and were used on the short overwater route from Los Angeles (Wilmington) to Santa Catalina Island. (USN-NA)

Douglas DWC & DOS

First flight: July 1923, Santa Monica.

Number built: Five DWCs and six DOSs by Douglas.

Type: Long-range record aircraft (DWC) and observation aircraft (DOS); fixed undercarriage or twin floats.

Background and significant events:

Two DWCs (*Douglas World Cruisers*) made the first flight around the world between 4 April and 28 September 1924, covering 28,950 miles in 371hr 7min flying time. Having to fly under widely differing atmospheric conditions, they were fitted with radiators of two sizes, one for use in cold weather, and the other in tropical conditions. The six DOSs (*Douglas Observation Seaplanes*) were essentially similar but had both smaller fuel tanks and provision for being armed with a pair of 0.30in flexible guns in the rear cockpit.

Data for the DWC fitted with floats

Dimensions: Span, 50ft; length, 39ft; height, 15ft 1in; wing area, 707sq ft.

Weights: Empty, 5,180lb; loaded, 7,795lb; wing loading, 11.0lb/sq ft; power loading, 18.6lb/hp.

Accommodation: Pilot and mechanic in tandem open cockpits.

Power Plant: One 400hp 12-cylinder *Liberty* water-cooled engine driving a two-blade, fixed-pitch, wooden propeller.

Performance: Maximum speed at sea level, 100mph; service ceiling, 7,000ft; maximum range, 1,650 miles.

Named Chicago, *serial number 23-1230 was one of the two* Douglas World Cruisers *that completed the first flight around the world in 1924. This photograph was taken 50 years later when it was rebuilt by the National Air and Space Museum.* (NA&SM)

Douglas C-1

First flight: 2 May 1925, Santa Monica.

Number built: 26 by Douglas.

Type: Single-engined military transport aircraft.

Background and significant events:

Two models of this transport aircraft, the first for the Air Service, were built. Seventeen C-1Cs had wings of increased span (60ft vs. 56ft 7in), an 8in longer fuselage, and redesigned vertical tail surfaces with a balanced rudder. The C-1 was used as a tanker during air refueling tests in 1929.

Data for the C-1C

Dimensions: Span, 60ft; length, 36ft; height, 14ft; wing area, 800sqft.

Weights: Empty, 3,900lb; loaded, 7,412lb; wing loading, 9.3lb/sqft; power loading, 17.0lb/hp.

Accommodation: Pilot and mechanic side-by-side in open cockpit; six to eight passengers, or 2,500lb of cargo, in an enclosed cabin.

Power Plant: One 435hp 12-cylinder *Liberty* water-cooled engine driving a two-blade, fixed-pitch, metal propeller.

Performance: Maximum speed at sea level, 121mph; cruising speed, 85mph; service ceiling, 15,950ft.

This C-1C (26-424) was assigned to March Field in California as the base transport. (Air Service)

Douglas Observation Biplanes (XO-2 through O-38 variants)

First flight: October 1924, Santa Monica.

Number built: 879 by Douglas and six under license.

Type: Most were built as observation aircraft but others were completed as attack aircraft (XA-2), record aircraft (O-2BS), basic/advanced trainers (BT-1 and BT-2), etc.

Background and significant events:
XO-2 prototypes were built with both *Liberty* and Packard 1A-1500 engines in response to an Air Service request for observation aircraft. The *Liberty*-powered model was retained for production in February 1925, starting a manufacturing program that only ended in 1936. Over the years, aircraft in this diversified family were also built with 600hp Curtiss *Conqueror* liquid-cooled engines (O-25 series) and various P&W *Hornet* and Wright *Cyclone* radials engines of up to 640hp (mostly for the O-2/O-38 series and export models).

BELOW *When radial engines (a Pratt & Whitney R-1690-3 for this O-38 of the Minnesota National Guard) replaced the ageing* Liberty *engines, the reliability of the Douglas observation biplanes increased markedly.* (Army Air Corps)

ABOVE *Using airframe and power plant similar to the O-2H observation aircraft, three O-2Js were unarmed aircraft used to transport VIPs (the Chief of Staff of the US Army in the case of this 26-420).* (Army Air Corps)

Data for the O-2H

Dimensions: Span 40ft 10in; length 30ft; height, 10ft; wing area, 362sq ft.

Weights: Empty, 2,857lb; loaded, 4,484lb; maximum; 4,550lb; wing loading, 12.4lb/sq ft; power loading, 10.3lb/hp.

Accommodation: Pilot and radio/gunner in tandem open cockpits.

Power Plant: One 435hp 12-cylinder *Liberty* water-cooled engine driving a two-blade, fixed-pitch, metal propeller.

Armament: One forward-firing 0.30in machine gun in the engine cowling and one flexible 0.30in gun in the rear cockpit.

Performance: Maximum speed at sea level, 134.5mph; cruising speed, 110mph; service ceiling, 16,900ft; normal range, 512 miles.

Data for the O-38

Dimensions: Span, 40ft; length, 31ft; height, 10ft 8in; wing area, 362sq ft.

Weights: Empty, 3,070lb; loaded, 4,343lb; maximum, 4,456lb; wing loading, 12.0lb/sq ft; power loading, 8.3lb/hp.

Accommodation: Pilot and navigator/mechanic in tandem open cockpits.

Power Plant: One 525hp Pratt & Whitney R-1690-3 seven-cylinder air-cooled radial driving a two-blade, fixed-pitch wooden propeller.

Armament: One forward-firing 0.30in machine gun in the engine cowling and one flexible 0.30in gun in the rear cockpit.

Performance: Maximum speed at sea level, 150mph; cruising speed, 120mph; service ceiling, 19,000ft; normal range, 275 miles.

Douglas Mailplanes (M series)

First flight: 6 July 1925, Santa Monica.
Number built: 59 by Douglas.
Type: Mail-carrying aircraft with possibility of carrying one or two passengers.
Background and significant events:

Developed from the military O-2 at the request of the US Post Office Department, the DAM-1 (Douglas Air Mail One) led to the production of improved M-2, M-3, and M-4 mailplanes with *Liberty* engines. The single M-4S was powered by a Pratt & Whitney *Wasp A* radial engine.

Data for the M-2

Dimensions: Span, 39ft 8in; length 28ft 11in; height, 10ft 1in; wing area, 411sq ft.
Weights: Empty, 2,885lb; loaded, 4,755lb; wing loading, 11.6lb/sq ft; power loading, 11.9lb/hp.
Accommodation: Pilot in open cockpit; two compartments between the engine and the cockpit for up to 1,000lb of mail or two passengers.
Power Plant: One 400hp 12-cylinder *Liberty* water-cooled engine driving a two-blade, fixed-pitch, metal propeller.
Performance: Maximum speed at sea level, 145mph; cruising speed, 118mph; service ceiling, 16,500ft; normal range, 700 miles.

This Douglas M-2, one of the six acquired by Western Air Express, was configured to transport mail in a compartment aft of the engine and a passenger. The pilot sat in the aft open cockpit. (Western Airlines)

Douglas *Commuter*

First flight: January 1926, Santa Monica.
Number built: One by Douglas.
Type: Two-seat touring monoplane.
Background and significant events:

Of modern appearance with its enclosed cockpit under the high-mounted wing, this light aircraft was well-designed but was not put into production.

Data for the *Commuter*

Dimensions: Span, 37ft 3in.
Accommodation: Pilot and passenger side-by-side in enclosed cockpit.
Power Plant: One 60hp Wright *Gale* three-cylinder radial driving a two-blade wooden propeller.
Performance: Maximum speed at sea level, 76mph.

First flown in January 1936, the Commuter *was a two-seat light aircraft powered by a Wright* Gale *three-cylinder radial engine.* (Douglas)

Douglas T2D & P2D

First flight: 27 January 1927, Santa Monica.
Number built: 30 by Douglas.
Type: Torpedo/bomber/maritime patrol aircraft with fixed undercarriage or twin floats.
Background and significant events:

The XT2D-1 was developed by Douglas from the XTN-1 designed at the Naval Aircraft Factory. Three prototypes were built in the Wilshire Boulevard plant with follow-on production in the Clover Field plant (nine T2D-1s and 18 P2D-1s). The latter were optimized for maritime patrol and differed externally in having twin tail vertical surfaces.

Data for the P2D-1 fitted with floats

Dimensions: Span, 57ft; length, 43ft 11in; height, 17ft 6in; wing area, 909sq ft.
Weights: Empty, 7,486lb; loaded 12,611lb; maximum, 13,052lb; wing loading, 13.9lb/sq ft; power loading, 11.0lb/hp.
Accommodation: Pilot and co-pilot/navigator side-by-side in open cockpit; two gunners in separate open stations.
Power Plant: Two 575hp Wright R-1820-E nine-cylinder radials driving three-blade, fixed-pitch propellers.
Armament: Two 0.30in flexible machine guns (one in the nose and one in the rear upper position); one torpedo or 1,500lb of bombs externally.
Performance: Maximum speed at sea level, 136mph; cruising speed, 108mph; service ceiling, 11,200ft; maximum range, 1,010 miles.

A Douglas P2D-1 of Patrol Squadron Three (VP-3) is shown flying over the Gatún locks on the Panama Canal. (Douglas)

Douglas DA-1

First flight: 7 September 1928, Santa Monica.
Number built: One by Douglas.
Type: Single-engine touring aircraft.
Background and significant events:

Second type of light aircraft designed by Douglas, this parasol monoplane was ordered by Ambassador Airways (hence its DA-1 designation). Following an engine failure, it was destroyed in a forced landing before delivery.

Data for the DA-1

Dimensions: Span, 35ft; length 22ft 6in; wing area, 212sq ft.
Weights: Empty, 1,750lb; loaded, 2,530lb; wing loading, 11.9lb/sq ft; power loading, 11.5lb/hp.
Accommodation: Pilot/instructor and passenger/trainee in tandem open cockpits.
Power Plant: One 220hp Wright J-5 *Whirlwind* nine-cylinder radial driving a two-blade, fixed-pitch propeller.
Performance: Maximum speed at sea level, 140mph; service ceiling, 14,500ft.

The two-seat Douglas DA-1 was built in 1928 for Ambassador Airways. (Douglas)

Douglas PD-1

First flight: May 1929, NAS North Island, San Diego.
Number built: 25 by Douglas.
Type: Twin-engine maritime patrol flying boat.
Background and significant events:
    The PD-1 was another aircraft designed at the Naval Aircraft factory and built by Douglas. Derived from the NAF-12, the PD-1s were in first line service until 1936 and remained as trainers until March 1939.

Data for the PD-1

Dimensions: Span, 72ft 10in; length, 49ft 2in; height, 16ft 4in; wing area, 1,162sq ft.
Weights: Empty, 7,453lb; loaded, 14,122lb; wing loading, 12.2lb/sq ft; power loading, 13.4lb/hp
Accommodation: Four crewmembers in separate open cockpits.
Power Plant: Two 525hp Wright R-1750-A nine-cylinder radials driving two-blade, fixed-pitch, wooden propellers.
Armament: Two 0.30in flexible machine guns (one in the nose and one in the rear upper position); 1,000lb of bombs or mines under the lower wing.
Performance: Maximum speed at sea level, 114mph; cruising speed, 94mph; service ceiling, 10,900ft; normal range, 1,310 miles.

This PD-1 of VP-7B was photographed taking-off from San Diego Bay on 15 September 1930. (USN-NA)

Douglas *Sinbad* & *Dolphin*

First flight: July 1930 (*Sinbad*), Santa Monica Bay.
Number built: 59 by Douglas.
Type: Transport flying boat (*Sinbad*) or multi-purpose amphibian (*Dolphin*).
Background and significant events:
    Named *Sinbad*, the prototype was a flying boat conceived as a 'flying yacht' for wealthy customers. 58 *Dolphins* were built in small lots to meet the needs of civil and military customers for amphibians for use as transports, sea rescue, or coastal patrol.

Data for the US Navy RD-3

Dimensions: Span, 60ft; length, 45ft 3in; height 15ft 2in; wing area, 592sq ft.
Weights: Empty, 6,764lb; loaded, 9,734lb; wing loading, 16.4lb/sq ft; power loading, 10.8lb/hp.
Accommodation: Two pilots and six to eight passengers in an enclosed cabin.
Power Plant: Two 450hp Pratt & Whitney R-1340-96 nine-cylinder radials driving two-blade, fixed-pitch, metal propellers.
Performance: Maximum speed at sea level, 149mph; cruising speed, 105mph; service ceiling, 15,100ft; normal range, 690 miles.

BuNo 9529, an RD-3 amphibian was photographed at Clover Field on 13 October 1934 just before its delivery to the USN. (Douglas)

Douglas Observation monoplanes (XO-31 through O-46A)

First flight: December 1930, Clover Field, Santa Monica.
Number built: 127 by Douglas (eight XO-31/YO-31Bs, 28 Y1O-43/O-43As, and 91 XO-46/O-46As).
Type: Observation monoplane with fixed undercarriage.
Background and significant events:

These aircraft were produced in three distinct series. The O-31s had gull wings with an upper mast and bracing wire tubular cabane for support; they were powered by Curtiss V-1750 inline engines. The O-43s retained this power plant, as well as the mast and bracing wire wing support, but had parasol wings. The O-46s had parasol wings with streamlined struts for lower support and were powered by radial engines. Assigned to National Guard units, the last O-46s remained in service until 1942.

Data for the O-46A

Dimensions: Span, 45ft 9in; length, 34ft 6¾in; height, 10ft 8⅛in; wing area, 332sq ft.
Weights: Empty, 4,776lb; loaded, 6,639lb; wing loading, 20.0lb/sq ft; power loading, 9.2lb/hp.
Accommodation: Pilot and observer/gunner in tandem under enclosed canopy.
Power Plant: One 725hp Pratt & Whitney R-1535-7 14-cylinder twin-row radial driving a three-blade, fixed-pitch, metal propeller.
Armament: Two wing-mounted forward-firing 0.30in machine guns and one flexible 0.30in machine gun in the rear cockpit.
Performance: Maximum speed, 200mph at 4,000ft; cruising speed, 171mph; service ceiling, 24,150ft; normal range, 435 miles.

This O-46A (35-1790) has been repainted by the staff of the Air Force Museum in the bright markings used by the Army Air Corps in the late 1930s. (USN-NA)

Douglas O-35 & B-7

First flight: June 1931, Clover Field, Santa Monica.
Number built: 14 by Douglas.
Type: Twin-engine observation aircraft (O-35) and light bomber (B-7).
Background and significant events:

The sole XO-35 was followed by the XB-7, seven Y1B-7s and five Y1O-35s. All had gull wings with underslung nacelles for both their Curtiss V-1570 engines and their retractable undercarriage.

Data for the Y1B-7

Dimensions: Span, 65ft; length, 45ft 11in; height, 11ft 7in; wing area, 621.2sq ft.
Weights: Empty, 5,519lb; loaded, 9,953lb; maximum, 11,177lb; wing loading, 16lb/sq ft; power loading, 7.4lb/hp.
Accommodation: Pilot, navigator/gunner, and gunner in three separate open cockpits.
Power Plant: Two 675hp Curtiss V-1570-53 12-cylinder liquid-cooled engines driving three-blade, fixed-pitch, metal propellers.
Armament: Two flexible 0.30in machine guns (one in the nose and one above the rear fuselage) and 1,200lb of bombs under the fuselage.
Performance: Maximum speed at sea level, 182mph; cruising speed, 158mph; service ceiling, 20,400ft; normal range, 410 miles; maximum range, 630 miles.

This Y1B-7 was assigned to the 88th Observation Squadron. (Douglas)

Douglas XT3D

First flight: August 1931, Clover Field, Santa Monica.
Number built: One by Douglas.
Type: Single-engined carrier-based torpedo bomber.
Background and significant events:

Conceived in 1930, the XT3D-1 was intended to replace torpedo bombers then embarked aboard USN aircraft carriers. Powered by a 575hp Pratt & Whitney *Hornet* S2B-1G radial and provided with open cockpits, the XT3D-1 did not meet performance requirements. It was not adopted by the Navy even after it had been rebuilt as the XT3D-2 with an 800hp Pratt & Whitney XR-1830-54 radial and separate canopies fitted over the cockpits.

Data for the XT3D-1

Dimensions: Span, 50ft; length 35ft 5in; height, 13ft 2½in; wing area, 624sq ft.
Weights: Empty, 4,238lb; loaded, 7,639lb; wing loading, 12.2lb/sq ft; power loading, 13.3lb/hp.
Accommodation: Bombardier/gunner, pilot, and rear gunner in three separate open cockpits.
Power Plant: One 575hp Pratt & Whitney *Hornet* S2B-1G nine-cylinder radial driving a two-blade, fixed-pitch, metal propeller.
Armament: Two flexible 0.30in machine guns (one in the nose and one in the rear cockpit) and one 1,835lb torpedo beneath the fuselage.
Performance: Maximum speed, 128mph at 6,000ft; service ceiling, 14,000ft; normal range, 560 miles.

The wings of the XT3D-1 were folded manually. (NMUSAF)

Douglas XFD-1

First flight: January 1933, Clover Field, Santa Monica.
Number built: One by Douglas.
Type: Single-engined, two-seat carrier-based fighter.
Background and significant events:

Flight-testing of the XFD-1 was fully satisfactory except for top speed that was slightly below specifications. However, the Navy did not order it into production as it had lost interest in using two-seat fighters.

Data for the XFD-1

Dimensions: Span 31ft 6in; length, 25ft 4in; height, 11ft 1in; wing area, 295sq ft.
Weights: Empty, 3,277lb; loaded, 4,672lb; maximum, 5,000lb; wing loading, 15.8lb/sq ft; power loading, 7.1lb/hp.
Accommodation: Pilot and gunner in tandem beneath a single canopy.
Power Plant: One 700hp Pratt & Whitney R-1535-64 14-cylinder radial driving a two-blade, fixed-pitch, metal propeller.
Armament: Two 0.30in fixed machine guns under the engine cowling and one flexible 0.30in machine gun firing aft and upward.
Performance: Maximum speed, 208mph at 2,000ft; cruising speed, 170mph; service ceiling 23,700ft; normal range, 575 miles.

The Douglas XFD-1, an experimental fighter biplane flown in 1933, should not be confused with the McDonnell XFD-1, the 1945 prototype of the Phantom *twinjet fighter.* (NA&SM)

Northrop *Gamma*

First flight: August 1932, Mines Field, Los Angeles.

Number built: 61 by Northrop (including 25 assembled in China).

Type: Single-engined aircraft adaptable to various roles; fixed undercarriage fitted to most aircraft with possibility of fitting skis or floats in the case of the *Gamma* 2B; retractable undercarriage for the *Gamma* 2J.

Background and significant events:

Using similar wings, the Gammas were powered by various engines and had fuselages adapted to their different uses. Five of the *Gammas*, the 2A, 2B, 2ED-C, 2G, and 2H, were built as record aircraft; three *Gamma* 2Ds were delivered as mail-planes; and the *Gamma* 2L was ordered to become a test bed for The Bristol Aeroplane Co. Finally, 49 *Gamma* 2Es, 2ECs, and 2EDs were built as attack aircraft for export to China.

Data for the *Gamma* 2D in postal configuration

Dimensions: Span, 47ft 9½in; length, 31ft 2in; height, 9ft; wing area, 363sq ft.

Weights: Empty, 4,119lb; loaded, 7,350lb; wing loading, 20.2lb/sq ft; power loading, 10.4lb/hp.

Accommodation: Pilot in enclosed cockpit; compartment for 1,400lb of mail located between the engine and the cockpit.

Power Plant: One 710hp Wright SR-1820-F3 nine-cylinder radial driving a two-blade, fixed-pitch metal propeller.

Performance: Maximum speed, 223mph at 6,300ft; cruising speed, 204mph; service ceiling, 23,400ft; maximum range, 1,970 miles.

The Northrop Gamma 2B, *fitted with twin floats, was photographed in Santa Monica Bay on 14 July 1934. In December 1935, flown by Herbert Hollick-Kenyon and Lincoln Ellsworth, the* Polar Star *became the first aircraft to fly across Antarctica.* (Douglas)

RIGHT *NR13758, one of the three* Gamma 2Ds *acquired by TWA, was modified to be used for experimental flights at high altitude.* (Douglas)

BELOW *The sole* Gamma 2J *was used by Douglas as a communication aircraft.* (Douglas)

Northrop *Delta*

First flight: May 1933, Mines Field, Los Angeles.
Number built: 13 by Northrop and 19 under license.
Type: Single-engined transport aircraft.
Background and significant events:

Planned as passenger transport aircraft, the *Delta* 1A through 1D-8 combined the wing of the *Gamma* with a new fuselage in which eight seats could be fitted (one on each side of the aisle). Built as a mail-plane, the *Delta* 1E had a fuselage similar to that of the *Gamma* 2D. Nineteen 1D-8s were built by Canadian Vickers in three versions and were used as for reconnaissance and light bombing; their undercarriage could be replaced by skis or floats.

Photographed at Mines Field before its delivery to Transcontinental and Western Air in August 1933, the Delta1A *was still carrying its 'X' for experimental registration.* (NA&SM)

Data for the *Delta* 1D-5

Dimensions: Span, 47ft 9in; length, 33ft 1in; height, 10ft 1in; wing area, 363sq ft.
Weights: Empty, 4,540lb; loaded, 7,350lb; wing loading, 20.2lb/sq ft; power loading, 10.0lb/hp.
Accommodation: Pilot and up to eight passengers in enclosed cabin.
Power Plant: One 735hp Wright SR-1820-F2 nine-cylinder radial driving a two-blade, fixed-pitch, metal propeller.
Performance: Maximum speed, 219mph at 6,300ft; cruising speed, 200mph; service ceiling, 20,000ft; maximum range, 1,650 miles.

Douglas DC-1

First flight: 1 July 1933, Clover Field, Santa Monica.
Number built: One by Douglas.

See Chapter 2.

Northrop XFT

First flight: 16 February 1934, Mines Field, Los Angeles.
Number built: One by Northrop.
Type: Single-seat carrier-based fighter.
Background and significant events:

The XFT-1 was ordered by the USN in May 1933. After its 625hp Wright R-1510-26 engine was replaced by a Pratt & Whitney R-1535-72 radial and its vertical tail surfaces had been enlarged, the aircraft was designated XFT-2. It crashed on 21 July 1936.

The Northrop XF-1 was photographed at Mines Field on 10 February 1934, six days before its first flight. (Douglas)

Data for the XFT-1

Dimensions: Span, 32ft; length, 21ft 11in; height, 9ft 5in; wing area, 177sq ft.
Weights: Empty, 2,469lb; loaded, 3,756lb; maximum, 4,003lb; wing loading, 21.2lb/sqft; power loading, 6.0lb/hp.
Accommodation: Pilot in enclosed cockpit.
Power Plant: One 625hp Wright R-1510-26 nine-cylinder radial driving a two-blade metal propeller with pitch adjustable on the ground only.
Armament: Two forward-firing 0.30in machine guns under the engine cowling.
Performance: Maximum speed, 235mph at 6,000ft; service ceiling, 26,500ft; maximum range, 975 miles.

Douglas DC-2 & military variants

First flight: 11 May 1934, Clover Field, Santa Monica.
Number built: 193 by Douglas and five under license.

See Chapter 3.

Douglas YOA-5 & XP3D

First flight: January 1935 YOA-5, Clover Field, Santa Monica.
Number built: One YOA-5 and one XP3D-1 by Douglas.
Type: Air-sea rescue amphibian (YOA-5) and maritime patrol flying boat (XP3D-1 and XP3D-2).
Background and significant events:

Douglas attempted to meet requirements from the Army Air Corps for an air-sea rescue amphibian and those from the Navy for a longer-ranged patrol flying boat with a common design. Even though it had set a world record, the YOA-5 was not ordered by the Air Corps while the Navy chose the Consolidated PBY-2 in preference to the more expensive XP3D-2 (designation given to the P3D-1 after it was rebuilt with wings moved to the top of the fuselage).

ABOVE *After test and acceptance flights were completed, the YOA-5 amphibian was briefly operated by the 1st Air Base Squadron at Langley Field, Virginia.* (Army Air Corps)

Data for the XP3D-1

Dimensions: Span, 95ft; length, 69ft 10½in; height, 22ft 5¼in; wing area, 1,295sq ft.
Weights: Empty, 12,813lb; loaded, 20,356lb; maximum, 25,748lb; wing loading, 15.7lb/sq ft; power loading, 12.3lb/hp.
Accommodation: Crew of four to seven in enclosed cockpit and cabin.
Power Plant: Two 825hp Pratt & Whitney R-1830-58 14-cylinder radials driving three-blade, variable-pitch, metal propellers.
Armament: One 0.30in machine gun in a nose turret and two 0.50in flexible machine guns in side hatches aft of the wings; up to 3,000lb of bombs or depth charges internally.
Performance: Maximum speed at sea level, 165mph; service ceiling, 17,800ft; normal range, 1,630 miles; ferry range, 3,010 miles.

BELOW *The XP3D-1 flying boat was tested from Santa Monica Bay in March 1935.* (USN-NA)

Douglas XO2D-1

First flight: March 1934, Santa Monica Bay.
Number built: One by Douglas.
Type: Single-engined observation amphibian with main undercarriage retracting in the central float.
Background and significant events:
Planned to be operated from cruisers, battleships or aircraft carriers, this amphibian lost the USN competition to the Curtiss XO3C-1 (future SOC-1 *Seagull*).

Data for the XO2D-1

Dimensions: Span, 36ft; span folded, 13ft 6in; length, 32ft; height on wheels, 16ft 4¼in; wing area, 302.8sq ft.
Weights: Empty, 3,460lb; loaded, 5,109lb; wing loading, 16.9lb/sq ft; power loading, 9.3lb/hp.
Accommodation: Pilot and gunner in enclosed cockpit.
Power Plant: One 550hp Pratt & Whitney R-1340-12 nine-cylinder radial driving a two-blade, fixed-pitch, metal propeller.
Armament: One 0.30in fixed machine gun under the engine cowling and one flexible 0.30in machine gun in the rear cockpit.
Performance: Maximum speed at sea level, 162mph; service ceiling, 14,300ft; range, 800 miles.

The amphibian XO2D-1 was tested by the US Navy at NAS Anacostia, District of Columbia, in May 1934 (USN)

Douglas TBD *Devastator*

First flight: 15 April 1935, Clover Field, Santa Monica.
Number built: 130 by Douglas.
Type: Carrier-based torpedo bomber.
Background and significant events:
Entering service in November 1937, the TBD-1 was the first monoplane with retractable undercarriage to be operated from US carriers. Unfortunately, it had become obsolete by the time *Devastators* were sent to war four years later. Losses during the first eight months of the war in the Pacific were very high. One aircraft was fitted experimentally with twin floats becoming the TBD-1A.

Data for the TBD-1

Dimensions: Span, 50ft; span folded, 25ft 8in; height, 15ft 1in; wing area, 422sq ft.
Weights: Empty, 5,600lb; loaded, 9,289lb; maximum, 10,194lb; wing loading, 22.0lb/sq ft; power loading, 10.3lb/hp.
Accommodation: Pilot, navigator/bombardier, and radio/gunner in a row under a long canopy.
Power Plant: One 900hp Pratt & Whitney R-1830-64 14-cylinder radial driving a three-blade, variable pitch, metal propeller.
Armament: One forward-firing 0.50in machine gun under the engine cowling and one 0.30in flexible machine gun in the rear cockpit; one torpedo or 1,200lb of bombs externally.
Performance: Maximum speed, 206mph at 8,000ft; cruising speed, 128mph; service ceiling, 19,500ft; range, 435 miles with a torpedo or 715 miles with 1,000lb of bombs.

This T3D-1 Devastator *was caught banking over the Santa Monica Mountains.* (USN)

Douglas B-18 *Bolo*

First flight: April 1935, Clover Field, Santa Monica.
Number built: 370 by Douglas.
Type: Twin-engined bomber.
Background and significant events:
> Combining the wings of the DC-2 with a broader fuselage, the DB-1 prototype was followed by 131 B-18s for the Army Air Corps, one DB-2 prototype, 217 B-18As for the Air Corps, and 20 *Digby* Mk Is for the Royal Canadian Air Force. B-18As retrofitted with an air-to-surface radar in a nose radome and a magnetic anomaly detection set in an extended tail cone were designated B-18Bs; they were used in the ASW role primarily along the US East Coast, in the Gulf of Mexico, and in the Caribbean.

This B-18A was photographed at Wright-Patterson AFB, Ohio, after it had been restored by the staff of the National Museum of the USAF. (NMUSAF)

Data for the B-18A

Dimensions: Span 89ft 6in; length, 57ft 10in; height, 15ft 2in; wing area, 959sq ft.
Weights: Empty, 16,320lb; loaded, 24,000lb; maximum, 27,673lb; wing loading, 25.0lb/sq ft; power loading, 12.0lb/hp.
Accommodation: Crew of six including two pilots.
Power Plant: Two 1,000hp Wright R-1820-53 nine-cylinder radials driving three-blade, variable-pitch, metal propellers.
Armament: Three flexible 0.30in machine guns (one in the nose, one in the dorsal turret and one in a ventral trap); 1,000lb (standard) to 2,000lb (overload) of bombs internally.
Performance: Maximum speed, 216mph at 10,000ft; cruising speed, 167mph; service ceiling, 23,900ft; normal range, 900 miles; ferry range, 2,100 miles.

Northrop 3A

First flight: July 1935, Mines Field, Los Angeles.
Number built: One by Northrop.
Type: Single-seat fighter.
Background and significant events:
> Intended to be offered to the Army Air Corps, this prototype was lost off the coast of Los Angeles shortly after testing had begun.

Data for the 3A

Dimensions: Span, 33ft 6in; length, 21ft 10in.
Weights: Loaded, 3,900lb; power loading, 5.6lb/hp.
Accommodation: Pilot in enclosed cockpit.
Power Plant: One 700hp Pratt & Whitney *Twin Wasp Jr* SA-G 14-cylinder radial driving a three-blade, variable-pitch, metal propeller.
Armament (Planned but not fitted):
> Two forward-firing 0.30in or 0.50in machine guns under the engine cowling.
Performance: Maximum speed at sea level, 279mph; service ceiling, 31,600ft; endurance, 3hr.

Shortly after this photograph was taken, the Northrop 3A fighter prototype disappeared off the coast of Los Angeles in July 1935. (Douglas)

Northrop A-17 & Douglas 8A

First flight: July 1935, Mines Field, Los Angeles.
Number built: 351 by Northrop (and then Douglas) and 102 under license.
Type: Single-engined attack aircraft/light bomber with fixed undercarriage (Northrop A-17) or retractable undercarriage (Northrop A-17A and Douglas 8A).
Background and significant events:

After the Army Air Corps tested two derivatives of the *Gamma* (the 2C which became the YA-13 and then the XA-16, and the 2F which ended up modified as the prototype for the A-17), Northrop obtained an initial contract for 110 A-17s (including the ex-*Gamma* 2F) with a trousered undercarriage. The Air Corps then ordered 129 A-17As and two A-17As with a retractable undercarriage. Douglas then developed its Model 8A-1 through 8A-5 for export customers. The 8A-1 was built under license in Sweden with SFA-built Bristol *Mercury* XXIV radial engines.

ABOVE *The A-17A of the National Museum of the USAF has been painted in the markings of the 90th Attack Squadron, 3rd Attack Group, of the Army Air Corps.* (NMUSAF)

Data for the A-17A

Dimensions: Span, 47ft 9 in; length, 31ft 8 in; height, 12ft; wing area, 363sq ft.
Weights: Empty, 5,106lb; loaded, 7,550lb; wing loading, 20.6lb/sq ft; power loading, 7.6lb/hp.
Accommodation: Pilot and radio/gunner in tandem enclosed cockpits.
Power Plant: One 825hp Pratt & Whitney R-1535-13 14-cylinder radial driving a three-blade, variable-pitch, metal propeller.
Armament: Four forward-firing 0.30in machine guns in the wings, one flexible 0.30in machine gun in the rear cockpit, and 400lb to 1,200lb of bombs (in overload) externally.
Performance: Maximum speed, 220mph at 2,500ft; cruising speed, 170mph; service ceiling, 19,400ft; normal range, 730 miles; ferry range, 1,195 miles.

BELOW *10 8A-3Ps were built by Douglas for the* Cuerpo de Aéronautica del Perú *(Air Corps of Peru).* (Douglas)

Northrop BT-1

First flight: 19 August 1935, Mines Field, Los Angeles.
Number built: 54 by Northrop.
Type: Single-engined carrier-based dive-bomber.
Background and significant events:

> The XBT-1 prototype was followed by 53 production aircraft, including one modified into the BT-1S test bed for a tricycle undercarriage. The US Navy withdrew its BT-1s from operational squadrons before America entered the war.

Data for the BT-1

Dimensions: Span, 41ft 6in; length, 31ft 8in; height 12ft 6in; wing area, 319sq ft.
Weights: Empty, 4,473lb; loaded, 6,527lb; maximum, 7,075lb; wing loading, 20.5lb/sq ft; power loading, 7.7lb/hp.
Accommodation: Pilot and radio/gunner in tandem enclosed cockpits.
Power Plant: One 825hp Pratt & Whitney R-1535-94 14-cylinder radial driving a three-blade, variable-pitch, metal propeller.
Armament: One 0.50in machine gun under the engine cowling and one flexible 0.30in machine gun in the rear cockpit; maximum of 1,200lb of bombs externally.
Performance: Maximum speed, 223mph at 9,500ft; cruising speed, 192mph; service ceiling, 25,500ft; range with a 1,000lb bomb, 550 miles; ferry range, 1,150 miles.

This BT-1 in the markings of VB-5 shows its 'Swiss cheese' dive brakes in the open position. (USN)

Northrop 5

First flight: October 1935, Mines Field, Los Angeles.
Number built: Three by Northrop.
Type: Single-engined attack aircraft.
Background and significant events:

> Final derivative of the *Gamma*, these two-seaters were exported to Japan (5A and 5D) and Argentina (5B).

Data for the 5B

Dimensions: Span, 47ft 8¾in; length, 30ft; height, 9ft 1in; wing area, 363sq ft.
Weights: Loaded, 6,995lb; wing loading, 19.3lb/sq ft; power loading, 8.5lb/hp.
Accommodation: Pilot and radio/gunner in tandem enclosed cockpits.
Power Plant: One 820hp Wright R-1820G nine-cylinder radial driving a three-blade, variable pitch, metal propeller.
Armament: Two forward-firing 0.50in machine guns in the wings; two rear-firing, flexible 0.30in machine guns (one firing upward and one downward); and 500lb of bombs externally.

The Northrop 5D was exported to Japan in 1936. (Douglas)

Douglas DST, DC-3 & military variants

First flight: 17 December 1935, Clover Field, Santa Monica.
Number built: 10,655 by Douglas and 5,396 under (and without) license.

See Chapters 4 and 8.

Douglas DF

First flight: September 1936, Santa Monica Bay.
Number built: Four by Douglas.

See Chapter 5.

Douglas SBD & A-24 *Dauntless*

First flight: 22 April 1938 (XBT-2), Mines Field, Los Angeles.
Number built: 5,938 by Douglas.
Type: Single-engined, carrier-based scout and dive-bomber.
Background and significant events:

> Developed from the XBT-2, a BT-1 fitted with a fully retractable undercarriage, this dive-bomber was built for the Navy (SBD-1s through SBD-6s) and the USAAF (A-24s through A-24Bs). During the war in the Pacific, *Dauntlesses* contributed significantly to the defeat of the Japanese Fleet.

Data for the SBD-5

Dimensions: Span, 41ft 6³⁄₈in; length 33ft 1¼in; height, 13ft 7in; wing area, 325sq ft.
Weights: Empty, 6,404lb; loaded, 9,359lb; maximum, 10,700lb; wing loading, 28.8lb/sq ft; power loading, 7.8lb/hp.
Accommodation: Pilot and radio/gunner in tandem enclosed cockpits.
Power Plant: One 1,200hp Wright R-1820-60 nine-cylinder radial driving a three-blade, variable-pitch, metal propeller.
Armament: Two 0.50in machine guns under the engine cowling; twin flexible 0.30in machine guns in the rear cockpit; and up to 2,250lb of bombs or depth charges externally.
Performance: Maximum speed, 255mph at 14,000ft; cruising speed, 185mph; service ceiling, 25,530ft; normal range, 1,115 miles; ferry range, 1,565 miles.

ABOVE *The most-built version of the Douglas dive bomber of WW II-fame was the SBD-5 which accounted for 2,964 of all 5,938 Dauntlesses.* (Douglas)

BELOW *This A-24-DE is yet another example of nicely restored aircraft at the National Museum of the USAF.* (NMUSAF)

Douglas DC-4E

First flight: 7 June 1938, Clover Field, Santa Monica.
Number built: One by Douglas.

See Chapter 6.

Douglas DB-7 & A-20 *Havoc/Boston*

First flight: 26 October 1938 (Model 7B), Mines Field, Los Angeles.
Number built: 7,098 by Douglas and 380 under license.
Type: Twin-engined light bomber with night fighter and photo-reconnaissance variants.

Background and significant events:

After Northrop had begun preliminary design work on the Model 7A with two 425hp engines, Douglas designed the Model 7B with a pair of 1,100hp engines. A further redesign led to the DB-7 first ordered by France in 1938. By substituting Wright R-2600 engines for the Pratt & Whitney R-1830 of the French aircraft, Douglas came up with the *Boston* for the Royal Air Force and the A-20 for the USAAF. Night fighter variants were obtained in Britain by modifying DB-7s and *Bostons*, and in the United States by manufacturing P-70s. Postwar, a number of surplus A-20s were modified into executive transport aircraft.

Data for the A-20C

Dimensions: Span, 61ft 4in; length, 47ft 3⅜in; height, 17ft 7in; wing area, 464sq ft.
Weights: Empty, 15,090lb; loaded, 21,500lb; wing loading, 46.3lb/sq ft; power loading, 6.7lb/hp.
Accommodation: Pilot, bombardier and radio/gunner in three separate enclosed cockpits.
Power Plant: Two 1,600hp Wright R-2600-23 14-cylinder radials driving three-blade, constant-speed, metal propellers.
Armament: Four forward-firing 0.30in machine guns in the forward fuselage; twin flexible 0.30in machine guns in the rear cockpit; one flexible 0.30in machine gun in a ventral hatch; and 2,000lb of bombs internally.
Performance: Maximum speed, 342mph at 13,000ft; cruising speed, 280mph; service ceiling, 25,320ft; normal range, 745 miles; ferry range, 2,300 miles.

ABOVE *This is a 'busy scene' staged for the benefit of wartime propaganda. The aircraft is a DB-7B built for the Royal Air Force but taken over by the USAAF to be used for training A-20 crews.* (LOC)

ABOVE *Fitted with SCR-540 radar (US development of the British AI Mark IV), the P-70s were the first American night fighters.* (Douglas)

BELOW *Beautifully restored in the markings of the* Força Aérea Brasileira, *this A-20K was photographed outside the* Museu Aeroespacial *at Campo dos Afonsos, Brazil.* (Museu aeroespacial)

Douglas B-23 *Dragon*

First flight:	27 July 1939, Clover Field, Santa Monica.
Number built:	38 by Douglas.
Type:	Twin-engined bomber.

Background and significant events:

Powered by 1,600hp engines but using the wings of the DC-3, this prewar bomber did not have the performance required for use in combat. Consequently, at least 18 were modified into UC-67 staff transport. After the war, many were used as corporate aircraft.

Data for the B-23

Dimensions:	Span, 92ft; length, 58ft 4¾in; height, 18ft 5½in; wing area, 993sq ft.
Weights:	Empty, 19,089lb; loaded, 26,500lb; maximum, 32,400lb; wing loading, 26.7lb/sq ft; power loading, 8.3lb/hp.
Accommodation:	Crew of six including two pilots.
Power Plant:	Two 1,600hp Wright R-2600-3 14-cylinder radials driving three-blade, constant-speed, metal propellers.
Armament:	One flexible 0.30in machine gun in the nose and another firing through side hatches on either side of the rear fuselage; one flexible 0.50in machine gun in the rear turret; up to 2,000lb of bombs internally.
Performance:	Maximum speed, 282mph at 12,000ft; cruising speed, 210mph; service ceiling, 31,600ft; normal range, 1,400 miles; ferry range, 2,750 miles.

This unidentified UC-67 was photographed at Ryan Field, southwest of Tucson, Arizona, in October 1967. (René J. Francillon)

Douglas XB-19

First flight:	27 June 1941, Clover Field, Santa Monica.
Number built:	One by Douglas.
Type:	Four-engined experimental bomber.

Background and significant events:

In response to an Air Corps request for an experimental long-range bomber, Douglas started work on the XBLR-2 in 1935. Six years later, this work resulted in the XB-19 which then was the largest bomber built to date in the United States. It was later re-engined with 2,600hp Allison V3420-11 liquid-cooled engines, becoming the XB-19A.

Data for the XB-19

Dimensions:	Span, 212ft; length, 132ft 4in; height, 42ft; wing area, 4,285sq ft.
Weights:	Empty, 86,000lb; loaded, 140,000lb; maximum, 162,000lb; wing loading, 32.6lb/sq ft; power loading, 17.5lb/hp.
Accommodation:	18 crew members (plus relief crew of six for very long flights).
Power Plant:	Four 2,000hp Wright R-3350-5 18-cylinder radials driving three-blade, constant-speed, metal propellers.
Armament:	Two 37mm cannon, five 0.50in machine guns, and six 0.30in machine guns distributed among four turrets and five hand-held mounts; maximum bomb load, 37,100lb.
Performance:	Maximum speed, 224mph at 15,700ft; cruising speed, 135mph; service ceiling, 23,000ft; normal range, 5,200 miles; maximum range, 7,710 miles.

The XB-19 photographed at March Field in 1942 after it had been fitted with its defensive armament. (Douglas)

Douglas DC-5 & military variants

First flight: 20 February 1939, Mines Field, Los Angeles.
Number built: 12 by Douglas.

See Chapter 7.

Douglas DC-4 & derivatives

First flight: 14 February 1942 (C-54-DO), Clover Field, Santa Monica.
Number built: 1,244 by Douglas and 71 by Canadair under license.

See Chapter 9.

Douglas A-26 (B-26) *Invader*

First flight: 10 July 1942, Mines Field, Los Angeles.
Number built: 2,452 by Douglas.
Type: Twin-engined attack aircraft and light bomber.
Background and significant events:

> Intended as a replacement for the A-20 *Havoc*, the A-26 was designed at El Segundo but production was entrusted to the Long Beach and Tulsa plants. The *Invader* was re-designated B-26 in 1948 but last operated in Vietnam under the A-26 *Counter Invader* designation. Post WW II, surplus *Invaders* were modified as executive transport aircraft.

Data for the A-26B-60-DL

Dimensions: Span, 70ft; length, 50ft 8in; height, 18ft 6in; wing area, 540sq ft.
Weights: Empty, 22,362lb; loaded, 26,000lb; maximum, 41,800lb; wing loading, 48.1lb/sq ft; power loading, 6.5lb/hp.
Accommodation: Pilot, navigator, and radio/gunner in enclosed cockpits.
Power Plant: Two 2,000hp Pratt & Whitney R-2800-79 18-cylinder radials driving three-blade, constant-speed, metal propellers.
Armament: Eight forward-firing 0.50in machine guns in the nose; six forward-firing 0.50in machine guns in the wings; two 0.50in machine guns in each of the dorsal and ventral turrets; 6,000lb of bombs internally.
Performance: Maximum speed, 322mph at 10,000ft; cruising speed, 278mph; service ceiling, 24,500ft; normal range, 1,680 miles; ferry range, 2,915 miles.

RIGHT *To counter light aircraft bringing weapons to Algerian rebels under the cover of darkness, the* armée de l'Air *had a few of its* Invaders *fitted with the AI Mark radar from* Meteor NF. 11s. *(Jean Cuny)*

BELOW *This A-26A* Counter Invader *was rebuilt by On Mark Engineering from a B-26B* Invader *airframe. (Peter B. Lewis)*

ABOVE *The three prototypes for the* Invader *(including the XA-26-DE) were built in the El Segundo plant but full production was undertaken in the Long Beach and Tulsa plants.* (Douglas)

Bowlus XCG-7 & XCG-8

First flight: 1942, Muroc Field.
Number built: Four by Douglas.
Type: Troop transport gliders.
Background and significant events:

William Bowlus, a sailplane manufacturer in San Francisco, designed two types of troop transport gliders, the XCG-7 (nine soldiers including the pilot) and the XCG-8 for 15. Lacking the industrial capability for building these gliders Bowlus turned to Douglas for assistance. Two prototypes of each model were built at El Segundo.

Data for the XCG-8

Dimensions: Span, 85ft 5 in; length, 61ft; wing area, 996sq ft.
Weights: Empty, 3,895lb; loaded, 5,900lb; wing loading, 5.9lb/sq ft.
Accommodation: Pilot, co-pilot, and 13 airborne soldiers.
Armament: None.
Performance: Towing speed, 120mph.

The Bowlus XCG-7 troop transport glider was tested at Muroc Field (now Edwards AFB) in the Mojave Desert of California. (USAAF)

Douglas XSB2D-1 & BTD *Destroyer*

First flight: 8 April 1943, Mines Field, Los Angeles.
Number built: 30 by Douglas.
Type: Two-seat carrier-based dive-bomber (XSB2D-1) and single-seat torpedo/bomber aircraft (BTD-1).
Background and significant events:

Conceived to replace USN Douglas SBD *Dauntlesses* and Curtiss SB2C *Helldivers*, the XSB2D-1 was a two-seat aircraft with defensive armament comprised of a pair of remotely-controlled turrets. Proving overly heavy and poorly performing, this two-seater was redesigned into the single-seat BTD-1 without the turrets. However, the *Destroyer* remained unsatisfactory and production contracts were cancelled. Two became XBTD-2s after being fitted with an auxiliary turbojet mounted at a downward-angle in the rear fuselage (see photograph on page 24).

Data for the BTD-1

Dimensions: Span, 45ft; length, 38ft 7in; height, 16ft 11in; wing area, 375sq ft.
Weights: Empty, 12,458lb; empty, 16,273lb; maximum, 19,140lb; wing loading, 43.4lb/sq ft; power loading, 7.1lb/hp.
Power Plant: One 2,300hp Wright R-3350-14 18-cylinder radial driving a three-blade, constant-speed, metal propeller.
Armament: Two forward-firing 20mm cannon in the wings and 4,000lb of bombs or torpedoes in a ventral weapon bay.
Performance: Maximum speed, 344mph at 16,100ft; cruising speed, 188mph; service ceiling, 23,600ft; normal range, 1,480 miles; ferry range, 2,140 miles.

One of the BTD-1 Destroyers *is shown warming up its engines at Mines Field.* (Douglas)

Douglas XB-42 *Mixmaster*

First flight: 6 May 1944, Clover Field, Santa Monica.
Number built: Two by Douglas.
Type: Twin-engined experimental bomber.
Background and significant events:

The XB-42 was of novel design with engines housed entirely in the fuselage and driving contra-rotating propellers mounted aft of the tail surfaces. The first had separate canopies for the two pilots but the other had them in a conventional cockpit. The first XB-42 was later modified into the XB-42A with auxiliary turbojets below the wings. In spite of its promising performance, the B-42 was not put in production once the war had ended.

Data for the XB-42

Dimensions: Span, 70ft 6in; length, 53ft 8in; height, 18ft 10in; wing area, 555sq ft.
Weights: Empty, 20,888lb; loaded, 35,702lb; wing loading, 64.3lb/sq ft; power loading, 13.5lb/hp.
Accommodation: Pilot, co-pilot, and bombardier/navigator.
Power Plant: Two 1,325hp Allison V-1710-125 12-cylinder inline engines driving contra-rotating, three-blade, constant-speed metal propellers.
Armament: Two remotely controlled 0.50in machine guns in a retractable turret on the trailing edge of the wings; 10,000lb of bombs internally.
Performance: Maximum speed, 410mph at 23,440ft; cruising speed, 312mph; service ceiling, 29,400ft; normal range 1,800 miles; ferry range, 5,400 miles.

The first XB-42 underwent testing at the Palm Springs Airfield in 1944. (Douglas)

Douglas XTB2D-1 *Skypirate*

First flight: 13 March 1945, Mines Field, Los Angeles.
Number built: Two by Douglas.
Type: Carrier-based torpedo bomber with tricycle retractable undercarriage.
Background and significant events:

Initially to be land-based for coastal defense when a Japanese invasion was feared, the XTB2D-1 was developed for use aboard large aircraft carriers (*Midway*-class CVBs). Its development was terminated at war's end.

Data for the XBTD-1

Dimensions: Span, 70ft; length, 46ft; wing area, 605sq ft.
Weights: Empty, 18,405lb; loaded, 28,545lb; maximum, 34,760lb; wing loading, 47.2lb/sq ft; power loading, 9.5lb/hp.
Accommodation: Crew of three (pilot, navigator/bombardier, and radio/gunner).
Power Plant: One 3,000hp Pratt & Whitney XR-4360-8 28-cylinder radial driving contra-rotating four-blade propellers.
Armament: (Planned but not installed)

Four wing-mounted 0.50in machine guns; two 0.50in guns in a powered dorsal turret; and one more on a flexible mount in the belly; 8,400lb of bombs or depth-charges carried externally.
Performance: Maximum speed, 340mph at 15,600ft; cruising speed, 168mph; service ceiling, 24,500ft; normal range, 1,250 miles; ferry range, 2,880 miles.

The XBT2D-1 was designed when a Japanese landing on the US West Coast was still feared. (Douglas)

Douglas AD (A-1) *Skyraider*

First flight: 18 March 1945, Mines Field, Los Angeles.
Number built: 3,180 by Douglas.
Type: Single-engined, carrier-based attack bomber, with electronic warfare, airborne detection and control, and other variants.

Background and significant events:

Designed as a carrier-borne attack aircraft, the *Skyraider* was built in numerous models as single-seaters (AD-1, AD-2, AD-3, AD-4, AD-4B, AD-6 and AD-7), two-seaters (AD-1Q, AD-2Q, AD-3Q and AD-4Q), and three-seaters (AD-3N, AD-3W, AD-4N and AD-4W), all of which retained the pilot's cockpit of the single-seaters (with additional crew members in a rear fuselage compartment as needed). The AD-5 was a multi-seat, multi-role aircraft with a broader fuselage. All AD designations were changed to A-1 designations in September 1962. The *Skyraider* was the last US combat aircraft powered by a reciprocating engine. The A-1s were withdrawn from use in the United States in 1972 but some *Skyraiders* flew with the presidential guard in Gabon for another 10 years.

Data for the AD-6 (A-1H)

Dimensions: Span, 50ft ¼in; length, 38ft 10in; height 15ft 8¼in; wing area, 400.33sq ft.
Weights: Empty, 11,968lb; loaded, 18,106lb; maximum, 25,000lb; wing loading, 45.2lb/sq ft; power loading, 6.7lb/hp.
Accommodation: Pilot in enclosed cockpit.
Power Plant: One 2,700hp Wright R-3350-26WA 18-cylinder radial driving a four-blade, constant-speed, metal propeller.
Armament: Four forward-firing 20mm cannon in the wings and up to 8,000lb of external stores.
Performance: Maximum speed, 322mph at 18,000ft; cruising speed, 198mph; service ceiling, 28,500ft; normal range, 1,315 miles.

ABOVE *The AD-1Q was a two-seat electronic warfare version of the* Skyraider. *Note the porthole above the fuselage insignia which provided limited lighting to the rear fuselage compartment in which the ECM operator was seated.* (Douglas)

ABOVE *This four-seat EA-1F (ex-AD-5Q) of VAW-13 was photographed aboard the USS* Independence *(CVA 62) during operations in the Gulf of Tonkin in 1965.* (Jerry Edwards)

BELOW *The 4407th Combat Crew Training Squadron, 1st Special Operations Wing was based at Hurlburt Field, Florida. One of its A-1Hs was photographed at McClellan AFB, California, after undergoing a major overhaul at the Sacramento Air Logistics Center.* (Peter B. Lewis)

Douglas C-74 *Globemaster I*

First flight: 5 September 1945, Long Beach.
Number built: 14 by Douglas.
Type: Four-engined military transport.
Background and significant events:

In addition to a cargo loading door on the left side of the forward fuselage, this large military cargo aircraft had a cargo lift beneath the rear fuselage. Too late for service in World War II, the C-74 was developed into the double-deck C-124.

Data for the C-74

Dimensions: Span, 173ft 3in; length, 124ft 2in; height, 43ft 9in; wing area, 2,510sq ft.
Weights: Empty, 86,172lb; loaded, 154,128lb; maximum, 172,000lb; wing loading, 61.4lb/sq ft; power loading, 11.9lb/hp.
Accommodation: Crew of six; 125 soldiers or 109 litter patients and five medical attendants; up to 48,150lb of cargo.
Power Plant: Four 3,000hp Pratt & Whitney R-4360-27 28-cylinder radials driving four-blade, constant-speed, metal propellers.
Performance: Maximum speed, 328mph at 10,000ft; cruising speed, 212mph; service ceiling, 21,300ft; normal range, 3,400 miles; ferry range, 7,250 miles.

Only 14 C-74 Globemaster I*s were built in Long Beach but they were followed by 448 C-124* Globemaster II*s with a double deck.* (Douglas)

Douglas DC-6 & derivatives

First flight: 15 February 1946 (XC-112-DO), Clover Field, Santa Monica.
Number built: 704 by Douglas.

See Chapter 10.

Douglas XB-43

First flight: 17 May 1946, Muroc Army Air Base.
Number built: Two by Douglas.
Type: Twin jet bomber.
Background and significant events:

The airframe of the XB-43 was essentially similar to that of the XB-42, but the inline engines of the earlier model were replaced by a pair of turbojets. The XB-43 thus became the first US jet bomber.

Data for the XB-43

Dimensions: Span, 71ft 2in; length, 51ft 2in; height, 24ft 3in; wing area, 563sq ft.
Weights: Empty, 21,775lb; loaded, 37,000lb; maximum, 39,533lb; wing loading, 65.7lb/sq ft; power loading, 4.9lb/lb st.
Accommodation: Pilot and co-pilot/navigator in side-by-side cockpits with separate canopies.
Power Plant: Two 3,750lb st General Electric TG-180 turbojets.
Armament: None fitted.
Performance: Maximum speed at sea level, 515mph; cruising speed, 420mph; service ceiling, 38,500ft; normal range, 1,100 miles; ferry range, 2,840 miles.

The Douglas XB-43, the novel US jet bomber prototype, was first flown from the dry lake surface at Muroc Army Air Base on 17 May 1946. (AFFTC)

Douglas *Cloudster II*

First flight: 12 March 1947, Clover Field, Santa Monica.
Number built: One by Douglas.
Type: Twin-engined light aircraft.
Background and significant events:

Of similar aerodynamic concept as the XB-42, this five-seater was powered by a pair of fuselage-mounted engines driving a pusher propeller aft of the tail. Too expensive, the *Cloudster II* was not put into production.

Data for the *Cloudster II*

Dimensions: Span, 35ft 4½in; length, 39ft 9⅜in; height, 12ft.
Weights: Empty, 3,200lb; loaded, 5,085lb; power loading, 10.2lb/hp.
Accommodation: Pilot and four passengers.
Power Plant: Two 250hp Continental E-250 six-cylinder air-cooled engines driving a two-blade metal propeller.
Performance: Maximum speed, 229mph at 1,200ft; cruising speed, 200mph; service ceiling, 22,200ft; normal range 950 miles; maximum range, 1,175 miles.

The Cloudster II *was powered by two internally-mounted Continental E-250 six-cylinder air cooled engines driving a single-pusher propeller.* (Douglas)

Douglas D-558-1 *Skystreak*

First flight: 14 April 1947, Muroc Dry Lake.
Number built: Three by Douglas.
Type: Transonic research aircraft.
Background and significant events:

Entertaining close working relations with the staff of the Bureau of Aeronautics, the El Segundo design team was asked by the Navy to design a high-speed research aircraft. On 25 August 1947, the *Skystreak* set a new world speed record of 650.796mph.

Data for the D-558-1

Dimensions: Span, 25ft; length, 35ft 8½in; height 12ft 11¹¹⁄₁₆in; wing area, 150.7sq ft.
Weights: Loaded, 9,750lb; maximum, 10,105lb; wing loading, 64.7lb/sq ft; power loading, 1.95lb/lb st.
Accommodation: Pilot.
Power Plant: One 5,000lb st Allison J35-A-11 turbojet.
Performance: Maximum speed at sea level, 650mph.

Three D-558-1 Skystreaks, *each powered by a single turbojet, were built as transonic research aircraft.* (Douglas)

Douglas D-558-2 *Skyrocket*

First flight: 4 February 1948, Muroc Dry Lake.
Number built: Three by Douglas.
Type: Supersonic research aircraft.
Background and significant events:

> The *Skyrocket* was initially flown on the power of a turbojet only; later, a 6,000lb st rocket engine was added. After the turbojet was removed, the D-558-2 had to be taken aloft beneath a Boeing P2B-1-S mother plane. In this configuration, the *Skyrocket* set an altitude record of 83,235ft and became the first aircraft to fly at twice the speed of sound.

Data for the D-558-2

Dimensions: Span, 25ft; length, 42ft; height, 12ft 8in; wing area, 175sq ft.
Weights: Take-off, 10,572lb with turbojet only and 15,266lb with mixed power; air launch weight, 15,787lb with rocket engine only.
Accommodation: Pilot.
Power Plant: One 3,000lb st Westinghouse J34-WE-40 turbojet and/or a 6,000lb st Reaction Motors XLR-8-RM-5 or -6 rocket engine.
Performance: Maximum speed, 585mph at 20,000ft on turbojet only; 720mph at 40,000ft on mixed power; and 1,250mph at 67,500ft on rocket power only when air launched.

As originally completed, the first D-558-2 was powered by a Westinghouse J34 turbojet with air intake on both sides of the forward fuselage, aft of the nose gear and cockpit. (Douglas)

Douglas F3D (F-10) *Skyknight*

First flight: 23 March 1948, Mines Field, Los Angeles.
Number built: 268 by Douglas.
Type: Twin jet, carrier-based night fighter.
Background and significant events:

> Even though the *Skyknight* was designed for carrier operations, it was mostly used from land bases as a night fighter during the Korean War and as an electronic warfare aircraft in Vietnam.

Data for the F3D-2

Dimensions: Span, 50ft; length, 45ft 5in; height, 16ft 1in; wing area, 400sq ft.
Weights: Empty, 18,160lb; loaded, 23,575lb; maximum, 27,681lb; wing loading, 58.9lb/sq ft; power loading, 3.5lb/lb st.
Accommodation: Pilot and radar operator side-by-side.
Power Plant: Two 3,400lb st Westinghouse J34-WE-36 turbojets.
Armament: Four 20mm cannons and up to 4,000lb of external stores.
Performance: Maximum speed, 565mph at 20,000ft; cruising speed, 390mph; service ceiling, 38,200ft; ferry range, 1,540 miles.

The first Navy and Marine Corps jet-powered night fighters, the Douglas F3Ds Skyknights *were used in combat in Korea and, after being modified into electronic countermeasure aircraft, in Vietnam.* (Douglas)

Douglas Super DC-3 & derivatives

First flight: 23 June 1949, Clover Field, Santa Monica.
Number built: 105 by Douglas.

See Chapter 11.

Douglas C-124 *Globemaster* II

First flight: 27 November 1949, Long Beach.
Number built: 448 by Douglas.
Type: Four-engined, double deck military transport aircraft.
Background and significant events:

Retaining the wings, engine installation, and undercarriage of the C-74, the C-124 had a larger and more capacious double deck fuselage. The floor between the two decks was folded when carrying large vehicles. Loading was mainly through clamshell doors in the nose with a built-in double ramp. A turbine-engined version was planned but only the YC-124B prototype was flown.

Data for the C-124C

Dimensions: Span, 174ft 1½in; length, 130ft 5in; height, 48ft 3½in; wing area, 2,506sq ft.
Weights: Empty, 101,165lb; loaded, 185,000lb; maximum, 194,500lb; wing loading, 73.8lb/sq ft; power loading, 24.3lb/hp.
Accommodation: Crew of six; troop seating for 200; medical evacuation configuration with 123 litters, 45 seats, and up to 15 medical attendants; maximum cargo load, 74,000lb.
Power Plant: Four 3,800hp Pratt & Whitney R-4360-63A 28-cylinder radials driving four-blade, constant-speed, metal propellers.
Performance: Maximum speed, 304mph at 20,800ft; cruising speed, 230mph; service ceiling, 21,800ft; range with 26,375lb of cargo, 4,030 miles; ferry range, 6,820 miles.

Nicknamed 'Old Shaky' by those who had to endure long flights in its cavernous fuselage, the C-124 had a long career which lasted until 1974. (Douglas)

Douglas XA2D-1 *Skyshark*

First flight: 26 May 1950, Edwards AFB.
Number built: 12 by Douglas.
Type: Turboprop-powered attack aircraft.
Background and significant events:

World War Two had not yet ended when the Bureau of Aeronautics asked Douglas to study the feasibility of developing a version of the BT2D-1 (future AD and A-1) to be powered by one or two turboprop engines. While the XA2D-1 and A2D-1s were themselves satisfactory, their turbine engines and reduction boxes remained unreliable. Production plans were cancelled.

Data for the XA2D-1

Dimensions: Span, 50ft 3/16in; length, 41ft 2 13/32in; height, 17ft ¾in; wing area, 400sq ft.
Weights: Empty, 12,944lb; loaded, 18,720lb; maximum, 22,966lb; wing loading, 46.8lb/sq ft; power loading, 3.7lb/eshp.
Accommodation: Pilot.
Power Plant: One 5,100eshp Allison XT40-A-2 turboprop (coupled T38 turbines) driving contra-rotating, three-blade propellers.
Armament: Four wing-mounted 20mm cannon and up to 5,500lb of external stores.
Performance: Maximum speed, 501mph at 25,000ft; cruising speed, 276mph; service ceiling, 48,100ft; combat range, 640 miles; ferry range, 2,200 miles.

The second XA2D-1 is shown undergoing preflight maintenance at Edwards AFB, California, in 1950. (Douglas)

Douglas F4D (F-6) *Skyray*

First flight: 23 January 1951, Edwards AFB.
Number built: 421 by Douglas.
Type: Single-seat, carrier-based interceptor.
Background and significant events:

With its aerodynamic concept inspired by the work of Dr. Alexander Lippisch in Germany, the F4D-1 (F-6A after September 1962) was an exceptionally fast climbing interceptor. Its range, however, was somewhat limited for safe operations far out at sea.

Data for the F4D-1

Dimensions: Span, 33ft 6in; span folded, 26ft 1¾in; height, 13ft; wing area, 557sq ft.
Weights: Empty, 16,024lb; loaded, 22,008lb; maximum, 27,116lb; wing loading, 39.5lb/sq ft; power loading, 1.4lb/lb st.
Accommodation: Pilot.
Power Plant: One 10,200lb st (dry) or 16,000lb st (with afterburning) Pratt & Whitney J57-P-8 turbojet.
Armament: Four wing-mounted 20mm cannon and either two AIM-9B *Sidewinder* air-to-air missiles or 4,000lb of external stores.
Performance: Maximum speed at sea level, 722mph; cruising speed, 520mph; service ceiling, 55,000ft; normal range, 700 miles; ferry range, 1,200 miles.

F4D-1s from several fighter squadrons are lined-up on the ramp at MCAS Yuma, Arizona, during a Navy air gunnery competition. (Douglas)

Douglas X-3 *Stiletto*

First flight: 20 September 1952, Edwards AFB.
Number built: One by Douglas.
Type: Supersonic research aircraft.
Background and significant events:

With two 6,000lb st (with afterburning) Westinghouse XJ46-WE-1 turbojets, the X-3 had been expected to cruise at Mach 2.0 for 10 minutes. The non-availability of these engines and their replacement by 4,900lb st J34 turbojets rendered the aircraft incapable of even reaching Mach 1.0 in level flight.

Data for the X-3

Dimensions: Span, 22ft 8¼in; length, 66ft 9in; height, 12ft 6⁵/₁₆in; wing area, 166.5sq ft.
Weights: Empty, 14,345lb; loaded, 20,800lb; maximum, 22,400lb; wing loading, 124.9lb/sq ft; power loading, 2.1lb/lb st.
Accommodation: Pilot.
Power Plant: Two 3,370lb st (dry) or 4,900lb st (with afterburning) Westinghouse XJ34-WE-17 turbojets.
Performance: Maximum speed, 706mph at 20,000ft; maximum ceiling, 38,000ft; endurance, 1hr at 590mph and 30,000ft.

Designed to fly at Mach 2 for 10 minutes, the X-3 was underpowered and could not even reach Mach 1 in level flight. (AFFTC)

Douglas A-3 (A3D) *Skywarrior*

First flight: 28 October 1952, Edwards AFB.
Number built: 283 by Douglas.
Type: Multi-role, carrier-based, twin jet aircraft.
Background and significant events:

The A3D-1 (A-3A after September 1962) and A3D-2 (A-3B after 1962) were built as carrier-borne nuclear bombers. Other versions of the *Skywarrior* were either built or modified as reconnaissance aircraft, electronic warfare aircraft, or test beds. However, it is best remembered for its use as a tanker, or tanker/EW aircraft, during the war in Southeast Asia. The last were retired in 1991 after taking part in the first Gulf War.

Data for the KA-3B

Dimensions: Span, 72ft 6in; wing folded, 49ft 5in; length, 76ft 4in; height, 22ft 9½in; wing area, 812sq ft.
Weights: Empty, 37,329lb; maximum take-off from carrier, 70,000lb; maximum take-off from land, 84,000lb; wing loading, 103.4lb/sq ft; power loading, 4.0lb/lb st.
Accommodation: Pilot, navigator, and crew chief.
Power Plant: Two 10,500lb st Pratt & Whitney J57-P-10 turbojets.
Performance: Maximum speed at sea level, 593mph; cruising speed, 495mph; service ceiling, 41,100ft; combat radius, 1,035 miles.

ABOVE *The EA-3B electronic reconnaissance version of the* Skywarrior *remained in use long enough to take part in the 1991 Gulf War.* (Rick Morgan)

BELOW *Built as an A3D-2 carrier-based nuclear bomber, this* Skywarrior *was modified as a KA-3B tanker. It was photographed over the Devil's Playground in California during an air refuelling exercise in November 1981.* (René J. Francillon)

Douglas DC-7

First flight: 18 May 1953, Clover Field, Santa Monica.
Number built: 338 by Douglas.

See Chapter 13.

Douglas A-4 (A4D) *Skyhawk*

First flight:	22 June 1954, Edwards AFB.
Number built:	2,960 by Douglas and McDonnell Douglas.
Type:	Single-seat carrier attack aircraft and two-seat advanced/carrier trainer.

Background and significant events:

The initial single-seat versions of the *Skyhawk* (A4D-1 through A4D-2N, then A-4A through A-4C after September 1962) were powered by Wright J65 turbojets. The next single- and two-seat versions had Pratt & Whitney J52 turbojets. Upgraded *Skyhawks* were re-engined in Singapore with General Electric F404-GE-100D turbofans.

Data for the A-4E

Dimensions:	Span, 27ft 6in; length, 40ft 1½in; height, 15ft 2in; wing area, 260sq ft.
Weights:	Empty, 9,853lb; loaded, 16,216lb; maximum, 24,500lb; wing loading, 62.4lb/sq ft; power loading, 1.9lb/lb st.
Accommodation:	Pilot.
Power Plant:	One 8,500lb st Pratt & Whitney J52-P-6A turbojet.
Armament:	Two wing-mounted 20mm cannon and up to 8,200lb of external stores.
Performance:	Maximum speed at sea level, 673mph; cruising speed, 485mph; service ceiling, 33,900ft; normal range, 1,160 miles; ferry range, 2,525 miles.

RIGHT *A TA-4J from Training Squadron Seven (VT-7) is about to come aboard the USS* John F. Kennedy *(CV 67) during a carrier qualification period in September 1996.* (René J. Francillon)

BELOW *A re-engined A-4SU belonging to 150 Squadron, Republic of Singapore Air Force, taxies at Cazaux, a French military airfield where this Singaporean training squadron is based.* (Michel Fournier)

ABOVE *This A-4Q (ex-USN A4D-2/A-4B) was at NAS Jacksonville, Florida, in January 1972, waiting to be ferried to Argentina and service with* Comando de Aviación Naval Argentina. (René J. Francillon)

Douglas B-66 *Destroyer*

First flight:	28 June 1954, Long Beach.
Number built:	294 by Douglas.
Type:	Twin jet bomber, reconnaissance aircraft, and electronic warfare aircraft.

Background and significant events:

Intended to have been a straightforward development of the naval A3D-1 *Skywarrior*, the B-66 ended up differing in several respects as the USAF kept making new demands. The EB-66 versions, obtained by modifying B-66 and RB-66 airframes, proved to be the most useful in service.

Data for the RB-66C

Dimensions:	Span, 72ft 6in; length, 75ft 2in; height, 23ft 7in; wing area, 781sq ft.
Weights:	Empty, 43,966lb; loaded, 64,085lb; maximum, 82,420lb; wing loading, 82.1lb/sq ft; power loading, 3.1lb/lb st.
Accommodation:	Crew of seven including five electronic warfare officers.
Power Plant:	Two 10,200lb st Allison J71-A-13 turbojets.
Armament:	Two 20mm cannon in remotely controlled tail turret (turret and guns later replaced by additional ECM equipment in a redesigned tail cone).
Performance:	Maximum speed at sea level, 640mph; cruising speed, 532mph; service ceiling, 39,200ft; combat range, 1,440 miles; ferry range, 2,935 miles.

The EB-66Es were electronic warfare aircraft obtained by installing additional electronic equipment in RB-66B airframes. This one, photographed at McClellan AFB, California, in April 1968, wore the markings of the 19th Tactical Electronic Warfare Squadron. (Peter B. Lewis)

Douglas F5D-1 *Skylancer*

First flight:	21 April 1956, Edwards AFB.
Number built:	Four by Douglas.
Type:	Carrier-based supersonic interceptor.

Background and significant events:

Intending to improve its F4D *Skyray* by increasing its range and flight endurance, Douglas began studies of an F4D-2N variant. This soon led to a new and larger aircraft retaining the configuration of the *Skyray*. In spite of its impressive performance, the *Skylancer* was not put into production. It did, however, prove to be a useful test bed for NASA.

Data for the F5D-1

Dimensions:	Span, 33ft 6in; length, 53ft 9¾in; height, 14ft 10in; wing area, 557sq ft.
Weights:	Empty, 17,444lb; loaded, 24,445lb; maximum, 28,072lb; wing loading, 43.9lb/sq ft; power loading, 1.5lb/lb st.
Accommodation:	Pilot.
Power Plant:	One 10,200lb st (dry) or 16,000lb st (with afterburning) Pratt & Whitney J57-P-8 turbojet.
Armament:	An all air-to-air missile armament (either four AIM-9 *Sidewinders* or two AIM-7 *Sparrows*) was planned but not fitted.
Performance:	Maximum speed, 749mph at sea level and 990mph at 44,000ft; cruising speed, 637mph; service ceiling, 57,500ft; combat range, 1,334 miles.

NASA F5D-1 of the Dryden Flight Research Center was photographed at Edwards AFB in March 1962. (NASA)

Douglas DC-8

First flight: 30 May 1958, Long Beach.
Number built: 556 by Douglas (then by McDonnell Douglas).
Type: Four-engined passenger, cargo, or combi jet transport.
Background and significant events:

After long delaying its entry into the jetliner market, in June 1955 Douglas announced that it would build a jet-powered successor for its DC-6 and DC-7. Initially two DC-8 versions were offered, differing by the engine type fitted and fuel tank capacity: the so-called 'Domestic' and 'Intercontinental' models. These designations soon gave place to 'series': The Series 10 with JT3C turbojets, the 20 and 30 with JT4As, the 40 with R-R *Conway*, and the 50 with JT3D turbofans. These versions were followed by the stretched Series 61, 62, and 63 retaining the JT3Ds of the Series 50 aircraft. After production had ended, Cammacorp came up with the DC-8-71/72/73s re-engined with CFM56s.

Data for the DC-8-32

Dimensions: Span, 142ft 5in; length 150ft 6in; height, 43ft 4in; wing area, 2,771sq ft.
Weights: Empty, 134,000lb; maximum, 310,000lb; wing loading, 111.9lb/sq ft; power loading, 4.4lb/lb st.
Accommodation: Cockpit crew of three; 127 passengers in two-class configuration or 176 passengers in high-density charter configuration.
Power Plant: Four 17,500lb Pratt & Whitney JT4A-12 turbojets.
Performance: Cruising speed, 588mph; range with 127 passengers, 5,450 miles; range with maximum payload (42,500lb), 4,605 miles.

Data for the DC-8-71 — *62   350,000LB*

Dimensions: Span 142ft 5in; length 187ft 4in; height, 43ft; wing area, 2,883sq ft.
Weights: Empty, 162,865lb; maximum, 325,000lb; wing loading, 112.7lb/sq ft; power loading, 3.7lb/lb st.
Accommodation: Cockpit crew of three; 212 passengers in two-class configuration or 259 passengers in high-density charter configuration.
Power Plant: Four 22,000lb st CFM56-2B turbofans.
Performance: Cruising speed, 550mph; range with 212 passengers, 6,045 miles; range with maximum payload (60,000lb), 4,600 miles.

ABOVE *This overhead view of a Panagra DC-8-31 undergoing pre-delivery acceptance testing was taken in January 1960.* (Douglas)

ABOVE *This re-engined DC-8-72, shown banking over the NASA installation at Edwards AFB was originally a DC-8-62H (fsn 46082 delivered to* Alitalia *as I-DIWK).* (NASA)

BELOW *Taken in 1975 at the* Aeropuerto Internacional Jorge Chávez *in Lima, Peru, this taxy shot emphasizes the length of the fuselage of the ultimate DC-8 stretched model.* (René J. Francillon)

Douglas C-133 *Cargomaster*

First flight:	23 April 1956, Long Beach.
Number built:	50 by Douglas.
Type:	Four-turboprop military cargo aircraft.

Background and significant events:

The C-133 was designed to be able to carry 96% of all types of military vehicles and was fitted with a capacious cargo compartment with easy access through large doors with built-in ramps at the rear of the fuselage. The *Cargomaster* never overcame the lack of reliability of its turbine engines.

Data for the C-133B

Dimensions:	Span, 179ft 7¾in; length, 157ft 6½in; height, 48ft 3in; wing area, 2,673sq ft.
Weights:	Empty, 120,263lb; loaded, 275,000lb; maximum, 286,000lb; wing loading, 102.9lb/sq ft; power loading, 9.2lb/eshp.
Accommodation:	Crew of five; maximum cargo load, 110,000lb.
Power Plant:	Four 7,500eshp Pratt & Whitney T34-P-9W turboprops driving three-blade propellers.
Performance:	Maximum speed, 359mph at 8,000ft; cruising speed, 323mph; service ceiling, 29,950ft; range with 52,000lb load, 4,000 miles.

The 60th Military Airlift Wing at Travis AFB, California, was the Cargomaster *unit on the West Coast. The aircraft in this August 1968 photograph is a C-133B.* (Peter B. Lewis)

Douglas DC-9 & derivatives

First flight:	25 February 1965, Long Beach.
Number built:	2,443 in Long Beach by Douglas (then by McDonnell Douglas and finally by Boeing) including 32 MD-80s assembled in China.
Type:	Twin-engined passenger, cargo, or convertible jetliner.

Background and significant events:

Douglas announced the development of a twin-engined jetliner in April 1963. The resulting DC-9 achieved considerable success and remained in production for 41 years. There were four DC-9 'generations': the original DC-9 models (Series 10 through 50) which were powered by JT8Ds; the stretched Series 80/MD-80 models with refanned JT8D 200 series engines; the MD-90 powered by IAE V500s; and the Boeing 717 (initially the McDonnell Douglas MD-95) with Rolls-Royce Deutschland BR 715s.

Data for the Douglas DC-9-15

Dimensions:	Span, 89ft 5in; length, 104ft 5in; height, 27ft 6in; wing area, 934.3sq ft.
Weights:	Empty, 49,160lb; maximum, 90,700lb; wing loading, 97.1lb/sq ft; power loading, 3.2lb/lb st.
Accommodation:	Cockpit crew of two; 70 passengers in two-class configuration or 90 passengers in single-class, high-density configuration.
Power Plant:	Two 14,000lb Pratt & Whitney JT8D-1 turbojets.
Performance:	Cruising speed, 495mph; range with 70 passengers, 1,700 miles; range with full payload (24,840lb), 690 miles.

Data for the McDonnell Douglas MD90-30

Dimensions:	Span, 107ft 10in; length, 152ft 7in; height, 30ft 6in; wing area, 1,270sq ft.
Weights:	Empty, 89,060lb; maximum, 156,000lb; wing loading, 122.8lb/sq ft; power loading, 3.1lb/lb st.
Accommodation:	Cockpit crew of two; 155 passengers in two-class configuration or 172 passengers in single-class, high-density configuration.
Power Plant:	Two 25,000lb st IAE V2500 turbofans.
Performance:	Cruising speed, Mach 0.76; range with 155 passengers, 2,300 miles; range with full payload (45,650lb), 1,380 miles.

Data for the Boeing 717-200

Dimensions:	Span 93ft 5in; length, 124ft; height, 29ft 1in; wing area, 1,000.7sq ft.
Weights:	Empty, 68,500lb; maximum, 121,000lb; wing loading, 120.9lb/sq ft; power loading, 2.9lb/lb st.
Accommodation:	Cockpit crew of two; 85 passengers in two-class configuration or 106 passengers in single-class, high-density configuration.
Power Plant:	Two 21,000lb st Rolls-Royce Deutschland BR 715 C1-30 turbofans.
Performance:	Cruising speed, mach 0.77; range with 85 passengers, 3,045 miles; range with full payload (32,000lb), 1,380 miles.

ABOVE *Northeast Airline had some of the most colorful jetliners back in the late 1960s, including this DC-9-31 on a predelivery flight.* (MDC)

RIGHT *The MD-88, the last JT8D-powered version of the Douglas twinjet, had an overall length of 147ft 10in, 41.6% longer than that of the original DC-9-11.* (Carl E. Porter)

BELOW *The top sign reminds one of the Douglas's glory days but that painted below is a sad commentary on the disappearance from the scene of one of the legendary aircraft manufacturers swallowed by its long-time competitor.* (Boeing)

McDonnell Douglas DC-10, KC-10 & MD-10

First flight:	29 August 1970, Long Beach.
Number built:	446 by McDonnell Douglas (including 60 KC-10 tankers for the USAF).
Type:	Wide-bodied passenger, freight, or combi jetliner (DC-10) or military tanker/transport aircraft (KC-10).

Background and significant events:

After unsuccessfully marketing a four-engined, wide-bodied jetliner that was too large and heavy to be of interest to airlines, Douglas set its sights lower by developing the DC-10 trijet. Intense competition against the Lockheed *TriStar*, a series of overly reported accidents, a drop in traffic growth, and the appearance of more economical wide-bodied twinjets led to a shortened production life. DC-10s converted into freighters (including the MD-10s with a two-pilot cockpit) had greater market appeal.

Data for the DC-10-30ER

Dimensions:	Span, 165ft 4in; length, 181ft 7in; height, 58ft 1in; wing area, 3,610sq ft.
Weights:	Empty, 265,750lb; maximum, 580,000lb; wing loading, 160.7lb/sq ft; power loading, 3.6lb/lb st.
Accommodation:	Cockpit crew of two; 255 passengers in two-class configuration or 380 passengers in single-class, high-density configuration.
Power Plant:	Three 53,200lb st General Electric CF6-50C2B turbofans.
Performance:	Cruising speed, 574mph; range with 255 passengers, 6,200 miles; range with full payload (102,250lb), 4,725 miles.

ABOVE *'Domestic' and 'Intercontinental' versions of the Douglas wide-bodied trijet that was first flown in 1970 are shown in this photo. A DC-10-10 of Hawaiian is in the foreground and a DC-10-40 of Northwest is taxying in the background.* (René J. Francillon)

BELOW *This MD-10-10(F) of FedEX was obtained by modifying and modernizing an ex-DC-10-10.* (Carl E. Porter)

McDonnell Douglas YC-15

First flight: 26 August 1975, Long Beach.
Number built: Two by McDonnell Douglas.
Type: Experimental, four-jet cargo aircraft.
Background and significant events:

When the USAF contemplated obtaining a successor for its Lockheed C-130, prototypes of STOL jet transports were ordered from Boeing (YC-14) and McDonnell Douglas (YC-15). Neither was put into production as the USAF kept on procuring more C-130s.

Data for the YC-15

Dimensions: Span, 110ft 4in; length 124ft 3in; height, 43ft 4in; wing area, 1,740sq ft.
Weights: Empty, 105,000lb; loaded, 216,680lb; maximum; 219,180lb; wing loading, 124.5lb/sq ft; power loading, 3.4lb/lb st.
Accommodation: Two pilots and a loadmaster.
Power Plant: Four 16,000lb st Pratt & Whitney JT8D-17 turbofans.
Performance: Maximum speed, 500mph; service ceiling, 26,000ft; range with 27,000lb load while operating from a short field, 460 miles; range with 38,000lb payload, 2,290 miles.

In 1977, the first YC-15 flew with its No 1 JT8D-17 replaced by a CFM-56. (MDC)

McDonnell Douglas T-45 *Goshawk*

First flight: 16 April 1988, Long Beach.
Number built: Two prototypes in the Douglas plant in Long Beach, with full production continuing in the McDonnell (now Boeing) plant in St. Louis.
Type: Two-seat, carrier-based trainer.
Background and significant events:

When in November 1981, NAVAIR (Naval Air Systems Command) announced its intent to acquire a single type to replace both North American T-2s and Douglas TA-4s, McDonnell Douglas entered into an agreement with British Aerospace to propose a US redesigned version of the BAe *Hawk*. The resulting T-45 won the VTXTS jet training system competition in November 1981. The current production model is the T-45C.

Data for the T-45A

Dimensions: Span, 30ft 9¾in; length, 35ft 9in; height, 13ft 5in; wing area, 179.6sq ft.
Weights: Empty, 9,394lb; maximum, 12,758lb; wing loading, 71lb/sq ft; power loading, 2.3lb/lb st.
Accommodation: Pilot and instructor in tandem cockpits.
Power Plant: One 5,450lb st Rolls-Royce F405-RR-400L turbofan.
Performance: Maximum speed, 620mph at 8,000ft; service ceiling, 42,250ft; ferry range, 1,150 miles.

Only the two T-45 prototypes were built in the Douglas plant at Long Beach. MDC chose to have production aircraft built in the McDonnell plant in St Louis. (MDC)

McDonnell Douglas MD-11

First flight: 10 January 1990, Long Beach.
Number built: 200 by McDonnell Douglas and finally by Boeing.
Type: Wide-bodied passenger, freight, or combi jetliner.
Background and significant events:

Although planning improved DC-10 models with increased seating, longer range, or a combination of both, McDonnell Douglas had to postpone launching these projects on several occasions. Finally, in 1985, work was restarted on a development of the trijet that became the MD-11 with a modernized cockpit (with two instead of three pilots), new engines, longer fuselage, and improved wings (with winglets). Unfortunately, this came too late as the newer Airbus A330 and Boeing 767 twinjet had better economics. The take-over by Boeing in 1997 brought an end to further developments.

Data for the McDonnell Douglas MD-11

Dimensions: Span, 169ft 6in; length, 200ft 10in; height 57ft 9in; wing area, 3,648sq ft.
Weights: Empty, 277,500lb; maximum, 602,500lb; wing loading, 165lbsq ft; power loading, 3.3lb/lb st.
Accommodation: Cockpit crew of two and up to 12 cabin attendants; 323 passengers in two classes or 410 in high density configuration; maximum payload for MD-11F freighter, 205,700lb.
Power Plant: Three 61,500lb/st General Electric CF6-80C2D1F turbofans.
Performance: Cruising speed, up to Mach 0.87; range with 323 passengers, 8,235 miles; MD-11F range with maximum cargo load, 4,075 miles.

ABOVE *Flying low over the Alps, this MD-11 appears to be posing for a Swiss Tourism Office poster.* (Swiss)

BELOW *This MD-11F, PR-LGD, of VARIG Log was photographed on approach to LAX (the Los Angeles International Airport) on 16 October 2005.* (Carl E. Porter)

McDonnell Douglas C-17 *Globemaster III*

First flight: 15 September 1991, Long Beach.
Number built: Including pending contracts, 269 had been ordered up to July 2011, with more than 230 already built in the Long Beach plant by McDonnell Douglas and then by Boeing.
Type: Four-engine military cargo aircraft.
Background and significant events:

Designed in Long Beach, the last in a Douglas facility, the C-17 first flew as a McDonnell Douglas but is now in production as a Boeing. *Sic transit gloria mundi.*

Data for the C-17A

Dimensions: Span, 169ft 9.6in; length, 174ft; height, 55ft 1in; wing area, 3,800sq ft.
Weights: Empty, 282,500lb; maximum, 585,000lb; wing loading, 153lb/sq ft; power loading, 3.3lb/lb st.
Accommodation: Pilot, co-pilot, and loadmaster; maximum cargo load, 170,900lb; alternate loads, 102 paratroopers on folding/storable canvas seats or 48-litter patients and medical attendants.
Power Plant: Four 41,700lb st Pratt & Whitney F117-PW-100 turbofans.
Performance: Cruising speed, 515mph; service ceiling, 45,000ft; range with 160,000lb load, 2,760 miles; ferry range, 5,400 miles.

The 3rd Wing in Alaska operates a variety of aircraft including C-17As assigned to its 517th Airlift Squadron. (USAF)

Index